Second Edition

MODERN POLICE MANAGEMENT

RICHARD N. HOLDEN

Prentice Hall Career and Technology

Englewood Cliffs, NJ 07632

Library of Congress Cataloging-in-Publication Data

Holden, Richard N., 1946--
  Modern Police Management/ Richard N. Holden. 2nd ed.
   p. cm.
  Includes bibliographical references and index.
   ISBN 0-13-097718-7
  1. Police administration–United States. 2. Police
Professionalization–United States. 3. Police –United States–
–Training of. 4. Organizational behavior. I. Title.
HV7935.H65   1994
352.2'068–dc20

      93–31193
      CIP

Acquisitions editor: **Robin Baliszewski**
Editorial assistant: **Rose Mary Florio**
Editorial/production supervision
  and interior design: **Mary Carnis**
Cover design: **Laura Ierardi**
Production Coordinators: **Ilene Levy Sanford and Ed O'Dougherty**

 © 1994 by Prentice Hall Career and Technology
Prentice-Hall, Inc.
A Paramount Communications Company
Englewood Cliffs, New Jersey 07632

Printed in the United States of America

10 9 8 7 6 5 4 3 2 1

ISBN   0-13-097718-7

PRENTICE-HALL INTERNATIONAL (UK) LIMITED, *London*
PRENTICE-HALL OF AUSTRALIA PTY. LIMITED, *Sydney*
PRENTICE-HALL CANADA INC., *Toronto*
PRENTICE-HALL HISPANOAMERICANA, S.A., *Mexico*
PRENTICE-HALL OF INDIA PRIVATE LIMITED, *New Delhi*
PRENTICE-HALL OF JAPAN, INC., *Tokyo*
SIMON & SCHUSTER ASIA PTE. LTD., *Singapore*
EDITORA PRENTICE-HALL DO BRASIL, LTDA., *Rio de Janeiro*

Contents

2   The Police Mission   20

THE PHILOSOPHY OF POLICING, 22

THE POLICE FUNCTION, 29

VALUES IN POLICING, 42

DISCUSSION QUESTIONS, 44

REFERENCES, 44

3   Leadership and Motivation   46

LEADERSHIP, 46

5   Decision Making   **106**

10 Labor Relations   237

11 Policy-Making and Ethics   259

13 Organizational Control   **304**

Illustrations

Tables

Cases

Preface

In writing a textbook, the question always arises as to what the author hopes to accomplish. I believe that a textbook should be written for only one of two reasons; to either present ideas that have never before been presented or to present what has already been said, but to present it in a manner better than what has previously been done.

In a book such as this one where there is a need to present information traditionally contained in such books, there is much that has already been said. Whether or not this book presents that information better than previous books is a question to be answered by those who are less partial. I believe I have, however, written this book from a perspective that is different than that of others in this field.

I have attempted to write a book with a view toward reality. I am not the first to make this claim, but this may be the only book on police management to highlight ineffective management practices that haunt police organizations, as well as the reasons why these practices continue and why they are so difficult to changed.

Managing a police agency is, in some respects, similar to releasing a magic djini from a bottle. Carefully controlled, they are both capable of great good. Uncontrolled, they are both capable of great mischief.

The chief executive is the person responsible for maintaining the organizational control of the agency. It is this person, holding in check the natural tendency of the officers to drift ever further into the political quagmire of ultra conservatism, that determines the ability of the agency to function effectively in a democratic society. Unfortunately, the controlling mechanism of most police agenices is a rigid bureaucracy devoted to maintenance of the status quo. Historically, police management has caused more organizational problems than it has solved, especially in the area of personnel.

This book, therefore, is based on three premises. First, many traditional police management practices are, for the most part, outdated and ineffective. Second, the evolving strategies of problem-oriented and community-oriented policing offer more potential for effective police management than any model yet conceived. Third, the secret for success in law enforcement management lies in personnel. Good people make good police officers, supervisors, and administrators. Simply stated, successful management entails hiring good people, providing good training, and developing and enforcing sound strategies.

Good police management should be simple; human nature and bureaucratic inertia ensure that it is not. Society is becoming a vastly more complex arena than in the past. Those who must police society must be better educated and better trained than at any time in history. The purpose of this book is to help those who are faced with the challenge of managing police organizations in a society becoming increasing chaotic.

ACKNOWLEDGMENTS

I would like to thank the following people for their contributions to this book:

Vic Kappeler and Betty Pine-Lockard for their assistance with the legal cases.

David Carter, Allen Sapp, and Bill Tafoya for their assistance on individual topics.

Robin Baliszewski, Mary Carnis, Eileen O'Sullivan, and the others at Prentice Hall for their assistance, support, and patience.

My wife, Denise, and our children, Julie, Jeff, and Greg for their love and continuous support.

DEDICATION

To Bill Davila, an excellent teacher, a fine human being, and a good friend

Richard N. Holden

Chapter 1

The Nature of Police Administration

The law enforcement administrator has the duties of other managers, plus two responsibilities unique to law enforcement. First, law enforcement policies often determine guidelines for life and death decisions. Outside the military in time of war, and to some extent custodial officers in correctional facilities, law enforcement is the only occupation empowered to take human life. This power is accompanied by an equally awesome responsibility, the full weight of which sits directly on the shoulders of the chief law enforcement executive.

The second unique feature of police management is the burden of the governmental image borne by the law enforcement agency. While the police are not the only agency of the government, they are the enforcement arm; and as such are the most visible element of government. Police actions are interpreted as governmental actions. A law does not become truly popular or unpopular until it is enforced. The police, therefore, have a direct effect on society's opinion of the government. This makes the law enforcement administrator unique because it forces the law enforcement agency to be the focus of attention for a large number of special-interest groups, politicians, the news media, and society in general. The way people feel about the quality of justice, institutions of government, and society itself are often crystallized by their attitude toward the law enforcement agencies they observe daily.

These two distinctions make law enforcement administration one of the most complex professions in the modern world. In the duration of this chapter we focus on what an administrator does and does not do, what an administrator is and is not, and what ground rules must be observed in the rewarding and frustrating task of police management.

ADMINISTRATION DEFINED

Administration is a process in which a group is organized and directed toward the achievement of the group's objectives. The complexity and sophistication of this process varies with the size and complexity of the organization and its goals. The functions of the law enforcement administrator, however, will retain a certain degree of consistency across all sizes and types of organizations. The administrative process can be broken down into functions, which have been the subject of management research since the early twentieth century, and will be discussed in detail shortly. Concurrent with these functions is the responsibility for successful fulfillment of these duties.

More important than functions and responsibilities, however, are the interrelated concepts of managerial philosophy and parameters of administration. These are more important because unlike functions and responsibilities, philosophy and organizational parameters vary greatly across organizations and administrators. These elements often determine the true effectiveness of the chief executive, for these respective variables determine how the administrator believes the agency should be managed and the willingness of the personnel of the organization to accept the manager's philosophy. Functions and responsibilities are a part of every organization and must be accomplished if the agency is to survive. Philosophical and organizational parameters vary across organizations and are the reason an effective manager in one type of agency has difficulty in maintaining that ability in another, regardless of the similarity in functions and responsibilities.

Prior to the discussion of functions and responsibilities, a number of definitions are in order. Although the terms *administrator, manager,* and *executive* are used synonymously in this book, it should be noted that administration, management, and supervision are unique concepts that occasionally overlap. *Administration* encompasses both management and supervision and provides organizational direction through policy design and interaction with oversight bodies (in private industry this would be the board of directors; in law enforcement it is the legislative body and higher administrators, such as city managers and mayors). *Management* is most closely associated with the day-to-day operations of the various elements within the organization. *Supervision* is direction provided on a one-to-one basis.

The confusion surrounding these terms occurs because the chief administrator often acts in all three capacities. When this person works with the legislative body in formulating policies and budgets, administrative duties are being performed. When this person directs the day-to-day activities of the organization through the mid-level managers, management is being performed. When the chief executive directs the activities of the administrative staff, supervision is

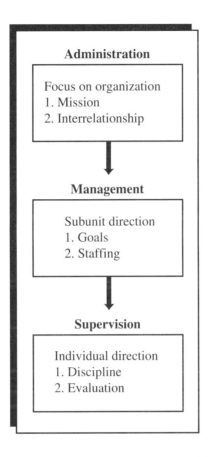

Illustration1-1 The Administrative Triad.

being performed. All three activities are, therefore, performed by those in managerial (administrative, management, supervisory) positions.

Perhaps the most useful, and easiest description is to define top-level personnel as administrators, mid-level personnel as managers, and those who oversee the work as it is being done as supervisors. Unfortunately, the necessity for all three levels to participate in the other two functions on occasion, renders this definition somewhat inaccurate. Illustration 1-1 provides a graphic description of these concepts.

Functions of the Administrator

The administrative functions can be classified under five categories: planning, organizing, staffing, directing, and controlling. Others have argued the necessity of including such topics as leading, budgeting, and coordinating in this list, but each of these duties can be placed into one of the categories listed above.

Planning is the process of preparing for the future. It may be conducted formally with a large amount of data collection and statistical manipulation or it may be the product of the chief executive's best guess. It may involve long-range predictions or it may be conducted on a minute-by-minute basis in a crisis. The planning function consists of a number of subfunctions which require that every manager have some skill in this area. The first and most prominent of these subfunctions is budgeting. Every organization operates within some form of budget, and fiscal accountability is an important measuring rod for administrative performance. It is impossible to prepare a competent budget without some notion of planning. Moreover, the administrator who consistently exceeds expenditure limitations in the budget will not remain an administrator long.

Another subfunction of planning is the establishment of the organization's mission, or reason for existing. The organization's goals, structure, staffing needs, and training needs are derived from the identification of the organization's mission. *If you don't know what you are trying to do, it is impossible to do it, regardless of the quality of the organization.* Failure to determine the agency's mission adequately, is the most effective method of assuring the organization's ultimate failure.

The second major function is *organizing*. The process of organizing determines the structure within which the personnel will be required to work toward accomplishing objectives. Often, the only major change accompanying a shift of the command personnel within an organization is in the structure of the organization. Just as often, this change has little or no impact on effectiveness. One of the unique aspects of the organizing process is that while a poor organizational structure will impede the effectiveness of competent personnel, a good structure will not help an improperly staffed organization. To be an effective administrator requires an understanding of the principles of organizing, but reliance on these principles alone will result in an ineffective agency.

The third major function is *staffing*. Personnel selection and training are crucial to the effectiveness of any organization. All organizations, especially those dealing in human services, are only as good as the personnel they hire. Good people do good work. No amount of administrative brilliance can overcome incompetent subordinates.

The fourth major function is *directing*. Directing an organization is similar to directing a stage play or motion picture. The director (administrator) supposedly knows what is to be accomplished and has the responsibility of communicating this to the cast (personnel). The quality of the final production is often determined by how narrow the gap is between what the director wants the crew to accomplish and what is actually accomplished. When this gap is narrow and this is accompanied by a director who began with a clear insight into what the objectives should be, the result is magical. In those instances when the director is not certain of the goals, cannot communicate the goals, or both, the result is often disastrous or, at least, ineffective.

To fulfill the function of directing requires an administrator knowledgeable about leadership, motivation, and one having a clear understanding of the capabilities and limitations of the organization. Equally important is a deep understanding of why the organization exists and the ability to communicate this clearly to the personnel.

The final function of administration is *controlling*. Controlling denotes a series of procedures designed to ensure compliance of personnel toward the desired objectives. The controlling process begins with selection of the proper personnel. Training, a controlling subfunction, should be designed to acquaint personnel with the organization's mission, goals, policies, and procedures. The foundation for organizational competence is thus determined. Follow-up procedures consist of a system of internal monitoring through various quality control or inspection techniques and a personnel evaluation system. Table 1-1 offers a summary of administrative functions.

Table 1-1
Administrative Functions

Function	*Duties*
Planning	Assessing future needs through the process of analyzing various trends including such variables as crime rates, inflation rates, technology, economic conditions, and changing demographics.
Organizing	Determining the agency's authority and communications structures. Specifying levels of specialization and division of labor.
Staffing	Determining job qualifications. Recruiting, screening, and employing qualified personnel. Creating a promotion and placement system that fulfills the organization's personnel needs.
Directing	Creating the organization's policies and procedures. Fulfilling leadership role within the organization
Controlling	Ensuring that employees' actions and decisions are within agency guidelines. Establishing a monitoring system to ensure that the agency remains on course. Creating and implementing evaluation systems for both personnel and organizational elements.

The idea behind the control function is that organizations are most effective when personnel are accountable for their actions within the organization. Controlling is necessary because the individual ability of workers to follow the purpose and goals of the agencies is as randomly distributed throughout the population as are the leadership abilities of administrators. While many employees need only the influence of competent leadership to accomplish the organization's objectives, others respond only to pressure applied from the rear. The latter are the people who are always looking over their shoulder to see if anyone is watching their performance. Every organization has its share of both types of worker. A competent manager is aware of this and provides both strong leadership and an effective system of controls.

Administrative Responsibilities

The ultimate responsibility for the fulfillment of organizational objectives rests with the chief executive. This responsibility cannot be delegated, nor can it be abandoned. The administrator's position is the focal point of the organization; it is the hot seat. A prerequisite to effective management is an understanding of this responsibility. The chief executive must bear the duties of office while maintaining allegiance to two diverse and often adversarial groups: the oversight body and the organization's personnel.

The administrator is always accountable to those in higher authority. This often translates into siding with the oversight body against the personnel. This is understandable, given the wish for job security among most administrators. The administrator, however, must not build too large or strong a wall between management and worker, lest the chief executive find it impossible to lead. One must always remember: The ability to lead is tempered by the willingness of others to follow. Few managers can long survive in an organization hostile to their presence.

The administrator is also responsible for the well-being of the employees. Factors included in the measure of how well an individual manager fulfills this responsibility includes such things as safety, promotional procedures, salary, benefits, and general organizational atmosphere. For example, it is important for the promotional procedures to be impartial and designed to promote only those with the most potential for success. The promotion process sometimes fails, however, and the wrong person is elevated in rank. The chief executive officer also has the responsibility to protect the personnel from incompetent supervision. The responsibility to decide how promotions will be awarded is coupled with the responsibility to provide a fair procedure for making demotions when necessary. Practically all administrative responsibilities are dual in nature, as this example demonstrates. A person unwilling to accept the unpleasant duties of management accompanying the positive aspects should avoid managerial positions—for everyone's sake.

There are other responsibilities of management. In varying degrees, administrators are responsible to society in general, and to the government in particular. All organizations are bound by governmental regulations and law. The person always responsible for compliance with these directives is the chief executive. The strategies and tactics employed by an organization to achieve its goals must always be in concert with the mandates of the law. The administrator must be prepared to defend or explain any organizational policy, procedure, or act of an organizational member to a legal or administrative tribunal. When the organization is in violation of a law or administrative regulation, the chief executive is ultimately responsible for that violation. If this were not the case, there would be no means of assuring that organization's accountability to the needs of the public they serve. Administrators are ultimately servants of both the organization and society. As long as they understand this and act accordingly, both the organization and society remain in proper perspective. The failure to recognize this often results in a change of administrators.

The following case offers a good example of a failure of administration and the tragic results that followed. It also provides insight as to how the courts view administrative responsibilities.

Popow v. *City of Margate* (1979)

476 F.Supplement 1237

Civil rights action was brought against the city and a police officer for death of the plaintiff's decedent. On defendant's motion for a summary judgment, the District Court, Brotman, J., held that gross negligence could constitute a constitutional violation and that the record created issues of fact as to officer's and city's gross negligence or recklessness precluding a grant of summary judgment.

In this civil rights action under 42 U.S.C. 1983, plaintiff Rosemary Popow, individually and as administratrix of the estate of her husband Darwin Popow, seeks damages for his death. Darwin Popow was shot dead by a city police officer who was pursuing another man he believed to be a fleeing kidnapper. An innocent bystander, the decedent was killed after stepping outside his home on a residential street in Margate in response to the commotion. Defendants include the city of Margate and George Biagi, the police officer who fired the fatal shot.

Officer Biagi argues that the allegations amount to no more than negligent conduct on his part, which is insufficient basis for a 1983 suit. The city of Margate argues that there is no allegation or evidence of unconstitutional official policy or custom sufficient to establish liability. Finally, both defendants assert that the factual allegations in the complaint state no claim of deprivation under the Fourth, Fifth, Eighth, and Fourteenth amendments.

Finding of the Court

Officer Biagi. In the instant case, the depositions testimony concerning the circumstances surrounding the shooting demonstrate a factual issue as to a level of culpability exceeding simple negligence on the part of Biagi. Both Biagi and the police officer with him at the time of the shooting, Officer Kertz, testified that they had no information or personal knowledge that the suspect was armed, had no specific reason to fear for their lives, and had not personally witnessed the suspect commit a felony. Under these circumstances, Biagi's firing his gun on a residential street at night could be determined by the finder of fact to constitute gross negligence or reckless disregard for the public's safety.

Gross negligence or recklessness on the part of a state official, that is, proceeding in the face of a known danger or the total disregard of potential danger, entails abuse of official power, which is the target of a 1983 action.

City of Margate. Liability in cases such as the present one must be based on an official policy or custom that causes the injury. Recognizing this principle, plaintiff argues that her theory of liability as to the city is direct misfeasance or nonfeasance in failing to train, supervise, and review and discipline members of the police force. Plaintiff further argues that deposition testimony indicates that the city's conduct is so inadequate as to amount to gross negligence or reckless disregard of public safety and constitutional deprivation.

First, as to the allegations of failure to train and supervise, the court finds that the deposition testimony as well as the answers to interrogatories, which we read in the light most favorable to plaintiff as we must on motion for summary judgment, create a question of fact as to whether the city of Margate's police department training and supervision procedures were grossly inadequate. Although police officers receive training at the state police academy in Sea Girt, New Jersey, when they first join the force, in Biagi's case that was ten years prior to the shooting incident.

The only continuing training was shooting instruction approximately every six months at a range in Atlantic County. However, there was no instruction on shooting at a moving target, night shooting, or shooting in residential areas. Margate is almost completely residential. The possibility that a Margate police officer will in the course of his duties have to chase a suspect in a residential area at night is not in the least remote; therefore, a finder of fact could determine that the city of Margate's training of officers regarding shooting was grossly inadequate. Furthermore, the officers viewed no films or participated in any simulations designed to teach them how the state law, city regulations, or policies on shooting applied in practice.

As to supervision, there was only one meeting to explain to officers the city's regulation on shooting. This was at the time it was adopted, about two years before this incident. The instructors at the shooting range may have discussed the rules, but not in any detail. Indeed, based on the deposition testimony, there could be a conflict between Officer Kertz's understanding of the city regulation on shooting and that of Chief Creaghe. This might indicate to a finder of fact that there was inadequate communication to officers of the city's policy and rules on this subject.

Also, Chief Creaghe's testimony, viewed in the light most favorable to plaintiff, might indicate that he considered the rules on firing in residential streets a matter of mere "common sense" requiring no detailed explanation. This evidence could be found by a finder of fact to demonstrate grossly inadequate supervision.

Finally, regarding the discipline of officers, the rule is that where a city's procedure of reprimand is so inadequate as to ratify unconstitutional conduct, the city may be liable under section 1983. A police chief's persistent failure to discipline or control subordinates in the face of knowledge of their propensity for improper use of force may constitute official custom or de facto policy, actionable under section 1983.

In Margate, every police shooting incident was referred to the Atlantic County prosecutor's office for possible action. There is a reasonable inference which may be drawn from the evidence that this was a grossly inadequate method of maintaining proper standards in the police department. The evidence shows no instance in which a prosecution actually resulted, and indeed the grand jury refused to indict Biagi based on this shooting incident. But while an officer's conduct may not be criminally actionable under state law, it may have caused a constitutional deprivation and therefore require reprimand or other punitive administrative action.

The depositions and answers to interrogatories reveal that there was no department investigation or reprimand procedure that resulted in punishment of police officers. Chief Creaghe indicated that Biagi was reprimanded after one prior shooting incident, but his record contains no such notation. Biagi has never suffered any disciplinary action whatsoever based on the shooting incident that is the subject of this suit or two prior shooting incidents in which he was involved. Chief Creaghe knew of these prior incidents, in 1972 and 1974, and acknowledges that Biagi's conduct in the earlier one was wrongful. They are close enough in time and substantial enough to create an issue of fact concerning the city's failure to control in the face of knowledge of past culpable conduct.

From all this evidence, a finder of fact could conclude that the city's practices were so grossly inadequate as to give police officers the idea that their unconstitutional conduct would have no substantial adverse consequences for them.

LAW ENFORCEMENT ADMINISTRATION

By their very nature, public service agencies are inefficient. This places the chief administrator in such an agency at a serious disadvantage compared with a private corporation. There are a number of reasons for this inefficiency. The first was identified by Peter Drucker as *mismanagement by budget* (1974, p.142). Public service institutions receive prestige in accordance with their size. The larger the staff and budget, the greater the regard afforded to the agency and its administrators both by people in the public service field and the public at large. Budget size has no relationship to the quality of the service rendered; therefore, the administrator has little incentive to be efficient. When chief executives of such organizations fail to spend all of their allotted monies within the fiscal year, they are often rewarded by having their next year's budget reduced by the amount they left unspent. This is hardly an incentive for efficiency. Instead, public administrators are rewarded for their ability to deplete their budgets, even if it means wasting large amounts.

A second reason for public service inefficiency is the nature of the work itself. Service is a more difficult commodity to measure than is a manufactured product. Often, this service is delivered only upon request of the client, a factor over which the agency has little control. Moreover, while it is difficult to measure quantity of service, measuring quality of service is even more difficult. This means that people are being paid to fulfill a function that is important but very difficult to evaluate. We simply do not know how efficient or effective many agencies are, and we are at a loss as to how this judgment can best be made.

Law enforcement agencies suffer from the foregoing factors, as well as others unique to the field. First, law enforcement agencies provide so many services that we have difficulty even determining what they do. To establish the efficiency and effectiveness of an organization, we must first determine what the agency does. Although functions, such as criminal investigation and traffic enforcement are obvious, other duties, such as domestic and business disputes, are more vague in nature, thus more difficult to define and measure. Many scholars have grappled with this problem. The debate continues. In the meanwhile it is sufficient to note that until the objectives can be defined clearly, the ability to achieve them will remain open to question.

Second, law enforcement has no input into the law-making process and little control over the causal factors of criminal activity. They are often asked to enforce unrealistic laws that reflect society's last ditch effort to solve problems created by social conditions over which the police have no control. With these issues in mind, it should come as no great surprise to learn that law enforcement in this country is neither efficient nor effective. The surprise is that it sometimes works as well as it does. This is a tribute to the dedication and hard work of law enforcement personnel, most of whom manage to find some measure of equilibrium in a rapidly changing environment.

Qualifications: Who Should Be a Law Enforcement Executive?

Studies centered on management over the past 50 years have not been kind to law enforcement administrators. From the Wickersham Commission Report in 1937, to the President's Task Force Reports in 1967, up to the present, the assessment of law enforcement management is that it is woefully inadequate. This indictment of police leadership was summed up concisely by Herman Goldstein in his classic book, *Policing a Free Society*.

> There is no need to dig deeply for an explanation of our failure to develop a reservoir of competent leadership in the police field. This country has tenaciously clung to the concept that leadership of a police agency should be drawn not only from within the police field, but from within the agency, and yet no provisions have been made to assure that police agencies systematically produce people with the requisite qualifications for leadership. Worse still, the citizenry and the police together have stubbornly adhered to provisions governing recruitment and promotion of police personnel that appear to have the opposite effect (1977, p. 231)

Goldstein concluded with the statement: "Indeed, if one set out to design a system to prevent and discourage the police from developing their own leadership capability, it would be difficult to come up with a more sure-fire scheme than that which currently exists" (pp. 231–232).

Why has law enforcement management failed so badly? Four interrelated factors appear to be most responsible for the inadequacies in law enforcement administration. The first error has occurred in the initial selection process for law enforcement personnel. Since the vast majority of administrators are taken from within the ranks of the agency, it is important that leadership potential be considered in the hiring process. It has not been, and as a result the pool from which managers are selected has been composed of people who were not hired with management skills as an employment criterion.

The second error has been in the promotional process. Promotions have, for the most part, been based on written examinations, usually taken from police management texts; past performance, in a nonmanagerial capacity as measured through some form of evaluation; and seniority. The written exams are supposed to test administrative knowledge, but often only test a person's ability to read and remember the material without giving any clue to whether or not the person can apply the information. Past performance gives some indication of competence at a lower level, or at least provides some indication of the ability to get along with peers and supervisors. It gives no indication of potential for competence in a higher position. Seniority is the least excusable factor in the promotion process. It should be used only when two candidates are too equal in all other categories to differentiate any other way; a phenomenon that rarely happens.

The promotion process is also frustrating in its slow progression. The most capable candidates must often wait for turnover in the higher ranks before they have a chance at promotion. If the agency stresses seniority, the personnel must wait out a slow process of senior officer promotion and turnover prior to getting a chance to move up, even though the younger personnel may be better qualified for promotion than many of the senior officers.

The third mistake is related to the training process. Law enforcement training in the past has been focused mainly at the operational level, and even this has been weak. Until very recently, managerial training for law enforcement administrators was virtually nonexistent. Police administrators were required to assume duties totally different than anything they had previously experienced and were presumed to be effective because they were good police officers. This has improved; there are a number of schools around the nation providing managerial training for law enforcement administrators, although many of these provide the training after the person is promoted rather than before.

The fourth error has been a rigid reluctance to participate in lateral entry. This has resulted in reduction of the pool of potential administrative candidates to those persons within the agency who were eligible to compete for promotion. This has had three serious negative effects on law enforcement agencies. First, the officer who has true potential for administration is limited to the immediate agency for promotion possibilities, resulting in frustration if there are insufficient promotion opportunities. Second, a jurisdiction that seriously wishes to improve the quality of its law enforcement is denied the most obvious method of doing so. Third, the absence of lateral movement stifles creativity and innovation, thus increasing the potential for organizational stagnation (Goldstein, 1977, pp. 231–238).

Reasons for Failure in Police Leadership

1. The initial selection process for law enforcement personnel is based on operational rather than managerial criteria.

2. Promotions have been competition oriented and have not focused on management skills.

3. Until very recently, managerial training for law enforcement administrators was virtually nonexistent.

4. There is a rigid reluctance to participate in lateral entry.

The problems listed above are not insurmountable, but it would be naive to argue that they can be alleviated quickly. Each of these problems is related to two, long-standing concepts: (1) only law enforcement personnel understand the problems, and (2) duties of law enforcement agencies and law enforcement should be subject to local control.

These ideas have led to the assumptions upon which the foregoing flaws are based. This philosophy has been complicated by a lack of understanding by both government officials and the public in general as to the complexity and importance of the law enforcement function. Because of this lack of knowledge, law enforcement agencies have been treated as political plums for politicians in many areas. Far too many chief executives have been appointed out of political loyalty or because the law enforcement administrator was a "good ole boy" who would be a team player.

The first criterion for professional law enforcement leadership is a solid education. Law enforcement encompasses so much more than merely enforcing the law. As pointed out earlier, the responsibilities of police administration include some of the most complicated and important duties in our society. Few public officials have more power to affect the daily lives of citizens than the police officer. The police executive must ensure that this power is correctly controlled. Knowledge of the technical aspects of policing is not sufficient to accomplish this task, nor is knowledge of management coupled with technical knowledge sufficient. The law enforcement administrator must have knowledge of government, law, social sciences, and a general understanding of the world in which we live. This is usually achieved through a broad-based college education. The law enforcement administrator must have as much understanding of the social arena in which the police operate as the chief executive of the entire jurisdiction. In America today, hardly anyone would consider hiring a city manager who did not possess a college degree. The public deserves no less in the selection of a police administrator since the duties and responsibilities are equally complex.

The requirement of a college education for the chief executive means that one of several other events must occur. If the law enforcement agency is going to maintain the policy of promoting only from within, college education becomes a necessity for all police personnel; or law enforcement personnel must accept the requirement of college education as a prerequisite for promotion. The third possibility is a greater emphasis on lateral entry. Of these possibilities, all are achieving some acceptance in today's law enforcement agencies. Lateral entry, especially at the chief executive position, is gaining the most popularity.

If law enforcement administration is to become more professionalized, another necessity is the establishment of better promotional procedures for middle management and prospective chief executive officers. The most encouraging trend in this area is the increasing utilization of assessment centers for the determination of management potential.

An obvious drawback to this approach is the expense of conducting these assessments. Only the largest police agencies have been able to participate in this type of promotional process. Even this approach is weakened if the pool of personnel fails to provide candidates with sufficient management potential. Sometimes, the assessment center merely selects a candidate with low potential from a list of personnel with less potential. In short, the assessment center concept is only as good as the personnel to be tested.

Managerial training is another important aspect of upgrading law enforcement administration. Ideally, there should be extensive training prior to the assumption of administrative duties. There should also be a systematized, ongoing management training process for all administrative personnel, the chief executive included. Management is a difficult process; one must continuously assess the organization in light of new information to become proficient. Successful people never stop learning. Above all, this applies to successful administrators.

In addition to these educational and training factors, there are equally important aspects to management that will always be vital to effective administration. Once again we return to the basic requirements of empathy and an understanding of people. The effective law enforcement manager must be able to work with people, because that is what law enforcement agencies do.

The Political Arena

All law enforcement executives are politicians. Some may refute this assertion, but only out of the misguided notion that politicians are evil or that an administrator cannot be a politician and still be a professional manager. Contrary to this idea, not only is there nothing wrong with the police executive being a politician, but good law enforcement administrators recognize the fact and use it to their advantage. A politician is really nothing more than a person accountable to the public for decisions made in the performance of duties. Although a small percentage of police executives are elected—such as sheriffs—the other police administrators are appointed by others who are elected. The vast majority of law enforcement administrators have little or no job security. Their tenure lasts only while they enjoy the support of people who must answer to the general public. Since the popularity of many government officials often rises and falls in direct relationship to the public's attitude toward the police, the police manager and the elected officials have mutual interests. Thus the law enforcement administrator is every bit as much a creature of politics as is the member of the city council or legislature.

Political survival is both art and science. For this reason many seemingly less qualified people are often promoted to top management above more qualified persons. This has always been the case, and will probably continue to be so for some time. Because of the nebulous nature of politics, it is difficult to pinpoint with any exactness the skills necessary to develop this art, although we will spend more time with organizational political behavior later in the book. The focus here is on the various political relationships all police managers are required to nurture if the organization is to succeed—indeed, if the administrator is to survive.

The most obvious relationship is the one already mentioned. The administrator is permanently tied to upper management. Upper management can take the form of a city manager, mayor, governor, city council, state legislature, or president of the United States. Police administrators have the responsibility of translating the laws, rules, and policies of these individuals and groups into organizational activities. The law enforcement executive has no choice but to listen to their concerns, ideas, and philosophies. All administrative policymaking must be completed within the parameters set by these people. The police executive who cannot or will not recognize this is doomed to early separation from the agency.

The failure to recognize the relationship between police and higher administration may explain why the average length of tenure for police chiefs in this country hovers around three years. A law enforcement administrator can wear out a welcome in a hurry, especially in a small or medium-sized jurisdiction, if attention is not paid to the powers from above. Smart police managers not only recognize the necessity of this relationship, but strengthen their position by actively courting the people in these positions. They develop a strong, personal relationship with members of both the executive and legislative groups. This ensures that their position will always receive a complete hearing and that those in oversight positions will see them as friends rather than as employees. It is relatively easy to dismiss Chief Jones, a person who is practically a stranger and who is only seen at city council meetings or on a news broadcast. It is much more difficult to dismiss Charlie Jones, member of the same organizations as the councilpersons, deacon of a local church, and friend and supporter of local politicians. This should not be the case, but until human nature changes, the secret to job security in police administration is often nothing more than the maintenance of strong personal ties to people who hold the political power.

Establishing these relationships does not mean that integrity and professionalism must be sacrificed; administrators need not prostitute themselves to their superiors in order to survive. The extra time and energy it takes for a police administrator to establish and maintain personal relationships with those above them, however, is well worth the effort.

The necessity to maintain close ties with superiors is also balanced against the necessity to maintain equally close ties with subordinates. If the law enforcement administrator is to initiate any meaningful changes within the organization, support must come from the organization itself. As much time and energy must be spent developing the support and confidence of the rank and file as is developed with top management. This cannot be done from the office of the administrator but must be accomplished through the efforts of the administrator to meet personally with agency members to discuss their concerns and sell the administrator's ideas. Respect and confidence are built far more rapidly in face-to-face discussions in neutral places than in direction by memo from the chief's office.

The needs of the elected representatives are sometimes in conflict with the needs of the agency employees. The chief administrator must be prepared to get caught in the cross fire as the two groups grapple with each other periodically over a variety of issues. How the manager handles these situations will have a significant impact on this person's image and effectiveness from the points of view of both groups. Above all, the administrator must be open and honest with both sides. The administrator is in a solid position to mediate the dispute with a minimum of organizational disruption, but only if both sides have faith in the manager's opinion and integrity. Once either side loses this faith, the administrator's future ability to lead the agency is seriously weakened, perhaps terminally.

Political skills are not necessary just to develop good relations with upper management and subordinates. Presenting the proper image to the public is also necessary. Elected officials tend to be pragmatic when assessing their own political futures. Friendship with these people will not save an administrator who is under intense pressure from the people. It is not sufficient to be seen by the public only when there is a crisis requiring a statement to the media. Skilled police managers establish good rapport with the public through a sound media relations policy. Frequently, the public attitude toward the administrator is determined by the attitude of the press. Law enforcement is a function constantly bringing the government into conflict with members of the citizenry. Police officers are only human; they will make mistakes, sometimes bad ones. The law enforcement administrator must accept this and be prepared to deal honestly and openly with problems of this nature. When the media representatives know the administrator can be trusted to discuss police issues candidly, this knowledge will be reflected by the media in their reports and editorials. If the media feel they cannot trust this person, that too will be reflected. The public attitude will then be shaped by the tone of these reports. Political skill must therefore be developed to satisfy the public through the representatives of the news media.

The Problem With People

Good managers care about and genuinely like people. The success or failure of any organization is dependent on the personnel within that organization. Many law enforcement administrators know this but often have trouble selling this idea to the elected representatives. Many an administrator has lamented that the legislative body will approve requests for large expenditures on expensive equipment but will balk at approving salary increases. This is because equipment expenditures are one-time expenses, whereas salary increases commit resources permanently. If we learn anything by studying the successes and failures of other organizations, including military units and professional sports franchises, it is that organizations placing the emphasis on people rather than things succeed; those with reverse emphasis ultimately fail. Public service agencies are slower to recognize this than are private organizations; they are protected monopolies whose resources are not connected to quality of service.

Despite the fact that good managers enjoy working with people, there are some disturbing elements in human nature that every person aspiring to administration must understand. People, including managers, do not always function in their own or the organization's best interest. All of us occasionally have personal problems interfering with our ability to exercise good judgment. We are all subject to sporadic bursts of jealousy, animosity, selfishness, and depression.

As with experience or self-discipline, intellectual capacity is not equally disbursed throughout the organization. In short, people are not all alike. This is as true of middle and upper management as it is of staff and line personnel. The true challenge for administrators is to mold this diverse group of individuals into a highly effective team. It is a difficult challenge because people, being adaptive creatures, learn how to play organizational games that thwart the goals of even the most effective administrators. If the administrator is not sincere, consistent, and confident, the subordinates will know. If the administrator plays games with people, game playing will become the major pastime of agency personnel. The administrator sets the tone of the organization. Everyone watches this person and learns. What they learn determines the ultimate effectiveness of the personnel and the organization.

PHILOSOPHIES OF POLICE MANAGEMENT

Later in the book management styles will be discussed with reference to how individuals manage their respective units. In this section we look at the styles employed in managing a police agency. This will reflect more on the philosophies of policing than on philosophies of management, which are discussed in Chapter 2. There are three contemporary philosophies of police management that have a direct impact on the management style of both the chief administrator and the overall organization: traditional, problem oriented, and community oriented.

Traditional Police Management

The traditional police chief executive officer is authority oriented. Based on the military structure, commands flow from top to bottom. Emphasis is placed on discipline and chain of command. The disciplinary process is punitive in nature; the organization's golden rule is, "don't make waves."

The development of this model is a product of historical forces. Early police agencies were often corrupt and mere tools of political machines. To change their image, and improve the quality of policing, the police developed the concept of police professionalism. This evolved into a powerful orthodoxy. Founded on the principles of military command and scientific management, this orthodoxy is responsible for both the theory and practices of police administration (Moore and Stephens, 1991, p. 1; Wilson, 1989).

Under this orthodoxy, a police managers' primary responsibility is for fulfilling the organizations' goals. They do this through traditional managerial functions such as planning, organizing, coordinating, and controlling. Additionally, the police are not responsible for setting these goals. Rather, they are established by law, formal policy, or tradition (Moore and Stephens, 1991, p. 1). This orthodoxy provides an aura around police organizations that acts as a shield against change. The police believe that since they are not responsible for determining their goals, their only option is to address those objectives as efficiently as possible.

Within the traditional police organization, therefore, emphasis is on control. The police executive is expected to maintain tight discipline. Rules and procedures are published with the objective of providing guidelines for every conceivable incident. Officers are held accountable for every rule, no matter how obscure or rarely used.

Moreover, this orthodoxy holds that politics is inherently bad and that one of the functions of the police manager is to protect the agency from the pernicious influence of the political system (Moore and Stephens, 1991, p. 3). The police were to be isolated from both the politicians they worked for and the public they served. It was believed that only in this manner could they develop into a fully professional organization.

As this orthodoxy has evolved, a number of changes have been offered. The proposed changes, however, have reflected a continuing preoccupation with means over ends. They always focus on operating procedure—on efficiency rather than effectiveness (Goldstein, 1990, p. 15). The guiding principle is that the police must always react. The reaction must always be within firmly established guidelines. Means have not only become more important than ends, in many instances the means have in fact become the ends.

Problem-Oriented Police Management

In its simplest form, problem-oriented policing (POP) is geared more toward effectiveness than efficiency. Rather than reacting to community problems within a set of structurally rigid guidelines, POP attempts to identify problems in their earliest stages of development. Once identified, steps are taken to eliminate or minimize the destructive effects of the problem. According to Goldstein, "problem-oriented policing is a comprehensive plan for improving policing in which the high priority attached to addressing substantive problems shapes the police agency, influencing all changes in personnel, organization, and procedures" (1991, p.32). The movement to the POP philosophy does not mean a total abandonment of traditional policing. Many of the positive elements are retained. High training standards and a commitment to professional policing are as revered in POP as in the traditional model. Similarly, the police in the POP model also respond to calls for service and investigate incidents after the fact. They still arrest suspects and present cases for court.

The change to a problem-oriented model does not so much change what the police do as it adds a new approach to police duties. Old functions are kept, but a new focus is added. The police become more than enforcers, they intercede before the fact. Rather than being isolated from the community and its leaders, they form a coalition with those people. Crime is seen as a symptom of a community problem rather than the problem itself. Problem-oriented policing is a model that integrates the police agency with other social service organizations and with the public. The traditional model is not abandoned; instead, it is improved.

The management style of the POP administrator is more participative than the traditional manager. Decentralization is stressed. The entire organization is allowed to participate in the identification of problems and solutions. Discipline in this system is a combination of punitive and corrective. Mistakes are tolerated more because experimentation is allowed.

Community-Oriented Policing

Community-oriented policing is related to problem-oriented policing but also differs somewhat in its orientation. The following description of community-oriented policing is from Robert Trojanowicz and David Carter.

Community policing seeks to intervene directly in the twin problems of crime and disorder in communities by direct involvement in the community. The community policing officer acts as a uniformed armed presence to deter crime, but equally important, he or she also takes action with citizen assistance to resolve problems before they erupt as crime. The officer performs a myriad of services, from educating citizens on preventing crime and organizing neighborhood organizations to gathering information that leads directly to the apprehension of criminals. In addition, the community policing officer also targets specific populations for special attention, typically children, women, and the elderly. The officers' efforts have a concrete impact on the day-to-day lives of community residents.

Community policing can also be distinguished from other forms of policing because it derives its priorities in part from community input. In addition, because physical and social disorder cluster closely with crime, the CPO also acts as the community facilitator in dealing with these problems. In the CPO's role as liaison, the officer acts as the community's link to public and private agencies, acting as ombudsman to deal with neighborhood decay (1988, pp. 17–18).

Community-oriented policing differs from problem-oriented policing in a number of ways. There is a greater emphasis on the relationship of the street-level police officer with the citizens of the community. Where the problem-oriented approach brings police management into closer touch with community leaders, the community-oriented approach does the same with officers and neighborhood leaders.

Managing the community-oriented police agency requires an even greater commitment to decentralized decision making. Problem solving is moved into the lowest ranks of the department. Each element is given the freedom to resolve problems at the neighborhood level. Punitive discipline is retained where necessary, but there is a strong emphasis on creativity and innovation.

DISCUSSION QUESTIONS

1. Define *administration* and identify its functions.

2. Compare the functions and duties of administration, management, and supervision.

3. In the case *Popow* v. *City of Margate*, which of the administrative functions did the chief of police fail to perform adequately?

4. What is the relationship between a police agency budget and the performance of its duties?

5. Discuss the unique features of law enforcement that complicate the administration and management of these agencies.

REFERENCES

Drucker, Peter F. (1974). *Management: Tasks, Responsibilities, Practices.* New York: Harper & Row.

Goldstein, Herman (1977). *Policing a Free Society.* Cambridge, Mass.: Ballinger.

_____ (1979). "Improving policing: a problem-oriented approach," *Crime and Delinquency*, Vol. 25, pp. 236–258

_____ (1990). *Problem-Oriented Policing*, New York: McGraw-Hill .

Moore, Mark H., and Darrel W. Stephens (1991). *Beyond Command and Control: The Strategic Management of Police Departments.* Washington, D.C.: Police Executive Research Forum.

Trojanowicz, Robert, and David Carter (1988). *The Philosophy and Role of Community Policing.* Community Policing Series No. 13. East Lansing, Mich.: National Neighborhood Foot Patrol Center, School of Criminal Justice, Michigan State University.

Wilson, James Q. (1989). *Bureaucracy: What Government Agencies Do and Why They Do It.* New York: Basic Books.

Chapter 2

The Police Mission

E very police agency should have a mission statement. It need not be long or complex; it is better that it be short and direct. The mission statement is nothing more than a series of sentences describing the agency's purpose. It identifies the direction for the agency and establishes the parameters within which organizational goals should be established.

Writing such a statement, however, is not always easily done. The mission statement should broadly encompass areas of police responsibility. Unfortunately, police responsibility often appears to encompass everything. The purpose of this chapter is to examine those factors that must be considered in determining the police mission.

The police are the most visible entity of the criminal justice system. This is by design, as the police are one of the few public service organizations responsible for handling emergencies. High visibility allows rapid recognition of law enforcement officers by innocent citizens as well as criminals. There are positive aspects to this visibility. The readily identifiable badge and uniform allow the officer to assume command of a situation quickly, thus eliminating the time-consuming procedure of producing identification to verify that the person is a police officer. Law enforcement officials have also argued that high visibility generates a feeling of safety among the general population. The thrust of the idea is that observation of marked police vehicles and uniformed officers makes people believe that the police are always close enough to aid those in need.

Furthermore, many in law enforcement believe that this same visibility strikes fear into would-be criminals, thereby deterring criminal activity.

There are also negative aspects to high visibility. Any member of a highly visible minority can attest to the problem of stereotyping. The police qualify as a minority in the sense that the actions of a few are generalized to the whole. Law enforcement personnel are rarely seen as individuals but as uniforms and symbols of authority. The world of the law enforcement officer is akin to life in a fishbowl: always under scrutiny and observation. In a sense we trade the police officer's security for our own. We may feel better seeing the uniform, but the person wearing it is always playing to an attentive audience. They cannot even eat a meal in public without being the center of attention.

Whether or not this visibility is useful in the prevention of crime is debatable. Evidence would indicate that it is not, although it does allow the officer a means of rapid identification in emergency situations. The uniform, badge, and gun signify power, and this can be useful in a number of situations. We could argue, therefore, that some degree of visibility is necessary. Past debates over the appropriate attire for law enforcement officers could be a meaningless dispute. Nazi Germany's Gestapo provided a strong example of a police agency without a uniform that symbolized fear and loathing. On the other hand, all Western democracies provide uniforms for their law enforcement officers. In truth, the respect that an agency receives is a result of the quality of the personnel wearing the uniforms and the competence of their performance.

This brings us to the major emphasis of this chapter, the duties of the police. To provide competent service a law enforcement administrator must first know what service is to be provided. Generally speaking, law enforcement management in the past has failed the public and the police personnel in three ways: (1) the inability to identify the police mission, (2) improper training, and (3) inadequate policies. The administrators of any organization must understand the business they manage. From this knowledge the staffing and training needs can be developed. Finally, policies and procedures must be formulated to guide the organization toward the desired goals. The failure to identify the police mission has resulted in a lack of appropriate staffing and training needs, and finally in a confused, and often conflicting, set of policies and procedures. How can a plan be designed to achieve objectives when no one knows what those objectives are? Clearly, all functions, policies, and procedures are dependent on the organization's goals. Those goals must be designed with an eye toward the overall mission of the organization. Many police agencies have not recognized this simple truth. The result has been fragmented and inconsistent delivery of police service.

The lack of a clear mission statement, however, is not totally the fault of various police managers. Law enforcement agencies have accumulated new and varied responsibilities at an alarming rate. Many of these duties were unanticipated and seemingly at odds with the traditional police function. The police administrators have not taken a stand on some issues regarding what should and should not be police responsibilities. They have taken on each new duty, often using the added responsibility to justify a larger budget and police force. Society has added each new responsibility to the police while forgetting they also share social responsibilities. As a result, law enforcement agencies find themselves doing far more for us than we have a right to expect, and far more than they may have the resources to accomplish.

To be truly effective, the law enforcement administrator must set down with the personnel, upper management, members of the public, and media to discuss openly the elements of a practical and appropriate mission statement. It cannot be stressed enough that while there will be similarities in the mission statements of law enforcement agencies, no two are likely to be identical. Different communities have different needs, and various agencies have varying resources and capabilities. The mission must be tailored to the individual agency and community.

To understand what the police attempt to do, it is necessary first to understand why they were formed. The modern American police force did not come into being until the late nineteenth and early twentieth centuries. Prior to this time, the law enforcement function was performed by the military or through the combined efforts of the military and civilian population. A growing urban population combined with a need for a more structured response to crime led to the creation of better structured and organized police agencies.

Concurrent with the development of the police has been an evolution in police philosophy. The duties and responsibilities of police organizations have changed with time and perspective.

THE PHILOSOPHY OF POLICING

How the police perceive their function is closely related to the administrator's philosophy of policing. Each administrator has a philosophy; each philosophy is a product of tradition, education, and experience. That philosophy will have a dramatic effect on the effectiveness of the organization. Only recently have we began to pay serious consideration to the organizational philosophy itself. This system of beliefs is widespread within an organization and has a great impact on organizational performance. Over the history of American policing, three distinct philosophical models of policing have emerged. Understanding which model is adopted by an administrator and an organization can tell an observer a great deal about the organization and where it is going.

If you spend enough time watching television cop shows, you might get the idea that all police agencies are pretty much alike. With the exception of the differences due to size, fictional police departments are very similar. In reality this is a far cry from the truth. Like other institutions, law enforcement goes through phases. The police of this country are in the midst of a transition period now. The phrase *philosophy of policing* is used to describe the differences in the focus of police agencies. Indeed, the philosophy of an agency determines many things about that department. It establishes organizational structure, the nature of superior-subordinate relationships, and organizational priorities.

Traditional Policing

Law enforcement in America developed sporadically for over a century. The socioeconomic factors that shaped this nation also shaped the structure and procedures of agencies from coast to coast. Although there were a number of attempts at police reform prior to the 1960s introduced by a few outstanding police leaders, it was not until the 1960s that the public became fully involved with the idea of police reform. Television was most instrumental in highlighting police shortcomings. Following the civil unrest associated with both the Vietnam War and the civil rights movement, the police were placed in the spotlight. What American citizens saw on their television night after night did little to foster the image of a professional police force. They saw brutality and intolerance. Something had to change and change it did.

It would be unfair to attribute all subsequent changes in policing to the turbulent 1960s. The majority of changes that occurred would probably have occurred anyway. Police agencies nationwide had already begun adopting higher standards and better procedures; the movement to professionalism was already under way. The combination of nightly television news stories combined with an activist U.S. Supreme Court, however, greatly increased the speed at which these changes occurred.

The widely held belief that the police were out of control led to the development of an organizational structure with rigid lines of authority and the appearance of strict accountability. The idea was not new. Following the Civil War in the United States, most American police organizations adopted a paramilitary structure, including rank designations.

Emphasis was placed on efficiency and control. The philosophical basis for the professional model was rigid bureaucracy. Efforts were made to improve personnel selection standards and training. Operating procedures were developed with the intent to speed up the flow of paperwork. The acquisition of modern equipment and investigative technology was also given high priority. The police began to see themselves as crime fighters; all other functions were considered of lesser priority. The police value system shifted to accommodate this new attitude. The police, and only the police, were responsible for crime control.

Efficiency and Discipline

The great strength of the professional model was its ability to control the organization. Street police officers operate with tremendous autonomy. Each officer decides the fate of numerous people throughout the course of the day. Only when an arrest is made is there likely to be any supervision. Otherwise, only the officer and citizen are aware of the officer's actions. Frequently, the citizen has no way of judging the officer's acts as legal or illegal, moral or immoral, ethical or unethical, right or wrong. Too many officers—past and present—have done what they pleased to whom they pleased.

In an atmosphere devoid of control, the first step in reform is gaining control. The professional model stressed this aspect of management. This was badly needed; police organizations were improved substantially because of this management model. Professional policing stressed consistency in policy and procedure, and personal accountability of police personnel. A high-priority item was police training. Standardized curricula were developed and (POST) police officer standards and training commissions evolved throughout the nation.

In the areas of managerial control, personnel selection and training, and technological innovation, policing in the United States took a giant leap forward. For the most part, the professional model was timely and necessary. Much good in modern police organizations is due to this model.

Community Isolation

An inevitable drawback to the shift to the professional model was the isolation of the police from the community they served

There had been serious problems with the police of earlier eras. The officers were poorly educated, untrained, and allied with partisan politics. It was not all bad, however; there were some positive aspects of this system. The police were close to the public, and much of that relationship was good. Neither street-level officers nor citizens were highly mobile; that is, they did not change jobs or residences often. Because of this, citizens and officers interacted over a long time period; they came to know one another. Despite the corruption and political favoritism, many officers were liked and respected by the people they policed. The structure of the political machine added to this relationship. Officers were hired out of their respective neighborhoods. Despite the lack of trust that people had for the police hierarchy, they knew their own officers on the street. Grassroots policing was reasonably effective even if police management was scorned.

With the introduction of the professional model, this changed. The officers gave up the intimacy of the foot beat for the mobility of the police car. Fewer officers could cover more territory and respond to more calls from a motor vehicle. Efficiency was seen as important; intimacy was seen as part of the corruption problem.

The professional model's emphasis on efficiency took the form of providing service. The police made a commitment to answer each and every call for service, regardless of the validity of the call (Goldstein, 1990, p. 19). Efficiency, therefore, meant handling calls rapidly.

Handling calls effectively was assumed, but this was not always the case. As demand grew, so did the drive to increase speed of call processing. As the police became consumed with their own priorities, all other functions assumed a lower value. Answering calls, taking reports, and returning to the streets became standard operating procedure. Effectiveness dropped as the need to take a report as rapidly as possible superseded the need to take as accurate a report as possible.

In most professional police agencies, the number of calls has long since outstripped the ability of the departments to respond either rapidly or effectively. The professional model has thus become trapped by its own priorities. The police became obsessed with immediacy. They adopted a "brushfire" approach to policing. They became so overwhelmed in the attempt to put out every little brushfire—respond to every call—they lost the ability to solve problems.

The focus for every single police-related event was now—today. Past and future became abstractions of little or no value. The police were aware that they were facing the same problems daily; arresting the same people and mediating the same disputes. The idea of looking at the causes of these problems and seeking a permanent solution was never seriously considered. The present-oriented values system was by then too firmly entrenched.

Perhaps the greatest drawback to the professional model was the altered relationship between police and policed. In the days of the political machine, the police were problem solvers. The machine stayed in power by solving any and all problems of the voters. The police were not crime fighters so much as mediators and social fix-it experts. They were expected to work closely with their constituents to solve problems at the neighborhood level.

The new philosophy meant that the police were law enforcers rather than problem solvers. The term *law enforcement* became the label of choice, for it clearly defined what the police believed they did and ignored those duties they saw as not being real police work. They ceased to be proactive—seeking to prevent criminal acts beforehand—and became a reactive force; always responding to events after the fact. The public came to be seen as outsiders. Not only did the police view crime as their province alone, but any public action regarding crime, unless as merely a witness or victim, was seen as an unwanted intrusion. The official position of the police was that law enforcement was to be left to the professionals; amateurs—average citizens—were not welcome.

Police isolation, was therefore self-imposed. With each passing year the relationship between police and public moved farther apart. By the late 1970s and early 1980s it was becoming clear that the gap had become too wide. Something needed to be done to bring the police and public back together.

Problem Oriented Policing

The term *problem-oriented policing* (POP) was introduced by Herman Goldstein in 1979. He was among the first to recognize the serious limitations inherent in the professional model of policing. The philosophy of this approach is based on the idea that police priorities are frequently out of touch with the community's problems.

Problem-oriented policing assumes neutral priorities. Instead, community problems are identified and priorities established in responding to those problems. The police management team, street officers, and community representatives may all be involved in both the identification of problems and the selection of priorities and solutions.

An interesting aspect of problem-oriented policing is that it may be instituted as a department-wide operation or may use ad hoc police units for specific problems. A police agency may therefore retain its professional model orientation and still adopt POP for specific problems.

Defining the Problems

The major emphasis in problem-oriented policing is on identifying problems. The quickest means by which some of the community problems may be identified is by an analysis of police calls. Traditionally, the police handle calls in a cursory manner with little view toward the factors that led to the call. They rarely, if ever, ask why a shoplifter stole or why a husband and wife continue to fight day after day, week after week. By grouping similar incidents into problem categories and analyzing the factors involved in the causes, possible long-term solutions to these problems may be identified (Goldstein, 1990, p. 33).

Adopting this view of police work requires two changes in current police procedure. First, it requires that officers identify the relationships between incidents, such as similarities of behavior, location, and persons involved. Second, it requires that officers begin to think in terms of causal factors. They must acquaint themselves with some of the conditions and factors that lead to such behavior (Goldstein, 1990, p. 33).

Community-Oriented Policing

Much of the early work done in community-oriented policing was accomplished through the national Neighborhood Foot Patrol Center at Michigan State University (later changed to the National Center for Community Policing). Through its research, primarily in Flint, Michigan, this organization, under the able direction of Robert Trojanowicz, lay the early foundation for the concept of community-oriented policing. According to Trojanowicz and Carter, *community policing* is:

> A philosophy and not a specific tactic...a proactive, decentralized approach, designed to reduce crimes, disorder, and, by extension, fear of crime, by intensely involving the same officer in the same community on a long-term basis, so that residents will develop trust to cooperate with police by providing information and assistance to achieve those three crucial goals. Community policing employs a variety of tactics, ranging from park and walk to foot patrol, to immerse the officer in the community, to encourage a two-way information flow so that residents become the officer's eyes and ears on the streets helping to set departmental priorities and policies (1988, p. 17).

The community-oriented model does not see the various communities of the jurisdiction merely as resources, but as partners. In that sense it is a more intensive approach to problem-oriented policing. The many communities of the area are mobilized into grass-roots organizations working in conjunction with the police and other public institutions. Problems are not only identified by these collective groups, but priorities are assigned as well as tasks and responsibilities. This is done at all levels of the organization, but the primary focus is on decentralization. The major decisions concerning a neighborhood are made at the neighborhood level by citizens and line officers, not at the top by police administration.

Not all community problems are police problems. The need to identify social problems is matched by the need to identify the agency most able to solve, or at least address, the issues. Occasionally, nonpolice problems are inherited by the police. An example is treatment of the mentally ill. At one time such people were institutionalized; they were warehoused in facilities that kept them out of the public eye. Beyond the need to identify such people occasionally, the police had little concern with the problems of the mentally ill. They were sick and needed medical care. That care was provided in mental hospitals.

The movement to deinstitutionalize the mentally ill had a disastrous impact on the police. Many of the mentally ill were suddenly evicted; they became outpatients. They then joined a growing army of the homeless. The police were once more left to deal with a social problem not of their making.

Proactive Policing

Problem- and community-oriented models differ from the traditional model in yet another aspect. By identifying problems as they develop, the police are free to adopt preventive strategies to stave off criminal behavior. Rather than sit and wait for something to happen, they take appropriate action beforehand. Instead of reacting, they act.

Proactive policing is not new. The early European police forces believed strongly in the crime prevention aspects of policing and established their organizations accordingly. The French developed a strong intelligence program as far back as the sixteenth century. The British were involved in various crime prevention programs, starting with creation of the London Metropolitan Police in the nineteenth century.

Proactive policing within American police organizations, however, is a recent phenomenon. The first real attempt was made with the creation of crime prevention units during the 1970s. The original idea was to make every officer a crime prevention specialist. Crime prevention could then have been included as part of the criminal investigation or as part of a beat officer's routine function.

Instead, American agencies fell into the old habit of creating specialized units. The crime prevention function became the duty of a handful of specialists and was therefore someone else's job. While there were some successes with crime prevention programs, the failure to make crime prevention part of the organization's philosophy doomed it to mediocrity, at best, and only a public relations gimmick, at worst.

Problem- and community-oriented policing goes well beyond the ideas developed in crime prevention. The police are encouraged to address situations that may lead to problems in the community, some of which are potential crime problems. Crime prevention is retained, but as a part of a much larger view of the police organization's role in society.

Table 2-1

Comparison of Policing Models

Methods and philosophies	Traditional	Problem-oriented	Community-oriented
Command structure	Bureaucratic	Formal, but less rigid	Localized
Discipline	Punitive	Punitive and Corrective	Punitive and Corrective
Decision making	Top down	Top-bottom interactive	Bottom-up
Agency emphasis	Law enforcement	Social problems	Community interaction
Tactics	Purely reactive	Proactive and reactive	Proactive and reactive
Training	Emphasis on criminal law, self-defense, and weapons	Traditional emphasis with focus on social problem identification and communication skills	Heavy emphasis on communication skills and human diversity. Less concerned with traditional training focus
Staffing	Military model; physical attributes over intellectual skills	More emphasis on education and training skills	High emphasis on education and training. Least emphasis on physical skills
Evaluation	Quantitative: heavy emphasis on productivity (focus on process)	Mixed: quantitative and qualitative. Focus on both process and outcomes	Quantitative: Emphasis on results. Less focus on process
Rulification	Heavy emphasis: vast array of intricate rules, policies, and procedures	Policies are more general. Retains substantial body of rules and procedures	Broad policy guidelines. Least restrictive rules and procedures
Media relations	Confrontational: heavy emphasis on secrecy and control of information	Consultive: works with media to identify problems and solutions	Open: views media as part of community team
Politics	Non-political: isolated from governmental	Apolitical: works closely with government leaders to identify problems and solutions	Political at grassroots level. Involves all members of organization with community leaders at all levels

Table 2-1 offers a summary of the three models of police management. It must be stressed, however, that few police organizations can be classified as purely problem oriented or purely community oriented. Although there are some traditional police organizations in existence, many of these have incorporated some of the ideas and values of POP/COP models. Moreover, many agencies have adopted the terminology of POP/COP without fully understanding the concept.

The reality of contemporary American police systems, therefore, is a hybrid mix of the three models. This means that with the exception of some traditional agencies, Table 2-1 (page 28) cannot be meaningfully applied to any current police agency. It is not the intent here to provide the definitive statement on how an agency should apply these models but rather to provide a view of these models from a perspective of theoretical purity: to highlight the differences in these models to the greatest possible degree.

Police administrators have the freedom to pick and choose those aspects of each model and apply it as an element of their own personal and organizational philosophy. This has been, and continues to be, the practice of many administrators and there is nothing wrong with that application. The result has been the evolution of an array of hybrid models adapted for the use of individual agencies.

The good news is that it is supposed to work that way; each agency adapts to it's own environment. The bad news is that each hybrid system has applied whatever label the chief liked; POP, COP, or traditional. This has confused the definitions of these concepts to the point that few people now understand the differences between these models. Table 2-1 is an attempt to clarify some of the confusion.

THE POLICE FUNCTION

Despite an organization's philosophy, all local police agencies provide certain basic services. As a rule, state and federal agencies are more specialized. Whereas they will provide some of the services outlined in Table 2-2, county and municipal agencies will provide all. Philosophy determines the priority with which the services are structured and the policies and procedures determining how such services will be delivered.

The police function can be divided into four broad categories under which their duties are grouped. These are: order maintenance, law enforcement, emergency services, and crime prevention (see Table 2-2). In addition, the police provide a variety of services that are not normally considered to be part of their function. Since the police provide 24-hour-a-day service at no charge, they may be asked to respond to almost any conceivable problem. In this capacity the police frequently act as a type of clearing house; if they cannot solve the problem, the police direct the citizen(s) to the appropriate agency or private enterprise.

Table 2-2

The Police Mission

Function	Responsibilities
Order maintenance	Providing for the community's sense of well being through a police presence; assisting to maintain an orderly flow of traffic; guaranteeing the constitutional rights of all people; assisting those in need; identifying problems within the community, and resolving interpersonal conflicts.
Law enforcement	Providing for the safety of the public by enforcing violations of laws and ordinances committed in their presence; investigating criminal activity and bringing criminal suspects before the court for trial.
Emergency services	Providing rapid response to people in physical danger, both police protective services and emergency first aid to those in need of such services.
Crime prevention	Deterring criminal activity through the use of uniform patrol techniques, crime prevention programs, and selective enforcement techniques.

Order Maintenance

The order maintenance function is the area to which law enforcement officers devote most of their time. Historically, the problem with this function has been the lack of legal authority given the police to adequately fulfill these obligations. Despite the proactive nature of problem-oriented policing, the legal system is reactive. It is geared to responding after the fact. Order maintenance is often proactive, requiring action to prevent a criminal or nonsocial act. As a result, some actions taken by the police in the name of public order are illegal or quasi-legal. Law enforcement problems usually need an immediate solution; they must be solved "now." The legal structure, especially when handled through the court system, is rarely prepared or structured to act in a timely manner. Although there have been some changes in this area with legislatures beginning to create some police powers to address such problems, many police solutions are still often creative and frequently of dubious legality. For the most part, these solutions seem to work out all right. When they do not, however, law enforcement officials sometimes find themselves entangled in legal difficulties.

A study by James Q. Wilson and George L. Kelling has provided strong evidence to support the contention that the police are more effective in order maintenance than in law enforcement (1982). They discovered a strong relationship between the perceptions of the public toward the acceptance of crime in an area and in the amount of actual crime. An example used by these authors concerns the psychological sensitivity of people to their surroundings. For example, when a person enters an empty subway car late at night, the mere condition of the car may determine how safe the rider feels. If the car is dirty, damaged, or is heavily marked by graffiti, the rider feels that no one cares about the car. More important, the rider feels no one is bothering to protect the car or the rider. Conversely, if the car is clean and cared for, the rider perceives that he or she, too, will be cared for.

Wilson and Kelling also point out that when a woman walks down a city street, she is not concerned about muggers and rapists in general. Such fears are abstract and most people believe that these crimes happen only to others. But if there is a group of young men loitering in her path, a wino sprawled across the sidewalk in front of her, or panhandlers approaching her for money, she will be frightened, for these are not abstract dangers but immediate unpleasant and concrete confrontations. Abstract fear of killers and rapists is not as likely to stifle business in the downtown area of a city as the actual fear of being confronted by bums, winos, prostitutes, and groups of bored, angry young men.

The implications of this for the police are dramatic. For the most part, groups and individuals such as those cited above are not always violating a law. Even youthful criminal gangs do not engage in crime most of the time. It would appear, however, that law enforcement can be far more effective in preventing crime by aggressively routing these people from the public streets, even though such action is often illegal and may even be unconstitutional. Thus the police can be most effective when they are proactive, but their legal foundation is purely reactive. This throws law enforcement into a direct confrontation with constitutional principles, and places the law enforcement administrator in a difficult situation concerning police policy and procedure.

We have been using the term *order maintenance* as if this concept were simple and all consuming. In fact, there are a number of police functions encompassed by this term. The order maintenance function consists of such duties as protection of constitutional guarantees, facilitation of movement, conflict resolution, aid for those in need, problem identification, and maintaining an image of security (Goldstein, 1977, p. 35).

Protection of Constitutional Guarantees

The U.S. Constitution was designed to protect the people from an overzealous government. This translates into protection from police abuse. In this sense, the American justice system differs from systems of other nations. Our courts, especially at the appellate level, devote a significant portion of their time and effort to police supervision. In a manner of speaking, the determination of guilt or innocence in a trial rests upon dual pillars of responsibility. The judge must determine (1) whether the information presented by the police was gathered in accordance with prescribed procedure, and (2) whether it supports the conviction of the accused. If the judge finds in the negative on either point, the accused goes free. Both parts must be found positive to achieve a conviction. No other justice system in the world, or in the history of the world, has placed this responsibility on the court.

Whether this is good or bad is not at issue here. The major police administrative concern is the belief that the emphasis placed on the U.S. courts, to the exclusion of all other elements, has unintentionally thwarted police development.

There is an unstated assumption that the courts are responsible for maintenance of the Constitution and are therefore the primary control point in the criminal justice system. Although this is theoretically true, according to the manner in which the system is designed, it obscures the fact that it is actually the police who have the most dramatic impact on implementation of the principles of the Constitution.

If the police choose to disregard these principles in one-on-one confrontations with the public, and are further prepared to commit perjury in court, there is little that either the individual or the court can do. The stronger the belief in the Constitution held by the police, the greater the likelihood that constitutional rights will be honored. If law enforcement officers believe that the Constitution is a nemesis whose only purpose is to thwart police effectiveness, it is likely to be ignored. The Constitution will be sacrificed to the gods of efficiency and effectiveness, at the expense of the accused, and ultimately of society. The lack of commitment to the Constitution is a problem inherent in our police and was aptly described by Goldstein:

> The model of a police agency that has emerged in this country has been a neutral, sterile kind of organization, devoid of a clear commitment to any values other than operating efficiency. It lacks specific standards by which the quality of its end product can be accurately assessed. Absent an effort to build a set of values into policing, those that prevail are the values of the police sub-culture. This accounts, in large measure, for the radically different judgments made about the quality of police service by police personnel as compared with those made by critics on the outside (1977, p. 12).

While the major emphasis had been on upgrading and professionalizing the courts, until 1968 little attention had been directed at professionalizing the police. With the advent of the Law Enforcement Assistance Administration (LEAA) and funding provided through the Law Enforcement Education Program (LEEP), there was a definite trend toward professionalization of the police through 1982, when these programs were terminated. It has only recently been realized that it is the police who have the greatest impact on our constitutionally guaranteed rights.

Of course, the Constitution is not concerned only with the law enforcement function. There are occasions when the exercise of rights by citizens must be protected from other citizens. When this occurs, the police have the responsibility of protecting the exercise of these rights. Some years ago this responsibility forced the law enforcement agencies of Skokie, Illinois to protect the right of the American Nazi Party to hold a rally, even though a significant portion of the citizens were Jewish and despised any vestige of Nazism.

The police also sometimes find themselves being both an adversary and a defender of a free press. They are adversaries when the press wishes to print something perceived by the police as critical of their actions. Simultaneously, they are defenders of the press by virtue of their responsibility for protecting the rights of the media as embodied in the Constitution.

Unfortunately, many law enforcement agencies have adopted a mostly adversary relationship with the media without realizing that ultimately, it is the press who ensure our freedom and that a free press is democracy's greatest ally. There are those in law enforcement who would willingly sacrifice a little freedom for more police effectiveness. They would do this never realizing that even police states have crime problems.

Facilitation of Movement

We live in a mobile, high-speed, society. Much more than most of us realize, we depend on the police to monitor and stabilize the constant flow of traffic. We have even developed law enforcement agencies for the sole purpose of facilitating the movement of traffic. While traffic control is rarely the only assignment given these elements, it usually is the predominant role of state police agencies.

Vehicular movement is vital to the economy of the nation. In other countries mass transportation systems reduce the law enforcement responsibility for traffic. The emphasis in the United States on private ownership of automobiles and a strong trucking industry, however, force the police to accept a major portion of the responsibility for supervising the flow of vehicular traffic. The highway is literally the lifeline of the nation, and the police monitor the highway.

Other forms of transportation (airplanes, ships, and trains) are monitored by various administrative agencies and have little contact with conventional law enforcement. Vehicular traffic, however, is controlled somewhat by a variety of administrative agencies, but actual movement is monitored by the police. Thus the facilitation of vehicle movement is a major objective of the police (Clark, 1982, p.27).

Other than highway patrol units, however, we find that law enforcement administrators frequently must use quota systems to pressure officers into enforcing the traffic code. Even though more people are killed annually on the highways than are murdered, many officers do not believe traffic enforcement to be real police work. Also, traffic stops are almost always negative contacts with the public. Few people enjoy being stopped by a police officer for a traffic violation and many react with erratic emotional responses such as anger or tears. Most officers do not enjoy such confrontations and therefore do not go out of their way to enforce the traffic codes unless it is an obviously flagrant and dangerous violation.

The same statement can also be said of accident investigation. Oddly enough, many officers would rather investigate serious accidents involving death or injury than minor, noninjury accidents. This is due to the emotional surge associated with incidents of major consequence. Serious accidents are real police work; minor accidents result in merely completing the proper forms. There is more prestige associated with the investigation of serious accidents than with minor ones. At any rate, all aspects of traffic control, law enforcement, and accident investigation are primary areas of police responsibility and must be treated as such by the law enforcement administrator.

Conflict Resolution

The domestic dispute is a task considered to be not only the most distasteful, but often the most dangerous of police duties. Interpersonal conflict is fraught with danger for anyone involved. The number of police injuries and deaths associated with domestic disputes is chilling evidence of the hazards involved. The danger only increases the necessity for the police to intervene rather than other social service agencies. The problem encountered by the police officers, and by the administrator from a policy point of view, is the lack of real legal authority given the police to deal effectively with these disputes. Most disputes occur on private property between spouses or people living together. Lacking a complaint from a neighbor or other outsider, the police are solely dependent on one or more of the participants in the conflict to provide legal grounds for police action. Since this rarely occurs, law enforcement officers must often create their own authority.

Claims of power not possessed, and threats of police action with no legal backing, are the primary weapons utilized by officers to bluff and cajole disputants into compliance with police orders. As long as the parties are ignorant of police powers, this approach often works. Once the participants become enlightened with regard to real police authority, law enforcement officers often find that they have no means of achieving even a temporary settlement of the dispute.

There has been some thought that conflict resolution is not a proper function of the police. Some people have argued the need to provide social workers on a 24-hour, 7-day-per-week basis for the response to such disputes. Those who support this idea believe that the police are ill prepared to address the root causes of the conflict and thus to resolve the problem permanently. They believe that social workers, who possess the proper education and training for this task, can be more effective.

The logic of this assertion is difficult to dispute. We should, however, have a better understanding of why the police are called in the first place. The most obvious reasons are (1) the availability of the police, and (2) the lack of costs associated with their service, but, there are other reasons that relate to the situation involving the people in conflict. First, many of the people involved do not believe they really have a problem. Calling in a specialist such as a social worker is an admission of a problem. Second, the police come only when they are called; social workers keep coming back to monitor progress, thus are a continuing reminder of the existence of a problem. The police pass no judgments and make no future demands. They come when called, keep the participants from hurting one another, then leave.

The police unintentionally reinforce the idea that the problem is a transitory, temporary conflict needing no special attention or treatment. The people involved want the police to protect them from each other, then leave. They do not want someone intervening in their lives. Finally, there is no evidence that intervention in domestic disputes is any safer for social workers than for police. The possibility that force may have to be used to protect one person from another, or the official from one or more of the participants, means that the police will still be required to respond in addition to any other agency.

How the police choose to respond is once more dependent on the police philosophy. The traditional model makes no attempt to provide long-term solutions. The problem-oriented model recognizes that long-term conflict sometimes turns to violence, even death. Long-term solutions may therefore become the police objective in these situations, despite the problems associated with bringing in specialists.

Aid for Those in Need

Law enforcement officers are expected to provide a measure of care for those who cannot care for themselves. They do not provide this service in the same form as that of mental health services or welfare agencies. Instead, they assume responsibility for helping elderly people when requested, children in trouble, those too intoxicated to care for themselves, and the physically or mentally ill when alone and uncared for. Although the police do not adopt these people, they are expected to know where to take them or which service agencies to contact so that care can be provided. In the case of the intoxicated person, either through the use of drugs or alcohol, this may take the form of an arrest. Although some would argue that an arrest is not very helpful, the reason behind the laws prohibiting a person from being intoxicated in public relates to the inability of such persons to care adequately for themselves. Many a wino has come to depend on the police occasionally for a warm dry cell and a decent meal. This has led to the development of detoxification centers in many states as a means of providing both care and cure for chronic alcoholics. In smaller jurisdictions, especially in rural areas, the law enforcement agency still provides this service.

The provision of aid for those in need sometimes takes a humorous direction. Officers have been called on to do everything from chasing skunks out of basements to prying locks off bathroom doors. The police have become the leading source for public services. Most citizens believe the police can either resolve the problem or locate someone who can. This is a useful and necessary part of the police mission. Of all public service agencies, the police are the most dependent on the good will of the people. As long as people feel that they can call on the police in any situation, the police can be comfortable in the knowledge that they are respected and liked. When the public no longer feels free to call the police, law enforcement agencies are in serious trouble.

The following case demonstrates the abuse of the responsibility to provide aid and care to those in need. This is a responsibility that cannot be taken lightly.

Parvi v. *City of Kingston* (1977)
394 N.Y.S. 2d 161

After plaintiff, while intoxicated, was transported by police officers to a spot that was only a short distance away from a busy thruway, he was struck by an automobile as he attempted to cross the thruway. In his subsequent action against the city for negligence and false imprisonment, the Supreme Court, Ulster County, John T. Casey, J., dismissed the complaint at the close of plaintiff's case. After the Supreme Court, Appellate Division, Third

Department, 51 A.D.2d 846, 380 N.Y.S.2d 781, affirmed the Court of Appeals, Fuchsberg, J., held, inter alia, that causes of action in negligence and false imprisonment were stated by plaintiff's complaint.

Sometime after 9:00 P.M. on the evening of May 28, 1972, a date that occurred during the Memorial Day weekend, two police officers employed by the defendant city of Kingston responded in a radio patrol car to the rear of a commercial building in that city where they had been informed that some people were acting in a boisterous manner. Upon their arrival, they found three men: Raymond Dugan, his brother Dixie Dugan, and the plaintiff, Donald C. Parvi. According to the police, it was the Dugan brothers alone who were then engaged in a noisy quarrel. When the two uniformed officers informed the three that they would have to move on or be locked up, Raymond Dugan ran away; Dixie Dugan chased after him unsuccessfully and then returned to the scene in a minute or two; Parvi, who the police testimony shows had been trying to calm the Dugans, remained where he was.

In the course of their examinations before trial, read into evidence by Parvi's counsel, the officers described all three as exhibiting, in an unspecified manner, evidence that they "had been drinking" and showed "effects of alcohol." They went on to relate how, when Parvi and Dixie Dugan said they had no place to go, the officers ordered them into the police car, and pursuing a then prevailing police "standard operating procedure," transported the two men outside the city limits to an abandoned golf course located in an unlit and isolated area known as Coleman Hill. Thereupon the officers drove off, leaving Parvi and Dugan to "dry out." This was the first time Parvi had ever been there. En route they had asked to be left off at another place, but the police refused to do so.

No more than 350 feet from the spot where they were dropped off, one of the boundaries of the property adjoins the New York State Thruway. There were no intervening fences or barriers other than the low Thruway guardrail intended to keep vehicular traffic on the road. Before they left, it is undisputed that the police made no effort to learn whether Parvi was oriented to his whereabouts, to instruct him as to the route back to Kingston, where Parvi had then lived for 12 years, or to ascertain where he would go from there. From where the men were dropped, the "humming and buzzing" of fast-traveling, holiday-bound automobile traffic was clearly audible from the Thruway; in their befuddled state, which later left Parvi with very little memory of the events, the men lost little time in responding to its siren song. In an apparent effort to get back, by 10:00 P.M. Parvi and Dugan had wandered onto the Thruway, where they were struck by an automobile operated by one David R. Darling. Parvi was severely injured, Dugan was killed.

Opinion of the Court

The Appellate Division upheld the dismissal of the negligence cause on the ground that it was not reasonably foreseeable that a person who is under the influence of alcohol will walk approximately 350 feet in the dead of night and climb over a guardrail onto the New York Thruway. Before treating that issue, we prefer to give our attention to the more basic duty owed by the city to the plaintiff in this situation, a question somewhat obscured by the jargon of negligence terminology.

In that connection we do not believe that it aids our analysis of the negligence count to speculate on the duty of a police officer to arrest or not to arrest intoxicated persons. Instead, we confront directly the duty of police officers to persons under the influence of alcohol who are already in their custody, as was the case here once Parvi was compelled to enter the police car. The case law is clear that even when no original duty is owed to the plaintiff to undertake affirmative action, once it is voluntarily undertaken, it must be performed with due care.

As Restatement of Torts 2d (324) puts it, "One who, being under no duty to do so, takes charge of another who is helpless adequately to aid or protect himself is subject to liability to the other for any bodily harm caused him by (a) the failure of the actor to exercise reasonable care to secure the safety of the other while within the actor's charge or (b) the actor's discontinuing his aid or protection, if by so doing, he leaves the other in a worse position than when the actor took charge of him."

We return now to the question of whether it was reasonably foreseeable that Parvi, who appeared sufficiently intoxicated for the police to take action, when set down in the dead of night in a lonely rural setting within 350 feet of a superhighway whose traffic noises were sure to make its presence known, might wander onto the road. To state the question is to answer it. To be sure, much has to depend on what the jury finds to have been the state of his sobriety and the nature of the surrounding physical and other circumstances. But traditionally, these are the kind of matters suitable for jury determination rather than for the direction of a verdict.

Finally, a word of clarification may be in order as to the legal role of plaintiff's voluntary intoxication. To accept the defendant's argument that the intoxication was itself the proximate cause of Parvi's injury as a matter of law would be to negate the very duty imposed on the police officers when they took Parvi and Dugan into custody. It would be to march up the hill only to march down again. The clear duty imposed on the officers interdicts such a result if, as the jury may find, their conduct was unreasonable. For it is the very fact of plaintiff's drunkeness that precipitated the duty once the officers made the decision to act.

Accordingly, the order of the Appellate Division should be reversed, both causes of action reinstated, and a new trial ordered.

Problem Identification

This aspect of the police function takes on a variety of forms. The police are the only public service agency routinely patrolling the entire geographic boundary of a city, county, or state. They are the most likely to observe potential problems as these trouble spots develop. Many governmental services are subject to failure within a given area. Water pipes break, bridges become unsafe, street lights burn out, and park equipment can break and become dangerous. All these problems are likely to be observed by the officer responsible for that geographic area. Since the officer is in position to observe the malfunction, usually before the appropriate agency, it is only natural that the police have responsibility for notifying the appropriate agency so action can be taken to remedy the situation in a timely manner. This can save time, damage, injuries, and resources lost through civil suits.

The same is true of "people problems." The officer on the street is in excellent position to pick up information on possible criminal conspiracies or dangerous acts. This information may also be transmitted to the proper person within the law enforcement agency or be acted upon by the officer. Information is vital to effective law enforcement. A major role of the police officer is to collect information and disseminate it to the proper personnel.

Promoting a Sense of Security

Law enforcement administrators attempt to justify the use of random patrol as preventing crime and promoting a sense of public security. The police argue that even if random patrol is ineffective in preventing crime, seeing a marked patrol vehicle in their neighborhood still makes people feel secure. This assumption is open to challenge. People may actually become more concerned when they see a police vehicle in their neighborhood because they feel that something bad must have happened to cause the police to be present. Of course, this is not true in all neighborhoods. In high-crime areas a frequent complaint of the people is that they do not see enough of the police (Radelet,1980, p. 219). From what research has been gathered (most notably, the Kansas City Preventive Patrol Experiment), it would seem that the ability to maintain an image of safety through high-visibility patrols is unsubstantiated.

Law Enforcement

The law enforcement mission is the most popular with individual police officers. Law enforcement is what police officers refer to when they speak of "real police work," as compared to the many order maintenance assignments making up calls for police service. Law enforcement is fairly self-explanatory. It is a process of coercing individuals into compliance with the legal codes through the use or threat of using formal legal sanctions. The police officer is most comfortable with this function, for it is the arena in which law enforcement officers have been most thoroughly trained and in which they have the most legally mandated authority. This function, and the aura that surrounds it, led to the following comments by the President's Commission on Law Enforcement and Administration of Justice:

> In society's day-to-day efforts to protect its citizens from the suffering, fear, and property loss produced by crime, and the threat of crime, the policeman occupies the front line. It is he who directly confronts criminal situations, and it is to him that the public looks for personal safety. The freedom of Americans to walk their streets and be secure in their homes—in fact, to do what they want when they want—depends to a great extent on their policemen (1968, p. 242).

The severity with which the law is enforced depends on a number of factors, not the least of which is the manner in which the individual officer views the police role. There are police officers who believe that the law is sacred and should be enforced to the letter (Broderick, 1977, p.11). Although this is a defensible view, it is unrealistic. All of the laws cannot be enforced all of the time; they are too numerous and all too often do not fit a particular situation sufficiently for appropriate application.

The law is merely one of a number of tools at the officer's disposal. Frequently, the law is the proper tool for the job at hand, and often it is not.

Other approaches may be better suited to solve the immediate problem. For example, it may be better to convince the participants in a dispute to separate temporarily, or the officer may determine that even though an arrest is possible, it would do more harm than good in that particular case.

The overzealous officer is not the only reason for the confusion surrounding what should be the appropriate degree of enforcement. Many states have statutes requiring the police to enforce all the laws all the time. This places the officer in the uncomfortable position of breaking the law every time that discretion is used and a formal charge is not filed against the violator, regardless of how minor the offense.

Similarly, enforcement of the law does not exempt the officer from caring for those in need or providing safety and security for the public. The following case provides an example of the failure to provide police protection following a lawful arrest.

Wood v. *Ostrander* (1989)
879 F.2d (9th Cir.)

Linda Wood brought this action under 42 U.S.C. §1983 against Washington state trooper Steven Ostrander and his wife, and Neil Maloney, chief officer of the Washington State Patrol and his wife. Wood appeals the district court's summary judgment dismissal of the case as to all defendants.

Trooper Ostrander pulled a car to the side of the road for driving with its high beams on. Ostrander determined that the driver, Robert Bell, was intoxicated and placed him under arrest. Ostrander called for a tow truck to have the car impounded, and returned to the car and removed the keys. Wood, who was sitting in the car, asked Ostrander how she would get home. Ostrander replied that he was sorry, but that Wood would have to get out of the car. These facts are not disputed. Wood claims that Ostrander simply returned to his patrol car and drove away. Ostrander claims that he offered to call a friend or family member who could give Wood a ride home, but that she declined the offer. Although Wood claims that she did not see any open businesses at the time when Ostrander drove away, Ostrander claims that a Shell service station and a Seven-Eleven store were clearly visible and open for business. Ostrander further claims that Wood was picked up by an unknown driver before Ostrander drove away, although Bell and Wood dispute this.

Ostrander left Wood near a military reservation in the Parkland area of Pierce County, which has the highest aggravated crime rate in the county outside the city of Tacoma. The temperature was fifty degrees and Wood was wearing only a blouse and jeans. Wood alleges that after walking one-half block toward her home, which was 5 miles away, and having turned down rides offered by three or four strangers, she accepted a ride with an unknown man. The driver took Wood to a secluded area and raped her.

The court ruled that although Ostrander did not himself assault Wood, he allegedly acted in a callous disregard for Wood's physical security, a liberty interest protected by the Constitution. Wood has raised a triable issue of fact as to whether Ostrander's conduct placed the plaintiff in a position of danger. The fact that Ostrander arrested Bell, impounded his car, and apparently stranded Wood in a high-crime area at 2:30 A.M. distinguishes Wood from the general public and triggers a duty of the police to afford her some measure of peace and safety.

The court also ruled that Wood raised at least a triable issue (if not an undisputed one) regarding Ostrander's knowledge of the danger: Official crime reports show that the area where Wood was stranded had the highest violent crime rate in the county outside the city of Tacoma. Ostrander, a state trooper stationed in that area since 1981, may well be chargeable with knowledge of these facts. Moreover, the inherent danger facing a woman left alone at night in an unsafe area is a matter of common sense.

The district court and the defendants too readily assume that Wood's travail would have been over if had she only gone to the Shell station or the Seven-Eleven. It is for the trier of fact to determine whether a reasonable person should have regarded a gas station or convenience store located in a high-crime neighborhood as a safe haven where she would have been given assistance or permitted to stay until daybreak before walking 5 miles home. Nor is a telephone much help to a person who allegedly has no money to place a call and no one to call. These factual assumptions, either expressly or impliedly made, are particularly inappropriate for the district court to make on summary judgment.

The court concluded that if Wood establishes at trial the facts that she stated in support of her section 1893 action, which the court must accept as true at this stage of the case, Ostrander would not be entitled to qualified immunity. A reasonable police officer who acted as Wood alleges Ostrander acted should have understood that what he was doing violated Wood's constitutional right to be free from an unjustified intrusion into her personal security in violation of her liberty interest under the Fourteenth Amendment.

A further complication to understanding the law enforcement function is generated by the mass media. Too many police movies and television series focus on the law enforcement function to the exclusion of all else. This tends to warp the public's perception of what the police should and can accomplish. *In truth, the police solve a crime when someone tells them that a crime has been committed, and when someone tells them who did it.*

Effective law enforcement is a product of citizen participation in the criminal justice process. Despite the emphasis placed on this function by both the officers and the public, police agencies are presently not very effective at law enforcement, especially if they fail to gain the respect of the public they serve.

Criminal Investigation

Of all police functions, perhaps none stimulates the imagination of authors and screen writers more than does criminal investigation. The image of the great sleuth ferreting out the criminal through the use of deductive and inductive reasoning has a powerful mystique in our culture. The truth, however, is a far cry from the image presented in works of fiction. Criminal investigation is a major portion of the law enforcement function. The primary focus of criminal investigation is the accumulation of physical evidence and statements from witnesses. Few cases are solved through intense mental reasoning; most are solved when a witness comes forward to testify.

There are scientific tools at the disposal of investigators; these are useful in placing a suspect at or near the scene of a crime. It is rare, however, that a case is solved by scientifically applied techniques alone. Effective criminal investigation has always been a product of developing informants and uncovering witnesses. To provide realistic policies concerning the investigative process requires an understanding of the realities of criminal investigation. Like good administrators, good investigators understand and like people; poor ones do not.

The investigator's greatest strength is similar to that of the crime lab. Investigators are not very successful at solving cases in which there is no identifiable suspect. When a suspect is identified, however, the investigator is proficient at collecting and organizing the evidence necessary to get a conviction in court. This is the real purpose of the investigative process and one frequently overlooked in discussions of criminal investigation.

Recovery of Property

Concurrent with the law enforcement mission is the responsibility for the recovery of property, either lost or stolen. Property recovery would seem to be most closely related to law enforcement due to the evidentiary value of recovered property in a criminal proceeding. In the past, law enforcement agencies have been somewhat lax in their fulfillment of this obligation. Police priorities appear to be attuned to apprehension and conviction of the culprit. More important, police personnel evaluation systems have been geared toward productivity in terms of arrests. Little incentive has been provided to encourage officers to seek out and recover lost property. Since officers gain nothing through the recovery of property, many do not go out of their way to accomplish this objective.

Most property recovered by the police is that which can be used in a criminal prosecution. For this reason the police are somewhat better at finding contraband than at finding property that can otherwise be legitimately possessed. Admittedly, part of the past difficulty in fulfilling this obligation has been the inability to communicate property descriptions, both lost and found, between various law enforcement agencies. The rapidly developing communications and computer industries may well reduce this problem in the near future, freeing the police to be more active in seeking out property and returning it to its rightful owner. Unless the police administrator is willing to reward officers who actively recover lost property, however, there will be no significant change in police procedure.

Emergency Services

The best argument for maintaining uniformed patrol lies in the delivery of emergency services. The deployment of personnel throughout the entire jurisdiction reduces the response time required for calls for service. Time is not relevant for most police calls, which may be categorized as routine completion of forms and investigations of past events. True emergencies, however, require a short response time. Thirty seconds may mean the difference between life and death to someone whose breathing has stopped or who has been involved in a serious accident. Since it is impractical to have ambulances and fire trucks patrolling an area for rapid response to emergencies, we must assume that the necessity exists for the police to fulfill this function.

Although this has always been a police function, it has only been in the past 20 years that the majority of police have routinely received serious first-aid training. It has, of course, only been within this same time period that the majority of governmental bodies required police training of any kind. Obviously, if the police agency is to be effective at providing emergency services, the officers must be trained in the techniques of delivery of those services.

The provision of emergency services may be second only to order maintenance in importance. When a police officer is given an emergency call, it is usually a situation concerning a threat of harm to an individual or group. The emphasis is on helping the person in need. As a result, law enforcement needs may even be relegated to a secondary position of importance. The community's need for a highly trained, rapid response emergency team justifies, as no other police function does, the existence of the police agency.

Crime Prevention

Crime prevention has been a recognized police function since formation of the first police agency. Formal crime prevention techniques, however, have only recently been developed for the police. People assumed that the police were experts in the prevention of crime, although no specific training had been established prior to the 1960s. Police administrators also believed that random police patrol would act as a deterrent by providing the image of a constant police presence. Law enforcement administrators are more sophisticated now. The theory of random patrol as effective crime prevention was seriously deflated by research, and techniques of physical security are now being taught to police officers throughout the country. The result has been new approaches to patrol utilizing computerized crime analysis techniques to direct the patrol officers, rather than depending on luck, as occurs with the random patrol approach. Crime prevention units have also been created to teach the public how to protect themselves. Crime prevention is therefore emerging as a major element of the police mission.

VALUES IN POLICING

Mission statements are clearly delineated statements of purpose for the organization. They explain why the organization exists. Value statements, however, are a new concept. Value statements provide the ideals the agency strives to attain. For example, the Houston Police Department publicly issued the following value statements:

1. The Houston Police Department will involve the community in all policing activities which directly impact the quality of community life.

2. The Houston Police Department believes that policing strategies must preserve and advance democratic values.

3. The Houston Police Department believes that it must structure service delivery in a way that will reinforce the strengths of the city's neighborhoods.

4. The Houston Police Department believes that the public should have input into the development of policies which directly impact the quality of neighborhood life.

5. The Houston Police Department will seek the input of employees into matters which impact employee job satisfaction and effectiveness (Wasserman and Moore, 1988, p. 4).

Value statements come in a variety of formats. Those above reflect the stated value system of the Houston, Texas Police Department, while the value system of the Madison, Wisconsin Police Department is embedded in its mission statement (Couper and Lobitz, 1991, p. 23):

> We believe in the DIGNITY and WORTH of ALL PEOPLE
> We are committed to:
> PROVIDING HIGH-QUALITY, COMMUNITY-ORIENTED POLICE SERVICES
> WITH SENSITIVITY
> PROTECTING CONSTITUTIONAL RIGHTS
> PROBLEM-SOLVING
> TEAM WORK
> OPENNESS
> CONTINUOUS IMPROVEMENT
> PROVIDING LEADERSHIP TO THE POLICE PROFESSION
> We are proud of the DIVERSITY of our workforce
> which permits us to GROW and which RESPECTS each of us as individuals
> and we strive for a HEALTHFUL workplace

Policing is a value-driven institution. Unfortunately, the predominant police value system has too often been that of the police subculture.* By defining those values that are important to the agency and the public, many police administrators are attempting to replace a dysfunctional set of values with those that are functional. A system of stated values acts as a constant reminder of what the organization is about. It is a statement that transcends what the police do and provides a clear statement of who they are.

* The collection of occupational mythology and informal organizational beliefs. "The police subculture is characterized by hostility toward the public, group solidarity, and secrecy" (Walker, 1992, p. 24; Westley, 1970).

DISCUSSION QUESTIONS

1. What must the administrator know before a mission statement can be prepared? Why?

2. Discuss the reasons for the development of the professional or traditional model of policing.

3. Identify the strengths and weaknesses of the professional or traditional model.

4. How do problem-oriented and community-oriented policing differ from the traditional model?

5. Why is the order maintenance function the most problematic for law enforcement?

REFERENCES

Broderick, John J. (1977). *Police in a Time of Change*. Morristown, N.J.: General Learning Press.

Clark, Warren E. (1982). *Traffic Management and Collision Investigation*. Englewood Cliffs, N J.: Prentice Hall.

Couper, David C., and Sabine L. Lobitz. (1991) *Quality Policing: The Madison Experience*. A PERF Discussion Paper. Washington, D.C.: Police Executive Research Forum.

Goldstein, Herman (1977). *Policing a Free Society*. Cambridge, Mass.: Ballinger.

_____ (1990). *Problem-Oriented Policing*. New York: McGraw-Hill.

President's Commission on Law Enforcement and Administration of Justice (1968). *The Challenge of Crime in a Free Society*. New York: Avon Books.

Radelet, Louis A. (1980). *The Police and the Community*. 3rd ed. Encino, Calif.: Glencoe.

Trojanowicz, Robert, and David Carter (1988). *The Philosophy and Role of Community Policing*. Community Policing Series No. 13. East Lansing, Mich.: National Neighborhood Foot Patrol Center, School of Criminal Justice, Michigan State University.

Walker, Samuel (1992). *The Police in America: An Introduction,* 2nd ed. New York: McGraw-Hill.

Wasserman, Robert, and Mark H. Moore. (1988). "Values in policing," *Perspectives on Policing*, Vol. 8, November.

Wesley, William A. (1970). *Violence and the Police*. Cambridge, Mass.: MIT Press.

Wilson, James Q., and George Kelling (1982). "Broken windows," *The Atlantic Monthly,* March, pp. 29–38.

Chapter 3

Leadership
and Motivation

The ability to get the organization from where it is to where it is supposed to be rests with the twin concepts of leadership and motivation. It might be said that leadership provides the organization's focus and objectives, while motivation provides the organization's will to succeed. A substantial amount of research has been conducted on both concepts. Theories offered to explain the why's and how's of leadership and motivation fill an array of books and articles. Despite the amount of material available, leading and motivating remain a mystery to many administrators.

In this chapter we look at a variety of theories that explain these concepts. Additionally, we will explore some ideas on what a person must do to be identified as a leader. Moreover, we will look at why motivating employees is so difficult a task to accomplish.

LEADERSHIP

The ability to lead is the single most important managerial skill possessed by an administrator. Many attempts to discover why some people are great leaders whereas others fail have been made by researchers over the years, with mixed results. When we acknowledge the significance of leadership in successful organizations or the lack of it in unsuccessful organizations, it should come as no surprise that organizations prize this ability in their administrators.

Leadership is a difficult term to define. It is made more so by the lack of relationship between ability to lead and who is chosen to lead. If only true leaders rose to power in society this discussion would be greatly simplified. Alas, such is not the case. We cannot even associate the ability to lead with some of those who have accumulated great power in the past. Such people as Adolph Hitler and Joseph Stalin attained the pinnacle of success in their respective nations, but their true leadership ability is open to question because of the manner, purposes, and results of their rise to power.

The problem lies in the variety of factors making up leadership ability. Leadership assumes a willingness on the part of others to follow. A person who no one is willing to follow is not a leader, regardless of how much authority or power he or she possesses. At the same time, leaders frequently have followers despite a lack of real power or authority. Leadership is therefore something internal to each person and is not controlled or dispersed by the organization. Unfortunately, even though an attempt may be made to identify true leaders when promotions are being determined, leadership is difficult to define and even more difficult to measure. The ability to lead, however, is crucial to the ultimate success of an administrator.

In the following section we will discuss various concepts of leadership, the most common being trait theory, leadership styles, situational approaches, and the normative model. First, however, we will discuss the role of theories and their applicability to management.

Trait Theory

Trait theory, which was very popular until about the 1950s, is based on the contention that good leaders possess certain character traits not possessed by poor leaders. The assumption is that leadership ability develops concurrently with personality during the formative years of a person's childhood. Those who developed this theory believed that a leader could be identified through a two-step process. First, leaders would be studied and compared to nonleaders to determine which traits were possessed solely by the leaders. Second, persons would be sought out who possessed these traits, and these people would be promoted into managerial positions.

A review of the literature on trait theory conducted by Joe Kelly revealed the traits most identified in research as being associated with leadership ability (1974, p. 363). These traits included intelligence, initiative, extroversion, sense of humor, enthusiasm, fairness, sympathy, and self-confidence (see Illustration 3-1). Prior to this review, a study of 468 administrators in 13 companies found successful administrators to be more intelligent and better educated; to have a stronger power need; to prefer independent activity, intense thought, and some risk; to enjoy relationships with people; and to dislike detail work (Mahoney, Jerdee, and Nash, 1960, pp. 147–163).

Trait theory has lost much of its support over the past 30 years. This is due partially to the basic assumption inherent in this theory that leadership cannot be

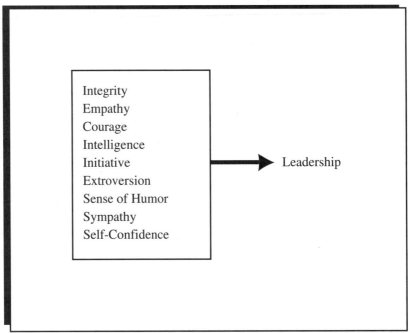

Illustration 3-1 Trait Theory.

taught. If this is true, attempting to improve leadership through education and training is an exercise in futility.

A stronger reason for the weakening support for this theory, however, is simply the growth of newer, more sophisticated approaches to the study of leadership. Trait theory served a valuable purpose in laying the foundation for future research. Its real weakness lies in the inability to quantify the traits it identified. What does it mean to say that a leader must be intelligent? Intelligent as compared to whom else in the organization or society? There was never a competent answer to this question other than the recognition that leaders may be more intelligent than subordinates. This is problematic since even proponents of trait theory never suggested using IQ tests as the sole basis for promotion. The same can be said of other traits: sense of humor, enthusiasm, fairness, and sympathy. Everyone has these in varying amounts. How does a person measure these traits to determine true leadership ability? The inability to measure these factors is really the flaw responsible for the subsequent decline in popularity of this theory.

Leadership Styles

In the 1950s, Edwin A. Fleishman began studies of leadership at Ohio State University. By focusing on leader behavior rather than personality traits, Fleishman believed that basic principles of leadership could be identified and taught (1953, pp. 205–222). Initially, leadership was thought to include eight measurable types of behavior. Eventually these eight were reduced to two dimensions: initiating structure and consideration.

Initiating structure refers to supervisory behavior that focuses on the achievement of organizational goals. *Consideration* is directed toward a supervisor's openness to subordinates' ideas and respect for their feelings as persons (see Illustration 3-2, p. 50). Even though the relationship between these two variables and productivity was not clear, it was assumed that high consideration and moderate initiating structure yielded higher job satisfaction and productivity than did high initiation of structure and low consideration (Sales, 1969, pp. 636–642).

Later it was discovered that productivity could be increased by increasing initiating structure. This was in direct opposition to the beliefs of those who proposed a human relations approach to management and who believed that there was a direct relationship between job satisfaction and productivity. In the later studies, job satisfaction was successfully sacrificed for the sake of increased productivity. These researchers learned that autocratic pressure can increase work output (Morse and Reimer, 1956, pp. 120–129).

The major focus of the style theory is the adoption of a single managerial style by individual managers, based on their position in regard to initiating structure and consideration. Basic to all managers.were thought to be three pure leadership styles: autocratic, democratic, and laissez-faire (Lewis, 1983, pp. 98–104).

Autocratic leaders are leader centered and have a high initiating structure. They are primarily authoritarians who prefer to give orders rather than invite group participation. They also have a tendency to be personal in their criticism while applying pressure on subordinates to accept their decisions. This style is most useful in emergency situations in which there is a need for strict control and rapid decision making. The problem with autocratic leadership is the inability of the organization to function when the manager is absent. This form of management stifles the development of leadership ability in subordinates, who are rarely allowed to make an independent decision.

Democratic leaders, or participative leaders, tend to work within the group and strive to attain cooperation from group members by eliciting their ideas and support. These managers are consideration oriented and work to attain a sense of mutual respect with subordinates. Democratic leaders operate in an atmosphere of trust wherein there is much more delegation of authority than with autocratic leaders. This style is very useful in situations where there is uncertainty about the course of action and where the problem is relatively unstructured. This form of management develops the leadership and decision-making ability of subordinates. In emergency situations requiring a highly structured response, however, democratic leadership may prove too awkward and time consuming to be effective. Although we may value the strengths of this style, we must recognize that major weaknesses also exist.

The third leadership style is laissez-faire. This is a hands-off approach to leadership. In this style the leader is actually a nonleader. The organization runs itself with no input or control from the manager. There are no positive aspects to

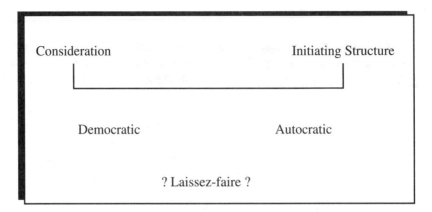

Illustration 3-2 Style Theory.

discuss with this style, and it is arguable that a manager who adopts this style will not manage long. This approach places the entire organization in jeopardy. Many authors on the topic of leadership styles no longer consider this to be an actual style. Rather, laissez-faire is considered to be administrative abdication.

Situational Leadership

Style theory assumes that each administrator will adopt one of the foregoing styles almost exclusively. This is based on the belief that there is a tendency for people to select a style which they believe works and to stay with it even when it fails. This assumption of managerial rigidity led later researchers to abandon the style theory for a more flexible approach. They realized that the impact of situations on leader behavior reduced the ability of the administrator to apply a single approach exclusively.

Early work in situational leadership was conducted by Fred Fiedler, who identified his concept as a contingency theory of leadership effectiveness (1967). His research was organized with the view that the personality characteristics relevant to leadership are stable over time and across situations. Some personality attributes are believed to contribute to effective leadership in particular situations, whereas other attributes improve effectiveness in other situations. An intriguing conclusion that Fiedler drew from studies he conducted was that leadership is not likely to be improved through either training or experience.

Fiedler's approach was called a contingency theory because he argued the absence of a single best approach to leadership. He believed that the influence of the situation determined the appropriate leadership style. Since, however, he returned us to the necessity of seeking out those who possess specific personality characteristics, which are once again difficult to measure, we must move on to other theories which provide us with insight into developing leaders within the organization.

P. Hershey and A. K. Blanchard refined the idea of the contingency approach and proposed a theory of situational leadership (1988). Based upon an analysis of organizational situations, these authors argued that a leader could behave in a combination of directive and supportive ways. They conclude that leaders use one of the following techniques to deal with all organizational situations: coaching, supporting, delegating, and directing. Table 3-1 highlights this theory. Directive leader behavior focuses on tasks, while supportive leader behavior is concerned with relationships.

Table 3-1
Situational Leadership

Leader Style	*Leader Behavior*	*Employee Behavior*
Delegating	Low directive Low supportive	High competence High commitment
Supporting	Low directive High supportive	High competence Variable commitment
Coaching	High directive High supportive	Some competence Low commitment
Directing	High directive Low supportive	Low competence High commitment

Normative Model

The normative model has been proposed to explain leadership behavior as a result of situational characteristics. Choices and decisions are incorporated into this model, together with the possibility of learning to examine situations and adapting the leadership style to fit various situations (Vroom and Yetton, 1976, pp. 1536–1549). Victor Vroom and Phillip Yetton have argued that supervisors use less consideration and more initiating of structure on poor performers than on good performers. He also noted that managers become more democratic when the situation is vague and unfamiliar, and more autocratic when problems are well structured and more precise (see Illustration 3-3). Vroom and Yetton stated: "It makes more sense to talk about participative and autocratic situations than it does to talk about participative and autocratic managers (1964, p.1545).

The normative model proposed by Vroom and Yetton provides a list of questions to be answered by the administrator in determining the appropriate response to the problem to be solved. Vroom and Yetton note that there are a number of discrete social processes by which organizational problems can be

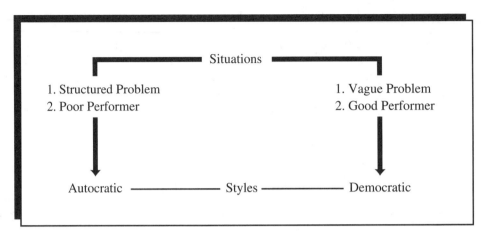

Illustration 3-3 Normative Model.

translated into solutions, and these processes vary in terms of the potential amount of participation by subordinates in the problem-solving process. Thus within leader-group situations, the degree of subordinate participation in problem solving varies. The range of variation is outlined below from the standpoint of the leader (Vroom and Yetton, 1976, p. 629):

1. You solve the problem yourself.

2. The subordinates supply the necessary information, then you make the decision.

3. You inform your subordinates of the problem, get their collective ideas, then you make the decision.

4. You bring your subordinates together, obtain their collective judgment about alternative solutions to the problem, and then implement the group's solution.

Since no one style is appropriate all the time, the manager must be aware of what type of process is appropriate for what type of problem. Vroom offered a list of "problem attributes" in the form of questions to be answered by the leader (1976, p. 1541):

1. Does the problem to be dealt with have a quality requirement, so that one solution would be more rational than another?

2. Do I know enough to make a sound decision?

3. Is the problem structured?

4. Must the subordinates accept the decision to implement it?

5. If I make the decision myself, is it certain that my subordinates would accept it?

6. Do my subordinates accept the organizational goals that will be achieved by solving this problem?

7. Is disagreement among my subordinates likely over the best solution?

Vroom further argued that leaders can be taught to break out of old habits of leadership style and make appropriate choices with regard to which style of leadership to implement.

The Art of Leading

What does all this mean? Are leaders born or made? What is more important, style or personality? In all probability a leader is a combination of all these things. Over the past 50 years there has been a substantial growth in the area of management training. Business schools continue to prosper; police management training is a growing phenomenon around the world.

Despite this trend it must be acknowledged that although administrative skills are often enhanced by these programs, leadership skills appear to remain relatively constant over time. It may well be that true leadership is found within the personality and character of each person. Invariably when subordinates identify a person as a weak manager, the cause is a personality defect. The same may be said of leaders.

Good Bosses-Bad Bosses

The topic of good management has been a source of best-selling books since early in the twentieth century. The cost to the organization, in terms of personnel turnover, poor decision making, low-quality products, and job actions by aggravated workers have led many in both private and public administration to seek the "Holy Grail" of effective management. Administrative theorists since the early masters, such as Henri Fayol, Max Weber, and Frederick Taylor, have professed to have the answer to these questions. Each year brings more articles and books on the subject, each arguing the virtues of a particular approach. Each of these theories rests upon a single assumption: that good management can be taught, learned, and applied. Those engaged in education sincerely hope this is to be the case. If it is not, many of us are wasting our time and energy.

For the sake of argument, however, let us explore the possibility that good administrators are born, not made. Anyone who has been involved with organizational life has known managers who were very good and many who were very bad. Often, both qualities are not products of a formal education or training. For example, how does one teach commitment to ethical behavior to a person who did not acquire this from parents and childhood friends? Honesty and integrity are crucial to effective management, but these traits are also learned early in life.

What about the characteristics of conceit, self-delusion, arrogance, and ignorance? How do you teach the danger of these negative characteristics to people who cannot view their own behavior and attitudes objectively? The hard truth is, you cannot teach such people, for they will not learn. Many people cannot be managers; they lack the foundations of character from which good management is derived. This does not mean that they were born weak, merely that they lack the foundation to prepare them for administration.

Good management can be taught but only to those willing to learn. A primary reason that poor managers cannot learn to be good managers may be their unwillingness to acknowledge that there is anything about management they need to learn. In short, a major cause of poor management is quite likely the inability of the manager to learn new techniques. People who do not know which of their behaviors is good or bad for the effectiveness of the organization are doomed to continue their present actions. Good managers are good because they are adaptable; bad managers may be this way because they are not adaptable.

What are the attributes of good and bad management? Beyond any shadow of a doubt, the primary skill necessary for effective management is the ability to interact well with people. Good administrators have the respect and admiration of their subordinates; poor managers do not.

Perhaps a better understanding of this topic can be derived by looking at what makes a bad manager. Michael M. Lombardo and Morgan W. McCall Jr. have done extensive research on the subject of bad management and have offered some powerful insights into this phenomenon (1984). Interestingly, managerial incapacities seem to be strongly related to character flaws in the personality of the manager. Lombardo and McCall identified 10 distinct types of weak manager:

1. Those who lacked integrity.

2. Hard-core autocrats.

3. Those who derive pleasure from their own sense of power.

4. Know-it-alls.

5. Those who are unable to make decisions.

6. Incompetents, managers who are prime examples of the Peter Principle—they are in over their head.

7. Those who delight in detail—most of their time is spent on minor issues.

8. People who, for some reason, often unknown, fail to achieve respect from anyone.

9. Those whose personal appearance or habits offend others.

10. Those who are not necessarily bad managers but who due to poor chemistry between the manager and worker, fail.

The connecting thread in each of these styles is the inability of the manager to elicit respect from subordinates. Good managers work well with people; poor managers do not.

The effect of poor leadership is an equally poor organization. As W. Edwards Deming observed:

> Leadership is the job of management, It is the responsibility of management to discover the barriers that prevent workers from taking pride in what they do. The workers know exactly what these barriers are: an emphasis on numbers, not quality; turning out the product [service] quickly rather than properly; a deaf ear to their suggestions; too much time spent on rework; poor tools [equipment].
>
> Rather than helping workers do their job correctly, most supervision accomplishes just the opposite (Walton, 1986, p. 70)

The following case demonstrates what can happen when there is a breakdown in leadership.

Horton v. *Charles* (1989)
889 F.2d 454 (3rd Cir..)

The city of New Kensington, Pennsylvania, and Sergeant William Dlubak, a police officer, appealed a judgment against them and in favor of the Estate of Douglas Powdrill, for Powdrill's wrongful death. The case was tried by a jury, which found in favor of the plaintiffs on liability. A separate trial was held on damages, and a separate jury returned a verdict of $65,899.00. Judgment was entered against the city of New Kensington and against Sergeant Dlubak in his official capacity.

The facts of the case are as follows: On November 10, 1982, the Cash Club was a private club at which alcoholic beverages were sold. It was owned by Charles "Pope" Flenory, recently retired from the New Kensington Police Department after 18 years of service, and who had enjoyed a reputation for violence. Shortly before November 10, 1982 the Cash Club was burglarized and some of the disc jockey's records were taken. Flenory called the New Kensington police and asked Sergeant Dlubak, with whom he had served on the police force, to come to the club. Before Dlubak arrived, however, Flenory and one of the disc jockeys began to interrogate Douglas Powdrill about the burglary. Powdrill, a casual employee of the club, was severely beaten.

When Sergeant Dlubak arrived at the club in response to Flenory's request, he also interrogated Powdrill who denied participation in the burglary and mentioned that he had actually informed the club manager, Mrs. Yolanda, about the crime. Dlubak instructed Powdrill to remain at the club while he went to question Mrs. Yolanda at her apartment. When asked why he did not take Powdrill from the club, Dlubak explained: "'Because I am talking to an ex-policeman that I worked with 14 years, and I know quite well; I figured that Mr. Powdrill is in good hands.'"

On September 10, 1982, the city of New Kensington operated under an official policy, reflected in the police department procedure manual, that the Department would maintain a hands-off policy with respect to events transpiring in private clubs. There is ample evidence that Dlubak's decision to leave Powdrill in the club in Flenory's "'good hands'" was made pursuant to that policy, and the defendants do not contend otherwise.

Following Dlubak's departure, Powdrill received another beating. Several hours later one of his relatives discovered him at the Cash Club and noted blood on the walls, and on the shirt of the club's disc jockey. The relative called the police. Two police officers responded and were met at the door of the club by Flenory. From Flenory's testimony the jury could find that he admitted to the police officers that a beating had taken place but that it had ended. The policemen did not investigate further, and there is evidence from which the jury could conclude that their failure to do so was pursuant to the township's official policy with respect to private clubs. Dlubak was not disciplined by the police department in any way for the manner in which he handled the incident at the Cash Club.

A half hour after the two police officers left the front door of the club, a relative took Powdrill to the New Kensington hospital, where, shortly thereafter, he died. Only after Dlubak learned of his death did he file a report on the burglary incident. The defendants contend that the evidence outlined above is legally insufficient to support a liability judgment under 42 U.S.C. §1983 (1982) either against Sergeant Dlubak or against New Kensington.

The court found that Sergeant Dlubak's role in the custody which led to Powdrill's death is sufficient by itself to prevent judgment notwithstanding the verdict. A further bar to such relief is the evidence respecting Flenory's role. From the evidence the jury could find that New Kensington delegated to Flenory its traditional police functions. The function of investigating crimes is clearly a governmental function. An official policy of deferring to private owners with respect to the investigation of crimes in private clubs, which the jury could have found from the evidence, suffices to permit a legal conclusion that Flenory, maintaining custody over Powdrill, was exercising a delegated state function. Thus even apart from Sergeant Dlubak's role in the custody, Flenory's role also precludes judgment notwithstanding the verdict.

The jury could have found from the evidence that this deliberate policy choice, duly implemented, exposed Powdrill to the risk that his constitutional right to be free of coercive custodial interrogation for purposes of law enforcement would be violated. That policy, the jury could find, resulted in Powdrill's interrogation in connection with a burglary investigation by a person not subject to the discipline of the police department, and thus likely to go to unlawful extremes. A factfinder could find that with deliberate indifference to the consequences, the city of New Kensington established and maintained, and Sergeant Dlubak enforced, a policy, practice, or custom that caused Powdrill harm. In this case it was the ultimate constitutional harm of death at the hands of an overzealous enforcer of the law.

If a person wishes to lead properly, what must the person do? A number of factors appear to be crucial to leadership within an organization. Despite the movement toward decentralization within police organizations, an absence of strong leadership will doom any organization to mediocrity or stagnation. The secret to success, if there is one, would seem to be the maintenance of a strong leadership role while allowing for substantial input from the personnel responsible for fulfilling the agency's mission.

To understand the problem, we must look at an organization from several points of view. All personnel see an organization from their respective positions within that organization. A patrol officer may have some good ideas about enhancing the patrol function but is ill prepared to solve the problems of the jail. Similarly, a commander of personnel will have better ideas about improving the personnel function than about improving the communications unit. Much of the infighting that occurs between units in the same agency is the by-product of specialization. All officers and commanders are more than willing to subordinate the interests of other elements to enhance the effectiveness of their own.

The point of view of the chief executive officer is therefore of prime importance. Only the CEO is in a position to view the needs of the overall agency from the perspective of neutrality. CEOs must have a clear understanding of the various strengths and weaknesses of an organization's many parts so that they can understand the capabilities of the agency as a whole. Additionally, the CEO must know what the organization is attempting to accomplish. Below the chief, all units view the world from within the limitations of their specialities. All other viewpoints within the organization are therefore limited. Like no other member of the organization, the leader must have vision and tenacity.

Vision

To lead, an administrator must know where the organization is going. The leader must have a future orientation. It is not necessary that the person spend every waking hour pondering the future; there are a frightful array of problems to be addressed here and now. What is important is that the administrator understand the forces shaping society and have a feeling for what this will mean for policing in the future. An administrator should be able to predict with some accuracy what the organization will be like in 5, 10, and 15 years.

It is true that the probability of accuracy drops with each passing year. Thus, the administrator's predictions for the 5-year mark should be more accurate than the those at 15 years. Complete accuracy is not important. What is important is that the administrator think in terms of future orientation. The person should always be asking: *What changes are taking place in society in general, and in my jurisdiction specifically? How will these changes affect this organization? How should this organization prepare for those changes?*

One thing that all great leaders have now, and have had in the past, is vision. The harsh reality of management is that if you do not know where you are going, you cannot possibly lead others there. A person may still manage or administer, but *without vision there is no leadership.*

Tenacity

History is replete with solitary visionaries who uttered their predictions to any and all who would listen. Some are called fools, others prophets; few are called leaders. Having a great vision is meaningless unless others are willing to adopt it as their own. The characteristic of a great leader is the ability to take a vision and transform it into a movement. To do this requires honest belief in the vision, sales ability, and most of all, tenacity. The transformation of an idea into action is a difficult and dangerous process. The administrator must first see the desired future, convince others that it is a desired future, then remove obstacles to the fulfillment of that destiny. Those obstacles are both internal and external.

A danger of problem-oriented policing is its reliance on decentralized decision making. Decentralization invariably leads to a parochial mind-set. It is a drawback to participative management. The further down the organizational ladder the decision is made, the closer it is likely to fit the problem to be solved. Unfortunately, the further down the chain of command, the further it is likely to be removed from the overall mission of the agency. The leader must be free to lead. Decentralization weakens that process if not carefully structured and delineated. The administrator must therefore be skilled in building a support network both within the organization and among various societal and political groups.

Finally, leaders have infinite patience. They do not quit. Changing an organization, especially one as entrenched as the police, takes time and unrelenting pressure. There are more failures than successes, especially at the beginning. Leaders stick with their agenda. With each setback they merely construct a new battle plan and attack once more. In a word, they are tenacious.

Principles of Quality Leadership

A major movement in management has been developing for several decades. Instituted in Japan by W. Edwards Deming, the concept of *Total Quality Management* (TQM) has been gaining acceptance in all types of organizations. Among the police leaders in this movement is David C. Couper, former chief of police for Madison, Wisconsin. Couper has adapted the principles of TQM into his management philosophy. He labels this philosophy *principles of quality leadership* (Couper and Lobitz, 1991, p. 48):

Anyone who wishes to be a leader in police management would be well advised to pay close attention to the chart on Page 59. This is a clear and concise description of sound leadership principles.

MOTIVATION

There are conflicting definitions of motivation. Traditionally, motivation is thought of as a means of stimulating a person to achieve an organizational goal. In this theory, supervisors provide external motivation to the subordinate, who then accomplishes the desired task.

The second approach to the study of motivation addresses the internal aspects of this concept. Those who hold this view propose that internal pressures created by some unmet need cause a person to seek a means to fulfill that need. These internal pressures are the actual motivators (Lewis, 1983, p. 185).

As with leadership, a number of theories have evolved over time to explain motivation and to predict appropriate methods of stimulating it within subordinates. Also, as with leadership, these theories possess varying utility, depending on the personal philosophy of the administrator.

Principles of Quality Leadership

1. Believe in, foster, and support teamwork.

2. Be committed to the PROBLEM-SOLVING process: use it, and let DATA, not emotions, drive decisions.

3. Seek employees' INPUT before you make key decisions.

4. Believe that the best way to improve the quality of work or service is to ASK and LISTEN to employees who are doing the work.

5. Strive to develop mutual RESPECT and TRUST among employees.

6. Have a CUSTOMER orientation and focus toward employees and citizens.

7. Manage on the behavior of 95 percent of employees not on the 5 percent who cause problems. Deal with the 5 percent PROMPTLY and FAIRLY.

8. Improve SYSTEMS and examine PROCESSES before placing blame on people.

9. Avoid "top-down," POWER-ORIENTED decision making whenever possible.

10. Encourage CREATIVITY through RISK-TAKING, and be TOLER-ANT of honest MISTAKES.

11. Be a FACILITATOR and COACH. Develop an OPEN atmosphere that encourages providing and accepting FEEDBACK.

12. With TEAMWORK, develop with employees agreed upon GOALS and a PLAN to achieve them.

Classical Approach

The classical or traditional view of motivation centers on the economic needs of the worker. Since money provides the means by which the worker supports the family unit and controls his or her life style, proponents of this theory argue that human beings are purely economic creatures. Managers who hold this view are predictable in their attempts to motivate workers. They will consistently utilize the carrot-and-stick approach to personnel management. Such administrators believe that to motivate workers it is necessary either to offer a reward for good performance or to inflict punishment for poor performance.

The classical approach to motivation can be traced back to the earliest organizations, and in spite of an impressive body of research denouncing this theory, it still retains a large measure of popularity among modern administrators. Those who adopt this philosophy tend to be autocratic leaders, or managers with high initiation of structure and low consideration.

Human Relations Approach

The philosophy of those who favor the human relations approach to motivation is based on people's social needs. These managers believe it necessary to recognize the power of the informal organization and strive to motivate workers by increasing job satisfaction. Sometimes called the Pet Milk theory, from an old Pet Milk commercial—"Pet, the milk from contented cows"—this theory revolves around the assumption that contented workers are productive workers.

The human relations theory had its beginning at the Western Electric plant in Hawthorne, Illinois in 1933. As a result of studies completed by Elton Mayo and his team of researchers, the impact of informal groups on productivity and organizational life was discovered (1961). Administrators adopting this approach will attempt to motivate workers through a distinctly democratic style. Every attempt will be made to make the subordinate happy. These are usually leaders with low initiation of structure and high consideration. The social aspects of the organization will be stressed by human relationists and economic considerations will be downplayed. Money will be a factor to be considered only for the effect it has on worker's contentment.

The philosophy inherent in this theory is based on people's need to be liked and respected by peers. Research has shown the willingness of workers to produce less than they are capable of producing, even when they are paid for piecework. This means that it costs the worker, financially, to maintain reduced productivity. The worker is willing to make this sacrifice in the name of social harmony: to maintain an image of solidarity with those who work at a slower pace.

Frederick W. Taylor first addressed this phenomenon in his work on scientific management. He labeled the tendency of workers to set informal production levels, *soldiering* (1947). Taylor did not, however, associate this tendency with the informal organization. He believed it to result from poor organization and lack of appropriate incentives for the workers. It was not until the Hawthorne studies isolated and identified the informal organization that soldiering was recognized for what it actually was. Soldiering is the product of peer pressure generated to protect less competent members while providing an easier pace for more experienced workers.

Human relations management is an attempt to motivate the individual through manipulation of the social environment of the organization. Administrators are nice to workers in the belief that happy people are productive people.

Hierarchy of Needs

The idea of a multidimensional approach to motivation was first presented by Abraham Maslow, who argued that people are not motivated by a single need, but by a hierarchy of needs (1954). Maslow believed that as people fulfilled one need, another need appeared which the individual strived to fulfill. These needs were listed in order of importance: *physiological, safety, love, esteem,* and *self-actualization* (see Illustration 3-4). In this theory a person moved up the ladder of needs as each level was satisfied and back down this ladder as lower-order needs reappeared. Maslow argued that since human beings are in a state of continual wanting, no need is ever fully satisfied.

Illustration 3-4 Hierarchy of Needs.

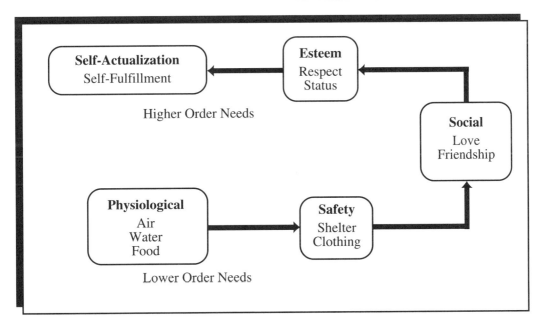

Items classified within each category were:

Physiological: air, food, water, and other items necessary for immediate survival.

Safety: clothing, shelter, and other items necessary for protection from external danger.

Love: Relationship with a member of the opposite sex and with members within the family.

Esteem: Respect from peers and family, as well as from the society in general.

Self-actualization: A sense of self fulfillment that comes only with the attainment of personal goals.

Although this theory was more sophisticated than earlier concepts, such as the classical approach or human relations management, it retained a lack of understanding of the true complexity of the person's mental makeup. Hierarchy of needs theory is useful in its attempt to demonstrate the variety of variables affecting actions, but has been abandoned as too simple to fully explain human motivation.

Maturity-Immaturity Theory

Chris Argyris offered still another approach to motivation theory. He proposed the development of individuals through the years from a state of immaturity to maturity (1957). Argyris argued for a seven-stage change in personality as people matured (see Illustration 3-5).

1. Individuals move from a passive state as infants to a state of increasing activity as adults.

2. Individuals develop from a state of dependency upon others as infants to a state of independence as adults.

3. Individuals behave in only a few ways as infants, but as adults they are capable of behaving in many ways.

4. Individuals have erratic, casual, and shallow interests as infants, but develop deeper and stronger interests as adults.

5. The time perspective of children is very short, involving only the present, but as they mature, their time perspective increases to include the past and the future.

6. Individuals as infants are subordinate to everyone, but they move to equal or superior positions with others as adults.

7. As children, individuals lack awareness of a "self," but as adults they are not only aware of, but are able to control "self."

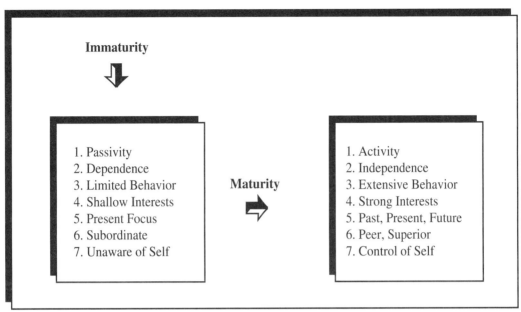

Immaturity

1. Passivity	1. Activity
2. Dependence	2. Independence
3. Limited Behavior	3. Extensive Behavior
4. Shallow Interests	4. Strong Interests
5. Present Focus	5. Past, Present, Future
6. Subordinate	6. Peer, Superior
7. Unaware of Self	7. Control of Self

Maturity

Illustration 3-5 Maturity-ImmaturityTheory.

Argyris argued that these changes exist on a continuum from immaturity to maturity. He further argued the existence of a stifling effect that most organizations have upon the natural progression to maturity. This occurs, he says, because most organizations utilize a classical approach that treats adults as if they were children, resulting in a tendency for workers to remain immature.

According to this theory, the administrator who wishes to motivate subordinates fully must generate an organizational environment that allows each person to grow to full maturity. The key to this environment rests with designing the job in such a manner as to allow each worker to grow into the job and the organization as a continuous process.

Motivation-Hygiene Theory

Frederick Herzberg conceived a theory of motivation similar to that of Maslow, but with more sophistication. Like Maslow, he argued the multidimensional quality of motivation. But he carried the idea well beyond that of previous theorists. He proposed the existence of a dual continuum for motivation and dissatisfaction rather than a single scale with motivation at one end and job dissatisfaction at the other (1968). He believed that the opposite of satisfaction was no satisfaction and that the opposite of motivation was no motivation. He was the first to argue the lack of relationship between motivation and lack of job satisfaction. Herzberg labeled these continuums *motivation* and *hygiene* factors (see Illustration 3-6).

Seven factors were identified with hygiene (the dissatisfaction-no dissatisfaction scale): *company policy and administration, supervision, interpersonal*

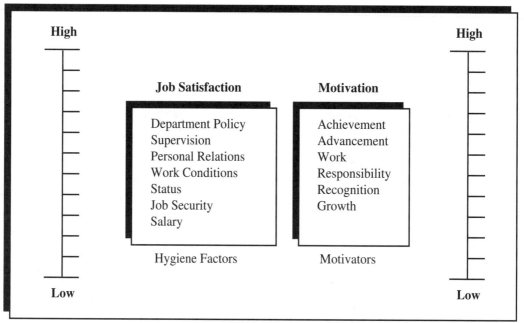

Ilustration 3-6 Motivation-Hygiene Theory.

relationships, working conditions, status, job security, and *salary.* Herzberg believed that hygiene factors could not motivate workers but could cause dissatisfaction with the job if these needs were improperly met.

He also identified six factors that led to motivation: *achievement, advancement, the work itself, responsibility, advancement,* and *growth.* While Herzberg believed that salary was not a motivator, he recognized the tendency of money to take on characteristics of such motivators as recognition, achievement, and advancement. In some instances, therefore, he believed that money could become a motivator. Herzberg also mirrored Argyris' contention about job design. He stressed job enrichment: designing jobs to stimulate individual interest and growth in an organization.

Critics of motivation-hygiene theory attack the manner in which Herzberg gathered his data. He asked workers to identify those factors in the organization that made them most happy and those that caused the most dissatisfaction. The motivators were constructed around those elements producing satisfaction while hygiene factors were those things producing dissatisfaction. Critics point out the tendency of people to identify things they themselves accomplish as good, while criticizing factors controlled by others. We all like to lay the blame for mistakes on others while taking credit ourselves for positive accomplishments.

Regardless of the criticisms, motivation-hygiene theory represented another step forward in the search for understanding what drives people to perform well. We should also be grateful for the spotlight that Herzberg placed on such elements of the organization as company policy and supervision as generators of low satisfaction. This is a constant reminder of the ability of the manager to destroy the effectiveness of operational personnel from behind a desk.

Acquired Needs Theory

David McClelland proposed that people acquire or learn certain needs from their culture (1962). This theory builds on that of Herzberg in that McClelland argues that when a need is strong enough it motivates the person to an action to fulfill that need. It is in the identification of needs that McClelland differs from Herzberg. Acquired needs theory recognizes only three acquired needs: *need for achievement, need for power,* and *need for affiliation.*

According to Andrew J. DuBrin, R. Duane Ireland, and J. Clifton Williams, "the need for achievement is the desire to accomplish something difficult for its own sake"(1989, p. 364). People with a high achievement need seek responsibility. They are more prone to take calculated risks and have a desire to get feedback on their progress (Stahl, 1983). A person who says that he or she climbs mountains because they are there is a person with a high achievement need.

The need for power is the need to control others. People with high power needs like to be in control of both people and resources. A person with strong power needs spends a significant portion of the time thinking about controlling and influencing others. This person also focus attention on obtaining a position of authority and status.

Research has shown that the power need is the primary motivator of successful managers (Cornelius and Lane, 1984). According to this theory, successful managers are driven to manage. They seek power over others and cannot obtain a feeling of satisfaction unless they obtain a degree of this power. The need for affiliation is the desire to be close to others. People with high affiliation needs may actually reject a formal leadership role. They are uncomfortable with managing others because they have difficulty with confrontation and hostility. Some research has shown that successful leaders have relatively low affiliation needs (McClelland and Boyatzis, 1982, p. 737).

This theory states that the combination of these needs and their relative influence on individuals determines their capacity for functioning within the workplace. It is most useful in explaining why some people seem driven to higher levels of management, others become task oriented and are neutral about management, and still others shun management and form extensive friendship networks within the organization.

Theory X-Theory Y

Douglas McGregor also challenged traditional theories of motivation when he proposed his *theory X-theory Y* (1960). He never implied that people could be classified in this manner but simply stated that managers' beliefs concerning the nature of people determined their managerial philosophy. Theory X and Theory Y, he argues, represent the opposing views of people as either inherently good or bad. A theory X manager treats people as if they cannot be trusted whereas theory Y managers tend to have faith in human nature. Theory X correlates very strongly with David Ricardo's _rabble hypothesis_, which states:

1. Natural society consists of a horde of unorganized individuals.

2. Every individual acts in a manner calculated to secure his self-preservation and self-interest.

3. Every individual thinks logically, to the best of his ability, in the service of this aim (Wren, 1972, p. 294).

Theory X states:

1. The average human being has an inherent dislike for work and will avoid it if he can.

2. Because of this human characteristic of dislike of work, most people must be coerced, controlled, directed and threatened with punishment to get them to put forth adequate effort to work.

3. The average person prefers to be directed, wishes to avoid responsibility, has very little ambition and wants security above all (McGregor, 1960, pp. 33–34).

Theory Y, on the other hand, assumed a much more positive attitude toward the nature of the worker. McGregor proposed six assumptions of the nature of man which underlie this theory:

1. The expenditure of physical and mental effort in work is as natural as play or rest.

2. External control and threat of punishment are not the only means of bringing about effort toward organizational objectives; man will exercise self-direction and self-control in the service of objectives to which he is committed.

3. Commitment to objectives is a function of the rewards associated with their achievement.

4. The average human being learns, under proper conditions, not only to accept, but seek responsibility.

5. The capacity to exercise a relatively high degree of imagination, ingenuity and creativity in the solution of organizational problems is widely, not narrowly, distributed in the organization.

6. Under the conditions of modern industrial life, the intellectual potentialities of the average human being are only partially utilized (1960, pp. 47–48).

According to McGregor, theory X and theory Y were not meant to be absolutes, but these represent merely two opposite ends of a continuum. Each administrator is believed to reside somewhere between the two extremes.

Goal Setting Theory

Goal setting theory was proposed by Edwin A. Locke. The essence of this idea is that conscious goals regulate a person's actions. Once committed to a goal a person will strive toward attainment. The goal will influence choice of behaviors, time allocated toward the goal, and methods of work to be employed (DuBrin, Ireland, and Williams, 1989, p. 373).

The basics of goal theory are as follows:

1. Difficult goals result in higher performance levels than do easy ones.

2. Specific goals get better results than do generalized "do your best" goals.

3. Feedback on performance improves effectiveness of goal setting.

4. Participation in goal setting improves performance only to the extent that it leads to high goals and to goal acceptance.

5. Goal setting improves performance when people believe that their performance against the goals will be evaluated (Latham and Locke, 1979, pp. 68–80).

Goal theory is closely related to the management philosophy known as *management by objectives* (MBO). Under that philosophy it is believed that an organization can be completely structured around specific goals and objectives. In theory, performance not only can be controlled and directed using goals, but it also provides an effective appraisal system that parallels the organization's mission.

There are negative effects related to goal theory. MBO systems have become very popular over the past 20 years. This popularity stems from the perceived objectivity of the administrative and supervisory process. The drawback is the reliance on quantification. If the goal cannot be measured numerically, it is usually "shelved" in favor of a measurable goal. As Deming says:

> A goal without a method for reaching it is useless. But setting goals without describing how they are going to be accomplished is a common practice among American managers.
>
> You can beat horses; they run faster for a while. Goals are like hay somebody ties in front of a horse's snout. The horse is smart enough to discover no matter whether he canters or gallops, trots or walks or stands still, he can't catch up with the hay. Might as well stand still. Why argue about it? It will not happen except by changing the system. That's management's job, not the people's (Walton, 1986, p. 77).

Expectancy Theory

Victor Vroom proposed a contingency theory of motivation known as expectancy theory. Vroom argues that motivation is the result of an individual's perception of a goal and of the path toward the attainment of that goal (1964). Under this concept each person identifies individual life objectives. Once these goals are identified, the person selects what is perceived to be appropriate means to attain these ends. The stronger the desire to achieve the goal and the greater the person identifies the means as appropriate, the greater the motivation within that person.

There are three variables identified with this theory: expectancy, instrumentality, and valence. An *expectancy* is defined as a person's subjective perceived probability that a given level of performance will occur. "The effort-to-performance ($E \rightarrow P$) expectancy refers to the individual's subjective hunch of the chances that increased effort will lead to the desired performance" (Dubrin, Ireland, and Williams, 1989, pp. 374–375).

An *instrumentality* is the person's assigned probability that performance will lead to certain outcomes. "The $P \rightarrow O$ instrumentality refers to the person's subjective evaluation of the chances that good performance will lead to certain outcomes" (Dubrin, Ireland, and Williams, 1989, p.375). Expectancies and instrumentalities range from 0 to 1.00 because both are probabilities.

Valence refers to the value that a person places on a particular outcome. People place negative valences on punishment and positive valances on rewards. The maximum positive valence is +1.00; the maximum negative valence is –1.00. Neutral valences carry a weight of zero (Dubrin, Ireland, and Williams, 1989, pp. 374–375).

In expectancy theory, therefore, motivation = ($E \rightarrow P$) ($P \rightarrow O$) (V). This means that motivation can be increased only if the expectancies, instrumentalities and valences are also high. The total range of motivation would be from -1.00, representing a total absence of motivation, to +1.00, complete motivation. As might be expected this formula is simplistic. The most obvious flaw is in the inability for accurate quantification of the variables within the formula. The assigned numbers, are therefore, little more than guesses, and not very educated guesses at that.

The strength of this theory lies in its recognition of the influence on motivation of situational and individual characteristics. Vroom also observed that motivation is such an individual phenomenon, that even knowing what needs a person wishes to fulfill does not guarantee the ability of the administrator and the employee to agree on the proper path to fulfill the goal. This theory goes a long way toward explaining why many administrators acknowledge a failure to understand their subordinates. They may have the same goals without agreeing on comparable methods of achievement.

Reinforcement Theory

Reinforcement theory differs substantially from other theories of motivation. Until now we have only looked at theories that address the internal processes of a human being. These include such internal concepts as needs, beliefs, perceptions, and desires.

The initial research on behavioral psychology was done by B. F. Skinner (1969). Reinforcement theory proposes that human behavior is determined by its consequences (Albanese, 1988, p. 435). These consequences occur in the external environment. The principles underlying reinforcement theory are simple and often repeated. Behavior that is reinforced is likely to be repeated, and behavior that is not reinforced or that is punished is likely to be avoided or eliminated. This idea was initially called the *law of effect* (Thorndike, 1911, p. 244). According to this law, it is not necessary that a person even know what reinforcers are at work. All behavior is a by-product of reinforcers and punishers applied, either intentionally or accidentally, to the person's behavior.

By definition a *reinforcer* is any consequence that increases the probability of a continuation of a behavior. A *punisher* is any consequence that tends to decrease or eliminate a behavior. The only way to know whether a behavioral consequence is a reinforcer or a punisher is to observe the effect on behavior (Albanese, 1988, p. 436).

This theory is built around a series of five contingencies. These contingencies are essentially *if-then* statements and are grouped into three broad classifications: *reinforcement contingencies, punishment contingencies,* and *extinction contingencies.*

The reinforcement contingencies are designed to increase the behavior. Within this general category are found positive reinforcement, negative reinforcement, and avoidance. Punishment and extinction contingencies differ in that they are designed to eliminate the behavior. Types and examples are provided in Table 3-2 (page 70).

Careful attention should be given to the use of punishment contingencies. Unlike the other contingencies, the use of punishment provides a strong potential for damage to the person on the receiving end. L. M. Miller has identified seven guidelines for the use of punishment (1978, pp. 197–202):

1. Use only when other behavioral contingencies will not work.

2. Use whenever the safety and well-being of employees are at stake.

3. Combine the use of punishment with the use of reinforcement. Use punishment to reduce undesirable behavior and reinforce the acceptable behavior with positive reinforcement.

4. Be consistent. Punishment should follow every occurence of the undesirable behavior.

5. Punishment should follow as soon as possible the occurrence of the undesirable behavior.

6. Administer punishment privately.

7. Punish the specific undesirable behavior, not the person.

Table 3-2

Types and Examples of Behavior Contingencies

Reinforcement Contingencies

Positive Reinforcement

Basic idea: Receiving a positive reinforcer is made contingent on a desired behavior.

Example: *If* you increase your score on the firing range by 30 points, *then* you will receive a firearms proficiency award.

Negative Reinforcement

Basic idea: Access to a desired outcome is made contingent on "escaping" from an obstacle to that outcome.

Example: *If* you complete the supervisory training program, *then* you will remove that obstacle to being promoted.

Avoidance

Basic idea: Avoidance of an undesired consequence is made contingent on some desirable behavior.

Example: *If* you show up on time, *then* you will not be suspended for tardiness.

Punishment Contingency

Basic idea: A punisher is administered after an undesired behavior occurs.

Example: *If* you fail to follow a lawful order, *then* you will be suspended for three days without pay.

Extinction Contingency

Basic idea: Undesired behavior is "extinguished" by not directly reinforcing or punishing the behavior.

Example: *If* you ask me for my advice on a problem that you should handle, *then* I will simply refuse to give it.

Source: Adapted from Robert Albanese, *Management* (Cincinnati, Ohio: Southwestern Publishing, Co.,1988), p. 437.

When reinforcement theory is used to modify human behavior it is frequently referred to as *behavior modification* (BMod). A newer version applied to formal organizations is *organizational behavior modification* (OBMod) (Daniels, 1985, pp. 225–236).

There are seven steps in the OBMod program:

1. A behavior that is a target for change is identified.

2. The target behavior is measured to determine frequency.

3. The current work situation is analyzed to determine the set of behavioral contingencies that is now reinforcing the target behavior.

4. A new set of contingencies is designed to obtain the desired behavior.

5. A new set of contingencies is implemented.

6. The new contingencies are evaluated to determine if they are working.

7. The new contingencies are monitored to make sure they continue to work and to determine if they need to be changed (Albanese, 1988, pp. 438–439).

Motivation and Job Satisfaction

Job satisfaction is an attitude that an employee has toward the job. Not just a single attitude, it is a set of attitudes toward the job in general and toward particular aspects of the job (Albanese, 1988, p. 441).

Many believe that job satisfaction is a single level of emotion. Still others see it as a complex set of dueling emotions. This is the basis of much of the debate between motivation researchers. Whatever the answer to that question, the variables that affect job satisfaction appear remarkably similar in all theories. They are: salary, the work itself, promotion opportunity, supervision, co-workers, and working conditions, all of which have an impact on job satisfaction (Albanese, 1988, p. 441).

An element in job satisfaction that is important to consider is the gap between the employee's expectations and the realities of the job. This is as true of the various aspects of the job as it is of the job itself. For example, if an employee expects to get paid $5.00 an hour but gets only $4.00, the person will be dissatisfied about the pay. On the other hand, getting both the expected $5.00 per hour plus a bonus will create satisfaction about the salary.

The existence of the gap between expectations and reality has dramatic implications for policing. There is probably no occupation in which this gap is greater than in that of law enforcement. The media bear much of the responsibility for this discrepancy. In "cop shows" there is only law enforcement; the world is one of felonies and felony investigations. Police officers are literally seen as soldiers in a war on crime. The reality of policing is that only a small portion of the job relates to enforcement of laws or criminal investigation. Moreover, there is the perception that officers have freedom to set their own priorities and choose to investigate whatever criminal activity is of interest to them. This perception is soon crushed under the realities of a rigid bureaucracy, an unbelievable number of rules and regulations, and an unending demand for reports; many of which are redundant and appear to have little value. Also, new officers are not prepared for the mundane aspects of the job. Wanting to investigate murders and robberies, they are soon innundated with barking dogs, parking complaints, false alarms, and domestic disputes. The officers' emotional response is ultimately a feeling of being let down. The job is not what they expected.

The police administrator's job is complicated by this discrepancy between expectations and reality. Job burnout, cynicism, and a police version of industrial sabotage (deliberately violating organizational procedures or damaging equipment because of boredom or frustration) are all by-products of failed expectations. The police administrator must know that each and every first-time officer hired by the agency is coming to the job with inappropriate expectations about the job. Eventually, this will have a negative impact on these officers' levels of job satisfaction.

Determining the causes of job dissatisfaction is further complicated by the relationship between three variables internal to each person on the job; the *cognitive component,* the *affective component*, and the *conative component.* The *cognitive component* is the set of beliefs the employee has about a job. The *affective component* is the employee's feelings toward the job. The *conative component* is the employee's tendency to behave in a certain way toward the job. Thus the officer may believe the occupation is a good career while at the same time hating the job. The result would probably be poor performance (Albanese, 1988, p. 441).

How much control does administration truly have over an employee's motivation? That is a difficult question and one that is dependent on which theory of motivation a person accepts. It may be that management cannot really motivate anyone. What should be obvious, however, is that management can crush the motivation out of just about everyone. W. Edwards Deming offered the following example:

> In a meeting of two hundred factory workers, a man said to me, "It's a matter of communication." I hear that word a dozen times a day—communication. I said, "Tell me about it." His machine had gone out of order and would make only defective items. He had reported it, but the maintenance men could not come for a long time. Meanwhile he was trying to run it himself. The foreman came along and said to run it. "In other words, he told me to make defective items."
>
> "'Where is my pride of workmanship?" he asked me. "If the foreman would give me as much respect as he does the machine, I'd be better off." He didn't want to get paid for making defective items.
>
> Talk about motivation. People are motivated. All people are motivated. Everyone? No. There are exceptions. Some are beaten down so often, so many times, that they have lost, temporarily at least, interest in the job (Walton, 1986, pp. 82–83)

What has this example to do with police management? There are police officers in every agency in the nation who attempt to write honest reports even when the officer has made procedural errors. Do the supervisors allow the honest report to go through the system that way? Not likely. Most of the time the supervisor will require that the report be rewritten to reflect what should have happened instead of what really happened. The supervisor demands dishonesty because the system cannot deal with variation from organizational policy or procedure (see Chapter 8). What is the impact on officer motivation and job satisfaction? Cynicism and frustration: two emotions that offer weak support for motivation and pride of workmanship.

Job Satisfaction and Performance

Of great importance to the administrator is the relationship between job satisfaction and job performance. There are three different theories concerning this relationship. The first is that happy workers are productive workers. Thus job performance is related directly to job satisfaction, with job satisfaction being the causal factor. This theory is central to the human relations school of management thought.

The second theory is that good performance causes job satisfaction. This is predicated on the idea that good performers reap the benefits of their performance. That is, good performers are recognized and rewarded for their performance, thus creating a high level of job satisfaction. This theory, like the first, argues a direct relationship between performance and job satisfaction, with job performance being the causal factor.

The last theory argues no relationship between job performance and job satisfaction. This is especially true when performance is measured through productivity. The argument posed is that productivity can be driven upward by autocratic command. The employees may not like the demands for increased outputs but will comply if their jobs are on the line. Using a police example, it may be observed that patrol officers do not like to issue traffic citations but will do so if they have no alternative. As the administrative demand for higher levels of traffic enforcement increases, job satisfaction may actually decrease. More citations will be issued despite the officer's dissatisfaction.

The reality is that all three theories are probably accurate. It depends on the job being performed and the individual employee. In situations where there is intense supervision and productivity is crucial, it is probably a mistake to assume a relationship between job satisfaction and productivity; or, it is equally likely that there is a reverse relationship. Many production-line workers would be happier sitting around the lounge swapping stories than working the line. In this case, job satisfaction might actually be an indicator of poor performance.

On those occasions where the employee must provide a difficult-to-measure service while operating with autonomy, job satisfaction might be crucial to performance. An employee unhappy with the job may not be the best person to deal with a citizen who needs help. Similarly, employees with a high achievement need may always perform well on their own. It is probable, therefore, that motivation, like leaderhip, may be more determined by situational variables than by any single theory.

Motivation is difficult to instill. It appears that men like W. Edwards Deming and Robert Townsend may be correct in their observation that organizations do not motivate people; they motivate themselves. It is the duty of managers, therefore, to do all in their power to keep the organization from crushing the motivation out of people.

DISCUSSION QUESTIONS

1. Compare leadership and motivation. How are they alike? How are they different?

2. Which theory of motivation is prevalent in law enforcement? Discuss the implications of your answer.

3. Explain poor management by using the four theories of leadership.

4. Discuss methods of motivating an employee with a "bad attitude" through the use of three different theories of motivation.

5. Discuss the relationship between productivity and job satisfaction. How can either, or both, be improved through the application of various theories of leadership and motivation?

REFERENCES

Albanese, Robert (1988). *Management*. Cincinnati, Ohio: Southwestern.

Argyris, Chris (1957). *Personality and Organization: The Conflict between the System and the Individual*. New York: Harper & Row.

Cornelius, Edwin T. III and Frank B. Lane, (1984). "The power motive and managerial success in a professionally oriented service industry organization," *Journal of Applied Psychology*, Vol. 69, No. 1 (February), pp. 32–39.

Couper, David C., and Sabine L.Lobitz (1991), *Quality Policing: The Madison Experience. A PERF Discussion Paper*. Washington, D.C.: Police Executive Research Forum.

Daniels, A. C. (1985). "Performance management: the behavioral approach to productivity improvement," *National Productivity Review*, Vol. 4, Summer, pp. 225–236.

DuBrin, Andrew J., R. Duane Ireland, and, J. Clifton Williams (1989). *Management and Organization*. Cincinnati, Ohio: SouthWestern.

Fleishman, Edwin A. (1953). "Leadership climate, human relations training and supervisory behavior," *Personnel Psychology*, 6, pp. 205–222.

Fiedler, Fred (1967). *A Theory of Leadership Effectiveness*. New York: McGraw Hill.

Hershey, P. and K. H. Blanchard, (1988). *Management of Organizational Behavior: Utilizing Human Resources, 5th ed.* Englewood Cliffs, N.J.: Prentice Hall.

Herzberg, Frederick W. (1968). "One more time: how do you motivate employees? Part II" *Harvard Business Review*. (Jan-Feb) pp. 53–62.

Kelly, Joe (1974). *Organizational Behavior: An Existential Approach,* Rev Ed. Homewood, Ill: Richard P. Irwin.

Latham, Gary A, .and Edwin A. Locke, (1979). "Goal setting: a motivational technique that works", *Organizational Dynamics*, Vol. 8, No. 3 (Autumn) pp. 68–80.

Lewis, Phillip V. (1983). *Managing Human Relations.* Boston:Kent.

Lombardo, Michael M., and Morgan W. McCall, Jr.(1984). "The boss is boss—but some are horrible," *The Kansas City Times*, February 15, section c.

Mahoney, T. A., T. H. Jerdee, and A. N. Nash (1960). "Predicting managerial effectiveness," *Personnel Psychology*., Summer, pp. 147–163.

Maslow, Abraham H. (1954). *Motivation and Personality*., New York: Harper & Row.

Mayo, Elton (1961). *The Human Problems of an Industrialized Civilization*. New York: Macmillan.

McClelland, David C. (1962). "Business drive and national achievement," *Harvard Business Review*, Vol. 40, No. 4, pp. 99–112.

_____ and Richard E. Boyatizis, (1982). "Leadership motive pattern and long-term success in management," *Journal of Applied Psychology,* Vol. 67, No. 12, p. 737.

McGregor, Douglas (1960). *The Human Side of Enterprise*. New York: McGraw-Hill.

Miller, L. M. (1978). *Behavior Management: The New Science of Managing People*. New York: Wiley, pp. 197-202.

Morse, N., and E. Reimer (1956). "The experimental change of a major organizational variable,"*Journal of Abnormal and Social Psychology*, Vol. 2, pp. 127–135.

Sales, Stephen M. (1969). "Supervisory style and productivity: review and theory," in Larry Cummings and William E. Scott, eds. *Readings in Organizational Behavior and Human Performance*. Homewood, Ill: Richard D. Irwin..

Skinner, B. F. (1969). *Contingencies of Reinforcement: A Theoretical Analysis.* New York: Appleton-Century-Crofts.

Stahl, Michael J. (1983). "Achievement, power and managerial motivation: selecting managerial talent with the job choice exercise," *Personnel Psychology,* Winter, p. 775–789.

Taylor, Frederick W. (1967). *The Principles of Scientific Management.* New York: W.W. Norton. (orig. 1947).

Thorndike, E. L. (1911). *Animal Intelligence.* New York: Macmillan.

Vroom, Victor H. (1964). *Work and Motivation.* New York: Wiley .

_____ and Phillip W.Yetton (1976). "Leadership," in Marvin D.Dunnette, ed., *Handbook of Industrial and Organizational Psychology.* Skokie, Ill.: Rand McNally.

Walton, Mary (1986). *The Deming Management Method.* New York: Perigee.

Chapter 4

Authority, Power, and Conflict

Effective management depends on the ability to coordinate and direct a group of people toward the completion of an organization's objectives. The primary tools of managers to attain these goals are power and authority. This does not mean that every act of an employee is coerced by management. On the contrary, power is often manifested through the ability to persuade a subordinate to complete a task. There are also a large number of tasks completed because the employee knows what is expected and is self-motivated to perform the job.

Authority, power, and conflict are forces within an organization that contribute to the dynamic characteristics of human groups. Conflict is inevitable whenever people work together. The terms *authority* and *power* denote formal and informal capacities to evoke actions from others. An understanding of these three elements is necessary to the ability to manage an organization of any size.

AUTHORITY

The terms *authority* and *power* are sometimes used to describe the same thing, the ability to incite actions from others. A more concise definition of these two terms separates and identifies their significant differences. Perhaps the clearest definition of *authority* was provided by Stephen Robbins, who defined it as *the right to act or cause others to act* toward the attainment of organizational goals (1976, p. 239). Curt Tausky defined authority as *institutionalized power* (1978, p. 131). The distinction drawn by these authors is the source of authority. Most argue that the organization is the only source of a person's authority. This is in direct contrast to a person's power, which comes from a variety of sources.

Authority, therefore, must be discussed in terms of an organizational entity. It is created and controlled by laws, rules, regulations, policies, and organizational hierarchical structures. Authority, within limitations, is also reasonably constant across the organizational chart. Authority resides in the position rather than within the individual.

Traditionally, authority is thought to originate at the top of an organization and flow downward, with each lower position having less authority than the position immediately above. In a law enforcement agency, therefore, authority begins with the people, who delegate it to the legislative body, from which it is delegated to the chief law enforcement executive, and on down to the lowest patrol officer. This view overlays the concept of authority onto the organizational chart. This is the basis for the chain of command within any organization.

Chester Barnard challenged the traditional view of authority (1938). He proposed that the control of authority actually rests with the bottom of the organization. According to Barnard's theory, authority is nothing more than the subordinate's willingness to submit to the demands of the supervisor. History would seem to vindicate Barnard's hypothesis. At the conclusion of World War II, there were trials in which soldiers were convicted of crimes against humanity. In these trials, the primary defense was based on the requirement of a subordinate to obey the orders of the superior. The courts ruled against the defendants, stating *the necessity of each individual to take responsibility for their actions, regardless of orders from above.* In effect, the courts have consistently ruled that *a person has no obligation to follow an unlawful order.* The determination of whether or not the order is unlawful rests with the person receiving the order rather than with the issuing person. The legal responsibility inherent in these decisions places the subordinate in the position of judging each command given by a superior to determine if it should be carried out. The subordinate, by law, must disobey an immoral or illegal command.

Authority must therefore, be discussed in terms of limitations and parameters. Barnard proposed four requirements which he states must be present if a subordinate is to accept a command as lawful:

1. Subordinates must be able to understand the communication.

2. At the time of the decision, the subordinate must believe that what is being asked is consistent with the purposes of the organization.

3. At the time of the decision, the subordinate must believe that what is being asked is compatible with the subordinate's personal interests as a whole; consequently, immoral or unethical requests, if they are viewed as such by the subordinate, may be disobeyed.

4. The subordinate must be mentally and physically able to comply with the request.

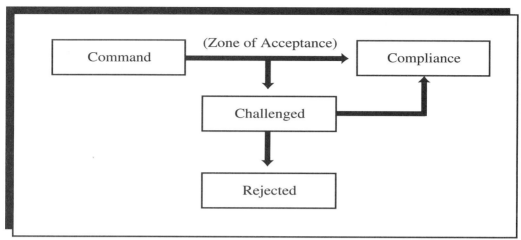

Illustration 4-1 Zone of Acceptance.

Barnard further refined his theory of authority and proposed a zone of acceptance.

Zone of Acceptance

The term *zone of acceptance* denotes the true limits of authority within a position (see Illustration 4-1). This area represents the authority a subordinate will accept without question. In this sense the zone of acceptance (which is referred to by some as the *zone of indifference*) is a graphic representation of the subordinate's screening process. There are two other zones, left untitled by Barnard, denoting those commands to be totally ignored and others to be carefully scrutinized prior to being accepted or rejected.

An instruction from a sergeant assigning a patrol officer to a specific geographic area within an agency's jurisdiction would undoubtedly be obeyed by the officer. An order from the same sergeant to the same officer to mow the sergeant's lawn would be an example of a command clearly outside the sergeant's lawful authority. Many commands, however, are not so easily defined. A new officer, insecure in the job, will possess a much larger zone of acceptance than a veteran officer who is more self-assured, experienced, and knowledgeable. The zone of acceptance, therefore, resides within the subordinate rather than within the position or the supervisor. The zone of acceptance represents a limitation of the superior's authority generated by the subordinate.

Delegation

In a public service organization, all internal authority below the chief executive is delegated. If we attempt to measure authority within a law enforcement agency, we discover that each level in the hierarchy has the same authority as the lower elements plus sufficient additional authority to supervise those below. At the top of the organization we find the possession of total internal authority. The person who holds this authority also has the ultimate responsibility for the actions of the agency, for authority and responsibility go hand in glove.

Internal authority is the ability to direct the actions of organizational employees. *External authority* is the right of organizational personnel to do their jobs. Internal authority varies in accordance with a person's position within an organization. External authority in a law enforcement agency is constant across all organizational lines. The chief executive has no more real police authority than the newest rookie. Both are controlled by statutory and constitutional law.

Another distinction can be drawn between *ultimate* and *operational responsibility*. A long-held principle of administration is the belief that responsibility cannot be delegated. Ultimate responsibility cannot be delegated, operating responsibility can and must be delegated. The chief administrator is responsible for the actions of each member of the agency as long as each member operates within the administration's directions. Subordinates, however, can be held accountable for their actions and decisions relating to specific assignments. This operating responsibility is a necessary element in maintaining accountability throughout an organization.

Delegation is another of those elements of administration that often determine the effectiveness of the manager. Many administrators have difficulty in delegating authority. As Robert Townsend said:

> Many give lip service, but few delegate authority in important matters. And that means all they delegate is dog-work. A real leader does as much dog-work for his people as he can: he can do it, or see a way to do without it ten times as fast. And he delegates as many important matters as he can because that creates a climate in which people grow (1984, p. 50).

There are a number of reasons why some administrators are reluctant to delegate meaningful authority. Some of these reasons are rational and some are not.

1. There is the old adage: "If you want something done right, do it yourself." The assumption inherent in this philosophy is either that subordinates cannot be trusted or the manager cannot adequately communicate to the subordinate the requirements of the task. Often, those who adopt this position are either uncomfortable with supervision or are attempting to demonstrate their superiority by outperforming the subordinate at the subordinate's tasks. Occasionally, this occurs when the subordinates honestly cannot fulfill the task requirements properly. This may be due to poor selection and screening of employees, to inadequate training, or to rapid turnover which hampers the ability to instill expertise in those assigned the task in question.

2. Some people were more comfortable with the position they held prior to promotion. They revel in the work responsible for their promotion. This occurs when someone is promoted too fast, or is promoted beyond their capabilities. They do what they do best, which was what they did prior to being promoted.

3. Some administrators fear their subordinates. They deliberately attempt to keep them uninformed and incapable of competing with the administrator for the administrator's job. These managers see job security in maintaining an image of themselves as difficult to replace. Occasionally, this is the result of vicious political infighting within an organization. The administrator may rightly feel pressure generated by subordinates who will resort to anything to force the manager out of the organization in the hope that one of them will be chosen to replace the manager. Usually, however, the fear is in the mind of the administrator rather than being true attempted sabotage.

4. Some administrators believe that since they are responsible for achieving the objectives of the organization, they should make the decisions. Those who hold this position argue that the accountability inherent in management requires firm control of all decisions. This view might best be described as one in which the administrator believes that those whose jobs are not jeopardized by the outcome of the decision, as the administrator's always is, should have little or no say in making the decision.

5. The responsibility of administration simply overwhelms the ego of the administrator. Those falling into this trap honestly believe that they genuinely are the only people with sufficient understanding of the needs of the organization to make competent decisions concerning its future. To these people, *they are* the organization rather than merely its administrator.

Delegation is really nothing more than the willingness of the administrator to stand behind decisions made by subordinates. Ultimately, all decisions are made by the chief executive, either through the authority to alter a decision of a subordinate or through willingness to let that decision stand. Delegation exists only to the extent that the administrator is willing to support decisions of subordinates and no more. One reason for the failure of a subordinate to complete a task is often the unwillingness of the manager to provide sufficient support for the subordinate's decisions regarding the task.

Delegation does not mean blind trust. The person to whom the authority is delegated must be held accountable for this authority. Just as a person must be given sufficient authority to accomplish a task, so must this person be held accountable for the use of this authority. Delegation without accountability is administrative abdication.

Authority Relationships

There are many authority relationships in this world. Some of these lie outside formal organizations, such as parent-child, teacher-student, and doctor-patient. Within the formal organization it is generally agreed that the most complicated authority relationship is between line and staff personnel.

Line Authority

Line authority rests within any position contributing to direct achievement of organizational goals. Any person within the chain of command between the chief administrator and personnel engaged in the delivery of the agency's services has line authority.

Staff Authority

Staff authority, on the other hand, is advisory in nature. Staff personnel do not give orders; they offer advice. Frequently, this advice is based on a high level of expertise, as in the case of the agency legal advisor, but the advice carries no formal requirement for acceptance. In reality, the advice of experts is usually accepted as if it were based on authority. This happens because of an understanding inherent in all organizations that in certain situations staff advice will be sought. Moreover, the assumption also exists that once offered, the staff advice will be listened to and given fair consideration. This idea is called the *principle of compulsory staff advice* (Davis, 1951, p. 453).

Conflicts arising between line and staff personnel usually occur between those who are clearly one or the other. Line personnel are sometimes envious of the apparent prestige of staff personnel. Staff personnel often have more than enough power to make up for their lack of authority, and this usually translates into the ability of staff personnel to have greater influence over the agency administrator. In a law enforcement agency this is usually due to a number of factors, which seem to be changing. First, staff personnel are usually better educated than line personnel. People such as attorneys, computer programmers, and accountants make up a good portion of the staff of a large organization. The expertise of these individuals is a result of their education and is the reason they were hired in the first place. It is only natural that they should develop a strong power base in their area of expertise. Second, staff personnel are often more articulate than line personnel. This also may be a product of a higher level of education. Third, because staff personnel are hired to advise the chief administrator, they have immediate access to the most powerful people in the organization. As a result, they develop high-level contacts early in their career, which adds to their ability to have more influence than line personnel. The line personnel recognize the superior ability of staff personnel to manipulate the administration into accepting the goals and methods of the staff personnel rather than those of the line personnel. This ability is resented by line personnel, who often have a different opinion of the direction the agency should be taking.

Although line personnel may resent the prestige of staff personnel, they rarely have the skill and expertise to compete. Line officers are also usually more rigid and out of touch with social change. Line officers often have a vested interest in opposing organizational change, whereas staff personnel, whose loyalties are often with their profession rather than with the agency, are more likely to be open to new ideas.

Over the past 15 to 20 years, however, a trend toward higher education in law enforcement has developed. As a result, line personnel are becoming better educated and more articulate, thus improving their ability to compete with staff personnel. This is a positive trend that can only improve law enforcement administration.

Functional Authority

Functional authority occurs when a person occupying a staff position is also given authority over a line function or unit. Functional authority is commonly used as a way of integrating the work between those who have staff authority and those with line authority.

Quasi-military organizations such as law enforcement agencies often complicate line-staff relationships by assigning both line and staff functions to the same personnel. Although the commander of a support unit, such as the records division, is technically a staff officer, this person will wear the insignia of a commander and have sufficient line authority to issue commands to lower-ranked line officers. This person therefore fulfills both line and staff functions. Line commanders also serve staff functions in the sense that they act as advisors to the chief administrator. For this reason senior administrators are often referred to as the chief's staff. In essence, most staff officers in a police organization also possess functional authority.

We should also remember that conflicts between line and staff focuses primarily on professional staff personnel, such as attorneys and accountants. This does not address the conflicts between organizational staff officers, such as commanders of support divisions, and line commanders. Conflicts between these groups take on the more traditional characteristics of power plays and internal politics, with neither side possessing a clear cut advantage in terms of superior education and articulation, although these will have some impact depending on the strengths of various individuals.

Authority and Responsibility

The administrator must delegate authority and responsibility in equal amounts. A person given authority without responsibility will often become a tyrant, since this person is not held accountable for the use of the authority. A person given responsibility without sufficient authority may simply become a scapegoat when the task to which this person was assigned is unsuccessful. Or the person will become an innovator, or manipulator, in the sense of utilizing unacceptable or unlawful means to complete the required end.

Authority must match responsibility if the objective is to be successfully completed through the use of legitimate methods. The following case represents a failure to provide accountability for the utilization of authority.

Black v. *Stephens* (1981)
662 F.2d 181

A civil rights action was filed against an undercover detective, a police chief, and a city as a result of confrontation between the plaintiffs and the undercover detective. After a trial, the jury found all three defendants liable and awarded $35,000 in compensatory and punitive damages. Defendants appealed. The Court of Appeals, James Hunter, III, Circuit Judge, affirmed the judgment.

    The parties hotly contest all but the basic facts. A review of the record, however, reveals the following: On March 21, 1977 at 11:15 P.M., Elwood Black drove his 1976 Cadillac Coupe de Ville to pick up his wife, who was finishing work. On his arrival he learned that his wife had offered to give Shirley Deily, a co-worker, a ride home. Ms. Deily got in the front passenger seat and Joyce Black got in the rear on the passenger side. They dropped Deily off at 7th and Lehigh Streets and then proceeded west on Lehigh to pick up some sandwiches at a local restaurant.

    The Blacks stopped for a red light in the westbound lane of Lehigh at the intersection of 8th Street, and Wayne Stephens, on duty as a plainclothes detective, pulled behind them in an unmarked patrol car. What transpired next is the subject of much dispute.

    According to the Blacks, when the traffic light changed, Mr. Black and another car proceeded through the intersection at a reasonable rate of speed. After crossing the intersection, detective Stephens suddenly raced up from behind and passed the Blacks' vehicle by crossing the double yellow lines on Lehigh Street. Black was startled by Stephens' recklessness and remarked to his wife about the driver.

    After passing the Blacks' car, Stephens and the unidentified third car stopped at the intersection of 10th and Lehigh. Black stopped about 6 feet behind Stephens, in the outside westbound lane. At this point, Stephens jumped out of his car and, without identifying himself, approached the Blacks' car and started screaming that Mr. Black was a "rotten" driver. Detective Stephens was wearing slacks, an open-collared shirt, and a nylon windbreaker. As Stephens approached, Black put his car in reverse and started drifting backward. After arguing with Stephens for a moment, Black said: "Why am I even bothering. Your car is in the way. It is blocking traffic. Will you move your car so I can move mine and get out of here?" Black then put his car in drive and attempted to pull around to the left of the approaching detective Stephens. At this point Stephens pulled out his service revolver and aimed it directly at Black's head, while Mrs. Black, who was still in the right rear seat, was in the precise line of fire. With gun drawn Stephens screamed that Black had driven onto his foot and threatened to shoot if Black did not move the car. Black testified that his car was nowhere near Stephens' foot, but he backed up and drove around the right of Stephens' vehicle and continued west on Lehigh Street.

    Terribly shaken by their encounter with the as yet unidentified gunman, the Blacks drove on toward the sandwich shop at about 40 miles per hour. As they approached 29th and Lehigh, approximately 2.1 miles from 10th and Lehigh, they saw flashing red lights and encountered a police roadblock and were arrested for aggravated assault by Officer Shoemaker of the Allentown police force.

    Detective Stephens' version of the events is, predictably, much different. According to his testimony, Stephens first noticed the Blacks' vehicle as he pulled behind their car at the intersection of 8th and Lehigh. When the light changed, the Blacks' car, originally in the outside westbound lane of Lehigh, started to swerve into the inside lane. As Stephens began to pass in the outside or passing lane, the Blacks' vehicle swerved back into the left lane and forced Stephens over both yellow lines, into the eastbound traffic. Stephens stopped for a red light at 10th and Lehigh and the Blacks' car screeched to a halt a few inches behind him. Stephens, worried that the driver might be intoxicated or that something was amiss, got out of his car and walked toward the Blacks' vehicle, which was now drifting backward slowly. Stephens inquired if there was anything wrong and Black screamed that Stephens was a "rotten driver." At this point the Blacks' car lurched directly at him and the left front tire rolled directly onto detective Stephens' foot. He screamed in vain for Black to get off his foot. Finally, because of the excruciating pain, Stephens drew his revolver and ordered Black to remove his car. Black then swung to the right through the intersection.

A high-speed chase ensued, with Stephens testifying that he traveled at 75 to 80 miles per hour to stay in visual contact with the Blacks' car. Stephens radioed for help and Officer Shoemaker set up a roadblock at 29th and Lehigh Streets. When Stephens arrived at the roadblock, Shoemaker was escorting Elwood Black into the squad car.

The parties have a general understanding as to what happened next. Elwood and Joyce Black were transported by Officer Shoemaker to the Allentown police station. During this trip, Black was very upset and promised to "get his [Stephens'] ass." Black was also concerned about a handgun, registered legally in his name, that was in the glove compartment of his car. Officer Shoemaker radioed the units to search the car for the gun, as well as some medicine that Black needed for his asthma.

At about 1:00 A.M. Wayne Stephens filed a criminal complaint for aggravated assault against Black. While filling out the complaint, Stephens testified that Black was still extremely upset and had promised to complain to Chief Gable and the mayor of Allentown. In addition, at the police station, Stephens testified that Black said he needed his handgun because "the world is full of nuts like [Stephens], and that if he had his gun, he'd shoot [Stephens]." Black was arraigned by Magistrate Stahl and released on his own recognizance at approximately 1:40 A.M.

Elwood Black returned to the police station on March 23, 1977 to register a complaint about Wayne Stephens and the events leading to his arrest on the evening of March 21. He spoke with Chief of Police Carson Gable, but was informed that no investigation of Stephens' conduct would begin until the charge against Black was resolved (this policy was written by Gable and was standard operating procedure in Allentown).

Stephens claims that in the morning following the arrests, he consulted the Lehigh County Assistant District Attorney, Lynn Cole, who recommended that three additional charges be filed against Black. This was unsubstantiated since Cole had changed positions and was no longer available at the time of trial.

On March 23 or 24, Chief Gable met with Stephens and informed him of the complaints by Black of excessive use of force during the March 21 incident. Thereafter, on March 29, Stephens filed three additional charges against Black based on the March 21 incident: recklessly endangering another person, carrying a concealed deadly weapon, and terroristic threats. The charges of carrying a concealed weapon and terroristic threats were subsequently dropped and Black was found not guilty of the recklessly endangering charge. Black was later found guilty of simple assault, but on appeal this verdict was vacated and remanded for a new trial, which is still pending.

Opinion of the Court

There is more than enough evidence from which the jury could find that Stephens' actions deprived the Blacks of their constitutional rights. While there was conflicting testimony at the trial, Elwood Black testified that his car was never on Detective Stephens' foot (an assertion supported by the testimony of medical personnel examining Stephens' foot immediately after the incident), and that he did not provoke Stephens to draw his gun. For an unidentified officer to brandish his revolver 18 inches from Elwood Black's head with Mrs. Black's head in the precise line of fire and then threaten to shoot is conduct that shocks the conscience.

Turning to the jury's finding of a connection between Gable's policy of promoting the use of excessive force and Stephens' conduct on the evening of March 21, while the evidence is not overwhelming, it is still sufficient to sustain the jury's finding. The court's task is not to review the record de novo, but rather to uphold the jury's verdict if the record contains that minimum quantum of evidence from which the jury could have rationally reached a verdict. Our examination of the record reveals such evidence. Chief Gable's policy concerning the use of excessive force ensured that a citizen's complaint about excessive force never went into an officer's permanent personnel file. Indeed, such a complaint could get into an officer's record only if the officer put it there himself. Although Chief Gable stated that he was in exclusive control of police discipline, he testified that he never initiated a disciplinary action against an officer based solely on evaluations of the officer's use of force. In addition, while Gable testified that an officer's use of force had no influence whatsoever on his chances for promotion, he added that Officer Stephens probably would not have been promoted to detective if he had been the type of officer who backed down when force was involved. Finally, Gable stated that any officer "worth his salt" would use force every week of his career because very few arrests are made without it. This testimony, when viewed in the light most favorable to the Blacks, supports the jury's responses to the interrogatories that establish the nexus between Gable's policy of promoting force and Stephens' use of excessive force in the incident with the Blacks.

Concerning the city of Allentown, Chief Gable may fairly be said to represent official policy for the city. He wrote and implemented the official police regulation concerning disciplinary hearings which the jury found proximately caused Stephens to file unwarranted charges against Elwood Black. Chief Gable is the final authority in charge of the police force in Allentown. He is a member of the mayor's cabinet, proposes and manages the budget, and establishes policies and procedures for the entire police department. There is sufficient basis for the municipality's liability under section 1983.

POWER

Power is a more difficult concept to measure and understand than authority. Unlike authority, power comes from both internal and external sources. Few will admit to seeking power, although most do to some extent. This makes us somewhat ambivalent to power and power seekers. We are taught at an early age not to trust those who quest for power, and this extends even to not trusting our own intentions (McClelland,1970, p. 29). Despite this, people who wield power ruthlessly are often respected and even adored by society in general. A case in point is the great popularity of novels and films centered around people obsessed with power and its attainment.

Power has been defined a number of ways. The most popular of these definitions resides around the ability to influence another person (Miner,1973, p.299). Stephen Robbins, for example, has defined power as the ability to influence the decision-making process (1976, p.86). This definition is suitable for our purposes, for it includes the ability to block decisions as well as to influence them. The blocking of a decision, or its implementation, is one of the more popular manifestations of power within formal organizations.

Power stirs strong emotions in people. This may have something to do with the ambivalence with which power is viewed. Although most people want power, few wish to be subject to the power of another. People strive, therefore, to keep others from attaining power as ardently as they strive to gain power for themselves. This is especially true in a society such as ours where independence and initiative are prized commodities. Americans both love and hate power; they want it, but would deny it to others. Most will also go to almost any length to avenge a perceived misuse of power, especially when it is misused against them.

Power Bases

The sources of power reside in a variety of areas. Each power base will vary with the time, place, perceptions of others, and the ability of the individual to take advantage of the potential for power. Moreover, there are different types of power. Some sources are strictly personal; other types of power are found within organized groups. The amount of power available depends on many factors. The sources of power and its types are the basis for the discussion in this section.

Organizational Power

Organizational power derives from the authority base of the agency itself. It is constrained by the limitations established through law and labor agreements. The power to reward and punish is provided to management so that the goals of the organization can be met. This power is legal and measurable. It is usually clearly defined in the organization. This power is manifested in three ways and is often referred to as legitimate power.

Legitimate Power. Legitimate power is derived from the organization. It is that portion of an organization's power that has been delegated to a person in order to provide administrative force. It puts the teeth in the manager's commands. It might be said that this is the power behind the person's authority. Such power is exercised through the auspices of the organization. The amount of legitimate power available is totally dependent on the amount of overall power available to the organization.

Position Power. The power of a manager's position, formal power, comes from three sources: legitimate power, coercive power, and reward power (Mulder and Associates,1986, pp. 566–567). It allows for the use of coercive and reward power, but only to the extent that the sanctions and rewards are made available by the organization. Such sanctions and rewards are validated through the manager's possession of legitimate power. The amount of position power is dependent on one's position within the organizational hierarchy. The higher one is in the chain of command, the greater the power that is available to that person.

Coercive Power. Coercive power is based on fear of the person holding the power. The true strength of this power base is directly related to the amount of harm the person holding the power can inflict. This power also has mythical strength, which is the amount of harm the person subject to the power believes the person holding the power can inflict.

There may be no relationship between real power and perceived power. In ancient Arabian societies, the shiek had the power to order the execution of anyone, without trial or without even a good reason. This is an example of immense coercive power. It is hard to imagine anyone seriously questioning the will of a person who held this amount of power.

Authority has a certain amount of coercive power built into the position. It might be said that power is the driving force behind authority. While authority gives a person the right to give an order, coercive power provides the person with a means of punishment for failure to comply with the command. In this sense there is a contradiction of the earlier statement that power resides in the person rather than in the position. When power is used to support authority, it becomes institutionalized. It becomes part of the position and takes on the characteristics of authority. An example of this is when a law enforcement administrator creates policies and provides penalties for their violation. This gives supervisors coercive power unrelated to the individual supervisor. This is position power rather than personal power and is found within the legitimate power base.

Not all coercive power is institutionalized. Peers may withhold social support from those who flaunt convention. Husbands and wives sometimes withhold affection as a means of punishment. Gossip, shunning, and ridicule are all forms of coercion used to keep members of the group in conformity with social values. The amount of coercive power held in this sense depends on how badly the recipient of the power is capable of being hurt by those using the power. Coercive power used in this fashion is an abstract force and difficult to measure. People with high social needs are more likely than the loner to be hurt by this type of coercive power.

A drawback to the use of coercive power is the aversion of others to being hurt. Those who wield coercive power liberally often find themselves alone, avoided by others who have no urge to be near a person who inflicts pain frequently. Coercive power must therefore be used sparingly and only as a last resort.

Reward Power. Sometimes referred to as remunerative power, reward power is the opposite of coercive power. This power is based on the ability to give something of value to others. Like coercive power, reward power is directly related to the value of the reward potentially given. Medieval kings could reward friends with vast estates and titles of nobility. U.S. presidents can give high government offices to those considered valuable allies. This is a potent form of reward power.

Like coercive power, the possession of a real reward is not always required. Sometimes it is enough for the person seeking the reward to believe that the reward is forthcoming to generate a power base for the individual holding the power. Perceptions of those at the bottom of the organization often create power bases where none exist in reality.

Reward power may also be institutionalized. Rewards such as merit pay, promotions, desirable transfers, and recognition may be provided for appropriate organizational behavior. In these cases the ability to reward is determined by the administrators' policies rather than by the individual supervisors. As in the case of coercive power, reward power may become an element in the support of authority and as such be a form of position power or legitimate power.

All rewards are not organizational. Friends, co-workers, and family members also have social rewards they may provide or withhold, depending on their perception of the person's worth. As with coercive power, the strength of this power base is heavily affected by the receptiveness of the recipient of the power to the use of the power.

Reward power is very different from coercive power in one major respect. Those who use reward power frequently have many friends. As coercive power repels, reward power attracts. Unfortunately, the abuse of reward power creates an atmosphere of expectation in which subordinates come to believe that they have a right to the rewards. In those cases, when the power base is depleted, those who have become dependent on these gifts take offense and turn away from the person who can no longer meet these expectations. Thus, like coercive power, reward power can be abused.

Personal Power

Personal power is distinguishable from organizational power in a number of ways. First, organizational power is limited to organizational relationships. To relieve oneself of the effects of organizational power, one need only resign from the organization: unless, of course, the organization is the military; and especially if the nation happens to be at war.

Personal power cuts across both personal and organizational lines. Moreover, although there are limits to the amount of personal power that any person can attain, it is often very difficult to determine the precise amount of such power that is possessed by a given individual. There are a number of sources of personal power. Each of these offers both problems and benefits to management. The two most common forms are expert power and charismatic power.

Expert Power. The influence exerted as a result of one's expertise, special skill, or knowledge is known as expert power (Robbins, 1976, p. 88). Knowledge is power, and the more necessary the knowledge to the organization or individual, the greater the power.

We might argue that the ability of an occupation to define itself as a profession, while others are mere occupations, is expert power. Most professions possess knowledge or skills of extreme value to society. Because they, and they alone, have this knowledge or skill, they decide the monetary value of their service and establish the definitions under which they function. Medical and legal personnel can charge exorbitant fees because they offer a service that is only obtainable from other medical and legal personnel, in agreement with the price structure.

Monetary value is not the sole criterion by which expertise is determined. For example, only certified ministers can perform the rituals of their religious denominations. Yet few ministers are highly paid. The source of expertise is knowledge. Expert power comes from having knowledge that someone else needs. The more they need this knowledge, the greater the power.

Expert power is not necessarily developed prior to a person's joining an organization. Administrators often fail to familiarize themselves with new techniques or technology. This paves the way for lower-ranked personnel to develop expertise in an area where little expertise exists within the organization. Sometimes the newest employee is assigned a task because of the lack of seniority held by this person. As a result, a new member of the organization gets placed in a position to develop expertise in a vital area where no one else wants to work. The chief administrator may find that the junior member of the organization alone has possession of knowledge necessary to the survival of the organization. In the case of computerization, this can easily happen.

Of all the power bases available, expert power may be the most practical and valuable at the lower end of the organization. As one group of authors stated, "expert power is the power to make one's superior appear either effective or ineffective"(DuBrin, Ireland, and Williams, 1989, p. 241).

Expert power is also usually the most substantial of all power bases within the area of expertise. For example, attorneys are not often challenged by non-attorneys on points of law; nor do laymen challenge physicians on medical questions. This power base, however, is also the narrowest. The same attorney may have no power to influence decisions that are not related to legal issues; one does not ask a physician how to repair a motor vehicle. Expert power is also directly related to the confidence that nonexperts within the organization have in the person possessing the expertise. Too many mistakes and the administrator will begin to doubt whether or not the person is truly an expert. As confidence decreases, so does the power base.

Charismatic Power. Charismatic, or referent, power is the product of a strong personality. A person with this form of power has socially desirable personality traits. Others identify with this person because this person is most like the kind of person they wish to be.

Of all power bases, charismatic power is the broadest and the most abstract or difficult to define and measure. The lowest member of the organization may have the most charismatic power, since this power is least related to position or knowledge. Old-timers frequently have strong charismatic power, due to the respect paid them by younger members of the organization. On the other hand, charismatic power bases have little with which to reward or punish others, except withholding or providing friendship. For this reason, charismatic power will ebb and flow within situations and individuals, and is sometimes unpredictable. Because it is broadly based, it may also be used in situations where it is not expected, and not be used at times when it is expected or needed.

Of all power bases, charismatic power is most mythical. It is seldom used directly, but is inferred. People follow charismatic leaders because they want to rather than because the leader has something with which to force compliance. Administrators often see the results of charismatic power without identifying the source or strength of the power. This power base can be the most useful to charismatic administrators, but also the most damaging to managers when possessed by subordinates.

Affluence Power. The ability of the individual to act independently because of outside financial resources is known as *affluence power* (DuBrin, Ireland, and Williams, 1989, p. 241). A person who is independently wealthy is in a position to quit a job at any time. Likewise, a person with a great deal of expertise in a high-demand area is never without job opportunities. Such people do not have power to influence their organization, but have sufficient power to nullify the organization's power over them. If they do not like what they see, they leave.

Subordinate Power

It is a human trait to seek to neutralize power. Since all legitimate power is in the hands of management, labor has found it necessary to develop competing power bases. Of these, the most common are collective power and legal power.

Collective Power. The power to influence management through collective action is known as collective power (DuBrin, Ireland, and Williams, 1989, p. 241). This power is generated through employee unity. It is most commonly established through the creation of labor unions or employee associations. The amount of power available is determined by the collective strength of the employees versus the ability of the organization to function without those employees. In other words, the effectiveness of collective power is determined by its ability to overcome an organization's coercive power.

Legal Power. Individual employees also have legal power available. Legal power is based on laws that protect workers from unsavory management practices. Such laws include, but are not limited to, the prohibition of discrimination based on sex, race, or nationality, sexual harassment, and violation of safety regulations. Table 4-1, which appears on the following page, provides a summary of the various types of power and their sources.

Table 4-1

Power: Types, Sources, and Limitations

Power type	Source	Limitations
Organizational		
Legitimate	The authority structure of the organization	Bound by legal and contractual constraints
Position	Chain of command	Organizationally imposed
Coercive	Organization	Limited to prescribed punishments
Reward	Organization	Limited to organizational rewards
Personal		
Expert	Knowledge	Range of expertise
Charismatic	Individual	Willingness of others to follow
Affluence	Personal wealth	Individual job satisfaction
Subordinate		
Collective	Group cohesion	Group goals and issues
Legal	Law	Useful only when organization violates law

Power Acquisition

The accumulation of power for power's sake is not everyone's goal. Most people, however, wish to have power in some form. If for no other reason, power usually carries a certain amount of recognition. The type of power sought says a great deal about the goals and desires of the person. The technique used to acquire power also provides this information. There are a number of strategies that may be employed to acquire power. These have been used successfully in the past and will probably be a factor in power accumulation within organizations well into the future.

Coalition Formation

Coalitions are formed primarily where tasks and resources are interdependent (Pfeffer, 1981, p. 57). The necessity to form a coalition springs from the realization that organization tasks are accomplished better and more quickly when there is support from other people and units. Gaining a power base helps to bring about this cooperation.

Cooptation

The cooptation technique involves changing the viewpoint of an adversary or potential adversary to one that favors the interests of another group (Dubrin, Ireland, and Williams, 1989, p. 247). The process of coopting involves the election of a person to the group by a vote of the existing members. Using this technique, senior patrol officers with a history of opposing change might be added to a team whose task is to redesign the patrol operation. Cooptation is effective because it exposes the potential adversary to the informational and social influence of the group. It also confronts this person with pressures to conform and the necessity of justifying the actions of the group (Pfeffer, 1981, p. 167).

Embrace or Demolish

Embrace or demolish is an ancient tactic and one that is difficult to use in public organizations. The principle involved is that when there is a takeover, the senior executives should either be welcomed warmly into the new organization and encouraged, or they should be removed. The reason is that if they are fired, they are powerless. If they are downgraded, however, they will remain united, resentful, and determined to get even (Jay, 1967, p. 6).

The obvious difficulty for police organizations is the inability to remove top police officials who are protected by civil service. Yet this tactic would be very beneficial for many chief executives who are brought in from outside agencies. The ability of command-level officers to stifle a new chief's ideas for innovation because they are resentful is almost legendary in police agencies. This is less of a problem in private organizations.The senior officers can either get on board completely or get off the ship.

Divide and Rule

The assumptions inherent in the divide-and-rule tactic are that enemies will unite forces and form a coalition opposed to one's interests. The basic power technique is to first precipitate a rift between or among the people who might form such an opposing alliance. This is often done by revealing to a selected person(s) negative comments made about them by another selected person(s).

This technique is more effective than one might imagine due to the all-too-human impulse to criticize. People talk about each other. On the average they spend more time on negative behavior than on positive behavior. This is primarily political behavior, which will be discussed in more detail later. The important aspect of this behavior is that it is related to the self-concept. People devalue others in an effort to appear more positive themselves. They are saying: "Look at how bad he is and how good I am by comparison." Needless to say, people also want to hear good things about themselves; nobody wants to be the object of the aforementioned comparison.

It is not necessary to make false accusations of negative statements by one person concerning another. Sooner or later everyone makes disparaging remarks about virtually everyone else in the organization. It is merely necessary to collect those statements and pass them on. Since most people are incapable of recognizing that such statements are meaningless expressions of self-worth, they can be expected to be appropriately offended, thus reducing the chances of cooperation.

Moreover, a person being informed of such statements is more than likely to respond with critical statements about the worth (and often more) of the first person. This can then be happily relayed back to that person. In a short period of time a well-managed series of misunderstandings can be manipulated into full-time war. The result is a failure of the coalition and a breakdown in power.

It might be added that this technique is used too often. Also, it is generally used by accident. Some members of the organization just like to gossip. They can be counted on to keep the pot stirred, thus automatically reducing the growth of alliances.

Exchange of Favors

Among legislators the exchange of favors is called *logrolling* or *good ole boyism.* Many informal agreements in organizations are based on the exchange of favors. To acquire power it is best to exchange favors with a more powerful person. The result may be either increased power or the ability to get an important return of the favor when it is needed (Dubrin, Ireland, and Williams, 1989, pp. 247–248).

Act Powerful

The first step in being successful is to act successful; the same is true of power. Appearance is a crucial aspect of the pursuit of power. Among business people it has become fashionable to hire wardrobe consultants to help acquire and maintain the proper appearance. At least one author advises people interested in acquiring power to study business etiquette (Gelles-Cole, 1985). Still another article advises upwardly mobile managers to invite important people to a power breakfast (Anon.,1986, p. 97). This is done by taking the person to a highly recognized and expensive restaurant. A finishing touch might be to order eggs with caviar (Dubrin, Ireland, and Williams, 1989, p. 249).

One of the concepts that all successful police officers master is the ability to take command. Despite the turmoil and confusion in a crisis, the people who are in control of themselves are also in control of the situation. The same is true with management and with power. Self-confidence and proper appearance translate into power. Within organizations it is easy to identify those subordinates with power over their superiors. Some people exude power. Even command-level officers are sometimes intimidated by lower-ranked officers. Yet if asked why, they may be unable to articulate what is happening (if they will even acknowledge the relationship—it is one of extreme discomfort for the superior).

Subunit Power

Not all subunits within an organization have equal power. Some units become surprisingly adept at accumulating and wielding organizational power. A theory posed to explain this anomaly. is the *strategic contingency theory.* The essence of this hypothesis is that those subunits with the best ability to cope with an organization's critical problems and uncertainties acquire relatively large amounts of power (McCall, 1978, p. 6).

An important component of this theory concerns the power that a subunit acquires by virtue of its *centrality.* "Centrality is the extent to which a subunit's activities are linked into the system of organization activities. A subunit has high centrality, whereas it is an important and integral part of the flow of work done by another subunit" (Dubrin, Ireland, and Williams, 1989, p. 242). The communications unit, for example, would have high centrality, whereas the school crossing guard unit would have low centrality.

Costs of Using Power

Power, like other resources, can be depleted. As D. J. Lawless said : "It may be nice to have power, but the use of resources is always costly. Power is effective when held in balance. As soon as power is used, it gets out of balance and the person against whom the power is used automatically resorts to some activities designed to correct the power imbalance (1972, p. 243)."

One of the factors affecting the amount of power that one person holds over others is the degree to which each person is compelled to maintain the relationship. Often, the person caring least about the relationship has more control than those who care more about maintaining the association. The person who can walk away without regret is less subject to manipulation than those who desperately wish to keep the relationship together. This is most apparent in relationships between lovers. The one most in love yields power to the person least in love, cruel though that may be. Of course, in relationships where the love is mutual, the power difference is negligible. It is the variance in the strength of the feelings by each participant that account for the competing power levels.

Power can be depleted. A person can threaten to break the relationship only so often before the other person calls the bluff. Eventually, even the most ardent of lovers will tire of continuous power plays. In associations of the heart, the use of power is tied directly to the willingness of one person to be the subject of the power. The power can be broken anytime that the person on the receiving end is willing to end the relationship. This is also true in most organizations. The exception to this is military situations, where personnel are not free to leave the organization, or penal institutions, where those subject to another's power are captive to those with the power.

Power ultimatums are almost always a mistake. In an organizational setting, the ultimatum usually results in a no-win situation for the issuing person. Once given, the ultimatum forces a person to do one of two things. The person may call the supervisor's hand, which forces the supervisor either to make good on the threat, often at the cost of a valuable employee, or to back down, causing the supervisor to lose power over future events. The other option is to bend with the threat and adhere to the command. Often, this results in the person completing this task but seeking a means of equalizing the power, otherwise known as "getting even." A favored form of equalization is the deliberate loss of initiative. The employee will continue to do as ordered but refuse to do anything without an order. This forces the supervisor to continue to use ultimatums to get minimal performance. The final product is a machinelike worker who does what the supervisor orders, but only what is ordered.

Power is used best when it is never used. The best managers never give orders; they make requests. They maintain the illusion of employee initiative. The worker is allowed to maintain an image of working due to a personal desire to fulfill organizational goals rather than because of a fear of organizational reprisals. Mythical power is also quite useful for administrators. Unfortunately, mythical power is not recognized as such until its use is attempted. At this point either the power base is real or it is exposed as being nonexistent thus reducing the administrator's effectiveness. The quickest method of depleting a power source is to use it frequently.

Each type of power has its own costs. Charismatic power, if overused, alienates people who eventually recognize that they are being manipulated. Reward power creates a need to keep increasing the reward to maintain its value. In this case reward power is akin to drug addiction. The person receiving the continued flow of rewards develops a tolerance to them. As with a spoiled child, they need more and more rewards of ever-greater value until the power source is used up.

Coercive power, if overused, will cause others to unite to counter the power. Many despots have been murdered while they slept—often by lovers or trusted friends—due to the fear that they, too, would receive punishment. Organizationally, those who rely on coercive power extensively create havoc while they last, but they seldom last long. Expert power is usually the most difficult to abuse, but if this is accomplished, others will also unite, and sometimes will bring in their own experts to counter or dilute the expert's influence. In the final analysis, any power base can be abused. When this happens, the person abusing the power will pay a heavy price for the abuse.

CONFLICT

A certain amount of conflict within an organization is normal and healthy. It becomes dysfunctional only when it takes a deflected form, such as focusing on personal disputes rather than organizational ones. When one person attempts to make a point by attacking the character or reputation of another, the conflict is destructive.

Conflict is most obvious when two or more persons, or groups, strive for limited resources. Many organizational decisions are *zero-sum games.* These are situations in which for every winner there is a loser. Every dollar allocated to one element of the organization means one less dollar for each of the other elements. An obvious example of this is the continuous dispute between public service workers and the elected officials over salary and benefits. The workers naturally desire more money and better benefits. Elected officials attempt to stay in office by holding down taxes. When one side wins, the other side loses. This is the clearest definition of a zero-sum game.

Another form of conflict is line-staff conflict. Both line and staff personnel seek to align the priorities of the organization in the direction with which they are most attuned. Since these groups rarely agree on priorities, conflict is inevitable.

The Importance of Conflict

Conflict produces change, without which the organization will stagnate. Disagreement over policies and goals forces the administrator to acknowledge the absence of a single best method or idea. It also forces proponents of a policy to research and present their ideas with care and thought. Conflict also contributes to the organization's identity and ideology, while providing a necessary organizational safety valve (Coser, 1954).

Organizational Identity

Conflict is essential for maintaining the identity of an organization. Every public service agency needs opposition to reaffirm its mission. Where would the U.S. space program have been without the Soviet Union? For that matter, what has happened to the status of the U.S. Army and Navy since the breakup of the Soviet Union? Firemen need fires, police officers need criminals, and environmentalists need polluters (McGurdy, 1977, p. 61). This is equally true within an organization. According to Howard McGurdy, "conflict between employees also helps to reinforce the formal hierarchy—by creating loyalties among persons who perform similar roles at similar levels in the organization" (1977, p. 61). Soldiers learn to hate the drill instructor. This hatred unifies them against a common enemy. Later, if necessary, this hatred can be shifted to the real enemy. Conflict is a stimulant; it keeps people alert and mentally prepared. Where there is no conflict, there is no growth, imagination, or creativity, and this is the definition of stagnation.

Safety Valve

Conflict also serves as a safety valve. "Conflict between people brings sources of hostility into the open where they can be resolved" (McGurdy, 1977, p. 62). If conflict is suppressed, internal pressure builds up encouraging groups to create fantastic beliefs, unchecked by reality. This often leads to the kind of rigidity frequently found in bureaucracies. Unrealistic conflict is also a product of this rigidity. This is the release of tensions against phantom objects without the expectation of attaining specific results.

The closer the relationship, the greater the potential for conflict and thus the greater need for friends to fight. This applies to top administrators and their staff as well as to husbands and wives and close friends.

Organizational Ideology

Organizational ideology is also dependent on conflict. When people fight with others, they tend to characterize their opponent as evil. The goal in this case is to defeat the enemy. The real objective, which caused the confrontation, is blurred or forgotten. When individuals stand together as an organization in a power struggle, however, they become more realistic. They begin to believe in themselves and their worth. They become less likely to compromise on basic principles just to end the conflict (McGurdy, 1977, p. 62).

This type of conflict does not drive the opponents apart, instead, it becomes a great unifier. Antagonists are brought together to fight, where they are forced to seek out new associates and alliances. They are forced to set up new administrative procedures and new norms so that they can institutionalize their conflict. It also helps to maintain the balance of power. Each opponent gains an appreciation of the comparative strengths of others, thereby serving to restrain antagonists from fantasies about their imagined invincibility—such as an impervious belief in total victory. "After a protracted conflict, if the power balance continues, the primary antagonists, who have learned to deal with each other through controversy, may learn to work together in a grand coalition" (McGurdy, 1977, p. 62).

Conflict Management

As with other elements of the administrative process, conflict must be managed; it cannot be allowed to run amok. A number of techniques are available for managing conflict, all designed to keep the conflict functional and within the parameters of organizational necessity. Conflict cannot and should not be eliminated. Dysfunctional conflict, however, must be guarded against diligently lest it act as a cancer and destroy morale. The techniques for managing conflict are: *confrontation, superordinate goals, resource expansion, avoidance, smoothing, compromise, autocratic command, behavioral change,* and *structural change.*

Confrontation

Confrontation attempts to resolve differences through face-to-face negotiations. No consideration is given to who is right or wrong. This is a useful technique when the conflict was created by a misunderstanding between the conflicting parties. Its value lies in the ability to hear each other out totally and focus on the points of conflict.

This approach is valid as long as the point of view of the participants is roughly equal. If the antagonists have different value systems, this technique is not only futile but may well increase the severity of the conflict. Confrontations between police and political activists during the late 1960s and early 1970s provide a striking example of this problem. Attempts to use the confrontation technique usually degenerated into shouting matches as frustration grew on each side. Each party was starting from a different philosophical point of view. There was no common ground from which to reach a settlement. Confrontation requires a common perspective if it is to be successful.

Superordinate Goals

Superordinate goals are those common objectives desired by all parties in the dispute which cannot be obtained without the mutual cooperation of these parties. Union-management disputes provide an excellent example of this concept in action. Labor demands higher wages while management attempts to hold down production costs. This deadlock may exist until the organization is threatened with destruction. At this point both labor and management are likely to make concessions not possible earlier in the dispute. Organizational survival supersedes the competing objectives of each party.

Superordinate goals are useful in reducing conflict, but have some disadvantages. First, their use may only delay conflict. When it reappears, it may be more severe than before. Second, the administrator does not always have the capability of generating a superordinate goal. Usually, these are produced as side effects of another conflict and are not always desirable.

Resource Expansion

When certain resources are scarce and valued, there will be intense conflict between people competing for the resource. If, for example, there are only two captain positions in a law enforcement agency and these positions carry great prestige and authority, the lieutenants (or sergeants) will be in constant competition against each other to attain one of these positions. By creating more captain positions, conflict will decrease. The resource is spread over a larger territory, making it less scarce and thus decreasing the conflict. There are some obvious limitations to this technique. Everyone in the agency cannot be a captain; the ability to expand resources is limited.

Law enforcement agencies have utilized this technique frequently in the past, with mixed results. Morale has increased with the addition of more managerial positions. Job satisfaction is temporary, however, due to the inability of the administration to meet increased expectations generated by expanding resources. Also, the resulting organization is top heavy, a situation that is difficult to alleviate later.

Avoidance

Avoidance may be the most common method of addressing conflict, although it is more correct to say that it is a method of ignoring conflict. This technique is useless for long-term problems but should not be overlooked as a method of gaining time to make a decision.

Avoidance is also a popular method of dealing with a problem when it can reasonably be assumed that the problem is of short term and will solve itself given a little time. Admittedly, this does not happen often, but it does happen. There are simply some situations that are temporary in nature, such as tension generated by a part-time or short-term employee. Since this person will not be around long, seeking methods of resolving conflict between this person and another may be a waste of time.

Most cases, however, are not as simple. There are some severe limitations with this technique. Used too often, it can create an administrative process known as *crisis management.* This happens when the administrator becomes entangled in one crisis after another. This is also called *brush fire management,* because the manager appears to spend every working minute putting out brush fires within the organization.

Crisis management occurs when problems are ignored until they can no longer be avoided. This is akin to a naval captain whose ship is caught in a storm. Everyone on board may be too involved in bailing water to notice that the ship is going in circles. Despite these limitations, however, avoidance may be the most used technique for responding to conflict within both organizations and society in general.

Smoothing

Smoothing is a technique wherein both sides focus on points of agreement and downplay conflict. This technique was used with some success by President Carter in his attempt to achieve an agreement between Israeli and Egyptian leaders at Camp David during the late 1970s. Smoothing is useful when both sides in a dispute have some points of commonality. Agreement is reached in areas that can be agreed on while areas of conflict are ignored. The limitations of this technique lie in the areas of disagreement. When the points of view are too far apart, complete agreement will never be achieved.

Compromise

Another of the more popular methods of conflict resolution is compromise. It is also one of the most controversial. Compromise often ensures mediocrity. When two parties feel strongly about a program but only one can be utilized, there is a tendency to give each a little victory. In theory, no one loses; in reality, everyone does. By compromising, two good ideas are often merged into one mediocre idea. The organization is usually better off when compromise is avoided, although this is not always possible.

Compromise also decreases accountability. When an idea succeeds, the author should receive full credit. When it fails, the author should also get the blame (Townsend, 1984, p. 34). If there is compromise and failure, the blame should go to the administrator who destroyed two perfectly good ideas in the mistaken belief that conflict is always bad.

Is compromise always avoidable? No, not always. Peter Drucker argued that there is a right and a wrong type of compromise. He says that there are always pressures to compromise to gain acceptance, to placate strong opponents, or to hedge risks. He further argues that:

> One has to compromise in the end. But unless one starts out with the closest one can come to the decision that will truly satisfy the objective requirements, one ends up with the wrong compromise—the compromise that abandons essentials.
>
> For there are two different kinds of compromise. One kind is expressed in the old proverb "Half a loaf is better than no bread." The other kind is expressed in the story of the Judgment of Solomon, which was clearly based on the realization that "half a baby is worse than no baby at all." In the first instance, objective requirements are still being satisfied. The purpose of bread is to provide food, and half a loaf is still food. Half a baby, however, is not half of a living and growing child. It is a corpse in two pieces (1974, p. 478)

Autocratic Command

Law enforcement administrators have been exceptionally fond of the technique known as autocratic command. This is the use of formal authority to force decisions on subordinates. This is based on the notion that the boss may not always be right, but this person is the boss.

Autocratic command can be useful in achieving short-term results. Its worst flaw is the inability to address anything but the symptoms of the conflict; the root causes are ignored. If overused, it helps generate a condition among subordinates known as *groupthink*. This occurs when members of a group silently go along with a decision with which they disagree. They will even publicly support the decision, or at least provide no opposition. This happens when the subordinates believe the administrator's mind is already made up and they wish to be thought of as team players.

A striking example of this phenomenon was provided during the presidency of John F. Kennedy when the decision was made to invade Cuba at the Bay of Pigs. Government officials and military commanders went along with a plan each admitted later was seriously flawed. The president and country were embarrassed because the advisors were unwilling to oppose a decision which they believed had already been made (Janis, 1972; Wyden, 1979, pp. 313–314).

Autocratic command is valuable when a decision must be made quickly. Otherwise, this technique stifles initiative and creativity within the organization.

Behavioral Change

One of the more difficult techniques of conflict resolution is the altering of human variables, or the changing of behavior of individuals or groups. The benefit derived from this method is a reduction in the causes of the friction as well as the symptoms. This is accomplished by actually changing the beliefs or values of one or more of the antagonists. Ways in which this can occur are *behavior modification, awareness training, human relations training,* and *education.* A word of warning should be given, however; some of these techniques can be harmful if not administered by professionals, which tends to make these techniques both costly and time consuming. These are among the least popular of conflict resolution techniques utilized by law enforcement administrators.

Structural Change

Structural change is among the more popular conflict resolution techniques used by law enforcement administrators. Simply stated, if two people are in conflict, transfer one of them. Problem employees are frequently placed in positions where their problem-causing capacity is limited. Often, it is easier to isolate a subordinate in a harmless position than it is to terminate the person. Every organization has its Siberia, where troublemakers are sent to minimize their destructive capacities.

The problem with this technique is the identification of a position as the organization's dumping ground. Every position needs some personnel who are competent. Once an element has been identified as a garbage dump, good people will not want to work there for fear of damaging their reputation and possibly their career. There is also a limit to how many subordinates can be subjected to internal exile.

Not all conflicts are the result of incompetence. Separating combatants usually does not require internal exile. It is often sufficient merely to separate two people by placing them in different units. When a troublemaker is transferred, however, it would be well to remember that the problem has not been eliminated, just moved.

Table 4-2
Conflict Resolution Techniques

Technique	*Definition*
Confrontation	There is face-to-face discussion of problem.
Superordinate goals	Ally opposing parties by shifting focus to common goal.
Resource expansion	Decrease competition by providing an increase in the sought-after resources.
Avoidance	Ignore the conflict in the hope that it will go away.
Smoothing	Focus on those aspects of the conflict where consensus can be achieved; ignores those aspects of the problem that appear to have no solution.
Compromise	Each side gives and takes so that everyone gets something as a result.
Autocratic command	Administrator makes the decision which is then imposed on the organization.
Behavioral change	One or both parties to the conflict are provided with training or education designed to change their point of view.
Structural change	The organization is changed so that the parties to the conflict no longer work in proximity to one another.

THE REALITIES OF ORGANIZATIONAL CONFLICT

Managers spend 45 percent of their time resolving conflicts (Graham, 1984, p. 6E). Because conflict is a predominant part of management, administrators must have a method of response. Researchers have identified five types of manager, based on their approach to conflict resolution. These were:

1. *Sharks*: win-lose managers who want to win all the time and use fear, force, and threats to get their way.

2. *Teddy bears*: lose-win managers who always give in to conflict. Teddy bears always fold under pressure.

3. *Turtles*: lose-lose managers who avoid conflict as if it were a communicable disease.

4. *Foxes*: compromisers who always seek the middle ground in any dispute. They are always willing to give up points to gain a consensus (win-win/lose-lose; everyone gains, everyone loses).

5. *Owls*: win-win managers who view conflict as inevitable and positive. They openly seek to find creative solutions to problems (Graham, 1984, p.6E).

Each type of manager has certain effects on the organization. The shark is stubborn, revengeful, and very competitive. Morale would seem to take a beating under this style. Teddy bears are often taken advantage of by subordinates. This style causes frustration and poor performance. The turtle creates more conflict among subordinates by overlooking problems until they become crises which must be addressed. The fox will reduce conflict, but the compromise approach will often ensure mediocrity. Finally, the owl is the most productive approach to management. This person gets the issues out in the open and seeks ways to prevent future problems.

Some evidence indicates that administrators tend to be naturally attracted to one of the five management styles described above. This provides support for leadership style theory, which we discussed in Chapter 3. The key issue would seem to be whether or not a person can recognize a personal deficiency in the handling of conflict and change to a more constructive approach. If this does not occur, the previous list of methods for resolving conflict are not useless, but are limited to the person's ability to adapt them to the situation. Administrators will continue to use the approach natural to their personality, and this is the sad reality of conflict management. It appears that few managers are able to change their approach to the handling of conflict. This should come as no surprise. Under the heading of behavioral change we observed that of all the approaches to resolving conflict, altering the human variable is the most difficult. This statement is as true of administrators as it is of subordinates.

DISCUSSION QUESTIONS

1. Contrast the traditional view of authority with that proposed by Chester Barnard. How do these views conflict? How do they interact?

2. Discuss the implications for the police administrator of the zone of acceptance.

3. Discuss delegation in view of the traditional police management model, the problem-oriented model, and the community-oriented model. What are the pros and cons of delegation?

4. Identify the various types of power and their sources. How do each of these affect an administrator's ability to lead an organization?

5. When is organizational conflict good for an organization? When is it bad? What conflict resolution technique would be best for a disagreement between division commanders over a tactical plan for a hostage situation? Why?

REFERENCES

Anon. (1986). "Power breakfasts: where the elite eat," *Business Week,* February 3.

Barnard, Chester (1938). *The Functions of the Executive.* Cambridge, Mass.: Harvard University Press.

Cosor, Lewis A. (1954). *The Functions of Social Conflict.* New York: The Free Press.

Davis, R. C. (1951). *The Fundamentals of Top Management.* New York: Harper and Brothers.

Drucker, Peter F. (1974). *Management: Tasks, Responsibilities, Practices.* New York: Harper & Row.

Dubrin, Andrew J., R. Duane Ireland, and J. Clifton Williams, (1989) *Management and Organization.* Cincinnati, Ohio: SouthWestern.

Gelles-Cole, Sandi, ed. (1985). *Letitia Baldridge's Complete Guide to Executive Manners.* New York: Holt, Rinehart, and Winston.

Graham, Gerald (1984). "Sharks and teddy bears and their management skills," *The Kansas City Star. April 15,* p. 6E.

Janis, Irving L. (1972). *Victims of Groupthink.* Boston: Houghton Mifflin.

Jay, Anthony (1967). *Management and Machiavelli.* New York: Holt, Rinehart and Winston.

Lawless, David J. (1972). *Effective Management.* Englewood Cliffs, N.J.: Prentice Hall.

McCall, Morgan, Jr. (1978). *Power, Influence, and Authority: The Hazards of Carrying a Sword.* Technical Report No. 10, Greensboro, N.C.: Center for Creative Leadership.

McClelland, David C. (1970)."The two faces of power," *Journal of International Affairs*, Vol. 24, No. 1, p. 26.

McGurdy, Howard E. (1977). *Public Administration: A Synthesis.* Menlo Park, Calif. Cummings Press.

Miner, John B. (1973). *The Management Process.* New York: Macmillan.

Mulder, Mark, and Associates (1986)."Power, situation and leaders' effectiveness: an organizational field study." *Journal of Applied Psychology,* Vol. 71, No. 4, pp. 566–567.

Pfeffer, Jeffrey (1981). *Power in Organizations.* Marshfield, Mass. Pitman.

Robbins, Stephen P. (1976). *The Administrative Process.* Englewood Cliffs, N.J.: Prentice Hall.

Tausky, Curt (1978). *Work Organizations: Major Theoretical Perspectives,* 2nd ed., Itasca, Ill. F.E. Peacock.

Townsend, Robert (1984). *Further Up the Organization.* New York: Alfred A. Knopf.

Wyden, Peter (1979). *Bay of Pigs: The Untold Story.* New York: Simon & Schuster.

Chapter 5

Decision Making

The responsibility for leading an agency through the myriad court decisions, social changes, and fluctuating economy requires a successive array of judgment calls. Although not required to make each decision personally, the chief administrator is ultimately accountable for each and every decision made. We assume the decision-making process of professional managers to be rational, although this is not always true. A number of common errors are made in decision making, including cognitive nearsightedness, assumption that the future will repeat the past, oversimplification, overreliance on personal experience, preconceived notions, unwillingness to experiment, and reluctance to decide (Nigro and Nigro, 1980).

Cognitive nearsightedness occurs when the future is sacrificed for the present. The administrator attempts to solve an immediate problem with no concern for the long-term effects of the decision.

Assuming that the future will repeat the past occurs when a decision is based on past information and events without considering changes in the department, society, or contributing variables.

Oversimplification is the tendency to view all problems in their simplest terms. This may be the most common mistake: the belief that complex problems can be adequately resolved with simple solutions.

Overreliance on personal experience occurs when the administrator equates rank or seniority with knowledge. The implications of this error are staggering. Not only does the administrator rely on one source—his or her own experiences—but the experiences and viewpoints of others are ignored. The implication is that others cannot be trusted.

Preconceived notions are those inherent biases found within all people. In all organizations there are myths or half-truths that over time become accepted fact. These beliefs often provide the basis for faulty decision making. Unwillingness to experiment is the tendency to use past practices without considering the possibility that there are better options.

General reluctance to make decisions is the last problem and is self-explanatory (Gaines, Southerland, and Angell, 1991, p. 384). This category, has, however, been sufficiently problematic to cause management scholars to investigate it as a problem in and of itself. This research has identified decision making as the crucial determinant in strong or weak management. Failure to make a decision therefore presents a major management problem. Five symptoms of indecisiveness have emerged; all are indications of weak management:

1. *Imitation.* Often without thinking about it, indecisive managers imitate their bosses. An employee of an indecisive manager said, "I asked him why we were doing the job the way we were doing it." The boss responded, "Because this is the way we did it when I was in your position." According to this study, only about 10 percent of any group have the ability and the desire to exercise decision-making authority.

2. *No plans.* Indecisive managers make few plans; they simply react to the situation. "I'm too busy putting out fires to plan" is the excuse they often give. To make a decision, you need a plan; otherwise, you are merely reacting to the situation.

3. *Not enough information.* Indecisive managers always seem to want more information before they can do anything. Everything must be known. Decisive managers also like information and try to get as much as they can. But they realize that they have to make decisions in the face of uncertainties and with incomplete information. In the case of complete information, the computer can make the decision.

4. *Fear of risks.* All decisions incur some risks. But the least doubt or uncertainty stops indecisive leaders in their tracks. When forced into a decision, indecisive managers want no record of their judgment. Indecisive managers do not want people following up on their decisions to see if they made them correctly. As an employee puts it, "When my boss makes a decision, he will have at least five people to blame if the decision turns out wrong."

5. *Excessive use of committees.* Effective committees can serve a valuable purpose in decision making. Committees are good at collecting data, analyzing alternatives, and making recommendations. But indecisive managers hide behind committees by saying, "We'll have to turn this over to such-and-such committee and see what they decide."

Although indecisive managers want to please everyone, they often have the opposite effect. Their delay and indecisions cause frustration, infighting, hostility, low morale, lack of confidence, and conflict within the group (Graham, 1984, p. 12F). In this chapter we focus on the decision-making process and factors detracting from the ability to make sound decisions.

THE DECISION-MAKING PROCESS

For a decision to be truly rational, there are four prerequisites: *problem identification, determination of alternatives, analysis of alternatives,* and *a selection of a course of action* (see Illustration 5-1).

Problem Identification

The first question in the decision-making process is, "Do we really need to make a decision?" Often the determination of a problem is a value judgment on the part of the administrator. The problem may only exist in this person's mind. If this is the case, any decision made may cause more harm than good. As with research, it is often more important to ask the right question than find the right answer to the wrong question. The decision-making process is really nothing more than a question-answer continuum. The first step is to ask the question, "What needs to be done to solve this problem?" The final step in the process is the answer to this question.

Decision making assumes the existence of a problem even though it is true that a nondecision is also a form of decision. If the administrator decides not to implement a change as a result of the decision-making process, this is an acknowledgment of the lack of a problem. The implementation of the formal decision-making process, therefore, assumes that a decision will be made, causing a change within the organization.

As important as it is to ask the correct question, it is equally important to identify the person best suited to make the decision. As a general rule, the person most affected by the decision should at least be consulted on the matter prior to the final selection of a solution. If at all possible, this person should actually make the decision. Obviously, this is not always possible, especially when a large number of people are equally affected by the decision. In these cases, the person responsible for implementing the decision is but one good source of input into the decision-making process.

Most decisions are not made through the formal process. The vast majority of decisions require a response in a short period of time. Most decisions are made within a few minutes of the discovery of a problem. Only decisions having long-term effects on the organization, for which there are sufficient time and resources to invoke the formal process effectively, should be subjected to formal decision making. Formal decision making is therefore applicable to a very small percentage of the decisions to be made by an administrator.

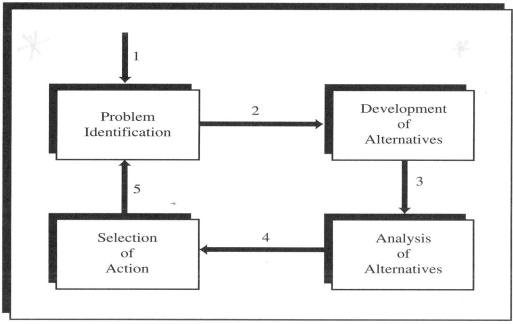

Illustration 5-1 Decision-Making Process.

Much has been made of Japanese management during the past 10 to 20 years. A major difference in American and Japanese management lies in the area of decision making. Americans tend to focus on the last step in the decision-making process, the point at which a solution is implemented. The Japanese focus on the first step, identification of the problem (Drucker, 1974, pp. 466–70).

The Japanese make decisions by first referring the question to all parts of the organization. The major emphasis is on the question, "Do we need to change?" Research is conducted addressing this question. Value judgments, alternatives, and benefits of making a decision are systematically ignored. The only issue is, "Do we need to change?" This can be a very long and involved process.

Once the organization decides change is necessary, however, alternatives selected to bring about change are often implemented with dazzling speed. This is a highly effective process for making major decisions. The results obtained by Japanese corporations are living proof of this effectiveness. Another aspect of the focus on the first step is the amazing flexibility this generates within the organization. Americans are often astounded at how quickly the Japanese can reverse a long standing policy once it appears to be in their best interest to do so. Japanese decision-making can be thus described (Drucker, 1974, p. 470):

1. The focus is on deciding what the decision is all about. The Japanese do not focus on giving an answer; they focus on defining the question.

2. They bring out dissenting opinions; because there is no discussion of the answer until there is consensus, a wide variety of opinions and approaches are being explored.

3. The focus is on alternatives rather than on the "right solution." The process further brings out at what level and by whom a certain decision should be made. And finally, it eliminates selling a decision. It builds effective execution into the decision-making process.

Americans, on the other hand, focus on the end of the process. Problems are identified hurriedly, and the majority of time is spent selecting and implementing a solution. With the Japanese, once the need for change is determined, the alternative comes naturally, and more important, everyone in the organization accepts the need to change.

The unwillingness of many American managers to spend sufficient time on the first step means that the selection of a solution will have to be sold to the remainder of the organization. Being presented with a solution before many of them were aware there was a problem means that not everyone will accept either the existence of the problem or implementation of the solution.

.Japanese decision making is not without fault. The Japanese have an excellent track record with major solutions. The process they use, however, is often too time consuming to be used for minor problems. Such problems are often allowed to fester until they become large enough to justify the expense, in both resources and time, of initiating the decision-making process.

Moreover, the socialization process of the Japanese is different from that of Americans. They are conditioned by centuries of subservience. The most highly sought attributes in workers are cooperation and compliance with those in authority. Achieving consensus in their system is much easier than in the United States, where independence is more highly prized than blind acceptance of authority (Briggs, 1982, p. 53).

Whether utilizing the Japanese approach to decision making or the American approach, the first step in the process is crucial. The manner in which the first question is asked, or in the way the problem is defined, determines the parameters within which the decision must be made. If the wrong question is asked initially, the likelihood of a successful solution is low. This first step therefore determines the direction of the remaining steps in the process. The identification of a problem should not be done quickly or halfheartedly. Success or failure is often ensured from the outset, by proper or improper isolation of a problem. As in the building of a physical structure, once the foundation is laid the superstructure must be built on that foundation. It is too late to repair the foundation after the roof is attached.

The first step in the decision-making process is the foundation. It must be done right prior to beginning the second step.

Development of Alternatives

Once the problem is identified, alternatives must be selected from which a solution can be derived. The first step in the development of alternatives is to get opinions from those with knowledge about the problem. Opinions can be gathered quickly and will provide a starting point. The administrator will also be informed of the points of view to be expected from those involved in making the decision.

Opinions, however, are not alternatives. Alternatives appear after the opinions have been tested against reality (Drucker, 1974, p. 470). This testing process is the trick to producing feasible alternatives. Reality testing consists of a number of questions to be asked of the ideas presented.

Conformity to Facts

Does the idea conform to what facts are available? An example might be a problem with how to provide police protection to a city. An opinion might be foot patrol. The facts, however, might indicate that the city is too large and spread out to accommodate foot patrol unless the budget and personnel were increased fourfold. The facts, in this case, would be a strong indicator of the inviability of foot patrol alone as an option, although it might still be reasonable in addition to another approach.

Feasibility

Is the opinion feasible? Can it be done with the resources available? Many projects sound good on paper but are simply impossible to transfer to reality. This concept not only encompasses economic costs of the idea, but also must take political beliefs, societal values of both the general public and the organization, and the organizational history into consideration. Alternatives must be measured against the expectations of society and of the organizational membership.

Realism

Is the opinion possible under any circumstances? For example, many theorists believe the crime problem to be a product of poor socialization in the home. To reduce crime, therefore, all one has to do is strengthen the family unit. This sounds good, but how does a law enforcement administrator accomplish this? The police chief cannot accomplish this; the theory may be sound, but it is not a feasible alternative for a law enforcement agency.

Rationality

Formal decision making assumes rationality by the decision maker. This assumption rests on the belief in the ability of the individual to identify every possible alternative. There are, however, limitations on the amount of knowledge an administrator can have concerning possible choices. According to Herbert Simon, actual behavior falls short, in at least three ways, of objective rationality (1976, p. 81):

1. Rationality requires a complete knowledge and anticipation of the consequences that will follow each choice. In fact, knowledge of consequences is always fragmentary.

2. Since these consequences lie in the future; imagination must supply the lack of experienced feeling in attaching value to them. But values can only be imperfectly anticipated.

3. Rationality requires a choice among all possible alternative behaviors. In actual behavior, only a very few of all these possible alternatives ever come to mind.

According to Simon, rationality also assumes a means–end chain. In other words, for a decision to be rational, it must be focused on a method of achieving some goal. The goal itself is often a value judgment. For example, two police officers are pinned behind a car by a sniper, who is injuring innocent bystanders. One stays under cover to keep out of the line of fire. The other officer leaves the protected area and kills the sniper, at the cost of his own life. Which behavior is rational? Both are; it is the goals that are different. The first officer's objective is survival; the action taken, therefore, is a rational approach to staying alive. The second officer adopts the goal of stopping the sniper from injuring anyone else. The action taken by this officer is designed to achieve this objective without regard for his own life. Rationality, therefore, depends on the person's perception of objectives.

Rationality is itself an abstract term. Perhaps it is best described in conjunction with a qualifier. We might say that a decision is *objectively rational* if it is the correct behavior for achieving maximum results. It is *subjectively rational* if it achieves maximum results relative to actual knowledge of the subject. It is *consciously rational* to the degree that the adjustment of means to ends is a conscious process. It is *deliberately rational* to the degree that the adjustment of means to ends has been deliberately brought about by the implementation of the decision. A decision is *organizationally rational* if it is oriented to the organization's goals. It is *personally rational* if it is oriented to the individual's goals (Simon, 1976, pp. 76–77).

Decisions that appear irrational at first glance often may be very rational once the person's goals are clarified. This is especially true where the person is making organizational decisions based on personal objectives rather than organizational ones. Generally, when we refer to rationality in decision making, we are referring to behavior that is organizationally rational. Hopefully, it is also consciously or deliberately rational as well.

Analysis of Alternatives

The third step in the decision-making process is the analysis of alternatives. Peter Drucker proposed a cardinal rule for this step. He says that a decision should never be made unless there is disagreement (1974, p.472). Until a person has considered all of the alternatives, this person has a closed mind. Consensus can come only after all alternatives are put on the table and thoroughly diagnosed in terms of strengths and weaknesses. When there is no dissent it is usually because the administrator has preconceived notions of how the decision should be made and has a habit of looking on those who disagree as troublemakers.

If the optimum decision is to be reached, groupthink and autocratic command must be avoided at this stage. The administrator must not view disagreement as a personal attack, lest the time and resources expended up to this point be wasted.

Sometimes it is desirable to seek information beyond the usual subjective sources in order to establish a clearer picture of what should be done. Computerization has made sophisticated mathematical models available to organizations of all types. There are a growing number of quantitative techniques developed by science and applied to management; these are useful in developing statistical data. Similarly, there are computer consultants who can create programs to provide whatever analysis the police administrator needs to aid the decision-making process. These techniques are not designed to make a decision but to provide a database from which decisions can be more accurately made. Each of these techniques shares a common feature: They are only as accurate as the information put into them.

Selection of a Course of Action

Once the alternatives have been analyzed, a selection must be made. At this point the process can break down if the decision maker is not cautious. Despite research and discussion, the final selection of an alternative is often the product of personal preference rather than scientific determination. Decision making is, after all, a human process, and human factors cannot be ignored. These human factors are the basis for Herbert Simon's concept of bounded rationality.

Bounded Rationality

According to Simon, every administrator has limitations on the ability to behave rationally. The administrator is trapped by personal limitations and resources. Rationality is bounded on three sides, like a triangle (see Figure 5-2). On one side, the manager is limited by skills, habits, and reflexes long forgotten. This is the *physiological* side. The ability to make decisions may be reduced by any number of health reasons. Fatigue, depression, and preoccupation with personal problems may all reduce the decision-making capacity. Anything affecting

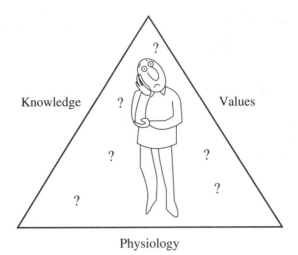

Knowledge

Values

Physiology

Illustration 5-2 Bounded Rationality.

the ability of the decision maker to process the available information mentally with sufficient speed limits the ability to make effective decisions.

The second boundary comprises the *values* and conceptions of purpose that motivate the individual administrator. No one is likely to make a major decision contrary to that person's beliefs or values. This sometimes causes problems for police officers who make decisions based on their own middle-class value system rather than on the value system of the minority with which they are dealing. The stronger the personal belief possessed by the administrator, the less likely the administrator is to deviate from this set of values in the making of a decision.

The third boundary is the amount of knowledge of the job possessed by the decision maker. No one person can know all there is to know about any job, but the extent of knowledge possessed by the administrator determines the ability to recognize options and foresee outcomes.

All decisions are made within these boundaries. The goal of the decision maker should be to expand these boundaries as far as possible. The more restricted the boundaries, the fewer the number of alternatives open to the administrator.

The Heuristic Process

Heuristic, or gut-level, decision making is not a scientific process, but it can be rational. Most decisions, whether organizational or personal, can be classified as heuristic. It is a rational process when the person making the decision has the ability to recognize the problem, understand the alternatives and the probable outcomes, and can select a proper course of action. This process is often so routinized that the decision jumps from step 1 to step 4 almost immediately. This occurs because the individual develops, through experience, standard responses to specific problems. A decision is made on the basis of similar past experiences. For the majority of problems this process is sufficient.

This process is less effective when an incorrect decision is applied consistently due to a failure to observe carefully the final results of the decision. Also, when conditions change, sometimes a previously correct decision is now wrong. This means that the problem is new and must be addressed as such.

Facts are less important in the heuristic approach than in the formal approach. "This is the arena in which intuition, judgment and rules of thumb hold sway" (McGurdy, 1977, p. 261). Major decisions must sometimes be made in this manner, due to a lack of hard facts. Also, because a decision is heuristic does not always mean that it was not a product of a formal approach.

Heuristic decisions are formal decisions when the chief executive calls together the other administrators and they engage in a formal discussion of goals and alternatives based solely on opinion and experience. This may be the only information available, thus the process is formal, but heuristic just the same.

There are a number of factors affecting the heuristic process. The effectiveness of this technique is determined by the parameters within which it is exercised. The limitations inherent in heuristic decision making are identical to the limitations discussed by Simon when he described bounded rationality. A number of these factors have an extensive impact on the heuristic process: *personal values, perceptions, limitations in human processing, political and power behavior,* and *time.*

The following case illustrates the competing interests inherent in police managerial decision making. Similarly, it also shows the willingness of the courts to balance these interests when determining police liability.

Waldorf v. *Shuta* (1990)
896 F.2d 723 (3rd Cir.)

This case presents an appeal and cross-appeals from an $8,400,000 jury verdict awarded a plaintiff who was rendered quadriplegic in a motor vehicle accident. Defendants—the borough of Kenilworth, New Jersey, and one of its police officers, Joseph Rego—appeal several issues of liability and damages. The plaintiff, Mark Waldorf, appeals partial summary judgments in favor of the borough of Kenilworth on two issues.

Waldorf's tragic accident occurred at approximately 11:45 P.M. on Wednesday, November 17, 1982, at the four-way intersection of Monroe Ave. and North Fourteenth St. in the borough of Kenilworth, New Jersey. On the night of the accident, the red light facing west at the intersection failed. Corporal Victor Smith of the Kenilworth Police Department discovered that the red light was out at approximately 11:00 P.M., when he was driving to the police station on his way to work. He radioed police headquarters to report the malfunction to his supervisor, Lieutenant Joseph Rego. Smith tried to get the light to work and then to switch it to blinking mode, but he failed in both efforts.

The intersection had little traffic on weeknights and there was none during the time Smith was at the intersection observing and trying to fix the light. Smith radioed police headquarters to report the malfunction to his supervisor, Lieutenant Joseph Rego, and proceeded to the station.

Lieutenant Joseph Rego, a 21-year veteran of the Kenilworth Police Department, was the officer in charge on the 11:00 P.M. to 7:00 A.M. shift on the night of the accident. Under his command were two other police officers, Corporal Smith and Patrolman Henry Moll. Rego assigned them to other duties that he considered more urgent than the intersection with the nonfunctioning red light. As soon as Corporal Smith got to the station, Rego ordered him to assist Moll in arresting Phillip Mathias. Mathias, whom Moll had seen outside a local tavern, was the subject of an outstanding bench warrant in an assault case. It was standard police procedure in the borough to use two police officers to make an arrest.

As soon as Smith and Moll got back to the station, Rego sent them to a hospital in a neighboring town to pick up a drunk driver who had been injured in an automobile accident. He had been arrested and taken to the hospital earlier by an officer who had gone off duty at 11:00 P.M. Shortly after they arrived at the hospital, Smith and Moll received a radio call from Rego about the accident involving Waldorf.

Waldorf sued the borough of Kenilworth, Corporal Smith, Lieutenant Rego, and the drivers of the two vehicles. The court granted partial summary judgments to the borough on two issues on grounds of immunity under the New Jersey Tort Claims Act, N.J.Stat.Ann. §§59:1-1 to 59:12-3, and denied it partial summary judgment under the act on a third issue. The jury found the borough 60 percent liable for its failure to provide emergency signaling devices, Lieutenant Rego 25 percent liable for his negligent deployment of police personnel once he had learned of the signal failure, Edward Shuta 10 percent liable for his negligent driving, Kenneth Spence 5 percent liable for improper installation of the bench in his van, and Corporal Smith not liable at all.

Lieutenant Joseph Rego claims that the evidence on which the jury found him 25 percent liable for Waldorf's injury was insufficient to sustain the verdict against him. The trial court disagreed and denied his motion for a new trial. Rego's alleged liability arises under N.J.S.A. §59:2-3, regarding public entity liability for discretionary activities.

Waldorf claims that Rego's conduct as police officer in charge on the night of the accident constituted palpably unreasonable actions and the jury agreed. This claim was based on the fact that Rego sent the only two police officers under his command to make two successive arrests between 11:00 and 11:45 P.M. rather than sending one or both of them to the intersection where the accident occurred. There was conflicting testimony as to whether Rego tried to call a maintenance worker to fix the light before the accident, but since both sides agreed that at least one police officer would have been needed to assist in the changing of the bulb, that issue is not separate from the allocation of police personnel. The verdict form that the jury was given asked only one question regarding Rego: "Was Lieutenant Rego's exercise of discretion as a shift commander, with regard to his utilization of police personnel, in the face of competing demands, palpably unreasonable and if so, was such conduct a proximate cause of the accident and plaintiff's injury?" The jury decided that it was. Lieutenant Rego contends that his discretionary decision to send the only police officers under his command to make the arrests, rather than to direct traffic at the intersection, was not, as a matter of law, palpably unreasonable.

We will not fault Lieutenant Rego for following police procedure and sending two officers, the only two under his command, to make the arrests rather than one. The realistic alternatives he had were to make the arrests or to guard the intersection. Suppose that Rego had sent the officers to the intersection rather than to the bar to arrest the man on whom there was an outstanding warrant for aggravated assault. Suppose that the man who was, as a result, not arrested and picked a fight during which he accidentally broke his opponent's neck, rendering him quadriplegic. There would have been no automobile accident, but Lieutenant Rego might now find himself being sued by another party for his palpably unreasonable allocation of police personnel in sending the officers to the quiet intersection rather than to make the arrest.

One can imagine a similar scenario occurring at the hospital where a man who was supposed to be in police custody was left unattended. Accordingly, we will reverse the judgment against Lieutenant Rego and remand to the district court for a new trial.

Personal Values

Every decision is biased by the decision maker's values, beliefs, and prejudices. The heuristic process is especially vulnerable. Lacking hard data, the heuristic decision must feel right to the administrator. The more closely the decision reflects the administrator's values, the more comfortable this person will be with the decision.

Personal values are important. They tend to provide stability in a rapidly changing environment. Values tend to act as society's anchor. They try to prevent change. Sometimes they succeed, other times they do not. The important thing to remember about personal values is that they are not universal. Individuals have individual values. Although these can often be categorized according to economic class or religious affiliation, they still differ considerably. When decisions are made within a group with strong homogeneity, values play a predominant part in the decision-making process. Without engaging the value system, the members of the organization may never accept the decision as legitimate.

On the other hand, if the decision affects a disparate group, the less likely the group is to accept a decision based on a value structure with which they do not agree. The greater the heterogeneity of the group, the less valid the use of personal values in decision making.

Perceptions

Like beauty, reality exists only in the eye of the beholder. Truth is relative; it is merely a reflection of an individual point of view. Each of us responds to others as a result of how we perceive that person. As with values, perceptions are developed over a lifetime. The old description of the optimist and pessimist offers a good example of perceptions. The optimist sees a glass of water which is half full while the pessimist sees the same glass as half empty. Some consider a difficult task a challenge, whereas others see it as a barrier.

Sociologists frequently describe criminal behavior as the result of a faulty socialization process. Psychologists see the same behavior and attribute it to a mental problem brought on by faulty mental processing. Nutritionists may observe the same individual and argue that the behavior is the result of physiological difficulties created by poor nutrition.

Some or all may be right, but the point here is that they are describing the same person. A human being cannot be broken into pieces for study but must be studied as a whole creature living in a dynamic environment. Scientific disciplines often act as if a person could be dissected, while alive, and cured by identifying the defective part for replacement. This cannot be done except by surgeons dealing with identifiable biological malfunctions. A person is a living, breathing creature who can be understood only in the context of the total environment.

Perceptions can dramatically affect the identification of problems and their solutions. Law enforcement agencies hired only white males in this country for well over 100 years due to the perceived incompetence of minorities and females. The destructive aspect of perceptions such as these lies in the person's inability to recognize a faulty perception. Rather, it is considered a factual observation based on experience and organizational wisdom.

Perceptions can lead to the labeling of a person, thus profoundly affecting the labeled person's career either for good or bad. Faulty perceptions can be a subtle destroyer of competent decision making. This is all the more true since people are inherently poor judges of character. Often, the factors utilized to judge character have nothing to do with character, but instead are elements of an image of character carefully maintained by the person being judged (this will be discussed in more detail in a later chapter).

One of the perceptions of the Kennedy administration that led to the disastrous invasion at the Bay of Pigs was the belief that Cubans would rally to the side of the invaders against the Cuban army. This assumption was based on information gathered from Cuban refugees—those who fled Cuba. No one thought to ask the opinion of those who stayed in Cuba, many of whom fought alongside Fidel Castro in the overthrow of the Batista regime. At the time of the Bay of Pigs fiasco, Castro was a hero in Cuba, a liberator. President Kennedy and his staff were greatly surprised when instead of joining the invaders as predicted, the citizens of Cuba attacked the invaders. The point is, perceptions are often deceiving and can result in a disastrous decision if the decision maker does not guard against their effects.

Limitations in Human Processing

No person can know all the possible information on which a decision can be based. We discussed this under Herbert Simon's concept of bounded rationality. We have not discussed the effect of this on the amount of dependency of the administrator on those who provide the data from which decisions are made. One of the reasons that Robert Townsend is so adamant in his belief that decisions should be made as low in the organization as possible is the realization that the higher the level of decision making, the greater the dependency on subordinates for necessary information (1970, p. 27). Since all data cannot be verified, the administrator must make decisions based on information gathered, filtered, and supplied by others. This opens the manager to manipulation through control of information, a problem in any organization.

Political and Power Behavior

Self-interest is a character trait in human beings. In our discussion of power we defined it as the ability to influence the decision-making process. What we often find in organizational decision making is *satisficing*, the selection of a minimally successful alternative, rather than *optimizing*, the selection of the option yielding the best results. A common example of this is the administrator's decision to focus on highly visible problems rather than more important problems which are less visible. Administrators also consistently sacrifice long-term success for the completion of short-term objectives.

This is most apparent at the federal level where there is a 2-4-6 mentality. Members of Congress focus on problems to be addressed within two years, senators expand this process to six years, and presidents do not look past four years. This, of course, represents the point at which each must run for reelection.

The nation as a whole seems to have a four-year mentality. Presidents are expected to correct, in just four years, problems that have taken centuries to develop. To a politician, therefore, a successful decision is often one that enhances a person's chances of being reelected, regardless of the long-range effect on the nation.

Public administrators are often guilty of the same kind of decision making. Law enforcement administrators prefer to deal with external problems, such as street crime and judicial leniency. They would rather not discuss internal problems, such as brutality and corruption, as these are no-win situations. Whether the allegations are true or not is irrelevant. Once the specter of corruption rears its head, many of the citizens will accept the allegations as fact before an investigation can be organized. The allegation may even be unfounded, but some will believe that it was covered up. Understandably, many administrators avoid looking too closely at their organizations, for if they do, they may discover that something must be done which will lessen the agency's reputation in the eyes of the public. Ignorance may be no defense to breaking the law, but it is certainly the most overused administrative response to internal problems. This is true of many organizations in addition to law enforcement.

Political behavior also affects decision making through the coloring, withholding, or overloading of data. Subordinates may present information in a manner calculated to inspire the administrator to make a decision in a manner advantageous to the subordinate. This person may also forget to provide data that would change a decision or may supply so much data that the administrator simply takes the subordinate's opinion of what should be done rather than to read personally through all the data. Also, administrators are frequently guilty of favoring one subordinate over another. In these cases the elements under the command of the preferred subordinate receive an excess of resources and preferential treatment at the expense of the other elements.

The most destructive quality in preferential treatment is the situation, often found in law enforcement agencies, where the tail appears to be wagging the dog. Units designed to provide support for the primary elements sometimes become predominant; they act as primary elements while line units support them. Unfortunately, "the decision of whether to initiate change or to maintain the status quo is not necessarily made on the basis of what is in the organization's interest, but rather of what is in the best personal interest of the decision maker" (Robbins, 1976, p. 167).

Time Constraints

Despite the need to get as many data as possible prior to making a decision, we must recognize the necessity to make many decisions quickly. Military commanders are well aware of this problem. Battles, indeed wars, have been won and lost because of decisions made with insufficient information or decisions not made in a timely manner. Few decisions can be put off indefinitely or even delayed long enough to engage the formal decision-making process.

Many bad decisions can be blamed on the lack of sufficient time to make a rational choice. There is no point in crying about this. There are simply times when a decision must be made quickly and damn the torpedoes. When this happens, the administrator must make the best decision possible and go on to other problems. Sometimes decisions will be right, often they will be wrong, but it is decision making under these circumstances that justifies administrative salaries.

PLANNING

"Management has two sets of problems, those of today and those of tomorrow" (Walton, 1986, p. 55). Planning deals with the problems of tomorrow. All administrators plan, although some fail to realize that they do so. Planning may be formal and structured or may be simply a heuristic process. Research indicates that organizations engaging in formal planning outperform those that do not (Herold, 1972, pp. 91–102). There is a danger, however, in becoming too planning oriented. Studies have isolated the variable "action orientation" among executives of effective organizations (Peters and Waterman, 1982, pp. 119–155). Good agencies "do" rather than "plan to do." Planning is therefore a tool to enhance effectiveness. It is not an excuse for failure to act.

In this section we focus on the planning process. First we discuss the pros and cons of planning. Then we will discuss the process itself, which includes determining goals, formulating strategy, selection of strategy, implementation of strategy, and evaluation.

Pros and Cons of Planning

There are two major reasons for planning. The first is to enhance the decision-making process in regard to directing an agency toward the future. Planning allows the administrator to justify future expenditures and accumulate sufficient resources to address future problems. The second reason for planning is the ability to demystify the future. Rather than sit idly by, worrying about what will happen and how it will be dealt with, the administrator attempts to predict the future and bases the selection of alternatives on this prediction. Thus the future is not a vague unknown but a series of predictable events. Although no prediction is totally accurate, by planning for a worst-case scenario, the administrator can be reasonably certain of few bad surprises. By planning for the worst, it is believed that most surprises should be pleasant.

The con, or negative aspect, of planning is the tendency to believe fully in the ability to predict the future. Invariably, predictions of the future are wrong as soon as they are made. The greater the distance in time, the greater the likelihood of error. Thus plans—especially long-range plans—are also likely to be wrong. Planning is also an expensive and often time-consuming process. Planning is a skill requiring personnel well versed in this type of analysis; poor planners produce poor plans. Because planning also requires the cooperation of personnel engaged in research, it becomes dependent on the quality of the research. A strong planning unit requires a strong research unit; lack of either makes the effectiveness of the planning unit questionable.

Finally, a strong commitment to planning frequently generates a planning mentality where nothing is attempted until it is planned for. As the planning element becomes overworked, there is a tendency to find reasons why something will not work rather than expend energy and resources to make planning successful. The planning unit can become a screen acting as a blockade to change. This has become institutionalized in the various levels of government by way of creating countless committees to study problems. Committees meet and file their report, usually after several months or years. They are thanked; the report is filed; nothing happens. This occurs primarily because committees are not designed to be decision-making bodies, but exist mainly to advise. The administrator must act on the committee report or no one will.

There appear to be more problems with planning than pluses. Planning done realistically by competent personnel, however, can provide valuable input into administrative decision making for future strategies. As long as the administrator is aware of the uncertainties of planning and remains flexible, planning can be quite beneficial.

Planning Process

The planning process is similar to the decision-making process. The major differences are in scope—the plan consists of a number of decisions—and time—the plan is for the future whereas decisions tend to have immediate effect. Prior to the implementation of the planning process, the administrator and planning team must first prepare to plan. Often, the success or failure of the plan can be traced to adequate or inadequate pre-plan preparation.

The first step in the preparation is to allocate resources and responsibilities to those involved in the planning. Next, the planning team must assess the present capacities and resources of the agency. To prepare for the future, you must first know where you stand today. Once these steps have been completed, the planning team is ready to begin planning. The planning process to follow consists of the following phases: *goal determination, strategy formulation, strategy selection, strategy implementation,* and *plan evaluation* (see Illustration 5-3).

Goal Determination

The selection of valid goals is crucial to effective planning. Normally, goals are expressed in terms of how they relate to the agency's mission (see Chapter 2). Ultimate or superordinate goals are those that when fulfilled combine to achieve the organization's mission. Subordinate goals are those that when fulfilled com-

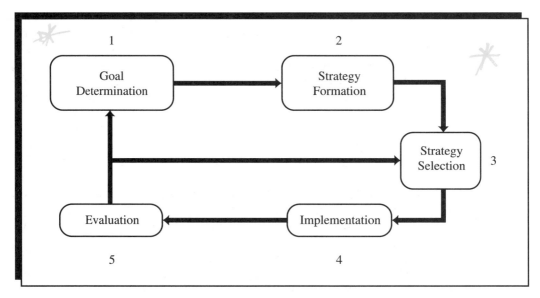

Illustration 5-3 Planning Process.

bine to achieve superordinate goals. Within the structure of the plan there is usually a hierarchy of goals that appear to be similar to graphic presentation of an organizational chart. The similarity is not accidental. Agency missions are fulfilled by divisions fulfilling their objectives. Division goals are fulfilled by completion of the objectives of the various units within the divisions. Finally, unit goals are fulfilled by the completion of the objectives of individual members of the various units.

The selection of objectives is therefore not determined merely by identifying the ultimate goals of the plan. The objectives of each and every person and unit responsible for the ultimate success of the plan must also be identified. The selection of goals must also discriminate between long- and short-range objectives. Frequently, the ultimate objective is one that cannot be achieved quickly, rather, it can only be fulfilled through the successful completion of a number of short-range goals. Long-range goals are those objectives that cannot be achieved in the near future. Long-range goals tend to be those that will take more time than is allocated in the current fiscal year; often, these may be objectives to be reached within five to ten years. The longer the time span, however, the less appropriate the plan is likely to be. Short-range goals are those that are designed to be fulfilled within the current fiscal year. Rarely will any short-range objective require more than a year to fulfill.

Considering the foregoing definitions of long- and short-range goals, it should be noted that there are some exceptions. These terms are relative; short-range goals are usually those that must be completed prior to the achievement of long-range goals. Thus, a tactical plan for dealing with a hostage crisis may call for a short-range objective of isolating the incident by sealing off possible escape routes while maintaining a long-range objective of freeing the hostages with minimum chance of injury. In this case the difference in the two objectives may only be a matter of hours, but the first objective must be met prior to fulfillment of the latter. Many plans may therefore be designed for problems of short duration; this is especially true of tactical plans.

Generally, however, administrative plans, especially those dealing with organization and direction of the organization, cover a number of years and can be divided into those objectives to be achieved this year versus those to be completed over a number of years.

A problem in the determination of goals is often the inability to differentiate between *stated goals* and *real goals*. *Stated goals* are those created for public consumption. There may be little intent to achieve these objectives, other than to influence public opinion. *Real goals*, on the other hand, represent the true focus of the organization. Earlier we discussed the origin of organizational prestige in a public service agency. Service organizations are seldom service oriented; they are geared toward continued growth. The real goals of the organization, therefore, are often growth and survival.

Unfortunately, too many law enforcement goals are stated rather than real. Stated goals tend to be addressed in simple terms; they are easily measured. Policies such as ticket quotas are a symptom of the attempt to fulfill a stated goal. Other items, such as arrest quotas and clearance rates, often measured without regard to quality, are further symptoms of the problem. These concepts generate numbers to be sold to the public to justify the police mission. Often these efforts at quantity have nothing to do with the quality of service provided. In fact, the placing of quantity above quality in terms of priority usually detracts from organizational effectiveness.

Ideally, real and stated goals should be identical. Human nature being what it is, however, few agencies are this well tuned. When real goals such as growth and survival are made subordinate to stated goals, the usual result is fulfillment of both. The secret is to keep the organization attuned to those objectives created through the planning process. In short, when the police takes care of the public, the public will take care of the police.

The selection of goals must be accomplished with as much care and thought as possible. Usually, this is a step-by-step process. In the preparation to plan, the unit first determines where the agency currently is and then attempts to determine where the agency wants to go. This may be accomplished heuristically, or intuitively, by the administrative staff. This method requires the administrative staff to think out what they would like the organization to accomplish in the future and what design it should take.

The second method, and most useful approach, is the determination of objectives via *need-demand indicators*. These are events, trends, or other information highlighting a problem not currently being addressed by the agency in an effective manner. They may point out short-range problems such as a dramatic increase in murders or robberies. They may also indicate long-range trends such as population shifts due to economic or energy factors. Either require a change in agency focus and whether the change should be immediate or in the future.

Another danger in goal selection is *suboptimization*. The organization selects subgoals that have little or no relationship to the agency's ultimate goals or mission. This can happen when the need-demand indicator is merely the symptom of the problem rather than the problem. As with medicine, the treatment of symptoms rather than causes tends to be cosmetic; it rarely solves the problem. The planning team must always be cognizant of the differences between problems and symptoms. Goals should always address problems; the symptoms sometimes provide a means of measuring the effectiveness of the plan.

Finally, the selection of objectives assumes that they can be measured. Goals should therefore be provided with operational definitions (they should be defined in terms of how they are to be measured), which allow the administrator to determine the degree to which they have been achieved. The real problem here is the inability to quantify many police functions. Goals that can be quantified should be, but never at the expense of quality. Further, techniques such as public opinion research can sometimes determine how effective nonquantifiable functions are. Many police functions are better measured through the media and public than through attempts to measure actual police activity. Felony arrests, citations for dangerous traffic offenses, and response times are adequate measures of some kinds of police performance. Empathy and fairness in handling various types of disputes is equally valuable to the police agency but is difficult to quantify. The planners must not become so enamored with quantification that they overlook the qualities of effective performance, which are difficult to measure.

Alternatives

The strategy is literally the plan of action. Step 3 in the planning process focuses on the formulation of possible strategies. The line between where the agency is and where it is attempting to go is determined by the strategy. As with the decision-making process, there is rarely a single possible strategy. Rather, the plan might take numerous possible forms. The purpose of this phase is not to eliminate strategies but to identify them and determine their strengths and limitations.

Much of the strategy formation process is an exercise in opinion and value judgment. The chief executive and the planning team put together their ideas as to the best possible approach to the achievement of objectives. As each plan is suggested, the team will add comments and refinements. The planning director should be careful to hold down criticisms of the various strategies at this point; the next step focuses on the elimination of faulty strategies. This phase is designed to provide alternatives rather than the master plan.

Strategy Selection

There are a number of factors that must be addressed by each strategy. The degree to which each strategy fits within the parameters in the following list will do much toward the elimination of poor strategies and ultimate identification of the proper plan:

1. *Cost.* To the extent that the administrator can project budget income and the commitment of expenditures, the strategies considered must be affordable. Any plan with a projected cost over the amount of funds available, therefore, is an unreasonable plan. To be acceptable as a plan, the strategy must be affordable.

2. *Staff.* The quality and training of the agency personnel are also factors to be considered in the plan. The organization can accomplish only what the staff is competent to perform. The goal of a baseball team may be to win the pennant, but unless the team players are of championship caliber, the goal is not likely to be reached. This is also true in law enforcement; the strategies must be accomplishable by the personnel within the organization.

3. *Time.* Time available for both planning and implementation of the plan is an important factor in the identification of an alternative. The best possible option is useless if there is insufficient time for implementation.

4. *Equipment.* For any plan to be successful, the correct equipment must be available and in proper working condition. A police program calling for increased patrol to saturate a high-crime area will not get off the drawing board if additional patrol vehicles are not available. Equipment necessary to fulfill the objectives of the strategy are a concern for any serious planner.

5. *Organizational history and philosophy.* One of the least considered but most important factors in strategy formation is the background of the agency. Obviously, the agency will be limited to activities in keeping with the organizational mission; the police are limited to police activities. For example, if research indicates that a breakdown in morality within the community is causing an increase in juvenile crime, the police could hardly be expected to round up all the teenagers and take them to church; this is clearly outside the law enforcement function.

6. *Political arena.* The political atmosphere will determine to a large extent whether or not the plan is feasible. No plan is going to be accepted by the legislative body if it poses a political risk to any of the members. Similarly, a plan designed for long-term results will be rejected in favor of a program promising immediate results when the politicians need positive publicity. Often, excellent plans must be abandoned because the political timing is not right. The administrator must be aware of the political climate in which decisions must be made. For any strategy to be successful, it must be politically feasible.

7. *Effectiveness.* Finally, the strategies must be evaluated in terms of their potential effectiveness. "Strategies should be integrated, continuous, cohesive, synergistic, and properly timed" (Robbins, 1976, p. 187). In other words, the strategy must be meshed with existing strategies. *Synergy* is the term used to denote the tendency of a whole to equal more, or in some cases less, than the sum of the parts. When the whole is greater than the sum of the parts, we say that it has positive synergy. When the whole is equal to less than the sum of the parts, it has negative synergy.

Duplication of work is an example of negative synergy. This can be seen in the overlapping of police jurisdictions in this country. A single city with local, county, state, and federal officers all performing similar functions is often a waste of resources. On the other hand, some jurisdictions have combined county and local law enforcement into a single entity, thus reducing the duplication of effort and increasing the effectiveness of both agencies. When a team works in close harmony, the result is often positive synergy. More is accomplished through teamwork than can be accomplished by groups or individuals working alone.

Less obvious is the impetus placed on the organization by its own history. A traditionally conservative agency cannot become ultraliberal overnight. Members of any organization resist change. The administrator must be aware of the agency's philosophy and plan accordingly. The chief executive must also be aware of what has been attempted in the past. Pronouncing a new program only to discover it was tried earlier without success is, at the very least, embarrassing. The following case is an excellent example of an organization's failure to break out of its flawed historical philosophy.

Webster v. *City of Houston* (1982) 689 F.2d 1220

Parents of a 17-year-old youth who was shot by police brought a suit against the city and six former police officers seeking damages for the death of their son. The U.S. District of the Southern District of Texas, at Houston, George E. Cire, J., entered the judgment on jury verdict, awarding them substantial amounts from individual officers and $2548.73 in actual damages from city, and the city appealed.

The Court of Appeals, Brown, Circuit Judge, held that:

1. The evidence was sufficient to establish that use of a "throw down," a weapon which police officers, having killed or wounded an unarmed suspect can put at the suspect's side to justify shooting, was a police department policy or custom, and that such a policy, along with the police department's cover-up of shooting of a 17-year-old unarmed suspect, supported the jury's verdict.

2. The city's conduct was not sufficiently outrageous to support an award of punitive damages against city.

3. The jury, in awarding no damages for violation of the victim's constitutional rights, committed an irreparable error.

We find that the evidence supports the jury's verdict in favor of the victim's parents in this section 1983 claim against the city of Houston, but since the jury misunderstood its instructions, we remand for a new trial as to damages alone.

Randy Webster, a 17-year-old native of Shreveport, Louisiana, stole a van from a Dodge dealership on the Gulf Freeway in Houston, Texas. Houston police officer Danny Mays spotted the van and gave chase. Officers Holloway and Olin, responding to his radioed calls, joined in. A Houston taxi driver, trying to do his part, tried to force the van off the road. Eventually, near the intersection of Telephone Road and Hall Road in southeast Houston, Randy lost control of the vehicle. It spun out of control and came to rest facing the direction he had come. The police cars screeched to a halt nearby. Mays, Holloway, and Olin ran up to the van and ordered Randy out.

At this point, the testimony diverges. According to the initial police report, Randy got out of the car with something in his hand. He resisted the officers' attempt to place him under arrest; a struggle ensued; and as officer Mays attempted to subdue him, his gun misfired, fatally wounding Randy in the head.

Ten minutes later, the story had changed. The officers related that Randy had emerged, armed, from the van and was shot immediately. Whichever story one prefers, when the ambulance arrived, a gun rested in Randy's hand.

The truth, which came to light after a long, and for Randy's parents, agonizing nightmare of involvement with the Houston Police Department (HPD), is not pleasant. Several witnesses, including the taxi driver, testified that Randy had no weapon. Further, subsequent testimony by members of the Houston Police Department revealed that using throw-down weapons was common practice among Houston police officers. Officer Dillon testified that it would be brought up at the police academy when instructors would casually mention that if you ever shot anyone accidentally, well, you had best have something to lay down to protect yourself. There was evidence offered that most officers of the HPD carried either a knife or an extra gun for such an occasion. According to Officer Holloway, probably more than 10 officers knew that Randy Webster had no weapon, but this never came to light in internal investigations. The HPD at first looked the other way and then, as that view became unpleasant, actively sought to conceal the truth.

Opinion of the Court

While acknowledging that one could imagine an extreme situation where taxpayers are directly responsible for perpetrating an outrageous abuse of constitutional rights, Justice Blackmun pointed out that "punitive damages imposed on a municipality are in effect a windfall to a fully compensated plaintiff, and are likely accompanied by an increase in taxes or a reduction in public services for the citizen footing the bill. Neither reason nor justice suggests that such retribution be visited on the shoulders of unknowing taxpayers."

The plight of Randy Webster, however reprehensible, however tragic, does not rise to the level of outrageous conduct to which Justice Blackmun referred. Since the trial court instructed the jury that it could assess punitive damages, which it then did, we must reverse that portion of the verdict.

We cannot delete this portion of the verdict and affirm the rest, however, for on examination of the instructions and the jury's answers, we find that the jury either misunderstood or ignored the judge's instructions. The jury, having found a violation of Randy's constitutional rights, could not ignore that finding in calculating damages (which they apparently did ignore). Violation of Randy's constitutional rights was, at a minimum, worth nominal damages.

We believe that, in awarding punitive damages, the jury thought it had covered all bases. It, of course, did not. Since it in effect disobeyed its instructions, we are obliged to remand to the District Court for a new trial on damages.

To be effective, the strategy must address the proper goals: those which are relevant to the organizational mission. Effectiveness should not be confused with efficiency. *Effectiveness* is doing the right job; *efficiency* is doing the job right. Ultimately, both effectiveness and efficiency are important, but in the planning stage effectiveness is crucial whereas efficiency is nice to have. Efficiency is a proper concern after the strategy has been determined to be effective.

Implementation and Evaluation

Implementation of the plan requires several prerequisites. First, the plan must be sold to the entire organization. Failure to adequately explain and elicit support from organizational personnel, those who must make it work, is a certain method of ensuring failure of the plan. Each member of the agency must know not only their individual objectives but how these objectives fit into the overall goals and mission of the organization.

The next step is building evaluation into the objectives and implementation. Evaluation techniques are difficult to add to a plan already in existence. A better approach is to design goals with evaluation in mind, and as the objectives are assigned and explained, the evaluation procedures are provided also. In this manner the agency personnel come to understand the plan, their role, and will know how their contributions to the strategy will be measured.

Evaluation provides for the systematic assessment of an activity or group of related activities. It also comes in different forms and guises. There are three evaluation perspectives and three types of program evaluation (Swanson, Territo, and Taylor, 1988, pp. 517–518). The perspectives are:

1. *Process*: focus on how evaluation is done, the steps and procedures involved in designing and conducting an evaluation.

2. *Product*: the findings or judgments that are made as a result of doing an evaluation.

3. *Purpose*: the end use of evaluation, such as for planning, policymaking, and decision making.

The various types of program evaluation are:

1. *Program evaluation*. This type of evaluation looks at whether or not the program has met its stated objectives. The focus is on the effectiveness of the program being assessed. An example might be the use of road blocks to deter intoxicated drivers over a holiday period. The police department would look at past accident rates for this time period and compare those with current rates during the same period after the use of the road blocks. If arrests for DUI offenses were up and accidents down, the conclusion would be that the program was successful.

2. *Process evaluation*. Looks at how program activities are being performed. This type is not concerned with outcomes or program utility, but instead, looks only at

the process. An example is the continuous staff inspection process wherein police activities are monitored to measure their compliance with procedures and policies. Using the example above, this type of evaluation would attempt to ascertain that the use of roadblocks and subsequent arrests were in conformance with department policy and state law.

3. *Impact evaluation.* More complex and costly than the other types, impact evaluation attempts to measure changes in the organizational-social-political environment that occurs because of the program. This evaluation not only looks at objectives but also evaluates side effects of the program. This type is used less by the police than other types. Using the example above once more, the police would look beyond the immediate arrest and accident rates and evaluate the public's perception of this program as well as the longer-term impact on driver behavior.

Each of the evaluation types has utility. A good plan will utilize both program and process evaluation; a sophisticated or complex plan should also include impact evaluation. To do this, monitoring points should be included in the plan. Time periods should be allocated for routine review of the plan in action. Also, there should be a system of warning signals for supervisors to watch for in case the agency gets off course. This dual warning system, periodic reviews and constant data monitoring, should keep the administrator informed as to the progress of the plan.

Despite the need for evaluation, many police administrators have resisted using assessment techniques. Even those agencies with planning and research elements have frequently used those units only for the tabulation of crime and budgetary statistics. There are several reasons for the failure to implement evaluation techniques. According to Charles R. Swanson, Leonard Territo, and Robert W. Taylor (1988, p. 520):

1. Police administrators did not understand, or would not acknowledge, the advantages to be gained from comprehensive program evaluation.

2. The policy preferences and positions of police administrators are translated into programs, and they were not very motivated to do anything that could discredit their stance.

3. The allocation of resources to the staff function of program evaluation was often viewed as a lower priority than the allocation of resources to the line functions.

4. A distrust of evaluation existed that was coupled with a preference for relying on subjective judgments gained through years of experience.

5. Disfavorable evaluations were feared as a powerful tool for "outsiders" to criticize the administrator personally or the department, whereas favorable evaluations would not be accorded very much weight.

6. Initiating evaluation and then using the results involves a commitment to being change oriented, and sheer organizational inertia was a frequent barrier.

The chief executive must always be aware of the need for flexibility. No plan, regardless of how well it is designed and carried out, is likely to exist for any length of time without the need for modification. As we discussed earlier, the longer the time period the plan is meant to cover, the more likely the plan is to require alteration. The future is just too unpredictable to allow for a perfectly designed plan. The day-to-day changes in personnel, expenditures, and society in general preclude perfect planning.

The plan is really nothing more than a guideline, often a very rough guideline at best. The administrator, should therefore, not be too enamored of the strategy selected, for it will require constant update and revision. The plan should be considered a living, dynamic document that grows with age and use. Should the plan be discovered to be faulty or inflexible, it should be discarded. New plans can always be drawn and old plans can always be revised; only the Ten Commandments were carved in stone.

BUDGETING

The major planning tool of law enforcement agencies is the budget. Whether or not the administrator believes in planning, the budget requires an estimate of needs for at least the next year. Thus the budget requires some planning. For those agencies engaged in long-term or sophisticated planning, the budget is an indispensable portion of this process. Both are eternally entwined; the budget determines the feasibility of the plan, while the plan determines what should be requested in the budget. Attempting to plan without considering the budget is futile; preparing the budget without a plan is irresponsible.

Selection of the format to be used in budgeting often determines the utility of the budget in planning. In this section we focus on the various types of budgets with their respective strengths and weaknesses. The budgets to be discussed are the *line-item budget, performance budget, planning-programming budget,* and *zero-based budget.*

Line-Item Budget

Initially, the line-item budget was conceived as a form of legislative control over the agency executive. Every budget format begins with this budget, but many agencies use this type as the only budget. The line-item budget is in the form of a shopping list wherein every perceived expenditure is listed with its probable cost. Generally speaking, the line-item budget is divided into four categories: *personnel, equipment, supplies,* and *contractual items.* Guidelines are designed to determine the selection of items to be placed into each category and the budget is constructed within these parameters.

The strength of the line-item budget lies in its simplicity; it is by far the easiest budget to prepare. It requires nothing more than a list of current expenditures, an educated guess as to cost changes in these items, and some idea of additional needs. The prices are listed and a total provided to the legislative body.

An additional advantage, or disadvantage depending on your point of view, is the inability of anyone to decipher the objectives of the agency through the study of a line-item budget. Since it is simply a list of expenditures, it defies evaluation. The administrator can hide any number of programs, or the lack of any clear mission, within the line-item budget.

The major drawback in this form of budget is the inability of the administrator to protect programs through the budget process. The legislative body sees only a shopping list and will frequently cut items resulting in the destruction of an effective program. More sophisticated budgets provide program descriptions that make indiscriminate budget slashing more difficult. While the easiest to construct, the line-item budget is the hardest type to defend.

Performance Budgets

The performance budget was designed to aid management. It derived its ethos and much of its technique from cost accounting and scientific management (Schick, 1978, p. 29). The idea behind the performance budget is to help administrators assess the work efficiency of operating units by (1) casting budget categories in functional terms, and (2) providing work-cost measurements to facilitate the effective performance of prescribed activities. The work-cost data are reduced into discrete, measurable units. In other words, how much production (output) are we getting for our tax dollars (input)?

The assumption inherent in performance budgeting is the ability to break work units into quantifiable elements. In public service this is often difficult, thus providing the real weakness in this form of budget. It is difficult to implement and is not easily understood by the personnel required to maintain this budget.

Planning-Programming Budget

According to Allen Schick, three important developments influenced evolution from the management orientation (performance budgeting) to a planning orientation (1978, p. 33):

1. Economic analysis—macro and micro—has had an increasing part in the shaping of fiscal and budgetary policy.

2. The development of new information and decisional technologies have enlarged the applicability of objective analysis to policymaking.

3. There has been a gradual convergence of planning and the budgetary process.

The planning-programming budget (PPB) was designed to use the budget process as a tool for planning. The PPB is constructed by dividing the organization into programs. For example, some of the police agency programs might be patrol, investigations, traffic, and record keeping. Instead of providing the legislative body with a lump sum to accept, reject, or modify, the agency administrator provides a list of programs with the budget computed on the basis of cost to operate each program. This allows the legislative body to pass judgment on programs rather than on individual items within the budget.

The strength of the PPB is the focus on planning. The administrators at each level are forced to identify and defend what they do. This is an excellent budget for defining agency mission and roles. It also allows for citizen input since programs are open for discussion in public forums such as legislative sessions. This means that the press has access to the administrator's proposed programs and methods of evaluation. Further, this budget places some responsibility on the legislative body for agency effectiveness; programs and objectives are evaluated and ruled on.

The negative aspect of the PPB is the heavy planning orientation. If the administrator lacks knowledge of agency mission and goals, or if this person is underqualified as an administrator, it will show up when this form of budget is used. This is a complicated budget to the extent that it requires a long-range orientation as opposed to a year-by-year approach. The planning budget considers the budget for the current fiscal year to be merely a small investment in a long-range plan. Other budgets we have discussed have a single year focus with no attempt to connect this budget with the next year. The planning approach connects a number of future budgets together to provide long-term programs. Planning budgets are full-time operations; as the plan is modified, so the future budgets must be altered.

Zero-Based Budgets

Zero-based budgeting was developed in 1969 at Texas Instruments. Georgia Governor Jimmy Carter adopted this approach in 1973 and ultimately applied it to the federal government when he became president.

The zero-based budget differs from PPB in the basic assumptions from which the two styles are derived. PPB provides for a continual stream of programs with no procedure for elimination of programs. Prior to the zero-based approach to budgeting, there was no budget designed to eliminate functions or programs.

The zero-based budget (ZBB) requires a review of each program every year as if it were being approved for the first time. The term zero-based means that the agency starts from zero, in terms of budget and programs, each fiscal year. No program is sacrosanct; all must be justified to receive continued funding.

Zero-based budgeting requires answering two questions about each program: (Phyrr, 1978, p. 254)? (1) Are the current activities efficient and effective? (2) Should current activities be eliminated or reduced to fund higher priority new programs or to reduce the current budget?

Also unique to the ZBB is the concept of decision packages. Decision packages are made up of decision units, which can be anything from a piece of equipment to personnel. The decision units are grouped into the larger decision packages, which are really programs. The decision-package is then presented at three budget levels; fourth would be the decision to eliminate the program:

1. The amount of funding needed to maintain the program at its highest reasonable, or optimal, leve l.

2. The amount needed to fund the program to maintain it at its current level.

3. The amount needed to maintain it at the lowest level possible while remaining reasonably effective. This level of funds should be the point at which any less funding would reduce the program's effectiveness so far as to justify its elimination.

The decision packages are put together and presented to the legislative body with the administrator's priorities stated. The legislative body then has the option of approving a budget by focusing on the amount to be budgeted on a program-by-program basis. This places a heavy responsibility on the legislative body to decide organizational priorities by way of their budget decisions.

The strength in this system is similar to the PPB; it is a planning budget that provides direction for the organization. As with PBB, however, it also is a time-consuming budget requiring administrative expertise and foresight. This budget forces the administrator to articulate the agency mission and break it into objectives and programs. It can be a powerful planning tool in the hands of competent management. It can also be an incredibly complex, incomprehensible paper generator in the hands of those less adroit with budgetary systems.

Ultimately, the choice of budget format depends on the size and complexity of the agency and the sophistication of the administrator and agency planners. Very small agencies of only 1 to 20 officers, for example, rarely need anything more sophisticated than the line-item budget. Agencies this small do not really have programs; they have personnel to be assigned in a manner that provides maximum police coverage of the area.

The larger the agency, however, the more varied the potential responsibilities and programs. Size of agency and planning needs are closely related topics. The mid-sized to large agency (100 or more officers) should operate with either the PPB or ZBB planning budgets to maximize planning effectiveness. The performance budget is least useful for a law enforcement agency. The demands for quantifiable measurements of outputs to be compared against budget inputs asserts too much pressure for the generation of production numbers. The maximum utilization of the budget requires its connection with planning; the two functions go hand in hand.

DISCUSSION QUESTIONS

1. Discuss the common errors made in administrative decision making.

2. Compare Japanese and American philosophies of decision making. What are the strengths and weaknesses of each?

3. Discuss rationality in decision making. What is bounded rationality? Why is it important in decision making?

4. Why is dissent important to the decision-making process?

5. Discuss the pros and cons of each type of budget. What is the best type for a small police agency, a medium-sized agency, and a large agency?

REFERENCES

Briggs, Bruce (1982). "The dangerous folly called theory z," *Fortune Magazine*, May, pp. 41–53.

Drucker, Peter (1974). *Management: Tasks, Responsibilities, Practices*. New York: Harper & Row.

Graham, Gerald (1984). "Strong managers are decisive; the weak ones are not." The Kansas City Star, August 5. p. 12F.

Herold, David M. (1972). "Long range planning and organizational performance: a cross validation study," *Academy of Management Journal,* March, pp. 91–102.

Locke, Edwin A. (1968). "Toward a theory of task motivation and incentives," *Organizational Behavior and Human Performance*, May, pp. 157–189.

McGurdy, Howard E. (1977). *Public Administration: A Synthesis*. Menlo Park, Calif.: Cummings Press.

Nigro, F. and L. Nigro (1980). *Modern Public Administration,* 5th ed. New York: Harper & Row.

Peters, Thomas J., and Robert H. Waterman, Jr. (1982). I*n Search of Excellence*. New York: Warner Books.

Robbins, Stephen P. (1976). *The Administrative Process*. Englewood Cliffs, N.J.: Prentice Hall.

Schick, Allen (1978). "The road to PPB: the stages of budget reform," in Fremont J. Lyden and Ernest G. Miller, eds.,*Public Budgeting: Program Planning and Evaluation.* 3rd. ed. Skokie, Ill.: Rand McNally, pp. 17–43.

Simon, Herbert A. (1976). *Administrative Behavior,* 3rd ed. New York: The Free Press.

Swanson, Charles R., Leonard Territo, and Robert W.Taylor, (1988). *Police Administration: Structures, Processes, and Behavior,* 2nd ed. New York: Macmillan.

Townsend, Robert (1970). *Up the Organization.* New York: Alfred A. Knopf.

Walton, Mary (1986). *The Deming Management Method.* New York: Perigee.

Chapter 6

Organizing

An organization may be defined as a group of people striving to fulfill a goal. When friends gather for a social event, they cannot be considered an organization. Should they decide to address an objective of mutual concern, however, they may become an organization. A great many social organizations, or even business enterprises, began in this fashion. Each organization has two elements, a formal and an informal element, that interacts as the group attempts to achieve the goal.

THE FORMAL ORGANIZATION

The term most used when discussing the formal organization is *bureaucracy*. It seems most appropriate, therefore, to begin this discussion with this often misunderstood concept. Max Weber, a German sociologist, is credited by some to have been the inventor of bureaucracy. Actually, he is responsible for the term rather than the structure. He coined the term to describe the structure he observed within industrial organizations. The term *bureaucracy* was used because the formal structure appeared to be made of bureaus, each providing a specialized task that complemented the tasks of other bureaus.

The first person to actually define principles of organization was a French mining engineer, Henri Fayol. He identified 14 principles of management and paved the way for later scholars, such as Weber. His principles are listed in Table 6-1 (Fayol, 1987).

Table 6-1
Fayol's Principles for Effective Management

Principle	*Meaning*
Division of work	Fayol believed that dividing labor into specialized units would reduce inefficiency through less waste and increased output and would simplify the task of job training.
Authority	The right to give orders and the power to exact obedience.
Discipline	Poor discipline is the result of poor leadership. Good discipline exists when workers and managers respect the rules governing activities in the organization.
Unity of command	No individual should have more than one supervisor.
Unity of direction	Tasks of a similar nature that are directed toward a single goal should be grouped under one manager.
Subordination of interests	Organizational goals should take precedence over individual goals. When the reverse is true there is conflict within the organization.
Remuneration	Rewards, in the form of pay and benefits, should be fair for all employees within the organization.
Centralization	The concentration of power and authority at the top of the organization.
Scalar chain	Chain of command; clarifies flow of authority.
Order	Resources should be coordinated in such a way that there is a place for everything and everything in its place.
Equity	Justice and kindliness in the manager-subordinate relationship.
Stability of tenure	Staffing should be conducted through planning to avoid high employee turnover.
Initiative	Employees should be encouraged to act on their own volition when they have an opportunity to solve a problem.
Esprit de corps	Managers should emphasize teamwork by building harmony and a sense of unity among employees.

As a result of his research, Weber praised the formal structure that he observed as being the most practical means of organizing and managing. He argued the necessity of organizing in this manner and proposed a number of elements composing the ideal organization (Tausky, 1978, p. 30):

1. The duties of each office are clearly specified, with the result that the division of labor among offices is clear.

2. An official hierarchy of authority exists. Each office is subject to discipline from a higher office, but only in regard to the duties of the office—the private life of the official is free from organizational authority.

3. The officeholder is an employee. The "means of administration" are attached to the office, not the officeholder, and there is no way to gain personal rights to the office.

4. Membership in the bureaucracy constitutes a career with distinct ladders of career progression.

5. Hiring and promotion are governed by competence, as measured by certified training or performance in office.

6. Impersonality, as contrasted to personal relationships, regulates activity. The body of specific and general rules regarding dealings with subordinates, peers, rank-and-file members, and clients is binding .

Fayol and Weber's organizational ideal is one in which personality and conflict do not exist. The pure bureaucracy would be an organization in which the organizational chart would correspond accurately with how the agency operated. Of course, Weber failed to consider the impact of the social environment within the organization. The informal group was not described until sometime later.

If it were possible to collect a group of people who would work selflessly, without envy or jealousy, with equal ability, Weber's structure would work well. Alas, such is not the case. The vast array of expertise, petty jealousies, and self-serving behavior undermines the clinical purity of Weber's ideal organization.

The structure of the formal organization is Weber's most prominent gift to organizational theory. The pyramid shape was best described by Weber and is a prominent portion of every organization, although it has been with us since the first organization was formed. It can be seen in the command structure of the ancient Egyptians, who, oddly enough, were in the business of building pyramids. Other portions of Weber's theory, however, are open to debate. It is not just the flawed nature of people that opens his theory to challenge, but the very concepts that he proposed may be flawed.

Although it is true that organizations do attempt to specify duties and responsibilities as clearly as possible, it is rare to find any organization without sufficient ambiguity within the division of labor to generate power struggles over jurisdiction and resources. There is a growing body of research indicating that strict delineation of duties and responsibilities hinders effectiveness of the organization (Peters and Waterman, 1982, pp. 121–125). Organizational fluidity appears to be a more promising approach to designing organizations.

Authority, as described by Weber, can also be criticized. He argued the necessity of considering authority in terms of position, as we discussed in Chapter 4. While authority may be provided for in the structural design of an agency, power differentials often serve to mitigate the effects of authority.

Within public service organizations a large portion of authority is delegated by the chief executive rather than being the product of organizational design. Chief executives do not delegate equally. While two subordinates of equal rank may have similar responsibilities, one may have far more authority as a result of the administrator's trust in this person's ability. There is no way in which this phenomenon can be described on an organizational chart, but it is a necessary fact of life in organizations. This is especially true in cases where the chief executive loses confidence in a lower manager's ability to make sound decisions.

Lacking the flexibility of the private industries to dismiss or demote personnel, the public administrator may be forced to retain the person at the current level. The only strategy left the administrator is to strip this person of any significant measure of authority. A few prerogatives may be retained, and these represent the true measure of positional authority; that which remains after delegated authority is removed.

Another aspect of the delegation process is the personal philosophy of the chief executive. Autocratic administrators delegate little, whereas democratic leaders delegate much. As a result, a division commander will have more authority under a democratic administrator than under an autocrat. Thus authority varies both within an organization and between different organizations for similar positions.

The requirement of nonownership is difficult to understand. Many of the most successful organizations are family-owned enterprises. Public agencies are never family owned, however, and to this extent the law enforcement agency adheres to this rule. Since no one can own a public institution, although some have acted as if they did, this commandment is followed totally.

The Weberian concept of career bureaucrats, his fourth facet, is partly true. Many do make careers in public service a lifelong occupation. Many, however, do not. For whatever reason—frustration, better opportunities elsewhere, or lack of promotions—many people who enter public service either leave it prior to retirement or shift from one agency to another, seeking the perfect agency. This is especially true in law enforcement, where there is a phenomenal turnover rate.

The notion given most lip service and heeded least is the hiring and promoting of personnel based on competence. The problem is the inability to identify and measure competence adequately. Also, the police function is so varied it is difficult to quantify for testing purposes. Promotional exams and personnel evaluations are therefore based not on specified capabilities, but on textbook testing and personal opinions. As a result, while often appearing to be fair, the promotion process sometimes screens out those people with reputations for challenging conventional wisdom. People who are easy to get along with and who support administrative positions without question often seem to get promotions over those who do not.

This can be seen in observing the effect of job screening activities over the past 100 years. Although these techniques have not significantly changed over the years, prior to the 1964 Civil Rights Act women and minorities found it exceedingly difficult to obtain law enforcement positions. The screening and evaluation systems, most of which are still in use today, effectively excluded these people. Whatever fairness is designed into the screening system for either hiring or promotion can be bypassed through the discretionary powers of the person doing the screening. Sadly, free thinking is often discouraged in public agencies. Blind compliance is rewarded far more than reasoned dissent. This is all the more disappointing since reasoned dissent is the most positive form of conflict and is the primary force behind adapting to changing conditions.

The idea of the rule of impersonality was invalid when presented by Weber. This is based on the concepts inherent in the traditional philosophy of management, such as: decisions are based on what is best for the organization; only competent people progress up the chain of command; and people act in accord with their position in the hierarchy. The organization was seen as a machine within which the workers were as mechanical parts, reliable and interchangeable. Today it is known that one of the secrets of the successful organization is informality and a lack of patience with a rigid system of authority and communications (Peters and Waterman, 1982, p. 122).

Weber's ideal organization, therefore, is far from ideal. Rather, it is a description of stagnant rigidity. Any approach that cannot accept the vast array of personalities and irrational behavior of the human species is doomed to fail in its attempt to describe actions within an organization. Weber has left us valuable information from which to begin the study of the organization. Others followed with added insight.

Principles of Organizing

After Weber described the structure of an organization, others immediately offered a number of principles to be considered when applying his approach to organizing. These principles are, however, occasionally contradictory (Simon, 1976, pp. 20–35). This problem is undoubtedly the result of observing the principles within organizations rather than using the principles in the original design. They only appear to be principles because of the consistency in which they appear within organizations.

If the above statement appears to be confusing, it is because there is a conflict in the logic being used to determine principles of organizing. It is one thing to establish principles and then apply these concepts to the building of an organization. It is quite another to build an organization without principles and then look at the completed structure and describe the elements appearing as principles. In the first case there are actually principles that can be used each time an organization is designed. In the second, there exists only a description of a single structure that may or may not be applicable to other structures.

In other words, the first approach creates principles of organizations, the second approach only provides a description of a single organization. Unfortunately, many of the following "principles" were the result of the latter process rather than the former and represent simple observations of how many organizations are structured. Because they are not true principles, they vary extensively in their application across differing organizations. They are better thought of as general descriptions of organizational design, occasionally usable and sometimes inappropriate in today's rapidly changing climate.

There are, however, three general principles applicable to all organizations. Their value lies in their broad view of organizational structure. First, the structure of an organization is dependent on its purpose and goals. The organization must be designed so as to fulfill its obligations. Second, the effectiveness of the entire organization is dependent on the effectiveness of the various parts of that organization. There is an old saying that the chain is no stronger than its weakest link. This is also true of organizations and the various elements from which they are made. Finally, since objectives and environments change, the organizational structure must be sufficiently flexible to accommodate the change. Failure to adapt leads to a pathological organization (the subject of the next chapter).

The Scalar Principle

The scalar principle refers to the pyramid design of the typical organization. The concept of this principle is control of the organization through the use of a cascading network of superiors and subordinates. The chief executive directly controls two to ten subordinates, who then control two to ten subordinates each, and so on until the bottom of the organization is reached. Everyone has a superior until ultimately the chief executive controls the entire agency. The scalar principle attempts to describe the level of authority within an organization and the results of the application of this principle can be observed by studying an agency's organizational chart (see Illustration 6-1).

Whether or not an organization is tall or flat can be determined by studying how this principle is applied. A tall organization is one in which there are numerous levels of management. A flat organization has few levels in the hierarchy. For example, the Catholic Church is an organization that serves several hundred million people and employs tens of thousands, yet has only five levels of management. In contrast, a typical law enforcement agency of only 500 to 700 officers may have as many as seven levels of management.

Illustration 6-1 The Scalar Principle.

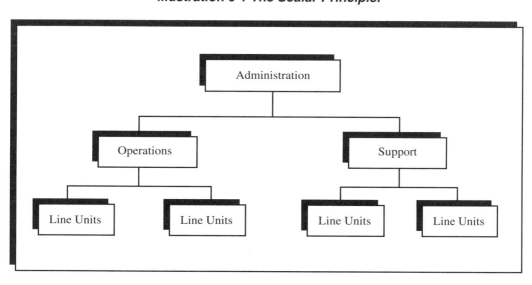

While we generally consider organizations with only one or two levels in the hierarchy to be flat, we must concede the flatness of the Catholic structure when size is considered. The epitome of the tall organization is the military, where there are often as many as 19 or 20 levels in the command structure.

The importance of command structure is related to the complexity of the organization. The more complex and formal the structure, or the more rigidly the scalar principle is applied, the less capacity the organization will have for adaptation. Recent research has identified two major indicators of organizational success related to the scalar principle. First, successful organizations have lean administrative staffs. They are relatively flat organizations with few personnel at each of the administrative levels (Peters and Waterman,1982, pp. 306–318).

Second, informality is encouraged to the extent that many of the agency personnel have never even seen an organizational chart and would be puzzled by it if they did. Informal communications among all personnel at all levels is one of the secrets of the productive organization, a concept totally at odds with traditional organizational philosophy (Peters and Waterman, 1982, pp. 121–125).

There is, therefore, an inverse relationship between the scalar principle and organizational effectiveness. The more formally the agency is structured, the less able it will be to react to new problems and the less effective it is likely to be.

Unity of Command

For the sake of stability, theorists propose the idea that each subordinate should answer to one, and only one, superior. Once more, this is to maintain control and is interrelated to the scalar principle. In theory, each group reports to an individual, who is part of a supervisory group that answers to a higher supervisor, and so on until a group of administrators reports to the chief executive. Unity of command is always traced from the bottom of the organization upward. There are often many subordinates for a supervisor, but only one supervisor for each subordinate (see Illustration 6-2).

Illustration 6-2 Unity of Command and Span of Control.

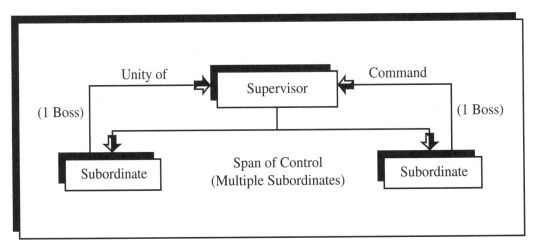

While the theory behind this principle is sound, in actuality it is often violated, especially in law enforcement agencies. The distribution of the patrol force over a large geographical area makes it nearly impossible for one supervisor to manage all of the needs of those assigned to this person. As a result, when a supervisor is called for, the one most convenient to the scene is often sent. This has the effect, however, of defeating the unity of command principle. This is especially true in military or quasi-military units, where levels within the hierarchy are given equal authority over all personnel. A sergeant is a sergeant is a sergeant, and few patrol officers will challenge any person occupying this rank, regardless of their relative positions on the organizational chart.

Span of Control

The number of subordinates or duties that one person can effectively supervise determines this person's span of control, sometimes known as the span of administration (see Illustration 6-2). The inability to determine a formula adequately for identifying the ideal number of subordinates or duties has complicated the application of this principle consistently. There are a number of variables associated with the capacity to supervise a variety of activities. Such spatial factors as proximity of supervisor and subordinate are important since a person can supervise the work of many people in a closed workspace much more easily than a person supervising others who are scattered across a large geographical area.

The capabilities of the supervisor, as well as those of the subordinates, must be considered in determining the span of control. Also, the job dynamics of the work itself play a role in identifying span of control. Is the job static, routine, or is it dynamic, requiring a great number of discretionary decisions? These factors have a definite impact on how much supervision is necessary.

As with unity of command, span of control is related to the scalar principle. It is also a principle of organizational control. Also, the inability to specify proper span of control makes this one of the least desirable of the principles to follow closely. Within most organizations, span of control is not designed up front, but seems to develop naturally as the organization evolves.

The Exception Principle

To save time and resources, theorists argue the necessity for making as many decisions as low in the hierarchy as possible. The exception principle is based on the concept that administrators should only make decisions of an exceptional nature. Routine decisions should always be made by those at the bottom of the organization. One of the complaints often voiced about many administrators is their inability to delegate. They get so tied up with trivial decisions that major decisions either do not get made or are late coming. The exception principle was espoused to prevent just this type of problem.

To accommodate the exception principle, however, requires a willingness to delegate authority, which is related to the amount of trust the administrator has in subordinates. The less the administrator delegates, the less this principle will be applicable. Again, this principle turns out not to be a principle at all, but rather a description of the delegation process within organizations.

The Aggregation Principle

Sometimes referred to as the division of labor, the aggregation principle stresses the need to departmentalize the organization according to various criteria. The criteria may include purpose (operations, technical services), time (shift or watch), area (beat or precinct), clientele (juveniles, rapists, burglars), and function (patrol, traffic).

The guidelines under which departmentalization occur should be *differentiation* and *integration*. *Differentiation* refers to the need to clarify tasks and functions of the organization. *Integration* involves the grouping of similar tasks and functions. Concurrently, responsibility for all tasks and functions, as well as sufficient authority and accountability, should be specified so that there is clarity regarding objectives, roles, and responsibilities.

The grouping of the organization into areas of specialization has both strengths and weaknesses (Duncan, 1979, pp. 59–80). Ramon J. Aldag and Timothy M. Stearns have provided a concise list of each (1991, pp. 274–275):

Strengths:

1. *Efficient use of resources.* By grouping common tasks together, economies of scale are possible. Each department can serve other departments efficiently by mobilizing problem-solving expertise quickly. Physical resources are also used efficiently because members who share facilities or equipment are in the same location.

2. *In-depth skill development.* More intensive training of members is possible within departments because of the similarity of knowledge and prior skill development. Members have the opportunities to specialize their skills to a greater extent by sharing information with colleagues in their unit.

3. *Clear career paths.* Employees have a clear understanding of job requirements and the path that will lead to promotion. By watching colleagues with similar backgrounds and expertise, an employee will learn quickly which activities are desired by the organization and which are not.

4. *Unity of direction.* A centralized decision structure helps in achieving unity of direction, as top management provides coordination and control of the organization. Departments can be provided with goals and objectives that will support the overall strategy of the organization.

5. *Enhanced coordination within functions.* Common backgrounds of members within a unit facilitate communication and enhance collegiality. This in turn helps the coordination process, as members of the unit are more likely to work as a team to accomplish the unit's goals.

Weaknesses:

1. *Slow decision making.* With decision making located at the top, senior managers may have an overload of decisions if multiple problems emerge within units. As a result,

decisions may be slowed or of lower quality, causing delays and additional problems in the organization.

2. *Less innovation.* Members of units may become focused only on unit goals rather than the overall goals of the organization. New ideas, innovations, or suggestions for new methods of solving problems often get lost because of the need to communicate or to generate support across units.

3. *Unclear performance responsibility.* The successes and failures of an organization are an outcome of activities by all departments. But the individual contribution of each unit to the success or failure of a goal is not easy to pinpoint.

4. *Limited management training.* While functional units excel at training members to solve problems related to specific skills, they do poorly at training members to solve problems affecting the organization as a whole. Top management must have an understanding of how units can be linked together effectively. Extensive training and experience in one unit reduces the opportunity for developing broader management skills.

5. *Poor coordination across functions.* Members of an individual unit may feel isolated from members of other units or even hostile toward them. As a result, they may be unwilling to support or compromise with other units to achieve organizational goals.

Distinction Between Line and Staff

Line personnel are those charged with the actual fulfillment of the agency's mission. These people are the reason the organization exists—theirs is the predominant function of the organization.

Staff personnel, on the other hand, exist to support the line function. Although necessary, duties performed by these people are of secondary importance to the line function. Staff commanders do have line authority within their respective units but should not have authority over line personnel. Few line patrol officers can safely contradict the commands of a service unit commander, however, even when the service division commander is out of line (no pun intended).

Formal Communications Network

In a formal organization, communications flow in accordance with the scalar chain. Usually, this takes the form of vertical communication. In rare instances, communications flow laterally, but formal organizations theory does not recognize the utility of lateral communications.

Communications may be oral, written, or silent. Formal communications are primarily written. These take the form of orders, policies, memos, and requests for information. Although this is supposed to be a two-way process, usually commands and requests come down, responses go up.

A major problem in many law enforcement agencies is a lack of control over the amount and type of written communications. Too many messages can clog up the communications network. Also, the inability to build all the subtle nuances accurately into a written message, usually contained in face-to-face communications, means that many messages will be misinterpreted.

Memo wars can have a disastrous impact on productivity. Misunderstood policy statements can also create confusion and apprehension until the intent is clarified. Written communication may therefore be the preferred medium in formal organizations, but if not carefully thought out and structured, they can cause more harm than good. Written messages are to be preferred when a record is needed of the thoughts being expressed on the subject of the message or the subject is too technical to be trusted to word of mouth.

Oral communications are not preferred among bureaucrats, but have a distinct advantage over written messages due to the ability of each party to provide and receive immediate feedback. As a result, the oral message is usually faster and clearer than other communication forms. Oral messages, however, are useful only when one person wishes to communicate directly with another. When the message must be sent to a variety of people, through a number of organizational layers, the message can become badly distorted before reaching the final destination. Because of this distortion problem, such messages must be written.

Silent communication refers to *body language*. Body language is most useful as a means of accenting or highlighting oral communication. Facial expressions or body posture can give meanings to the spoken word which are inconceivable to a person not present at the conversation. The lack of body language available to the written message is the reason it is difficult to fully grasp the intent of the message. Most people have difficulty fully hiding their emotions. Thus their reaction to oral messages often tells the communicator more than their verbal response. Silent communications are invariably classified as informal, as are oral messages generally. This is due to the inability to store oral or silent messages for future reference.

THE INFORMAL ORGANIZATION

Human beings are social creatures. Because of this, they can never be expected to function within a group in the manner prescribed by advocates of formal organization theory. People act with regard to how they perceive themselves and how they believe they are perceived by others. People will often sacrifice personal gain to maintain social cohesiveness with peers. This can be observed in organizations where people are paid on a piecework scale; they are paid for each piece of work they complete. One would expect each person to produce as much as possible to maximize earnings. Often, however, an informal rate will be established to protect slower workers from the faster ones. Usually, the informal rate will be well below the worker's capabilities but will appear to be reasonable. Personal gain will thereby be sacrificed for the image of the group.

This informal rate setting, called *soldiering* by Frederick W. Taylor, does not happen because the workers do not need the money. It happens because peer acceptance for most people is more powerful than financial rewards. This system is enforced also. Those who flaunt the group convention do so at their own risk. The group will invariably retaliate, first through mild kidding, then through increased joking with escalating viciousness. Finally, if all else fails, the errant member will be ostracized. Because of this phenomenon, the organization rarely sets the production rates of the employees; they set it themselves.

In police organizations this can most often be observed with the issuance of traffic citations. New officers learn quickly how many citations they can issue in an evaluation period without drawing unwanted attention from senior officers.

The organizational subculture is a by-product of several factors. One, just discussed, is the need of human beings to be social; to have friends and shared values. There is a negative reason for the development of this subculture as well. According to Sam S. Souryal:

> Criminal justice agencies are bureaucratic organizations. As such they are pyramidal, formal, impersonal, and to a large extent, frustrating. Within traditional bureaucracies, it is not uncommon that authority is abused by unethical supervisors, that power is manipulated in favor of a group of "insiders," that rules are stretched to accommodate a cohort of "benefactors," and that discipline is applied in a vindictive manner. As a result, the work environment may become dissatisfying, stifling, and, at times, intolerable. As in other public agencies, criminal justice practitioners perceive such practices as hypocritical and hostile. In response, they naturally develop informal ways and means for coping with unhealthy environments and, perhaps, getting even with uncouth managers. Thus, an *occupational subculture* emerges, consisting of a set of beliefs, attitudes, and schemes that determine in large measure what workers *have to do to survive* (1992, p. 43).

Conformity

All groups have established norms dictating acceptable standards of behavior. This is true not only for work production, but for all other aspects of the group's interaction, including absenteeism, tardiness, and goofing off (Robbins, 1976, p. 282).

Research has also indicated that when a member's interpretation of data relevant to the group is significantly different from the interpretation held by the rest of the group, the majority will apply intense pressure on the deviant member to align the individual's interpretation with that of the group (Asch, 1964, pp. 304–14). There is also evidence indicating that a person's ability to withstand this attack is increased significantly if the person does not have to stand alone. A minority position can be held longer and more successfully if there is more than one person in the minority (Robbins, 1976, p. 283).

Another important facet of group behavior is the concept of status, a prestige grading position or rank within a group. Status may be formally imposed by a group (i.e., organizationally imposed through titles or amenities) or acquired informally by such characteristics as education, age, gender, skill, or experience.

Often people claim that status is unimportant. Most of us, however, spend the better part of our lives collecting status symbols. Organizational status symbols may be such things as: keys to the executive washroom, office location, quality of office furnishings, size of expense allowance, possession of company car, and private secretary. Titles such as chief, sheriff, director, captain, and sergeant are much more than designations of authority level; they are status symbols. Personal status symbols take a variety of forms: make and year of automobile owned, level of education, size and value of home, size of salary, relative status of acquaintances, and membership in select organizations.

Status is responsive to management only to the extent that the administrator has control over factors which enhance or decrease status. Status is determined by that person's relative position within the group, and many of the criteria by which status is determined are controlled only within the group. For example, promotions and raises in salary may provide increased status for an individual, but only if the group believes that the rewards were deserved.

Informal Communications Network

Informal communications are primarily oral, although not exclusively so. Within an organization, the most highly recognized informal communications network is the *grapevine,* a name derived from the American Civil War when telegraph lines were strung through the trees, like grapevines to connect various command posts.

Unlike formal communications, information fed into the grapevine travels rapidly due to the lack of necessity of operating along the chain of command. The first person to hear the information tells every acquaintance who can be contacted within a short period of time. They, in turn, tell all of their friends, and so on until everyone has the news. Through this process a rumor can spread through a large organization within an hour. This same organization may spend 3 days to 2 weeks transmitting a similar message through formal channels before everyone in the organization receives the message.

Rumors can devastate organizational effectiveness. Although they cannot be stopped, they can be limited. Rumors can only be controlled by the truth, quickly and publicly spoken. The longer the delay in transmitting the truth, the harder the task of controlling the rumor.

The best policy for the control of rumors is the rapid dissemination of information of concern to the employees as soon as it is available. Secrecy generates rumors. When people are not informed of events and decisions affecting their job, they tend to fill in the information void with guesses. Many times the guesses are far worse than the truth, but this just makes them travel that much faster.

The danger created by rumors lies in the focus of the misinformation, which usually addresses areas of vital concern to employees and usually have just enough truth in them to make them plausible. Time on the job can be lost while employees gather to discuss the new rumor and worry about their job security.

Some organizations have found it necessary to publish memos concerning major policy issues on agency bulletin boards prior to the next day's working hours. This means that some administrator must get to work during the early morning hours to post the information, so that the grapevine will not have a chance to generate misinformation. If rumors get out first, they cause confusion and dissatisfaction. They may even cause the truth to be ignored as rumor or propaganda. Employees may spend several days in a state of anxiety and agitation, worrying and meeting secretly to console one another or to plan a counter strategy, at the expense of production. A good rumor can stop production for 3 or 4 days. A really spectacular rumor can initiate a labor strike. The only antidote is truth, spread quickly before the rumor mill has a chance to start.

Gossip is a slightly different matter. It can be neither stopped nor controlled, and there is no reason why it should. Gossip focuses on individuals, whereas rumors are concerned with organizational matters. Gossip is much less destructive to the organization. Gossip serves a dual purpose; it acts as a means of social control and provides entertainment. There are certain consistent elements inherent in gossip: (1) it is usually negative information that is (2) self-serving in the sense that the person delivering the news is trying to impress the recipient, and (3) the information contained in gossip is often true. It is the accurate nature of gossip that makes it an effective mechanism of social control.

To limit gossip would require total control over every member of the organization. Since organizations are made up of people, all of whom are imperfect, people will transgress and others will gossip about their misadventures.

The fear of gossip keeps many in line with the social standards of the group, for gossip is the means by which each miscreant is notified that the misadventure is now public news and the person is being watched. The hostility observed in those subject to gossip is understandable only when one considers the deep desire of these people to keep the topic secret.

Once negative information becomes public the person can expect embarrassment at the least, with a possibility of occupational, social, or legal problems at the worst. Gossip is therefore one of the most potent weapons that the group has to enforce group standards.

Administratively speaking, gossip is also a valuable source of information on potential personnel problems. An employee's peers detect flaws and potential problems in the individual long before the supervisor or manager. These defects often become the subject of gossip which if listened to can forewarn the administrator of future difficulties or provide information on which the problem can be diverted.

It is a mistake to attempt to stifle gossip. It is a natural human endeavor; attempting to stop it would constitute a waste of time and energy and ultimately would be an exercise in futility. It should be noted, however, that there is an overlap between rumor and gossip. This is especially true when the gossip involves significant organizational personnel. Moreover, people often want to believe negative information about others. Gossip can be generated maliciously or be the product of false perceptions. Because of the effects of gossip it is a wise administrator who listens to the gossip, then tracks down the truth. It is important to protect personnel from the debilitating effects of inaccurate information or innuendo. As to those who suffer because of their own indiscretions, there is little the administrator can do except to monitor the situation and take actions when agency effectiveness is in danger of being sacrificed.

The importance of informal communications lies in its ability to solve problems rapidly. Effective managers use informal communications with the operational personnel much more than they utilize formal channels (Peters and Waterman, 1982, p. 121). Formal communications are just too slow. Much more can be accomplished in a quick face-to-face discussion of the problem at hand.

To be effective, however, the employee must feel free to be frank with the administrator. Important information can be lost when the operative is too frightened to be candid. The proper use of informal communications depends on the administrator having sufficiently thick skin not to be offended by what lower-level employees have to say. This is easier said than done, for often the employee will have a number of criticisms of agency policies and procedures. There is a tendency in all people to assume that criticism of decisions is a personal attack.

Those who aspire to administration must constantly be aware of the separation between attacks on one's person and attacks on one's opinion. Those who cannot maintain this separation should avoid administration. Those who cannot maintain this separation and are already administrators, should stay hidden in their offices and continue to use formal communications channels. They will be ineffective, but their feelings will not be hurt.

EFFECTIVE ORGANIZATIONS

Over the past 25 years a number of books have been published describing the elements of the effective organization. Such people as Robert Townsend *(Up the Organization,* 1970; *Further Up the Organization,* 1984), James Ouchi *(Theory Z,* 1980), and Thomas J. Peters and Robert H. Waterman, Jr. *(In Search of Excellence,* 1982) have written best-sellers based on their observations of what makes organizations operate the way they are supposed to operate. What we have learned from these observations should form the foundation for designing a more effective law enforcement organization.

Unfortunately, these works have focused on the private sector, with little or no mention of the administration of a public agency. This does not mean that the information is not valid for the police administrator; it only means that a certain amount of adjusting must be done to make the ideas fit.

A word of warning is appropriate before we discuss elements of effectiveness. A private organization often has the ability to reorganize quickly. This includes reclassifying personnel as well as dismissing those who are nonproducers. Public agencies such as law enforcement are much more limited. Police organizations are created by statute; any change in the agency must be accompanied by a change in the law. Personnel are often protected by civil service rules far in excess of what would be considered fair. The net result of these restrictions is the inability of the chief executive of the agency to change the organization rapidly. This does not mean that the organization cannot be changed. It just means that the organizational renovation will have to take place over a longer period of time, usually measured in years rather than weeks or months.

Simple Structure–Lean Staff

What have the Japanese, who have created successful organizations, learned that we have failed to detect? The answer to that question may well be the secret to organizational effectiveness. The first lesson is a simple and lean structure.

Two elements of the organization appear to be crucial to effectiveness: top administration and operational personnel. Middle management poses a threat to the agency in its propensity to act as a barrier between these elements. Research has shown an inverse relationship between the size of the hierarchy in an organization and its effectiveness (Peters and Waterman, 1982, pp. 306–17). The closer the administrator is to the operations, the more effective the agency. A top-heavy organization generates numerous problems (which are discussed in Chapter 7).

Informal Communications Stressed

Lesson 2 is related to lesson 1. People in effective organizations talk to each other. This facet of administration has even been titled in some organizations; United Airlines calls it *visible management* and Hewlett-Packard calls it *MBWA* (management by wandering around) (Peters and Waterman, p.122).

Effective managers have realized that problems do not cause an organization to be ineffective; delays in solving the problems do. The further the administrator is from the operative, the longer the delay in solving problems. Also, when the top administrator is constantly seeking input from those who actually do the job, administrative policies tend to be clear cut and relevant.

Administrative decisions tend to be better when they are based on the realities of life in the actual operations. The people who do the work of the organization every day have a much clearer picture of the agency and its problems than do administrative personnel locked away in their air-conditioned offices.

Focus

The third element of effectiveness is understanding what business the organization is in. Effective organizations stay with their specialty and do not sail into unfamiliar waters. They understand their business, their competition, and their objectives. They then pursue their goals with fanaticism. If this seems unrelated to law enforcement, it is not.

Many police agencies have diverted resources and time from efforts they were good at, to new ideas they were uncomfortable with, simply because the larger department down the road did it or because it was the current fad. Effective organizations know what they can and cannot do. They do what they can as well as they can and they do not attempt what they cannot accomplish.

Staying Close to the Customer

The fourth element is willingness to stay close to the customer. Successful organizations make it a point to seek out constantly their customer's advice on the service they provide. Often the customer has a better understanding of the organization and its product than does the agency administrator. The person who uses the service is in a unique position to judge its quality. Law enforcement administrators would do well to keep this in mind.

Law enforcement is almost totally dependent on the willingness of the public to support the police agency. Anything law enforcement personnel can do to build public trust and confidence in the police is worthwhile. Any action or policy that causes the public to mistrust or dislike the police is detrimental to the mission of the agency and should be changed.

The question asked at the beginning of this book, "What business are we in?", is crucial to the organizational function. Law enforcement agencies are in the people business. People determine the effectiveness of the police agency by their willingness to come forward and report criminal acts and to act as witnesses in courts. If the police executive expects public cooperation, people must be nurtured with the same loving care that a farmer provides to crops in the fields.

An example of the way that law enforcement has failed in this regard can be seen by observing the treatment of witnesses in large courtrooms. In the typical law enforcement agency, witnesses to a crime must fend for themselves at court. They must drive their own cars (or take a bus) to the courthouse, find a parking place, find the courtroom—which can be confusing in a large courthouse—and then sit around for hours in a witness chamber wondering what is happening and vowing never to do this again. This process is further complicated by the delaying tactics of defense attorneys, which always seem to include at least one postponement. This means that the ritual may have to be repeated a number of times before the case comes to trial. Is it any wonder the police often have difficulty getting witnesses to testify in court?

Consider how much easier it would be on the witness if the investigating officer took the effort to pick up the witnesses at their residences, took them to the courthouse (in many jurisdictions, law enforcement personnel have specified parking for official vehicles), escorted them to the proper courtroom, saw to their comfort (including getting them coffee), and kept them company through the court process while keeping them informed about what was happening and why. Of course, this is not always possible; sometimes witnesses are from outside the jurisdiction and cannot be picked up by agency vehicles. Many witnesses, however, can be picked up by the officers, especially witnesses who are elderly or insecure. These people need special care due to their increased anxiety.

Great care should also be taken with victims who are also witnesses. They have suffered enough trauma without the additional burden of a confusing and irritating court experience. The police can and should relieve as much of this anxiety as possible.

In many cases police officers on their way to court have driven past the homes of witnesses. In the courtroom, officers gather together in their own special rooms and ignore the people on whom they depend to get the criminal convicted. This represents a lack of understanding of the police mission. The witnesses are not the responsibility of the court or prosecutor, but of the police. People make the law enforcement agency effective and ineffective. Those agencies determined to be effective know where their bread is buttered; they take care of the people who take care of them. And no one needs police support like victims and witnesses; this is one way in which the police can stay close to the customer.

Decentralization

The reality of organizational life is that no one knows the needs of the organization better than those who must deliver the service. The administrator cannot sit up on Mount Olympus and make grand pronouncements and policy statements having any practical value unless those who must implement them concur. Effective organizations place the decision-making responsibility on those who must deliver the service.

In private organizations research has shown the necessity of breaking large units into smaller elements to enhance their ability to refine their service or product. This enhanced ability is accompanied by increased autonomy. Each unit is accountable for its product; management does not interfere with the means by which the objectives are accomplished, as long as the means are legal. In other words, the administration assigns the personnel and the task, then gets out of the way and allows the people to do the job they are being paid to do. This includes the freedom to make occasional mistakes and to alter organizational policy when circumstances dictate. The necessity for this freedom was most aptly stated by Robert Townsend in a quote from Napoleon:

> A commander in chief (manager) cannot take as an excuse for his mistakes in warfare (business) an order given by his minister (boss) or his sovereign (boss's boss), when the person giving the order is absent from the field of operations and is imperfectly aware or wholly unaware of the latest state of affairs. It follows that any commander in chief (manager) who undertakes to carry out a plan which he considers defective is at fault; he must put forward his reasons, insist on the plan being changed, and finally tender his resignation rather than be the instrument of his army's (organization's) downfall (1984, p. 60).

Decentralization implies trust. The administrator must trust both the knowledge and judgment of operational personnel and line supervisors to make this work. Sound organizations have this trust, weak agencies do not. Administrators must realize that it is not they who determine organizational effectiveness, but the people who do the job. The tightly run ship approach, where the chief executive holds the reigns and makes all the decisions, does not work now, will not work in the future, and has not worked in the past, despite the beliefs of traditional managers who long for a return to the good old days. The hard truth is that there were no good old days, just a failure to remember how bad things really were.

Production Through People

Law enforcement is a people-oriented operation. It is people serving people. Effective organizations consistently foster in their employees a strong sense of organizational values, self-respect, a strong sense of responsibility, and freedom to deliver the service according to their own judgment. The key to this success lies in the area of judgment. The law enforcement administrator must strive to provide an organizational atmosphere where each person's judgment is allowed to grow to its full potential. The duty of the managerial team is to encourage this growth and to remove those with an inability to exercise sound judgment. Good police work is dependent on the individual officer's ability to make correct decisions quickly. Judgment is therefore the most important trait among officers and should be the major criterion for selection, retention, placement, and promotion. All other factors pale in comparison.

Another factor involved in productivity through people is an emphasis on success rather than failure. Peters and Waterman found a major distinction between successful organizations and those that are unsuccessful is the focus of management. Good organizations are constantly praising success, and more important, constantly finding ways to allow as many people as possible to be successful.

Weak organizations focus almost totally on failure. Administrators in these organizations spend most of their time with operational personnel on disciplinary matters. They take little or no time praising success or providing incentives for better productivity (Peters and Waterman, 1982, pp. 235–278).

A closely related factor is the willingness of many executives in successful organizations to act as cheerleaders for the workers. The effective administrator can be found in the field, talking to operatives and providing encouragement, as opposed to remaining locked away in the palace, guarded by an unapproachable mob of staff personnel and secretaries sworn to protect the chief from any outsiders, including patrol officers. (At the height of the public relations problems that the Los Angeles Police Department faced as a result of the Rodney King incident,* it was stated by a former commander that Chief Darrel Gates was so isolated that even deputy chiefs had no access to the chief without an appointment; no one got past the chief's secretary.)

Any open-door policy must be real. Too many open-door policies are paper policies only; everyone knows they are meaningless because of the rigid requirement that personnel always follow the chain of command. By the way, the latter

---

* Rodney King, a black man, was beaten with nightsticks and shocked several times with an electronic stun gun by white Los Angeles police officers. This occurred over a 20-minute period and was videotaped by a passing citizen. The resulting controversy generated into rioting when an all-white jury found the officers innocent of charges stemming from this incident.

is a policy that guarantees the protection of incompetent supervisors and middle management by allowing them to stifle any criticism proceeding up the formal communications channel while reducing the flow of informal communications between field personnel and the chief executive.

People must not only be *allowed* to grow, they must be *forced* to grow if they wish to stay with the organization. Those who cannot develop to their full potential should find other employment where their potential can be reached. The ultimate achievement of a chief executive is having the ability to take an extended leave of absence without being missed. The better the people at the bottom of the organization, the less those at the top have to worry.

DISCUSSION QUESTIONS

1. Discuss the strengths and weaknesses of the bureaucratic structure.

2. Discuss the principles of bureaucracy as proposed by Max Weber.

3. Discuss the strengths and weaknesses of formal and informal communication.

4. Compare and contrast the formal and informal organization.

5. Discuss the factors that distinguish effective organizations from those that are ineffective.

REFERENCES

Aldag, Ramon J., and Timothy M. Stearns. (1991). *Management,* 2nd ed. Cincinnati, Ohio: South-Western.

Asch, Solomon (1964). "Opinions and social pressures," in Harold J Leavitt and Lewis R. Pondy, eds., *Readings in Managerial Psychology*. Chicago: University of Chicago Press.

Duncan, R. (1979). "What is the right organizational structure? Decision tree analysis provides the answer." *Organizational Dynamics,* Winter, pp. 59–80.

Fayol, Henri (1987). *General and Industrial Management* (revised by Irwin Gray). Belmont, Calif.: David S. Lake.

Ouchi, James G. (1981). *Theory Z: How American Business Can Meet The Japanese Challenge*. New York: Avon Books.

Peters, Thomas J., and Robert H. Waterman, Jr. (1982). *In Search of Excellence*. New York: Warner Books.

Robbins, Stephen P. (1976). *The Administrative Process.* Englewood Cliffs, N.J.: Prentice Hall.

Simon, Herbert A. (1976). *Administrative Behavior: A Study of Decision-Making Processes in Administrative Organizations,* 3rd ed. New York: Free Press.

Souryal, Sam S. (1992). *Ethics in Criminal Justice: In Search of the Truth.* Cincinnati, Ohio: Anderson.

Tausky, Curt (1978). *Work Organizations: Major Theoretical Perspectives.* 2nd ed., Itasca, Ill.: F.E. Peacock.

Townsend, Robert (1984). *Further Up the Organization.* New York: Alfred A. Knopf.

Townsend, Robert (1970). *Up the Organization.* New York: Alfred A. Knopf.

Chapter 7

The Police Organization

Depending on the size of the organization, police agencies follow a fairly consistent pattern of dividing responsibilities. Obviously, size and amount of specialization among subunits are directly related. If we were to observe the small one- to 10-officer agency we would find a single administrator and a body of generalists with little or no specialization, whereas the very large organizations have a high degree of specialization within numerous semiautonomous elements (see Illustration 7-1). Of the three major organizational divisions of a law enforcement agency (operations, administrative services, and technical services), operations is the most critical, regardless of agency size.

OPERATIONS

The police organization revolves around operations. The elements that compose this portion of the agency have the responsibility of addressing the needs of the public. All other units are created for support purposes. Operations is the reason that police agencies exist. Within operations, certain types of elements will always be found: patrol, criminal investigations, and some specialized units designed to address specific crime-related problems.

Patrol

The patrol officer is the primary agency representative. The majority of contacts between the public and police occur between citizen and patrol. The first and

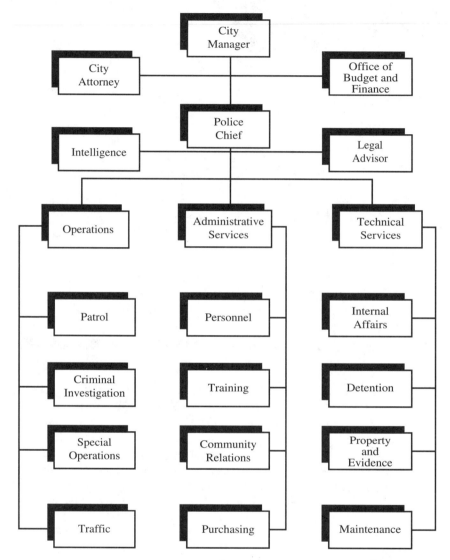

*Ilustration 7-1 **The Police Organization.***

foremost police element is patrol; all other units exist to augment and support this function. This is the only police element to be distributed in a geographic manner calculated to provide rapid police service anywhere in the jurisdiction.

Patrol provides the initial response to almost every event requiring police presence; whether this is a major crime, a serious injury, or a cat up a telephone pole. The patrol officer is the only member of the law enforcement agency to be involved in practically every incident calling for police action.

If the last statement appears to be a somewhat heavy-handed description of patrol, it is due to the incredible importance of this unit. To state the case more bluntly: patrol is the only element the law enforcement administrator cannot afford to disband. Patrol officers can, and have, assumed the duties of other police elements in times of financial crises requiring agency cutbacks. No one but patrol can assume the patrol function.

Distribution

Since the patrol force has 24-hour responsibility, patrol officers must be assigned in such a manner to facilitate constant coverage of the jurisdiction. The time requirements are best understood by noting that to maintain 10 officers on patrol for three shifts requires approximately 40 officers, allowing for two days off a week and vacation time. Thus while it is possible to concentrate other agency elements, such as the administrative elements, into five 8-hour blocks from Monday through Friday, patrol must be dispersed over every hour of every day.

The determination of how the patrol force is to be distributed can be made in a simplistic manner or through the use of sophisticated computer models. All distribution methods share certain characteristics; they are all based on time and geographical requirements. More complex systems also consider work loads by time of day, day of week, and month of year. The most sophisticated systems also figure in type of call, amount of time required to complete each type of call, and work load by geographic subunit within the jurisdiction.

The most simple distribution technique involves dividing the patrol force into three equal-sized platoons or squads and assigning them in 8-hour segments so that each element is coming on duty as another element is going off. This is often accompanied by assigning beats of roughly equal size to each officer or team of officers in the platoon. Such decisions are made without regard to population within each beat or amount of work by either beat or time of day. An obvious drawback of this system is the unequal distribution of work among individual officers and between entire platoons.

Through the addition of a fourth patrol element, sometimes called the fourth watch or swing shift, some of the problems of equal staffing can be eliminated. The fourth platoon is assigned during periods of peak police activity, thus providing additional officers when they are most needed and relieving the pressure on the officers with the highest work load. An example of this would be assigning 10 officers to work from 6:00 P.M. to midnight and 10 more to work from midnight to 8:00 A.M. The swing shift might bring an additional 6 to 10 officers on duty from 8:00 P.M. to 2:00 A.M., providing additional personnel during the period of peak activity.

This system can be improved further by designing beats according to number of calls for police service rather than by attempting to allocate by geographic size alone. Techniques for defining geographic beats can get extremely complicated with the utilization of computers. Both beat design and the determination of number of police elements to be assigned can be improved through computerized mathematical models.

The problems associated with the more sophisticated approaches are often too serious to overcome, especially in small to midsized agencies. First, computerization requires computer experts and programmers. People with these qualifications are not often found among law enforcement personnel. Administrators also tend to be distrustful of systems they do not understand. Second, computer models need a constant supply of accurate data to maintain an up-to-date design. When the beats constantly change, as they can in the sophisticated models, patrol officers are not allowed to adjust to one design. The continual changing of beats can generate confusion and low morale.

Third, the data required to drive the computer models must be accurate, but more important, it is data that police agencies do not normally collect. A new system of record keeping must be instituted, therefore, to provide the necessary data. This requires significant alterations in patrol and records procedures. As a result, personnel in both divisions must be retrained to work within the new system. For the very large department this is practical. For agencies of less than 400 officers there is some question as to the validity of the more sophisticated approaches.

The smaller the agency, the easier it is to heuristically determine proper beat design and number of patrol units to be allocated. Computer-designed beats and patrol car allocation is not really necessary unless the size of the jurisdiction and agency make data analysis impossible without a computer.

Patrol Strategy and Tactics

The means by which the patrol force meets its objectives is determined by a variety of techniques. Traditionally, the patrol force operates under the philosophy of random patrol; units randomly drift around assigned beats awaiting calls for service. The concept was based on the idea of *omnipresence of the police.*

Administrators have put their faith in the idea that a high-visibility patrol will create fear in the mind of potential criminals due to an inability to predict when and where the police officer would next appear. Research has challenged this assumption. New ideas have evolved, however, and their application has had mixed results.

One of the first of these new approaches was saturation patrol. In this technique one or two beats would be inundated with patrol units, while other beats would be stripped of patrol elements. The basis of this concept was placing patrol elements in high-crime areas or where they were needed most. The method of selecting which beat to saturate changed from agency to agency. In some, the determination was made by work load; in others the decision was made randomly to confuse potential criminals.

There are still variations of saturation patrol in use today. The terminology has changed, however. It is now called high-visibility patrol. The major emphasis in this technique is on crime-specific, temporary saturation patrol with clearly marked police vehicles. A variation of this system is low-visibility patrol. The saturation tactics are identical, but the patrol vehicles are unmarked. *Crime-specific* means that the focus of the patrol is on a certain crime problem, such as robbery or burglary, identified as a specific threat to the area to be patrolled.

Another approach to patrol is the *directed deterrent patrol.* "Directed deterrent patrol (DDP) differs from routine patrol methods in that patrol officers perform certain specific, predetermined, preventive/deterrent strategies on a regular and systematic basis" (Hale, 1981, p. 115). This form of patrol is based on strategies developed in a crime analysis unit. The concept is designed to attack a specific crime problem at a precise location. The patrol officer is not only told what problem exists but is also told in detail how to approach the problem during the tour of duty. The agency primarily responsible for the developing of this technique is New Castle County, Delaware. The directed deterrent patrol method is reported to be a successful crime reduction technique (Hale, 1981, p. 116).

Another approach to patrol is the *decoy method.* New York City has had some success with this technique in fighting street crime. The officers engaged in this form of patrol do so in disguise, within a specific location, in an attempt to attack a certain type of crime. Although this technique has been successful in the apprehension of street criminals it has also been controversial. If not carefully supervised, the decoy units can easily step over the line from decoy to entrapment. Some police agencies have had to curtail decoy activities due to adverse public reaction (Knickerbocker, 1977, pp. 3–4).

Two other strategies, similar to low-visibility patrol, have been developed. These, called *apprehension-oriented patrol*, use low-visibility tactics. The first is location-oriented patrol and is directed at places or geographic areas where certain crimes are occurring. The second is *perpetrator-oriented patrol* and is focused on individuals who, based on reliable information, are likely to commit a criminal act. Both systems rely heavily on intelligence and crime analysis information to identify target areas and persons to keep under surveillance (Hale,1981, p. 120).

Research conducted by the Kansas City, Missouri Police Department indicated that both location- and perpetrator-oriented patrol were superior to traditional patrol in effectiveness. Both, however, generated more citizen complaints than were generated by routine patrol. The administrator must therefore weigh the good points and bad to determine which approach is most suitable.

Another concept has been implemented in Wilmington, Delaware. It is known as the *split-force concept.* Early results indicate some merit to this strategy. The split-force concept calls for division of the patrol force into two elements. One provides traditional random patrol and responds to calls for service while the second utilizes directed patrol. These officers do not respond to calls unless absolutely necessary. Instead, the directed patrol elements operate in accordance with the directives of the crime analysis unit. Under this system preventive patrol becomes a primary activity rather than something to do between calls. Research indicates that patrol effectiveness is enhanced by this approach (Tien, et al.,1977).

Future patrol strategies will undoubtedly include increased utilization of directed patrol and declining use of random patrol. As computer and other technologies improve, the capacity to predict criminal activity and other community problems will require an appropriate patrol technique.

There are, however, some negative aspects of directed patrol requiring serious discussion. The first and foremost problem is the effect that directed patrol has on morale and job satisfaction. One of the real attractions of law enforcement is the freedom of individual officers to devise personal strategies for attacking crime in their sector. Directed patrol removes this freedom. The officer becomes the tool of the computer and crime analyst to be moved around like a puppet or a chess piece. Although the agency and administration find increased fulfillment of objectives through increased effectiveness, the patrol officer loses motivation and interest. This is despite the increased activity of each officer as the crime analysis unit improves its ability to predict. Part of the problem may be that as a specialized unit such as crime analysis gains prestige, the patrol force loses prestige. Of course, the Wilmington split-force concept can alleviate some of this problem if the administrator is willing to rotate patrol assignments so that every officer is required to work both random and directed patrol.

A second problem is personnel. If there are insufficient personnel to handle both calls for service and engage in directed patrol, the system is useless. No matter how good the crime analysis section becomes, if there is no patrol officer free to respond to the directions, the efforts and resources are wasted. Directed patrol strategies assume the existence of sufficient patrol time available to respond to directives.

Regardless of the problems inherent in directed patrol, the weakness of the traditional approach requires a shift in strategy. Traditional patrol has only one administrative advantage; it is easy to manage. Directed patrol requires highly developed crime analysis skills and an understanding of probability theory and trends. Directed patrol is a sophisticated technique requiring knowledge beyond that required for the traditional approach. Effective patrol requires ever-increasing complexity and application of new technology.

Types of Patrol

Patrol is the term used to identify a means for the delivery of police service. The ways by which the patrol function can be accomplished are as varied as the imagination of the police administrator.

Automobile Patrol. The most common form of patrol is motor vehicle patrol. The officer is assigned an automobile with which to cover the assigned area. The advantages of the automobile are many. It can cover a large geographic area quickly, it provides a mobile office for the officer, and it allows for the easy transportation of prisoners.

There are also disadvantages to patrol by auto. The officer becomes somewhat isolated from the public. The emphasis of this type of patrol is mobility; the chief measures of performance are usually tied to response time and number of calls for service handled.

Foot Patrol. Foot patrol was once the primary means by which the uniformed units performed their duties. The introduction of the automobile changed this in many jurisdictions. Most large cities, however, especially those with congested downtown areas, retained foot patrol as the most appropriate means of patrolling areas of heavy foot traffic.

Studies conducted by the National Neighborhood Foot Patrol Center at Michigan State University over the past decade have revived interest in the use of foot patrol as a major component of the patrol function. Those police departments shifting to a community-oriented policing have been especially pleased with the utility of foot patrol in the enhancement of police-community interaction and understanding. According to Robert Trojanowicz and David Carter: "While today's community policing often puts officers on foot in the community as was done in an earlier era, today's officers do much more than patrol a beat. The same officer day after day diagnoses the beat area and then develops problem-solving approaches ranging from organizing neighborhood associations to referring people to appropriate community social agencies" (1988, p. 19).

Bicycle Patrol. Bicycle patrol is also gaining more acceptance as a means of delivering police service. The bicycle offers the close personal interaction of the foot patrol officers with a mechanized mode of transportation that extends the officers' geographic range. The bicycle is especially useful in areas difficult for automobile travel.

Horse Patrol. Equestrian units are also regaining popularity. Horses are being successfully used in city parks and in urban shopping areas. A mounted officer has the advantage of elevation, which is especially useful in crowd control situations. The officer can observe both pedestrian and auto traffic for several city blocks. Of equal importance, the mounted officer can be seen from the same distance.

Air Patrol. Air patrol has gained in popularity, especially the use of helicopters. The helicopter has tremendous utility as a patrol vehicle. By observing fleeing vehicles from the air, the on-ground pursuit vehicle can be guided to the proper location without endangering the lives of officers or innocent citizens. Additionally, helicopters offer air surveilance of building rooftops, a favored point of entry for burglars and a place not readily accessible to ground police units. Rural and state agencies have also found air units, both helicopter and fixed-wing craft, useful for monitoring traffic and for search-and-apprehend or search-and-rescue services in remote areas.

Water Patrol. In jurisdictions where there are large bodies of water or rivers, the use of marine vehicles has become popular. The increasing use of lakes, rivers, and oceans for recreation has placed a patrol responsibility on government agencies to provide police services for these areas. Many police departments now have watercraft for search and rescue as well as for routine patrol. The demand for police services in aquatic areas is becoming sufficiently high that some agencies are developing a high degree of specialization in aquatic law enforcement.

Criminal Investigations

Criminal investigation becomes a specialized function when the patrol force becomes too overworked to complete follow-up investigations adequately. The investigations element is usually the first specialized unit created as the agency grows. There is no magic formula that tells the administrator when to create this element. It is created when the administrator feels that the patrol element can no longer provide both patrol coverage and handle investigative duties.

The Rand Analysis

The investigative function has been the subject of numerous works of fiction. The detective is always portrayed as colorful, inventive and capable of solving crimes through the use of logic in the organizing of slim bits of evidence into a solid case. The truth, of course, is somewhat different. In 1975, the Rand Institute completed an in-depth study of the investigative function. They reached the following conclusions (Hastings, 1977):

1. Department-wide arrest and clearance rates are unreliable measures of the effectiveness of investigative operations. The vast majority of clearances are produced by activities of patrol officers, by the availability of identification of the perpetrator at the scene of the crime, or by routine police procedures.

2. Department-wide arrest and clearance statistics vary primarily according to the size of the department, the region of the country in which it is located, and the crime workload (number of reported crimes per police officer). Variations with investigative training, staffing, procedures, and organization are small and do not provide much guidance for policy decisions.

3. While serious crimes are invariably investigated, many reported felonies receive no more than superficial attention from the investigators. Most minor crimes are not investigated.

4. An investigator's time spent on case work is preponderantly consumed in reviewing reports, documenting files, and attempting to locate and interview victims. For cases that are solved (i.e., a suspect has been identified), an investigator's average time in post-clearance processing is longer than the time spent in identifying the perpetrator. A substantial fraction of the time is spent on noncasework activities.

5. Many police departments collect more physical evidence than can be productively processed. Allocating more resources to increasing the processing capabilities of the department is likely to lead to more identifications than some other investigative actions.

6. In many large departments, investigators do not consistently and thoroughly document the key evidentiary facts that reasonably assure that the prosecutor can obtain a conviction on the most serious applicable charges.

7. Investigative strike forces have a significant potential to increase arrest rates for a few difficult target offenses, provided they remain concentrated on activities for which they are uniquely qualified; in practice, however, they are frequently diverted elsewhere.

After the completion of this research, the Rand Corporation made the following recommendations based on their findings:

1. Postarrest investigative activity is not only important for prosecution but it is also one of the major activities now performed by investigators. This activity can perhaps be performed in a less costly and more effective manner. Police and prosecutors should make explicit the types of information that are appropriate to collect and document for each type of crime. Above and beyond merely improving coordination between police and prosecutors, it is worthy of experimentation to assign the prosecutor responsibility for postarrest investigations.

2. Assigning all apprehensions of known suspects to investigators does not appear to be cost effective. Certain patrol officers, whom we call generalist-investigators, should be trained to handle this function. Only when apprehension proves difficult should investigative units become involved.

3. Any steps a police department can take to convert investigative tasks into routine actions will increase the number of crimes solved. Information systems and well-organized manual files help produce routine clearances. We believe an experiment should be conducted to determine the cost and effectiveness of lower paid personnel performing these routine tasks.

4. A significant reduction in investigative efforts on crimes without known suspects would be appropriate for all but the most serious offenses.

5. Establish a Major Offenses Unit to investigate serious crime.

6. Assign investigators of serious offenses to closely supervised teams rather than individual investigators.

7. Police departments should employ strike forces selectively and judiciously. The advantages of strike force operations are unlikely to persist over a long period of time. Departments must accustom themselves to creating and then terminating strike forces.

8. Evidence processing capabilities should be strengthened.

9. Police departments should initiate programs to increase the victim's desire to cooperate with the police and to impress on citizens the crucial role they play in crime solution.

The PERF Study

In 1979 the Police Executive Research Forum conducted its own study of criminal investigations (Eck, 1979, 1983). This research identified two perspectives of the investigative function. The first was the *circumstance-result hypothesis* first identified by the Rand study. This hypothesis argues that investigative success is the by-product of the curcumstances surrounding the criminal event. According to this hypothesis, the activities of the follow-up investigator play a minimal role in solving the case (Eck, 1992, p. 28).

The second perspective was the *effort-result hypothesis*. This perspective argued that the activities of investigators played a significant role in the successful conclusions of criminal cases. This theory argued further that the amount of investigative effort expended was directly related to the ability to conclude a criminal case successfully (Eck, 1992, p. 28).

The results of this research were ambiguous. Both perspectives were supported. They found that preliminary investigations were significant, thus supporting the circumstance-result hypothesis. They also found, however, that follow-up investigations were significant, thus supporting the effort-result hypothesis.

In conclusion, John Eck proposed a triage approach to managing criminal investigations. He states that it is necessary to differentiate among types of cases. He offers a classification of three groups (Eck, 1992, pp. 31–32):

1. Cases that *cannot be solved* with a reasonable amount of investigative effort.

2. Cases *solved by circumstances,* which require only that the suspects be arrested, booked, interrogated, and a prosecutable case prepared.

3. Cases that *may be solved* if a reasonable level of investigative effort is applied to them, but will not be solved otherwise.

By identifying which category a case may be classified, it is believed that the appropriate assignment can be made. Either the case is filed away with no investigative effort expended, or assigned to an investigator for either follow-up or preparation for prosecution. In classifying cases, it is necesary to consider solvability factors.

Solvability Factors

A key factor in managing an investigative unit is understanding the capabilities of this unit. Not all cases can be solved through the investigative process. The good investigator knows when to devote full efforts to the assigned case and when to walk away. The old idea, that every case must be assigned to a detective and investigated, is counter productive. Not only are unsolvable cases still left uncleared, but valuable time is wasted that could be used on cases for which a solution is possible. The result is fewer cases solved due to the overworking of investigators on hopeless investigations.

Since investigative resources are scarce, the focus of the investigator should be on those cases that can reasonably be expected to end in success. Researchers at Stanford University devised a system for predicting investigative success through the use of probability theory (Greenberg, Yu, and Lang, 1972). This system utilized quantitative weights assigned to leads developed by the preliminary investigator. If the combined weight of the factors was too low, the initial investigator recommended no follow-up investigator be assigned.

The police department in Rochester, New York also experimented with solvability factors. They analyzed 500 cases to determine what factors had led to the solution. From this analysis, 12 factors were identified; one or more of which was present in every case cleared through investigation. These solvability factors were (Hastings, 1977, p. 216):

1. The suspect could be named.

2. The suspect could be identified.

3. The address of the suspect was known.

4. The suspect could be located.

5. The vehicle plate number used in the crime was known.

6. The vehicle could be identified.

7. There was traceable property.

8. There were identifiable latent prints.

9. A significant modus operandi could be developed.

10. It was reasonably suspected that there was a limited opportunity to commit the crime.

11. There was reason to believe that the crime would arouse such public interest that public assistance would be forthcoming.

12. There were reasons to believe that further investigative effort would lead to the solving of the crime.

After reaching the conclusions noted above, Rochester decided to submit cases for follow-up investigation only when one or more of the factors above were present. The result has been an increase in clearance rates for this agency. The police administrator can utilize investigative resources to their maximum capacity through the use of solvability factors in the assigning of cases to investigators.

Coordinating Patrol and Investigations

The follow-up investigation is a natural extension of the preliminary investigation performed by the patrol officer. Since the follow-up is normally conducted by a detective, it would seem appropriate for patrol personnel and detectives to maintain close contact. Alas, such is not the case in many agencies.

V. A. Leonard and Harry More labeled departments with severe communications problems between these units as *detective dominated* (1971, p. 272). They further identified the conditions leading to this problem. First, investigators are paid more and are awarded more prestige. Second, an attitude develops wherein anyone who stays in patrol for any length of time is considered incompetent as a police officer. Third, the investigators become elitist and refuse to communicate with personnel they consider beneath them, especially patrol officers.

A serious administrative concern arises when communications between patrol and investigations breaks down. These are the two most important elements in the agency; they must communicate openly and honestly with each other. The failure to do so generates serious administrative headaches. The response to this problem has usually been to ignore it. Not every agency, however, has allowed this error to continue. Some have developed different methods of relieving the conflict. The first technique is to force the two elements to work together and more important, to talk to each other face to face to work out their problems.

The second technique is known as team policing. Team policing probably qualifies as a transitory phase of police organization. It is a precursor to problem-oriented policing. It is considered a relatively new concept, although it is based on policing techniques dating back to the era prior to the advent of the two-way radio. The theory is developed around the idea of having a close-knit team of generalists confined to a relatively small geographic area. Supposedly, both police expertise and police-community interaction will increase. The organization of the team approach varies from department to department, but generally it consists of the following elements (Hale, 1981, p. 112):

1. *Unity of supervision*: intended to enhance consistency of police policies and procedures and to provide greater uniformity in developing solutions to community problems.

2. *Low-level flexibility in decision making*: by which team members are encouraged to share and exchange ideas and work together in solving problems within their area of responsibility.

3. *Unified delivery of services*: which places emphasis on the development of generalist rather than specialist skills among team members.

4. *Combined investigation and patrol functions*: which is designed to bridge the gap between patrol officers and investigators, thereby leading to a more cooperative approach to problem solving.

Whether the team policing approach is adopted or not, the administrator must maintain a close watch on the relationship between patrol and investigations. Any indication of a breakdown in communications should be addressed immediately. Success or failure of the agency to fulfill its mission rests with operations, and none is more important than patrol and investigations.

Traffic

Besides the investigations element, the traffic detail is most likely to be the next specialized unit created. Even the smallest police agencies often have a traffic detail, sometimes consisting of only one officer. There are a variety of reasons for the creation of this unit. First, more people are killed annually through traffic mishaps than as the result of criminal activity. Second, in urban areas traffic problems tend to consume an inordinate amount of a patrol officer's time, thus distracting patrol from other activities. Third, while political leaders and law enforcement administrators dislike admitting it, traffic fines contribute an enormous amount of money to the jurisdiction's treasury. Without the contribution of traffic enforcement, many communities would have to raise taxes substantially.

While none of these factors alone is sufficient justification for the creation of a traffic detail, together they make a formidable argument. These are added to another factor. Job satisfaction can be increased among the officers. Even though most officers do not care for the traffic function, a small percentage in every department has a keen interest in this area.

There are a number of drawbacks to operating traffic details, especially motorcycle units. Patrol officers tend to assume that the traffic detail has traffic responsibility for all traffic and many patrol officers cease to involve themselves in traffic law enforcement. Many agencies have been forced to institute citation quotas for the patrol officers to force their commitment to traffic enforcement. Traffic elements are subject to the same dysfunctions as all specialized elements, although the effects appear to be less pronounced. This may be because many in patrol actually look down on the traffic function and feel no jealousy toward those assigned to this detail.

Motorcycles offer their own problems. First, they are expensive to purchase and maintain. Second, they are difficult to assign to various officers on various shifts as is done with patrol cars because the motorcycle seat is usually permanently set for one person. Third, they can only be used in good weather, which is fine in southern California or Florida, but not so good in the northern portion of the nation. Fourth, the special uniforms are much more expensive than regular uniforms. Fifth, an officer on motorcycle is limited in the number of services that can be performed. This person is generally limited to traffic duty, whereas patrol officers in cars can be assigned any detail. Finally, motorcycles are dangerous. In many agencies utilizing motorcycles, the majority of officer injuries are the result of motorcycle accidents.

On the positive side, motorcycles offer access to areas otherwise unobtainable to automobiles due to excess traffic congestion caused by rush-hour traffic or accidents. Also, as has already been mentioned; traffic officers tend to have higher-than-average morale. The question facing the police administrator is whether or not the traffic situation within the jurisdiction is severe enough to justify the creation of such an element. The decision to buy motorcycles should be made with caution.

Tactics

Traffic units provide three basic functions: traffic law enforcement, traffic direction, and accident investigation. Traffic law enforcement usually takes one of two forms, random or selective.

Random enforcement occurs when a police officer engaged in patrol takes enforcement action on any violation observed. This form of traffic enforcement has limited, if any, effect on the accident rate within the community. There is, however, an interesting side effect. Patrol officers often use the traffic stop as an excuse to check out suspicious persons. Many felony and serious misdemeanor arrests take place as a direct result of the routine traffic stop.

Selective enforcement was designed with specialized traffic units in mind. Accidents tend to group at specific locations and times. Although there are random accidents everywhere, good record keeping will identify those locations that have more than their fair share. By identifying which offenses are causing the accidents at given times and places, a traffic officer can be assigned the location at the proper time and by strictly enforcing the accident-causing offense, accidents can be reduced. This is the real strength of the traffic detail. When used correctly, it can save lives.

Tactical Teams

The tactical, or SWAT (special weapons and tactics), concept developed as a result of the turmoil of the 1960s and early 1970s. As internal friction threatened to erupt into more urban riots and as violent crime increased dramatically, the large metropolitan agencies recognized the limitations of the average officer when confronted with increased hostage situations and trained terrorists. Rather than provide the entire agency with expensive and time-consuming training, the police agencies created small specialized units and provided intense training and modern weaponry. The tactical team was born.

The concept was quite simple: to bring superior firepower and discipline to the scene of an armed confrontation. The idea caught on and has been quite successful in larger jurisdictions. It has not been so successful in smaller jurisdictions where there was lack of demonstrated need.

There are a number of real problems with tactical teams. First, they are expensive; they require a great deal of special equipment and training. Budgeting in a police agency is a zero-sum game; each dollar placed into one unit is taken from someone else. Second, because the purpose of having a tactical team is to handle special situations, which by their very nature are unpredictable, the team must be either large enough to operate 24 hours a day or must be kept on standby far beyond what is demanded of regular officers. This means either excessive overtime, compensatory time off, or long uncompensated work hours, which inevitably leads to a high rate of job burnout.

Unless the agency has a continuing problem with tactical situations which patrol is unable to handle, and unless the agency is large enough to create a special unit without jeopardizing the patrol function, the creation of a tactical team is usually a waste of time, personnel, and resources.

SERVICES

Service elements of the law enforcement organization are designed to support the operations units. Service elements are staff or support functions. They have developed in response to a number of factors. In an effort to keep up with private industry, large law enforcement agencies have occasionally adopted a variety of private industry philosophies. Also, smaller agencies have attempted to copy trends adopted by the larger departments. As a result, many police agencies are structured in a manner similar to large industrial organizations.

There are both positive and negative aspects to the staff structure. Service elements can be invaluable to the administration but only as long as they remember they are staff and strive to simplify the line functions. If staff units become sufficiently powerful to overrule line command, there is no end to problems that can occur.

In this chapter we discuss two major types of service division, administrative services and technical services. Both fulfill functions that must be accomplished if the agency is to achieve full effectiveness. The function of the services differ, however, in the focus of their respective service.

Administrative service units are designed to increase the chief executive's capacity to fulfill administrative functions. Such management duties as budgeting, planning, staffing, and training are enhanced by the creation of a specialized unit to work with these areas on a full time basis. *Technical services*, on the other hand, provide services designed to enhance the line function. Such duties as record keeping, communication, criminalistics, and jail management are accomplished by this division.

Possibly the best method of determining how a unit should be classified is to ask the question: Who does this unit directly support? If the unit provides direct support to the administration, it is an administrative services element. If the unit directly supports the operations function, it is a technical services unit.

ADMINISTRATIVE SERVICES

The second major division in many law enforcement agencies is administrative services. People assigned to this division are predominantly staff personnel. Administrative services exist to serve operations, in theory. In reality, administrative services usually have a dramatic impact on the effectiveness of operations. If a staff element is going to generate an authority inversion (tail wagging the dog), it will most likely be a unit in administrative services. Service elements have a long and tiresome history of usurping operational prerogatives. The purpose of administrative services is to enhance operational effectiveness by relieving the operations personnel of time-consuming detail work which is only incidentally related to the police mission.

The administrative services division is important; its contribution to agency management is substantial. However, administrative services exist to support operations. Decisions in this division should always be made with thought given as to what impact the decision will have on operations. The administrator must be certain that nothing done in this division detracts from the operational effectiveness of the agency. Units normally found under this division are: personnel, purchasing, training, research and planning, and inspections.

Personnel

Personnel may be an entire division within very large agencies. In most, however, it is a subunit of administrative services. The primary function of personnel is to maintain proper levels of agency staffing through recruiting, selection, and promotion. This unit also administers the personnel records and benefits such as hospitalization and life insurance.

The personnel function is important but has the potential to offer the law enforcement administrator significant problems. The first problem is the violation of a crucial principle of decision making. Decisions should always be made by those who are directly affected by the decision or who must implement the decision. Personnel decisions are some of the most important issues addressed in any organization, yet personnel units are neither affected by the decisions they make nor must they implement them. This makes this unit responsible for decisions in which they are not truly accountable for the outcomes.

Second, within all major organizations, law enforcement and otherwise, no unit has as unsavory a history of administrative usurpation as does personnel. Consider the situation in the U.S. military. A cardinal rule for everyone, enlisted and officer, is: Never make someone in personnel angry; they may lose important records or be instrumental in providing an undesirable transfer. This means that decisions affecting the ability of the nation to defend itself effectively are in the hands of people not accountable for these decisions. The same is true of personnel divisions in every organization.

Unfortunately, the larger the organization, the more necessary this unit is to agency effectiveness. The ever-growing array of law, both civil and criminal, that affect personnel decisions makes the existence of personnel experts mandatory. This unit can complicate the lives of other members of the organization, but it can also save the organization time and resources that might otherwise be expended in court defending personnel decisions.

Training

Training is normally a function of administrative services, but not exclusively so. In some agencies, especially small ones, this duty may be assigned to someone in operations or some other element. Where the agency is large enough to have a specialized training unit, however, it is normally a service or support function.

The most thorough development of training has been mostly in state agencies, federal agencies, and large urban departments. This is only a small portion of the overall number of law enforcement officers currently providing police service in this country. The majority of these officers still operate under training requirements of only a few hundred hours. Moreover, there are still a large number of officers who, because of their employment prior to the implementation of training standards, still have no training, and many have little formal education.

Training is crucial to effective law enforcement and is treated in more detail in Chapter 12. This function is worthy of considerable administrative attention and resource allocation. This may well be the most important support element in the agency.

Purchasing

Purchasing is another unit with a tendency toward empire building. In theory, purchasing units provide the administration with a centralized means of providing equipment and supplies for the organization. Like personnel, they tend to accomplish this task through a promulgation of rules, regulations, and specialized forms.

Many law enforcement administrators prefer a centralized purchasing unit because it appears to allow for tight administrative control. It also slows down the process of obtaining supplies and equipment, for the following reasons:

1. Once again we have people making decisions in situations where they are not affected by the outcome.

2. A centralized purchasing unit operates strictly through channels. Forms must be submitted, signatures obtained, and the item finally purchased. This is often a time-consuming process.

3. It costs more to operate a centralized purchasing unit. Not only is the agency required to pay salaries of purchasing personnel, but the promulgation of rules and directives actually detract from the ability to find the best price for the material needed. As Robert Townsend pointed out, "I'm told that the federal government, with all its joint-use purchasing economies, really pays 20 percent more for a pencil than you do at the five-and-ten" (1984, p. 189).

The better approach to purchasing is to make individual unit commanders responsible for both their budgets and the condition of their equipment and supplies. Each unit should do its own purchasing; the agency will get better supplies with less problems and at no greater cost. This includes items that must be purchased by bid. If only one unit needs the item, that unit should submit it for bids.

Centralized purchasing officers tend to have the minimum number of suppliers they can notify since they are often more interested in simplifying their own job than in getting the best price. The person who is actually going to use the item, and must pay for it out of a specific budget, will go to greater lengths to get as many bids as possible, thereby increasing the probability of getting the best price.

There are exceptions, such as items that must be submitted for bids and will be used by a variety of elements, such as police vehicles. In these cases the administrator should put together an ad hoc committee composed of persons who must use the item, then let them articulate the specifications and submit it for bid. The agency still comes out ahead.

Research and Planning

The function of this element is to provide the chief executive information from which to make policy decisions. The two functions of research and planning are placed together because they are interdependent. This is a unit requiring both specialization and centralization, although individual units should not be discouraged from engaging in either. Centralization and specialization are necessary because there are skills required of researchers and planners not normally possessed by law enforcement personnel.

Neither research nor planning skills are originally developed through on the job training. The skills required are knowledge of statistics and research methodology, knowledge that is best acquired at institutions of higher education. These skills will improve, however, through constant use. They can be enhanced even further with help from professional researchers found in all colleges and universities. The dramatic results of research in police departments such as Kansas City, Missouri and San Diego, California attest to the positive results of capable departmental researchers coupled with professionals from outside the agency.

Planning and research can be an invaluable unit, but only when it is properly staffed and given sufficient freedom to conduct research and seriously plan. Numerous agencies have staffed these units with patrol officers, and sometimes administrators, who lacked the basic skills required.

Research and planning require information correctly and completely gathered and processed. The term used among those who design computer models for research is GIGO (garbage in, garbage out). The quality of the final plan is dependent on the quality of information used to obtain the plan. The person fulfilling this task must know what to do and how it is done. Lightweight staffing in this unit is worse than having no unit at all; it will provide the agency with bad information. Decisions made from poor information tend to be poor decisions.

Data Analysis

Law enforcement agencies collect an enormous amount of data. Many organizations do nothing more than file this information away for possible future use. A recent addition to law enforcement, however, is the data analysis unit. This unit has a number of functions, all of which can be of value to the organization.

Some of the possible duties of data analysis include crime analysis, which attempts to predict criminal activity based on modus operandi and crime statistics by using probability theory; traffic analysis, which is similar to crime analysis except in the utilization of accident information rather than criminal acts: budget control, which provides an accurate accounting tool through the constant monitoring of expenditures; equipment analysis, which allows the administrator to monitor equipment breakdowns and repair costs to determine the cost-effectiveness of each item; and personnel management, which allows for work load projections based on past needs. Although this is not a complete list, it should provide an idea of the possibilities of such a unit.

The data analysis unit can be a part of research and planning or be a separate entity. Either way, data analysis must work closely with research and planning due to the overlapping nature of their respective functions. Probably, the two elements should operate as one for simplification of communications.

Inspections

Ultimate responsibility for the police function lies with the chief executive. The larger the agency, however, the further this person is removed from the provision of these services. Therefore, the administrator rarely has consistent knowledge of the degree to which there is compliance with policies and procedures. The need to ensure compliance with directives mandates departmental inspections.

There are two general types of inspections, line and staff. Each has the purpose of maintaining administrative control over the police operation.

Line Inspections

Line inspection is a command responsibility. In small departments the chief executive fulfills this function. As the size of the agency increases, this duty is passed down to lower-ranked supervisors. The person usually responsible for the line inspection is the immediate supervisor of the unit being inspected. "These inspections seek to exercise control through the processes of observation and review by those directly responsible for a particular function and activity" (Swan, 1977, p. 334).

Line inspections suffer from a number of weaknesses, which make staff inspections necessary. There is a natural tendency to protect one's own unit and personnel, which translates into a tendency to cover up errors rather than document them. Line inspections may also be self-serving; the supervisor can appear to be a good guy to the subordinates by allowing them to slough off. Finally, an incompetent or corrupt supervisor can cover this ineptitude by falsifying inspection reports. Because of these problems, the line inspection is suspect. It is still necessary, however, because good supervisors can use the line inspection to maintain positive control over their units.

Staff Inspections

Staff inspections are conducted for the purpose of providing answers of vital importance to the chief administrator (Swan, 1977, p. 335). There are several aspects to the staff inspection. First, the staff should review the reports of line inspections to familiarize themselves with current problems. They should also use the information derived from the line inspections to design and implement staff inspections.

Staff inspections are independent of the chain of command. The officers assigned to the staff inspection must be impartial and free of any affiliation with the element under inspection. The staff inspection itself is a detailed observation and analysis of departmental elements, procedures, and practices designed to inform the administrator about performance and effectiveness. The staff inspection should encompass everything in the organization. There are five broad objectives of the staff inspection (Swan,1977, p.335)

1. Are established policies, procedures and regulations being carried out to the letter and in the spirit for which they were designed?

2. Are the policies, procedures and regulations adequate to attain the desired goals of the department?

3. Are the resources at the department's disposal, both personal and material, being utilized to the fullest extent?

4. Are the resources adequate to carry out the mission of the department?

5. Does there or could there exist any deficiency in personal integrity, training, morale, supervision, or policy which should be corrected or improved?

The inspection team should be led by a person in whom the administrator has complete confidence. This person should have personal integrity above reproach and have a high degree of objectivity and good judgment. The members of the team should also have these qualities as well as being respected by the personnel in the element being inspected.

Finally, the inspection should follow a plan. The team should design an appropriate checklist for the unit to be inspected. No one, however competent, can simply walk around and inspect without having a specific idea of what and how to inspect. Walk-through inspections are meaningless and doomed to failure. If the inspection is going to be concise and all encompassing, it must be conducted in a systematic manner with a clear understanding of the chief executive's operating philosophy as well as an understanding of policies and procedures.

Moreover, the staff inspection should never be a surprise. The purpose of the inspection is to discover problems. When those to be inspected know that the inspection is coming, they will attempt to operate at maximum effectiveness. The only problems visible will be errors due to poor interpretation of policy and procedures or chronic deficiencies that cannot be hidden; precisely the kinds of problems the staff inspection is designed to discover.

Staff inspections should be made by neutral, trustworthy people, and the inspection should be an up-front operation with no secrets and no surprises. Inspections are much more valuable when the unit under inspection is operating at maximum capacity.

TECHNICAL SERVICES

Technical services provide expertise in a variety of areas not normally available to the officer in the field. Technical services provide hands-on support, while administrative services provides logistical support. Units within the technical services division work much more closely with line units than do administrative services units. This provides one reason why their appears to be less friction between this division and operations than between administrative services and operations.

Some of the units most often found in the technical services division are records and communication, identification, jail management, and physical plant. Occasionally, if the agency is large enough, there will also be a crime lab.

Records and Communications

The primary function of the records and communication unit is information management. The amount of information entering a law enforcement agency daily is staggering. It must all be received, recorded, analyzed, and filed for future use. The capacity of the agency to fulfill its goals depends on the ability to obtain accurate information and utilize it.

Records

Records systems of the past have been unsophisticated. Often, law enforcement personnel used "coat pocket" files; these were kept individually by every officer in the agency. There was almost no cross-indexing and a large amount of information was misplaced.

Even before the advent of computers, law enforcement administrators began to appreciate the value of a good up-to-date record system. Thus, 3- by 5-inch cards became popular for indexing reports, which were processed more formally and filed carefully for future reference. The introduction of computers has aided record keeping immensely, even more than the invention of microfilm. Law enforcement now has the capability of keeping an almost infinite amount of information in a relatively small space, with high-speed access through computerized indexing. No element of a law enforcement agency has evolved faster and taken better advantage of improving technology than the records element.

The purpose of the records system should be no secret. It is designed to allow the agency to keep track of crime trends, specific crimes, criminal tendencies of certain individuals, lost persons and property, wanted persons, stolen property, and resource utilization. Law enforcement agencies usually maintain files on every police-citizen contact. These files frequently take on one of the following forms:

> **1.** *Police reports.* Every report submitted by an officer is kept to provide a record of incidents requiring police response. This includes criminal offenses, arrests, lost and found property, and general information.

2. *Accident reports.* To determine high accident locations and causes of accidents accurately, a report of each accident is reported, filed, and analyzed.

3. *Modus operandi (method of operation).* These files are maintained to develop identifiable patterns of criminal behavior. Once the pattern is identified, predicting future incidents is possible, thus improving the chances of capturing the suspect.

4. *Warrant files.* This file is maintained for the purpose of rapidly assessing if a person is wanted. Many times, people are arrested on a warrant due to a routine check of this file during a traffic stop. An updated, computerized warrant file provides street officers with rapid access to information on wanted persons.

5. *Identification.* Fingerprints and photographs are also filed for future comparisons with suspects. Finding a latent fingerprint is useless unless it can be matched with a suspect's finger. For this reason, files of this type are maintained. The same is true of pictures. Photographs of possible suspects can be a valuable investigative aid when there are eyewitnesses who do not know the suspect's name.

6. *Field contact cards.* Patrol officers frequently submit information cards obtained by interviewing people in suspicious places at suspicious times. Should it be discovered later that a crime was committed in this area, the police have a potential lead.

7. *Personnel records.* Civil service requires documentation of improper conduct when personnel charges are filed. Promotion and transfer are also affected by officer performance. The personnel file holds a complete record of each employee's performance, reflecting strengths and weaknesses.

8. *Intelligence files.* Perhaps the most sensitive, these files are important to the agency. They are sensitive because they are made up of information that may or may not be substantiated. They may contain only rumors or bits and pieces of data. The sensitivity lies in the ability of this type of information to inflict damage to the subject's reputation without a shred of hard fact to back it up. Intelligence information often has the ability to hurt innocent persons. The greatest care must be taken, therefore, to keep this information confidential.

Not all records are as sensitive as the intelligence file, but most must be managed as if they were. Information open to the public should be made so, but responsibly. Access to police files must be limited to a need-to-know basis. For this reason, and the necessity that all police units have access to the records unit, the unit must be centralized and concentrated in a secure area.

Communications

Communications is usually concerned with two different but related technologies, the two-way radio and the telephone. This unit is responsible for receiving information from either the public or agency personnel, briefly analyzing the data and dispatching a police unit when appropriate. The larger the agency the more complex the function. As the size increases, so does the number of calls for service, number of dispatchers, and number of different frequencies required to handle the radio traffic.

The advent of computers has also had a significant impact on the communications process. Computer-aided dispatch (CAD) has allowed the computer to select the most appropriate patrol element, in terms of location and capability, for each call for service. Many of the very large departments now have the capacity to monitor the constant location of the various patrol vehicles. Although the individual officers have shown little enthusiasm in being constantly monitored, this has been an invaluable aid to the dispatcher and administrator.

The major objective of the communications element is to provide the public with the most efficient service possible while maintaining as much safety as possible for the officer on the street. By one of those strange quirks of organizational design, the dispatcher is often one of the lowest positions, in terms of remuneration and prestige, while providing one of the most important functions. The dispatcher operates in many ways as a patrol supervisor.

Some agencies have recognized the critical nature of this position and have assigned senior officers to dispatch duty. While a good argument can be made for this arrangement, it represents a waste of talent needed more on the street. Civilian dispatchers would appear to be the most practical, but only with adequate training and supervision.

Evidence Processing

Evidence technicians often provide the service of most use to the criminal investigation units. As the Rand analysis of criminal investigation noted, the police gather more information than they can process. An emphasis on collection of physical evidence and its subsequent analysis is likely to increase the effectiveness of the investigation units.

The evidence technician is a person specializing in the in-depth inspection of major crime scenes in order to collect evidence linking the perpetrator to the crime. This is a technical field requiring extensive training. This unit is sometimes connected to other units, often without regard to logic. This unit, or person in many smaller agencies, may be located in any operations or service element. If the agency is large enough to have its own criminalistics laboratory, the evidence technician will usually be located within the crime lab.

This unit is crucial to law enforcement effectiveness, but few agencies acknowledge this fact. The persons assigned this function are often poorly trained; this unit is usually understaffed, and sometimes personnel are assigned here to get them out of other elements where they are having problems. Many agencies underestimate the potential of this unit.

Jail Management

The management and operation of incarceration centers have been a responsibility of law enforcement administrators since creation of the first police force. The jail should not be confused with a prison or correctional center. It is primarily a holding unit for criminal suspects: those who are accused of crime but not yet convicted.

Ideally, law enforcement personnel should neither manage nor maintain detention facilities; this should be done by those trained in corrections (Kassoff, 1977, p.477; President's Commission, 1967, p.90). Despite this acknowledgment, however, few governmental bodies, especially at the local level, have shown any desire to take the jail out of the hands of the police. There is no indication of a change of this attitude in the near future. We must assume, therefore, that the police will be held responsible for jail management for some time to come. The following case demonstrates the importance of sound jail management while pointing out the administrator's responsibilities concerning supervision and training.

McClelland v. *Facteau* (1979)
610 F.2d 693

Action was brought under civil rights statute against two police chiefs and subordinate officers for alleged deprivation of plaintiff's constitutional rights during arrest and custody. The U.S. District Court for the District of New Mexico, Howard C. Bratton, Chief Judge, granted summary judgment in favor of defendant police chiefs, and plaintiff appealed.

McClelland was stopped by Officer Facteau for speeding, and after refusing to sign the traffic citation he was taken to the Farmington city jail. McClelland was not permitted to use the mobile telephone in his truck to call his attorney, nor to call for his employee to pick up the vehicle. Instead, he was locked in the patrolman's car to await the arrival of a tow truck called by Officer Facteau. He was booked at the jail by Jimmie Brown, who eventually set bond at $50. McClelland was released after he paid this amount. Apparently McClelland was questioned during custody by Conn Brown, but not informed of his constitutional rights, was denied phone calls, and was not brought before a magistrate. Prior to his release he was made to lean against a wall, where he was beaten and injured by Officer Facteau in the presence of the Browns. McClelland alleged a number of specific deprivations under the Fourth, Sixth, and Fourteenth Amendments.

McClelland does not claim that the police chiefs are liable under respondeat superior. Rather, he asserts that the police chiefs are directly liable through breach of their duty to train and supervise subordinate officers properly.

Opinion of the Court
McClelland sets out basically two duties that we consider. First, he alleges negligence in the police chief's duty to train subordinates and to establish department procedures that will provide protection for people's constitutional rights. Both Schmerheim and Vigil brought forward affidavits and documents showing that adequate training was given to the three subordinates and that departmental procedures then in effect would have secured McClelland's rights if they had been followed. Supervisors cannot automatically be held liable for a subordinate straying from the established path.

Next we consider the police chief's duty of supervision to correct misconduct of which they have notice. The standard to be applied is the conduct of a reasonable person, under the circumstances, in the context of the authority of each police chief and what he knew or should have known.

To establish a breach here, plaintiff must show that the defendant was adequately put on notice of prior misbehavior. Although both Schmerheim and Vigil denied any knowledge of wrongdoing by the subordinates, McClelland countered by tendering newspaper articles and affidavits indicating that it was well known that rights were being violated in the Farmington jail and by state police officer Facteau, and showing that Schmerheim was a party in two law suits involving the deaths of prisoners incarcerated in the Farmington jail. We hold that McClelland's showing was adequate to raise an issue of fact on the sufficiency of notice because the accusations contained in the material were recent and serious.

If publicity of police misconduct was widespread and credible it may be inferred that police chiefs who admitted reading the daily newspapers knew of it. They had ultimate responsibility for what went on in the departments, and it might be found that they should and could have taken steps that would have prevented the deprivation of McClelland's rights.

The case is affirmed in part (opinion on inadequate supervision and training), reversed in part (opinion on failure to act in the face of knowledge of prior misconduct), and remanded for further proceedings consistent with this opinion (summary judgment overruled and new trial ordered).

Physical Plant

Every law enforcement agency operates from physical facilities. These must be maintained constantly, which requires custodians, replacement of worn-out equipment, and a program of continual upkeep. Much of this is accomplished through a contractual system wherein service representatives of equipment manufacturers provide for maintenance.

Other methods of facility and equipment maintenance require full-time personnel assigned to these functions. In some agencies inmates are used for custodial services, but this is not universal. Some hire civilian custodians or use those hired by the local government for the provision of these services in all government offices.

Proper facility care and maintenance are important for the morale and job satisfaction of personnel. When equipment and facilities are in bad shape, the morale of the employees suffer accordingly (Holden, 1980, p. 126).

Crime Laboratory

The crime lab will be found in the very large law enforcement organizations. Few small or intermediate-sized agencies can afford either the space or the personnel required to maintain such a facility. The crime laboratory exists to analyze evidence recovered at the scene of a crime. This evidence is usually recovered by identification technicians, or by patrol officers and detectives if there are no technicians available. In the larger metropolitan areas, evidence may also be gathered by members of the medical examiner's staff in cases involving homicide.

The crime lab, or criminalistics laboratory for scientific purists, cannot work miracles. The quality of the analysis is directly related to the quality of the crime scene search and finally to the collection of potential evidence. The lab cannot analyze what is not obtained during the investigation.

The crime lab has three general functions (Fox,1977, p. 457):

1. Reconstruction of the crime: aids the detective in the reconstruction of the crime by piecing together the physical evidence. They attempt to discover the sequence of events leading up to and during the criminal episode.

2. Corpus delicti: establish the elements of the offense.

3. Connective-disconnective: establishes whether a link does or does not exist between the suspect and the crime. Rarely does the crime lab solve cases on its own or through the analysis of evidence by itself. The real value of the crime lab is the ability to compare the analyzed evidence against a suspect, thus establishing a connection or removing the person as a suspect.

DISCUSSION QUESTIONS

1. Of the three major organizational divisions of a police agency, which is most critical? Why?

2. What is the most important element in a law enforcement agency? Why?

3. Discuss the function of administrative services elements. What are the positive and negative effects of creating specialized units within this area?

4. Discuss the function of technical services elements. What are the positive and negative effects of creating specialized units within this area?

5. Discuss the different types of inspections. What are the pros and cons of each?

REFERENCES

Eck, John (1979). *Managing Case Assignments: The Burglary Investigation Decision Model Replication.* Washington, D.C.: Police Executive Research Forum.

_____ (1983). *Solving Crimes: The Investigation of Burglary and Robbery.* Washington, D.C.: Police Executive Research Forum.

_____ (1992). "Criminal investigation," in Gary Cordner and Donna Hale, eds., *What Works in Policing: Operations and Administration Examined.* ACJS Monograph Series, Cincinatti, Ohio: Anderson. pp. 19–34.

Fox, Richard H. (1977). "Criminalistics," in Bernard L. Garmire, ed., *Local Government Police Management.* Washington, D.C.: International City Management Association.

Greenberg, Bernard, Oliver S. Yu, and Karen I. Lang (1972). *Enhancement of the Investigative Function.* Vol. 4, Menlo Park, Calif: Stanford Research Institute.

Hale, Charles D. (1981). *Police Patrol: Operations and Management.* New York: Wiley.

Hastings, Thomas F. (1977). "Criminal investigation," in Bernard L. Garmire, ed., *Local Government Police Management.* Washington, D.C.: International City Management Association.

Holden, Richard N. (1980). *A Study of Motivation and Job Satisfaction in the Houston Police Department.* Dissertation. Huntsville, Tex: Sam Houston State University.

Kasoff, Norman C. (1977)."Jail Management" in Bernard Garmire, ed., *Local Government Police Management,* Washington, D.C.: International City Management Association.

Knickerbocker, Brad. (1977). "Police decoys: crime stoppers or traps," *The Christian Science Monitor,* October 5, section 3, pp. 3–4.

Leonard, V.A. and Harry W. More (1971). *Police Organization and Management,* 3rd ed. Mineola, N.Y: The Foundation Press.

President's Commission on Law Enforcement and Administration of Justice (1967). *The Challenge of Crime in a Free Society.* New York: Avon Press.

Swan, John K. (1977). "Internal controls," in Bernard L. Garmire, ed., *Local Government Police Management.* Washington, D.C.: International City Management Association.

Tien, James M., et al. (1977). *An Evaluation of an Alternative Approach in Police Patrol: The Wilmington Split-Force Experiment.* Cambridge, Mass.: Public Systems Evaluation, Inc.

Townsend, Robert (1984). *Further Up the Organization.* New York: Alfred A. Knopf.

Chapter 8

Organizational Pathology

The sick organization is one in which the agency loses sight of its mission. It is a place where ends and means become immersed in self-serving power struggles. Sadly, the speed with which healthy organizations become sick, or pathological, is frightening. Time and evolution play an important role in this process, but the sickness can begin with creation of the agency. To make matters worse, there are a number of standard administrative processes that increase the problem. Such activities as training and socialization of personnel into the agency subculture can actually be harmful. Great care must be taken in properly accomplishing these activities.

In this chapter we discuss the evolutionary process of an organization, symptoms of bureaupathology, and organizational politics. We further attempt to discover the means by which administrators can avoid the factors responsible for the incapacitation of many law enforcement agencies.

ORGANIZATIONAL EVOLUTION

Studies concerning organizational development have identified an evolutionary process affecting most organizations. This provides some prediction of where agencies are going and the changes likely to take place along the way. The frightening aspect of this progress is the dependency on time. This is frightening because while private organizations rise and fall in accordance with this life cycle, public agencies progress along the same cycle but do not self-destruct. Most law enforcement agencies have been in the latter portion of the cycle, the bureaucratic stage, for many years. This is a difficult stage to break out of and is the least effective of all positions within the life cycle of organizations.

Five stages have been identified in the life cycle of an organization: adolescent stage, prime stage, maturity stage, aristocratic stage, and bureaucracy stage (Ray and Eison, 1983, pp. 32–33; Adizes, 1979, Katz and Kahn, 1979).

> *Adolescent stage.* This is the time of creation, the genesis of the organization. Productivity is low while the personnel adjust to each other. Original policies are formulated; training cliques develop as an organizational value system begins to form. Planning is the predominant concern; the focus of this stage is on the future. Generally, morale is high and there is strong informal interaction as the organization takes shape.

> *Prime stage.* In this period the organization is results oriented. The system is stable and there is optimum productivity. The organization establishes an acute awareness of external demands and individual subunits grow to meet needs. Support services are predictable and tuned to the needs of the line elements. There is still an emphasis on planning, but it is coupled with high expectations on the part of management, which are generally fulfilled by the operational personnel.

> *Maturity stage.* The organization's sense of urgency declines. Risk taking declines and there is less emphasis on research and development. Aspirations are held low as both management and labor enjoy yesterday's fruits. Procedures and policies become more important as a formal climate develops. Internal relationships begin to become very important. There is a birth of internal political systems seeking increased power at the organization's expense.

Politics begin ↗

> *Aristocratic stage.* The guiding policy is business as usual. The organization becomes backward looking as admiration is developed for past successes. Ritual becomes important, tenure is most important, and dress codes are well developed and understood. This is the jargon stage, where the subculture language has become fully developed and universally adopted throughout the organization. At this point more control systems are developed and there is more employee training ritual as understanding the organization becomes more important than understanding the job.

> *Bureaucracy stage.* Production falls as the agency slips into stagnation. Research and development are ignored. There is managerial paranoia, political infighting, and blame placing. The better people leave the organization, which sinks deeper and deeper into a rut. At this point the guiding principle is, "put it in writing." The left hand doesn't know what the right hand is doing. If the organization is private,

Table 8-1

Life Cycle of Organizations

Stage	Symptoms
Adolescent	Focus on future; productivity low; morale high.
Prime	Focus on production; high expectations by management; production high; morale high.
Maturity	Focus on present; birth of internal political systems; production decline.
Aristocratic	Focus on past; understanding organization more important than understanding job; subculture fully developed.
Bureaucratic	Loss of focus; managerial paranoia; political infighting; blame placing.

the next stage is bankruptcy, unless it is large enough to get government assistance or retains a monopoly that allows it to survive despite itself. In the public sector, however, there is no competition and no means of adequately disbanding a law enforcement agency. Because of this many police organizations reach the bureaucracy stage and stay there, blissfully ignorant of how ineffective they truly are (see Table 8-1 above).

BUREAUPATHOLOGY

The pathological organization was perhaps best described by Robert Merton in his classic work, "Bureaucratic structure and personality" (1969). He defined four types of inappropriate behavior that are symptomatic of the bureaucratic stage of organizational development: *trained incapacity, occupational psychosis, goal displacement,* and *sanctification.*

Trained Incapacity

According to Merton, "Trained incapacity refers to that state of affairs in which one's abilities function as blind spots"(1969, p. 84). In other words, training a person to do a job in a manner appropriate to today's conditions may be inappropriate under tomorrow's conditions. You might say that training a person to do a job one way simultaneously trains the person not to do it any other way.

Trained incapacity is closely related to the psychological concept known as *operant conditioning.* A person becomes programmed to respond to stimulus in a certain manner. Long after the response becomes inadequate to the conditions, the person continues to respond that way. The only means of breaking the cycle is to retrain the person to respond more appropriately. This means that training must be an ongoing feature of organizational life.

Law enforcement agencies have numerous examples of this phenomenon as a result of firearms training. For many years police agencies trained their officers on the PPC (practical pistol course). This course required the officers to fire from a variety of positions and distances and sought to simulate actual conditions. Two problems developed almost immediately. First, to keep the scoring simple, officers loaded their weapons with only five rounds at a time, thus allowing the scoring to be in multiples of five. Second, to encourage neatness, officers were encouraged to police the brass, i.e., pick up the empty bullet casings immediately after they were fired. Many officers developed the habit of emptying the brass into their hand and stuffing it into their pocket so that it would never hit the ground. For years after this course was instituted, officers involved in actual armed confrontations would in the heat of battle load their weapons with only five bullets and were taking the time to place the empty brass in their pocket, thus wasting valuable time. The officers were only doing what they were trained to do, but the training was dysfunctional.

In a similar vein, many officers wounded in action have fallen to the ground in the assumption that they were dying, and because they gave up were subsequently killed by the criminal. Why did this happen? Because on television and at the movies when someone is shot they fall down and die. Not all gunshot wounds are fatal or even disabling, except in media fiction. The media, in this case, have provided dysfunctional training.

The foregoing are examples of dysfunctional training with drastic consequences. Most examples of trained incapacity are less dramatic, but crucial to organizational effectiveness just the same.

For many years law enforcement management has been based on the traditional military model. Police executives have been hammered with the principles of organizing until they have become rigid disciples. Everyone knows that the span of control in a law enforcement agency should never exceed six people. Patrol officers must be closely supervised because they are lazy or cunning or both. There must be strict adherence to the chain of command. Insubordination must never be allowed. The chief executive and the administrative staff know what is best for the organization. No one below the rank of lieutenant is either intelligent or mature enough to have any concrete ideas concerning solutions to agency problems. The administrators must have extensive and detailed policies to protect them from incompetent underlings, and so on and so on. Then researchers come along to say that this is all nonsense; organizations do not work well under these conditions.

Administrators have been trained too long to think traditionally; many are incapable of changing. But some will listen and sometime in the distant future conventional wisdom may side with those who see the problems clearly, but it will take time. Overcoming trained incapacity is a difficult task.

Occupational Psychosis

Occupational psychosis is a product of the socialization process. New members learn to adopt the organizational value system while discarding or altering their own values in the process. All institutions seek to impose their values on society.

Naturally, this cannot be accomplished until there is conformity of values among the organizational members. To accomplish this, new members are placed under tremendous pressure to identify with the agency's values. All organizations socialize their members, but law enforcement agencies do so with the intensity of elite military units. The young officer, as a result, develops a warped perspective of life. Tunnel vision develops wherein the organization is seen as right and any person or group offering criticism of the agency, no matter how justified, is wrong. The stronger the pressure to conform to the values of the organization, the stronger the resulting effects of this syndrome.

Within law enforcement, this is known as the *John Wayne* or *Wyatt Earp syndrome.* It is recognizable by the loss of sense of humor, belief that everyone is either all good or all bad with no middle ground, feelings of overimportance, and isolation from those not associated with the job. The John Wayne syndrome is a form of defense mechanism wherein the young officer is shielded emotionally from the vast array of conflicting feelings that must be dealt with in the day-to-day activities of law enforcement.

This is a growing period in which the individual shifts roles from civilian to police officer. The new officer begins to lose naivete and learns to cope with the awesome authority entrusted in the position. All people go through a similar experience when entering a new organization, but the law enforcement socialization process is greatly intensified. The progression of the syndrome over time can be understood by the following observation made by a veteran police officer:

> When I first entered police work I was told there were three types of people: police officers, honest citizens, and jerks. After two years I found there were only two types: police officers and jerks. After four years I came to the conclusion there was only one type: jerks.

Occupational psychosis is not totally dysfunctional if its effects are only moderate; the new member must adapt to the organization. In a severe form, however, the person becomes hard to be around. The high divorce rate among young police officers is testimony to this problem.

Occupational psychosis frequently generates a related problem known as *fundamental ambivalence.* This refers to a form of occupational blindness or a rigid form of tunnel vision. A way of seeing something becomes a way of not seeing something else. The rigidity of viewing life from only one perspective prevents the person from accepting another point of view. Officers become rigidly conservative in their outlook. Because they see only the bad side of people, they conclude that all people must be bad. Every event is screened through the value-laden perspective of the police viewpoint. The job becomes the be-all and end-all of life; all other elements—home, family, and friends outside the organization—become unimportant in comparison. This phenomenon is dysfunctional. It is also rewarded by uninformed administrators who are pleased to see young officers so dedicated to their job that they volunteer for excessive hours and spend most of their waking hours in the company of other officers, to the exclusion of their families and outside friends. The trade-off is more work hours at low cost now, for serious family problems that will reduce officer effectiveness in the future. It may eventually result in employee burnout, thus losing the officer permanently.

Goal Displacement

Perhaps the most recognizable form of irrational behavior within an organization is goal displacement. Adherence to rules, originally conceived as a means, become transformed into ends. The discipline designed to maintain the conformity necessary for the smooth operation becomes a value to the bureaucrat. Rules and procedures become ritualized with no allowance for flexibility. "Discipline is maintained by a *tyranny of proceduralism* that ensures absolute compliance with agency rules of operation "(Souryal, 1992, p. 185).

This may happen to the extent that maintaining the rules and procedures actually jeopardize the goals of the organization. To the pathological bureaucrat, the rules are all that is important. "Regulations, for all practical purposes, are effectively used to silence the nonconformists who dare to deviate from the administrative line" (Souryal, 1992, p. 185).

This person may not even be aware of the agency objectives. As long as the rules are enforced, all is well. "An extreme form of this process of displacement of goals is the bureaucratic virtuoso, who never forgets a single rule binding his action and hence is unable to assist many of his clients" (Mannheim, 1936, pp. 12–13).

Goal displacement is a characteristic of the bureaucratic stage of organizational development. People developing this pattern can find a myriad of reasons why something new will not work. They can be depended on to use the policy manual as a weapon against anyone not in total conformity with the prevailing administrative philosophy.

Sanctification

Sanctification is a process wherein bureaucratic norms become sacred values in their own right. This is often a finalizing aspect of goal displacement. The rules and procedures come to be seen not only as the right way of doing things, but the only way of doing things. Further, organizational symbols, such as who gets the largest office or who gets the first new squad car, also become sacred.

The saddest aspect of this problem is the tendency to sanctify procedures and policies long since obsolete. The employees develop a strong emotional dependence on the bureaucratic symbols and provide them a legitimacy of their own. These symbols are no longer merely a technical means for expediting administration, but a sacred portion of agency's myths. Altering these symbols becomes no less difficult than amending the Ten Commandments. The following case provides an excellent example of a pathological organization.

Herrara v. *Valentine* (1981)
653 F.2d 1220

Jo Ann Yellow Bird filed a lawsuit in federal district court alleging violations of her federal civil rights as well as various state law claims. She named 14 parties as defendants in the case, including Officer Valentine and the city of Gordon. After a lengthy trial, the jury returned a verdict that found the city of Gordon and Valentine liable for violating Yellow Bird's federal civil rights. The jury awarded the plaintiff $300,000 in compensatory damages. The defendant's posttrial motions challenging the verdict were denied and this appeal followed.

On September 15, 1976, Jo Ann Yellow Bird, an Indian woman visibly in the later months of pregnancy, was kicked in the stomach by Clifford Valentine, a police officer employed by the city of Gordon, Nebraska. Valentine was attempting to arrest Yellow Bird's husband at the time of the incident. As Yellow Bird went to the aid of her husband, Valentine kicked her in the abdomen, throwing her to the ground. After he had kicked her, Valentine handcuffed her and forced her into the back of his patrol car. Yellow Bird's pleas for medical attention were ignored. Instead of driving her a few blocks to the nearest hospital, Valentine drove her 20 miles to the county jail. On the way to the jail, Valentine stopped the car and threatened to take Yellow Bird out into the country and shoot her. She was arrested and jailed; her requests for counsel were also ignored. As a result of the beating and inattention to her medical needs, she suffered physical and emotional injuries; her unborn child died in her womb and was delivered dead two weeks later.

Opinion of the Court

The city asserts that Yellow Bird's claim against it is based solely on the doctrine of respondeat superior. It is clear that a municipality cannot be held vicariously liable under section 1983 for the acts of its employees. Yellow Bird does not, however, assert that the city is liable under the doctrine of respondeat superior. Her claim is that the city's failure to properly hire, train, retain, supervise, discipline, and control Valentine and the other police officers directly caused her tortuous injury. To prove her case, Yellow Bird had to establish that the city had notice of prior misbehavior and that its failure to act on such knowledge caused her injury.

We are satisfied that Yellow Bird proved her case against the city of Gordon. It is undisputed that racial tension was at its peak before, during, and after the incident giving rise to this lawsuit. Well before she was injured by the Gordon police, Yellow Bird, and her husband and many other Indians and Caucasians as well, complained to the authorities of continuing police misconduct. Use of excessive force, sexual misconduct, racist conduct, and selective enforcement of the laws were among the many infractions cited. The Yellow Birds were essentially spokespersons for the dissident group. Their complaints were a subject of community-wide knowledge.

Dissatisfied with the city's failure to remedy their complaints, Yellow Bird wrote to the acting director of the Nebraska Indian Commission, Stephen F. Janis. Because of the numerous other complaints regarding the misconduct of the Gordon police, the commission went to Gordon and convened a hearing in early 1976. At that hearing, attended by both Indians and Caucasians, the commission received nearly 40 separate complaints of police misconduct. These complaints were taken under advisement and later submitted to the mayor of Gordon.

A few months later, the commission reconvened in Gordon and heard more complaints. After this meeting, Janis appeared at a city council meeting and personally handed the mayor the citizen's complaints. The entire city council was given a summary of the complaints that had been prepared by an attorney with Panhandle Legal Services. The Yellow Birds also appeared before the city council and once again made known their various complaints. The commission asked the city to remedy the problem and report back to it. The city neither remedied the problem nor reported back. The matter was apparently turned over to the Sheridan County Attorney's office, which later reported to the mayor of Gordon that it was obvious that the city's police force considered themselves "overlords," whose orders were to be obeyed without question. A similar conclusion was reached by Security Services of Lincoln, Nebraska, an outside agency investigating the Gordon police department.

The foregoing demonstrates that the city was notified that its five-member police force needed close and continuing supervision. However, it permitted its overzealous police force to continue its overlording. The inevitable result was the kind of misconduct that caused Yellow Bird's physical beating, loss of her unborn child, and her medical and emotional problems. The plaintiff's section 1983 verdict stands as rendered.

A by-product of the sanctification process is *organizational fear*. The process is so accepted and so institutionalized that no one is willing to challenge the system. Nor is it only law enforcement that is cursed with this problem. It is a major concern of industrial analysts. In discussing this problem, Mary Walton said:

> People are afraid to point out problems for fear they will start an argument, or worse, be blamed for the problem. Moreover, so seldom is anything done to correct problems that there is no incentive to expose them. And more often than not there is no mechanism for problem solving. Suggesting new ideas is too risky. People are afraid of losing their raises or promotions, or worse, their jobs. They fear punitive assignments or other forms of discrimination and harassment. They are afraid that superiors will feel threatened and retaliate in some fashion if they are too assertive or ask too many questions. They fear for the future of their company and the security of their jobs. They are afraid to admit they made a mistake, so the mistake is never rectified. In the perception of most employees, preserving the status quo is the only safe course (1986, p. 72).

According to W. Edwards Deming while discussing this same problem, "The economic loss from fear is appalling. Fear takes a horrible toll. Fear is all around, robbing people of their pride, hurting them, robbing them of a chance to contribute to the company. It is unbelievable what happens when you unloose fear" (Walton, 1986, pp. 72–73).

ORGANIZATIONAL POLITICS

No organization is immune from internal politics. People are often concerned with their own interests and to the extent that they are not challenged to reach their full potential working for the agency will sometimes expend excess energy working for themselves, at the agency's expense. Stephen Robbins defines self-serving behavior as political behavior (1976, p. 64). Although political scientists might disagree with this, it is a useful definition. The following discussion centers on individual or group behavior that is self-serving.

Political behavior is functional when the goals of the individual coincide with the objectives of the organization. In this situation the individual is seeking to fulfill personal goals, but in so doing the agency objectives are also satisfied. Political behavior becomes dysfunctional when the interests of the individual are in conflict with those of the organization. This can be destructive, for when there are a number of organizational members engaged in this behavior, the goals of the agency become obscured by the infighting and the power struggles that ensue. There is no way to eliminate dysfunctional political behavior completely, but too much of it can cripple the organization.

Types of Political Behavior

Political behavior can be grouped into three distinct forms. These forms, or philosophies, represent techniques of manipulation for either survival or gaining unfair advantage over other members. These types of behavior are: *offensive, defensive,* and *neutral* (Robbins,1976; pp. 78–79).

Offensive

Offensive political behavior can be identified by its aggressive nature. Actions classified as offensive are attempts to build a power base through empire building, developing personal loyalties, sabotaging, and exploiting others. Persons engaged in this activity will often develop "good ole boy" networks; these are systems of mutual back scratching wherein network members strive to make each other look good. This same network will develop a sophisticated communications system so that crucial information can be provided to team members in advance of others in the organization.

Since, to a real extent, knowledge is power, this clique will attempt to penetrate as many information sources as possible. Individuals in this group will constantly seek ways of gaining access to confidential information, always keeping in mind the possibility of exploiting such information for personal advantage. Another aspect of offensive political behavior is the taking of credit for someone else's ideas. Although the theft of an idea is not necessarily offensive politics, taking credit for it is.

The most obvious technique of offensive politics is empire building. This takes the form of unit commanders attempting to obtain personnel and resources beyond justification. Remember that there is the tendency to judge public officials by the size of their budgets and staffs. This drive for prestige often leads people to constantly seek ways of increasing the size of their unit or organization far beyond rationality. Empire building may be the most formidable obstacle confronting administrators who wish to improve organizational effectiveness significantly. It is a major reason why the majority of law enforcement agencies are top heavy.

Defensive

The term *defensive political behavior* is self-descriptive. The person seeks ways of self-protection through the dodging of accountability for mistakes. A common technique can be observed in young children who "tattle" on others. The idea is: *if you cannot look good, make someone else look bad.*

Another form of this behavior is the deliberate falsification of information to cover up mistakes. The cover-up, made infamous by the Watergate scandal during the Nixon presidency, is alive and well in most organizations. A related activity is the manipulation of the focus of the information. The person may go to great lengths to present the positive side of a report while ignoring or lightly touching on the negative aspects. If this occurs several times over various levels in the hierarchy, the problem becomes compounded to the point where the data are useless. It may show a project to be a glowing success when it was really a dismal failure.

Manipulation of statistics is a similar form of defensive politics. Law enforcement administrators sometimes dabble with crime statistics. Crime rates can be raised or lowered to meet the administrator's desires by a variety of techniques having nothing to do with actual crime. Statistics are only as good as the method by which they are obtained and evaluated. It is relatively easy to design a research instrument capable of providing data supporting a certain position, instead of obtaining the truth.

Neutral

Persons engaging in this type of behavior are easily identified; they are classic bureaucrats. They never make a decision, to them, *the buck can always be passed.* If forced to make a decision, they call for a vote of all parties affected. In essence they will syndicate the decision; they will spread responsibility sufficiently to diffuse any attempt to hold them personally accountable. They can also be counted on to keep detailed records of all conversations. All memos and requests will be passed along the formal communication channel. This prevents anyone from accusing them of withholding information of any kind. These people generate massive amounts of paperwork, hold numerous meetings (for which there must always be a published agenda), and refuse to screen anything out of the communications channels. Items of real importance will often be buried in a mountain of trivia and just as often be slow in arriving due to the information logjam that is created by these people. A person who has really developed neutral

Table 8-2
Organizational Politics

Type	*Symptoms*
Offensive	Empire building; aggressive tactics used to build power base and support network. Attempts to crush the opposition.
Defensive	Negative attacks on competitors; belittles co-workers.
Neutral	Buck passing; failure to make decisions or be held accountable.

politics to a science can maintain an image of being totally occupied while accomplishing almost nothing (see Table 8-2 above).

Survival Instincts

Within a sick organization, politicians rule. These people usually have keen survival instincts. In these organizations, appearances can be deceiving. Neatly pressed suits and uniforms often act as camouflage for barbarians.

Image Management

One of the basic techniques for survival is centered around image management. Looking good is often more important than being good. Survivors always look good when it counts. Office workers frequently complain of the tendency of the supervisor never to be around when they work but seem to appear always when they are on a break. The more astute worker observes the habits of the supervisor and plans breaks at times when the boss is not around. Even administrators are creatures of habit. They are as predictable as everyone else, and just as likely to develop a routine. Any worker who cares to take the effort can maintain an image of total dedication while doing no more than anyone else.

There is no real secret to this ability. Students have been observed using the same techniques to obtain higher grades than others while doing work of equal quality. Simply by using more expensive paper and dark high-quality typing, the paper of one student looks better than equal work presented on cheap paper by a lower-quality typewriter. When a report looks good, there is an automatic assumption of quality in the content also. This applies to dress, hair style, and language as well as the work itself. Everyone can manage his or her own image by taking the time and trouble. Survivors always take the time and trouble.

Parkinson's Law

To understand the skills associated with image management, a person must first know something about bureaucratic behavior. An assumption made by many is that people are paid to do a particular job. When the job is completed successfully, the worker has fulfilled the obligations of employment. Within organizations in the bureaucratic stage nothing could be further from the truth. People are paid for putting in hours, usually 40 per week, often without regard for amount of work accomplished. People can actually be too efficient for their own good. If the assigned task is completed too soon, another task will be assigned, and another, until the work period is over, with no additional rewards. What is more, the efficient person will be expected to maintain this level of work without increased compensation. Worse, efficient personnel will appear to have more break time, due to the rate with which they complete tasks, while less efficient people will slowly plod along accomplishing little but always appearing to be industrious. The cardinal rule in a bureaucracy is to look busy. Being busy is relatively unimportant.

One of the first to discover this was C. Northcote Parkinson, who after researching formal organizations, found that there was no relationship between the size of an organization and the amount of work to be done (1957). This observation led to his pronouncement of *Parkinson's Law*: Work expands so as to fill the time available for its completion. He was referring to the phenomenon in which people manage, often unconsciously, to stretch their work assignments out until they have totally utilized the time allocated for the assignment, regardless of the speed with which the job could be accomplished.

Parkinson's Law goes hand in hand with empire building. Unit commanders convince higher administrators of the need to provide more personnel in their units. Rather than bring in someone to share the work, such as an assistant, the commander attempts to obtain two or more subordinates to share the work without reducing the commander's power or prestige. In turn, these people will attempt to accomplish the same feat. Eventually, a vast division may spring up with an extensive number of personnel. This occurs despite the lack of sufficient work to justify this element's existence. Also, as long as the lower echelon, those actually doing the work are busy, no one questions the efficacy of having the unit. The number of levels in the element's hierarchy make the unit appear more important than it is in reality.

This is the dilemma facing the American taxpayer. Governmental organizations have grown at a much faster pace than the amount of work needed to be accomplished by those organizations. This happens because the members of those agencies have been highly successful at convincing the legislators and special-interest groups that they are overworked.

Peter Principle

The promotional procedures in most organizations are based on past performance. As long as the person looks good in the present position, chances for promotion are excellent. When a person finally gets promoted to a position that is beyond the person's capability, promotions are no longer likely. Neither, however, is demotion. The person remains at the level of incompetence. This is, of course, a paraphrase of Lawrence Peter's *Peter Principle*, which states: "In a hierarchy every employee tends to rise to his level of incompetence" (Peter and Hull, 1969). The final application of this theory is the realization that sooner or later every position in a hierarchy will be filled by an incompetent person.

Although this is a useful theory, it has some weaknesses. There is an assumption of total promotability of all employees. Given the pyramid structure of law enforcement organizations, each level is more competitive than the former. Many people never reach their level of incompetence. They become trapped at a level far beneath their abilities, and this may be as damaging to the organization as the Peter Principle, for this causes frustration and resentment.

Alliances

Another survival technique is the careful selection of allies. The old saying "who you know is more important than what you know" has more than just a little truth. Agency administrators learn early of the value of having strong contacts with legislative officials. This provides job protection beyond the capacity of the top executive, such as president, governor, or city manager. Lower-ranking employees have also discovered this fact, and many nurture their own relationships with people in positions above the chief law enforcement officer.

Successful administrators recognize the value of alliances. This is why so many become such obviously political creatures on their ascendency to the position of chief executive officer. Survival dictates making the right connections and maintaining them. Failure to do so results in a lack of social supports that are necessary for a strong administrative position. Although this is often obvious to top administrators, they sometimes fail to see the validity of this technique among lower-ranked employees. Many a police chief has been shocked to discover the difficulty encountered in firing an obviously incompetent officer due to an outpouring of support from strong community factions with which the officer has become associated. It is one thing to fire Officer Smith. It is quite another to fire Officer Jones, deacon of the First Baptist Church and president of the local Jaycees. Survivors seek ways of protecting themselves, and the sicker the organization, the more developed will be the alliances between organizational members and powerful interests outside the agency.

Team Behavior

Team behavior is another form of self protection. Many of the problems besetting law enforcement can be traced to this tendency. A formal definition of a team has been provided by Erving Goffman:

> A team is a set of individuals whose intimate co-operation is required if a given projected definition of the situation is to be maintained. A team is a grouping not in relation to social structure or social organization but rather in relation to an interaction or series of interactions in which the relevant definition of the situation is maintained (1959, p. 104).

A major portion of the socialization process of new police officers is focused on what behavior is expected in order to maintain the public's belief in the agency's definitions. Attention is given to image management or how to present to the public the image that is most advantageous to the members of the organization. The public must believe in the competence of the law enforcement agency. For police officers to feel they are worthwhile, the police function must be viewed as worthwhile and necessary by the public.

Although there is nothing inherently wrong with attempting to maintain a positive public and self-image, there are damaging aspects to this activity which are related directly to the amount of sickness within the organization. The most damaging aspect is the "we versus them" tendency. Officers develop an almost paranoid belief in the inability of outsiders to understand them or their problems. Any team member thus becomes more valuable than any outsider. We can argue, with conviction, that the reason we have bad police officers is due to their protection by good officers. Corruption, brutality, and blatant incompetence can exist only with the implicit cooperation of officers who would never engage in these acts themselves. Neither, however, would they ever complain or testify against an officer who does engage in these activities. The team's image must be protected, and this includes protecting bad members.

Another aspect of this form of behavior, which can be damaging to the organization, is the systematic development of individual arrogance among personnel. The individual officer represents a powerful organization whose members will protect this person even when undeserved. The citizen represents no such institution. Officers therefore begin to feel that they are the organization and see no need to treat the citizen with respect. The officers see themselves as powerful and all-knowing; the citizen is just some jerk infringing on their time. Rudeness and arrogance are a major problem in most large organizations, especially monopolies and public service agencies. In some police agencies it has reached chronic proportions.

Team behavior is not isolated to entire organizations. Small teams also develop within the larger organization, with all the attributes of the larger team. The we versus them syndrome applies to every unit within an organization in their relationships with other elements. The amount of hostility and mistrust in an organization gone wild with internal politics has to be seen to be believed. It can reach a point where information is withheld from one team by another to prevent "those people" from accomplishing more than us.

CAUSES OF BUREAUPATHOLOGY

The organization need not succumb to terminal bureaucracy simply because it is old. There are administrative and organizational actions responsible for the development of the illness. Michael Crozier has identified five conditions leading to the pathological organization: *rulification, centralization, isolation, acceptance of isolation,* and *resultant power struggles* (1964). After discussing these conditions we discuss the organizational atmosphere fostered by the administrator and the role this plays in nurturing the illness.

Rulification

The first step toward a pathological organization is the attempt by the administration to provide rules for every conceivable situation. As the policy manual grows, the initiative and creativity of personnel decline. The mistaken belief, on the part of management, in the ability to foresee every decision in advance not only insults the operational personnel, it stifles their ability to solve problems quickly. Rulification attempts to treat people as mechanical units absent the intelligence to make sound decisions on their own. This appears to happen automatically in the maturity stage of organizational development. From that point on, the rules and policies just get longer and more complicated, with no resultant improvement in effectiveness.

Centralization

The attempt to maintain control of the organization from the top is doomed to failure. The larger the agency gets, the less control the executive can truly have. Centralization is the by-product of rulification. The rules and policies are generated in order to maintain centralization. Decision making in lower echelons is discouraged, resulting in a still greater reduction in creativity and ingenuity. This is coupled with a comparative loss of job satisfaction and morale as the lower-ranked personnel become what the administration already thinks they are, unmotivated dullards simply putting in their time while doing as little as possible.

Isolation

So that team behavior can be maximized, each hierarchical level, as well as each individual unit, is isolated from each other. Usually, this is done to the extent that they never have to look each other in the face. This is a marvelous method for generating internal jealousy and friction. Isolation guarantees an increase in the use of formal communications while decreasing the ability to use informal communications. It also guarantees a greatly reduced ability to solve problems and meet objectives.

Acceptance of Isolation

As each group becomes consolidated as a team, they generate pressure to accept the isolation. They lose interest in communicating informally with other groups and resent any perceived intrusion into their affairs. The isolation becomes sanctified, and those not associated with this particular element are looked on with suspicion. In time, everyone in the organization becomes comfortable with the isolation and subsequent territoriality.

Resultant Power Struggles

The obvious conclusion to this tale of woe is the shift from units attempting to defend their turf to an aggressive position where each element attempts to claim territory not already staked out. In its most sinister form, units will attempt to steal functions and responsibilities from other units. Budgetary battles become agency bloodlettings as each element tries to establish its prestige by taking money that could be better used elsewhere (see Table 8-3).

Table 8-3
Causes of Bureaupathology

Factors	*Symptoms*
Rulification	Attempt to regulate every aspect of organizational life. Characterized by rigid disciplinary system that stifles creativity and initiative.
Centralization	Attempt to maintain complete control of organization from top. Characterized by low levels of delegation and a rigid hierarchy.
Isolation	Segmentation of organization into self-contained units with little or no need for face-to-face communication with other elements.
Acceptance of isolation	The acceptance of the isolation as natural, with the tendency to view others in the organization as hostile competitors.
Power struggles	The result of the segmentation process wherein each element engages in no-holds-barred battles with other elements for control of resources, values, and the organization's objectives.

Unfortunately, many authors believe in the inevitability of this process. Howard McGurdy argues that once rigidity sets in, the only time it can be broken is during a crisis, but this flexibility is short lived. Usually, a crisis requires strong action by top management. This regenerates a strong central administration and starts the bureaucratic process again, rapidly leading to the old dysfunctions (1977, p. 95).

We must recognize, however, that many organizations have escaped the evolutionary process by refusing to succumb to attempts to formalize the operation and by focusing on what made them successful in the beginning. Bureaupathology is inevitable only if the organization initiates the foregoing conditions. After those conditions are allowed to set in, change is difficult indeed.

Political Atmosphere

Political behavior can be found in all organizations. The extent to which it is a problem is subject to the climate fostered by the administrator. Like other life forms, organizational politics thrives better in some atmospheres than in others. As with other forms of evil, dysfunctional politics grows best where there is secrecy, mistrust, and favoritism. Such things as double standards, selective screening, ambiguity, administrative abdication, and isolation also increase the likelihood of political game playing.

Double Standards

There is always a tendency on the part of administrators to favor managerial personnel over those at the operational level. This may happen due to the closeness of the relationship between various levels of administration while the operative is isolated from the chief executive. It may be associated with the hostility between management and labor that has become apparent over the past century. Then again, it may just be the result of the administrative philosophy of supporting management to increase their ability to manage. Although it is easy to rationalize any of these reasons, it is a mistake to take them too seriously. Policies intended for all personnel should say so and be enforced accordingly.

This problem occurs frequently in most organizations and is a source of discontent. There always appear to be some who can get away with anything. Those who appear to be beyond the reach of the rules are a source of irritation to those required to abide by the regulations. The lack of consistent policy application can cause destabilization within the agency and create an atmosphere ripe for political manipulation.

Selective Screening

Perhaps the most destructive process within a law enforcement organization is selective screening. In this process personnel who do not agree with the administrator's philosophy are systematically screened out of the promotion process and sometimes out of the organization. One might call this loading middle and upper management with "yes people." Many law enforcement administrators have come to believe that they have all the answers and only need personnel to support their positions. Those with the audacity to dispute their opinion are viewed as agency traitors who must be purged from the organization.

Unfortunately, people with differing viewpoints are most needed within any organization. These are the people with new ideas or at least a willingness to try something new. These are also the people who can be counted on to tell the administrator when policies or procedures are likely to be ineffective. Those whose jaws are permanently locked in the yes position offer nothing constructive for the agency; they are paper passers who only take up space.

The only ideas likely to emerge from agencies where selective screening is practiced is from the chief administrator. Since no one is capable of a constant stream of new ideas, the chief's well of originality usually dries up after a few short years. From then on it is a downhill ride to stagnation. Every administrator desperately needs people around to support good ideas and kill bad ones. In the long run, selective screening can deplete the organization of those critical thinkers needed so desperately if the agency is to remain dynamic.

Ambiguity

Another way in which the administrator can set the stage for organizational politics is by failing to provide personnel with clear objectives and responsibilities. Ambiguity can be useful in small doses, where the problem is ill defined and outcomes are uncertain. Too much ambiguity can generate power struggles. These power struggles will be based on temporary alliances and momentary advantage and therefore will act as a destabilizing force within the organization. Ambiguity breeds political in-fighting, which generates more ambiguity. The process feeds on itself and eventually saps the productive energy of the organization.

People must know where they stand and for what they are responsible. If objectives and accountability are not clearly defined the members will attempt to provide their own definitions in a self-serving manner. The choice rests with the administration; either management defines the organizational variables or the definitions are left to individual determination. No other option exists.

Abdication

Abdication occurs when the administrator delegates all authority to subordinates then fails to provide effective follow-up to ensure accountability. Unit commanders may attack each other viciously as each attempts to become the predominant member of the managerial team. Rifts already apparent in the organization may be torn wide open as personnel at various levels perceive a leadership vacuum. Isolation of elements occurs more rapidly as each unit seeks to protect itself from the political manipulation of those in other elements.

A critical function of administration is the need to look at problems and objectives from a total organization perspective. Subunits cannot do this because their perspective is limited to the needs of their element. When the chief executive fails to coordinate the separate units, they tend to go their own way, often at the expense of the entire agency. Administrative abdication results in fragmentation and a loss of a sense of organizational purpose.

Isolation

Administrative isolation differs from the organizational isolation discussed earlier. When administrators become isolated from the actual work of the organization, any number of negative things can occur. First, the executive becomes dependent on lower-level administrators for operational information. Decisions thus initiated are made with second- or third-hand information. The danger here is the loss of reliability of any information over a number of hierarchical levels, regardless of the dedication of personnel within those positions. Reliability is also affected by timeliness of the data. The slower the communication process, the older the information on which critical decisions are based. There is also a danger of political manipulation of the chief executive by lower managers through the control of the communications channel.

At the very least, isolated administrators are seriously out of touch with their organizations. When problems occur, these executives are frequently the last people to know. Sometimes the administrator does not even discover the problem at all until notice is received of a civil suit.

Another problem with isolation is the frequent unwillingness of lower-level managers to be the bearer of bad tidings. Many well-intentioned individuals will do almost anything to protect the chief from bad news, even though the chief executive needs this information as soon as possible. Isolation is a cardinal administrative sin and encourages political behavior in its worst forms.

Secrecy

There is a direct relationship between the amount of secrecy in an organization and the amount of destructive political behavior. Secrecy protects incompetence and nothing else. This is not to say that all information within a law enforcement agency should be open to the public; this is not only impractical, but illegal. The problem is with administrative secrecy. People usually attempt to keep only mistakes secret. Successes are trumpeted throughout the organization. The ability to continue making the same mistakes over and over is related directly to the ability to keep those mistakes from public knowledge.

If you recall the discussion on informal communications; the only manner in which rumors can be controlled is by publishing the truth as soon as it is known. This includes policy decisions, disciplinary actions, personnel decisions of any kind, and responses to criticisms.

As Robert Townsend noted, "Secrecy is totally bad. It defeats the crusade for justice, which doesn't flourish in the dark. Secrecy implies either:

1. What I'm doing is so horrible I don't dare tell you.

    or

2. I don't trust you (anymore)" (1984, p. 201).

CURING THE SICK ORGANIZATION

The best treatment for the pathological organization was offered in Chapter 7. These concepts are best initiated, however, when the organization is originally conceived. This does not mean that law enforcement agencies cannot change to this format, for they can if given sufficient time to overcome their own traditions and obstacles. There is a long history of organizational turnarounds where failing businesses became successful with appropriate leadership. Robert Townsend, for example, took over Avis Rent A Car when it had not made a profit in years and within a few years had turned it into an industry leader.

The first step in the treatment process is to recognize that police agencies are in the people business. Participative management is more than a catch phrase, it is the most applicable means of establishing agency objectives and obtaining consensus of the organization's members. Even if the chief administrator cannot dismantle the monstrous bureaucracy immediately (which probably evolved over several decades), this person can reduce its harmful properties by communicating directly and informally with the operational personnel, those who actually fulfill the agency's mission.

The second step is to develop an open-door policy and mean it. This includes not only all organizational members, but also media personnel. The news services can be the best friend an administrator has or they can be a vicious enemy. The determination of which is usually a by-product of administrative activities. When the administrator attempts to hide agency activities, the news media often assume that there is something to hide and attempt to find out what. Open departments diffuse media hostility by allowing the press to act as professionals and by aiding them in the completion of their objectives. The mistake made by many law enforcement administrators is to assume that any criticism leveled at the agency is unjustified, when many times it is honest criticism. When the press continues to report occurrences of corruption, brutality, or incompetence, it is usually because the problem exists. Corruption, brutality, and incompetence do not flourish in the cold light of media inspection. A competent free press with full access to the organization is better than an internal affairs unit and vastly more neutral.

The third step is honesty. Mistakes, which will be made, should be admitted openly and corrected as rapidly as possible. Administrators must be honest with employees, superiors, the public, and most of all with themselves. There is no valid reason for supplying the legislative body or chief executive officer with incorrect information. Sooner or later they will discover the perfidy and the administrator's credibility will be shot. The same holds true for subordinates, and especially for the press.

Everyone makes mistakes and most are willing to forgive them if they were honestly made and openly admitted. Cover-ups are almost always an unsalvageable error. Also, why waste valuable time and energy defending a decision that you already know is wrong? This is the worst mistake of all.

Fourth, the organization should be led, not only through words but through actions. The chief executive officer should demonstrate the unacceptability of dysfunctional political behavior. Excellent performance should be rewarded, but the organization should never reward poor performance. Responsibility and accountability should be clarified and the members held accountable. All decisions should have an author, and this person should receive the glory when the decision is right and take the blame when it fails, but allowances should be made for good attempts that end in failure.

Fifth, rebellion should be encouraged rather than mutiny. Every person in the organization should feel free to walk into the administrator's office and tell the boss off, to let off steam, or to submit a real grievance. Disagreement among subordinates should be encouraged, for this is where initiative and creativity are generated. The chief does not have all the answers, but they probably exist somewhere within the organization. Unless everyone has the ability to offer suggestions or objections, the agency will be limited to the administrator's own narrow view.

Sixth, walls should be torn down. Everyone in the organization should be forced to deal with each other face to face. Isolation is often an effectiveness-destroying monster. If the administrator does nothing more than require that all shift briefings be attended by every unit working that shift, there will be some improvement. Better yet, the offices should be scrambled so that no unit is allowed to become a castle within a castle.

Members of different units should be forced to work together, and above all, questions, requests, and complaints should never be transmitted in written form unless the author is present when it is delivered. It is easy to get angry at a faceless name who resides somewhere else in the building and is always sending nasty notes. It is something else to sit across from that person day after day and compare problems. It is amazing how rapidly solutions are derived when people talk to each other. This includes throwing out that absurd policy requiring everyone to adhere rigidly to the chain of command.

Chain of command is nice for routine reports and matters that must be dispersed to every employee. Other than these instances, the only purpose the chain of command serves is to allow middle management to prevent negative information from reaching higher levels. So what if this means that some officers will make routine stops at the chief's office to complain about a supervisor or unit commander. If this person is lying, the chief needs to know so that this person can be removed from the organization. If the officer is telling the truth, the chief needs to know so that something can be done about the supervisor. At the same time the policy on insubordination should be eliminated. Better yet, all the titles should be eliminated and everyone required to address each other by first names only. Deep conviction and emotion go hand in hand; all personnel should be allowed to express both without fear of offending someone of higher rank.

Seventh is fairness. Injustice can destroy agency morale like the plague. There is no room for favoritism or prejudice in good organizations. People know when the administration is just; so do middle managers. The chief cannot assume that supervisors are always right and operatives always wrong. Each side must be listened to openly, and decisions should be based on facts rather than intuition. Most people are terrible judges of character; they see only what others want them to see. When opinions conflict with facts, the administrator should always trust the facts.

Finally, someway, somehow, that monstrous bureaucratic hierarchy must be torn down. No law enforcement agency in the country needs more than five levels from patrol officer to chief. The vast number of agencies, those below 500 employees, usually need only three, four at the most. This is the difficult and time-consuming task. It may take years, but sooner or later someone is going to do it, and when they do a lot of administrators are going to have to follow suit, without the luxury of time.

DISCUSSION QUESTIONS

1. Discuss police operations and management in light of the five stages of organizational evolution.

2. Why is occupational psychosis a problem for the police administrator? What can be done to minimize the problem?

3. What effect does goal displacement have on the attempt to introduce problem-oriented or community-oriented policing to a traditional law enforcement agency?

4. Discuss political behavior. Why is it a problem in large organizations?

5. Discuss the causes of bureaupathology. Is it possible to prevent an organization from becoming pathological? Explain your answer.

REFERENCES

Adizes, Ichak (1979). "Organizational passages: diagnosing and treating lifecycle problems of organizations," *Organizational Dynamics,* Summer, pp. 2–25.

Crozier, Michel (1964). *The Bureaucratic Phenomenon.* Chicago: University of Chicago Press.

Goffman, Erving (1959). *The Presentation of Self in Everyday Life.* Garden City, N.Y.: Doubleday Anchor Press.

Katz, Daniel, and Robert L Kahn (1979). *The Social Psychology of Organizations,* 2nd ed. New York: Wiley.

Mannheim, Karl (1936). *Ideology and Utopia.* New York: Harcourt, Brace.

McGurdy, Howard E. (1977). *Public Administration: A Synthesis.* Menlo Park, Calif.: Cummings Press.

Merton, Robert K. (1969). "Bureaucratic structure and personality," in William Sexton, ed., *Organizational Theories.* Columbus, Ohio: Charles E. Merrill.

Parkinson, C. Northcote (1969). *Parkinson's Law.* Boston: Houghton Mifflin.

Peter, Lawrence J. and Raymond Hill (1969). *The Peter Principle*. New York: Bantam Books.

Ray, Charles M., and Charles L. Eison (1983). *Supervision.* New York: Dryden Press.

Robbins, Stephen P. (1976). *The Administrative Process.* Englewood Cliffs, N.J.: Prentice Hall.

Souryal, Sam S. (1992). *Ethics in Criminal Justice: In Search of the Truth.* Cincinnati, Ohio: Anderson.

Townsend, Robert (1984). *Further Up the Organization.* New York: Alfred A. Knopf.

Walton, Mary (1986). *The Deming Management Method.* New York: Perigree.

Chapter 9

Staffing the Organization

The secret to organizational effectiveness is really nothing more than hiring the best possible personnel and then getting out of their way so they can do the job for which they were hired. The staffing function exists to find and employ the people on which the organization's capabilities will depend. This is a crucial part of the administrator's duties; the road to agency success begins here. The earlier concerns expressed toward personnel units must be reiterated here. The most important organizational decisions concern personnel, either in selection, promotion, transfers, or discipline. All decisions should be made by personnel directly affected by the decision. Personnel officers are rarely affected by their decisions concerning personnel; this is the real weakness in the concept of the personnel unit. Personnel decisions are too important to be delegated to a unit that will not be required to face the consequences of poor judgment. Some of the steps in the personnel process can and should be centralized, but the steps requiring discretionary judgments must be made by those whose duties require them to work with the new recruits. The final decision should be made by the chief executive in consultation with those involved in the selection process.

In this chapter we look at the selection process. First we examine the factors currently used to determine applicability for a law enforcement career. Next we discuss why the current system is flawed and how the future police selection process might change.

JOB ANALYSIS

Prior to the selection process, the administrator must know what qualities the new recruit must possess to function adequately in the law enforcement role. The proper method for making this determination is through job analysis. Job analysis is used to determine the kind of people needed to fill the job and culminates with a job description identifying specific details about the job and the qualifications necessary for successful completion. The data necessary to obtain this analysis may be obtained in a number of ways (Robbins, 1980, p. 251):

1. *Observation.* The employee is either watched directly or filmed on the job.

2. *Individual Interview.* Selected job incumbents are interviewed extensively, and the results of a number of these interviews are combined into a single job analysis.

3. *Group interviews.* Same as individual except that a number of job incumbents are interviewed simultaneously.

4. *Structured questionnaire.* Employees check or rate the items they perform in their job from a long list of possible task items.

5. *Technical conference.* Specific characteristics of a job are obtained from experts, who usually are supervisors with extensive knowledge of the job.

6. *Diary method.* Job incumbents record their daily activities in a diary or notebook.

On completion of the data-gathering process, the job is evaluated and a job description is published, usually in the following format:

1. Job title

2. Duties to be performed

3. Distinguishing characteristics of the job

4. Authority and responsibility

5. Specific qualifications necessary, such as required knowledge, skills, abilities, training, and experience

6. Criteria by which job incumbents will be evaluated

The failure to determine job qualifications adequately for law enforcement personnel has perhaps been most noticeable in the undue attention given physical qualities as opposed to intellectual capacity. This has led to extreme physical requirements, such as 20/20 vision with no correction allowed, height requirements at 6 feet, nearly perfect physical conditioning, and so on. At the same time, the intellectual requirements were the ability to pass a civil service exam, in some cases, and a high school diploma or its equivalent. If a person were to attempt to assess the law enforcement function by studying entrance requirements, one might have to conclude that the police role requires brute force and little intelligence. Nothing could be further from the truth. Stated qualifications for many police agencies simply have little relationship to the job requirements. For this reason, the job analysis is useful; you cannot determine qualifications until you know what the job requires.

Physical Qualifications

Since the physical requirements of most law enforcement agencies are most pronounced, this provides a good starting point for our discussion of entrance qualifications. The major areas of focus for law enforcement organizations are vision, hearing, general health, height, and weight.

Vision

The topic of vision standards is one of continuing controversy. A 1984 study of 323 major police departments indicated that law enforcement agencies have consistently adopted high standards for corrected vision, but there is no consensus as to how much correction should be allowed (Holden, 1984, pp. 126-127). Eighty-three percent of the departments surveyed required a corrected vision of 20/20. Requirements for uncorrected vision ranged from no correction allowed (2 percent) to no requirements for uncorrected vision (26 percent), with the remaining agencies distributed between these extremes. Clearly, there is little in the way of standardized vision requirements (see Tables 9-1 and 9-2, adapted from Holden, 1984, p. 127).

Table 9-1
Police Corrected Vision Standards

Corrected Vision	*Agencies*	*Percentage*
20/20	271	83
20/30	39	12
20/40	5	1.5
20/50	1	.01
Acceptable to physician	5	1.5
None listed	2	.06

Table 9-2

Police Uncorrected Vision Standards

Uncorrected Vision	Agencies	Percentage
20/20	8	2
20/30	6	2
20/40	58	18
20/50	40	12
20/60	10	3
20/70	29	9
20/80	2	1
20/100	71	22
20/200	8	2
None	84	26

The controversy centers around the perception that an officer must be able to function without the benefit of eyewear. There is a belief, strongly held by some police administrators, that officers may engage in a struggle that causes the eyewear to be knocked from the officer's face. It is believed that the officer may then be required to use either a firearm or drive an automobile in this condition. These beliefs are held without supporting documentation. In fact, what little research is available on this topic reports that such fears are unfounded (Holden, 1993).

Moreover, as with many physical requirements, there is a broad gap between what is required for entry standards and what is required for officers already employed. Most departments have no eyesight requirements for officers already employed. This is a questionable practice and one that has now been noted by the courts. It has also been observed that some of the largest police agencies in the nation require only that the applicant's vision be corrected to 20/20. Departments such as Chicago, Detroit, and Newark have used this standard for years without apparent problems. This fact alone makes it difficult for other agencies to require a more rigid standard. The police department of Philadelphia, Pennsylvania, for example, agreed to a settlement in Federal District Court that significantly altered vision requirements. As a result of the lawsuit in Philadelphia, the department now allows an uncorrected vision of 20/200 correctable to 20/20.

The courts have now entered the debate on eyesight requirements. One by one, rigid requirements are being struck down in favor of more defensible standards. This process is likely to continue into the future. The following case is typical of the attack on police vision requirements.

Brown County v. *Labor & Industrial Review Commission* (1985)
124 Wis.2d 560

In May 1974, John Toonen applied for a job as a deputy sheriff with the Brown County Sheriff's Department. He was well qualified by experience and education for the position. He had served as a military police officer and had received an associate degree in police science. Before applying for employment with Brown County, he had served without any difficulties as a jail deputy, a dispatcher, and a traffic patrolman in Shawano County. He was told by the Brown County Sheriff's Department that on the basis of his preliminary examination and experience, he would be hired as a traffic patrol officer by the county if he passed the physical. The physician examining for the county reported, however, that Toonen's uncorrected vision in each eye, 20/400, failed to meet the county's uncorrected vision requirement of 20/40 in the better eye and 20/100 in the poorer eye. By use of glasses or contact lenses, Toonen's vision was corrected to 20/20. Because his uncorrected vision did not meet the hiring standard, however, Toonen was not hired.

In March 1980, Toonen filed a complaint with the Department of Industry, Labor and Human Relations (DILHR) alleging that Brown County had discriminated against him on the basis of a handicap. The record developed at a hearing in March 1981 before a DILHR hearing examiner reveals that Toonen never had any difficulty in performing his duties as a traffic officer because of his vision—that he had on occasion in the course of duty been in fights, sustained blows to the head, but had never lost his contact lenses. There was expert testimony that modern contact lenses were very unlikely to be dislodged, and that even if one were lost, a person could see adequately with one lens. There was also evidence that patrolmen on the job with Brown County were not required to maintain the entrance level of uncorrected visual acuity and that serving traffic officers had visual acuity that did not meet the hiring standard.

In May 1981, the hearing examiner issued her decision. The hearing examiner found that Toonen was handicapped because of his visual impairment, that he had met the required burden under the act to show that he had been denied employment because of his handicap, and that Brown County had failed to meet its burden of showing that Toonen's handicap was reasonably related to his ability to perform on the job. The examiner held that Brown County had discriminated against Toonen in violation of WFEA and ordered Brown County to offer Toonen the next available position and to pay him back pay from January 1, 1980.

This decision was ultimately upheld by the Wisconsin Supreme Court.

Hearing

Hearing is a less controversial topic; it also results in fewer disqualifications than does vision. The usual hearing requirement for entrance to most police agencies is normal. This means that the person can hear noises within the standard audible auditory range at an acceptable sound level, without sound enhancement devices.

Poor hearing can often be corrected with a battery-powered amplification system. Modern technology allows these amplifiers to be small enough to fit into the stems of eyeglasses or be placed directly in or over the ear. Many police officers who met the hearing standards when hired have found it necessary to utilize a device such as this. By all accounts, these officers continue to perform well. Hearing is therefore similar to vision to the extent that both are somewhat correctable. The safest procedure for law enforcement administrators is probably to require normal hearing after correction. Even this may be open to future legal challenge.

General Health

The topic of general health covers a number of factors. First, the person must be physically capable of performing the duties of the job as determined by the job description. The person should not have any lingering illnesses or injuries that might decrease this person's ability to be productive throughout a full career. Anyone with a history of chronic illness or injury should be looked on with some wariness. Medical retirements are expensive. To hire someone who cannot fulfill a complete career due to previous injury or illness can be a costly mistake.

Another consideration in the area of general health is physical agility. Many agencies have adopted physical agility courses to ensure that recruits possess minimum coordination and are in reasonable physical condition. These goals are worthy in and of themselves, under two conditions. First, if the goal is the maintenance of physical condition, recruits should not be required to have a higher standard of conditioning than is required for experienced officers assigned similar duties. If the administrator believes that police officers should be in good physical condition, all officers should be in good shape, not just the recruits.

Second, the requirement may be to test for a minimum level of coordination. This means, however, that candidates unfamiliar with the techniques of physical agility courses should be coached prior to an official attempt and be allowed practice time to achieve the required technical competence. After all, the test is one of physical coordination and conditioning, not of athletic technique, which can be taught if it is necessary to job performance.

Height and Weight

There was a time when height and weight requirements were narrow and rigid. Court rulings have changed this greatly. No other physical requirement has been subjected to as great a revision as this area. Standards for height and weight for men were originally established on the "Wild West" image of the law enforcer as the toughest and usually the biggest man in town.

Logic and civil suits have changed this perception somewhat while altering the requirements substantially. The standard of most agencies today is no height requirement, with weight in proportion to height. This standard is reasonable and needs no further comment, except for a somewhat deceptive technique that many law enforcement agencies have developed to bypass the standard.

The oral interview has been used to eliminate candidates from the selection process in cases where the interviewers believed the candidate to be of improper stature, usually too short. This is not the purpose of the oral interview, but due to the ability of law enforcement agencies to eliminate candidates without providing a specific reason for the rejection, this phase in the selection process has been subverted by many agencies to get around legal mandates in a subtle manner. This practice is wrong. The oral interview has its purpose, and will be discussed in more detail later, but it was not designed to eliminate qualified applicants. The misuse of any step in the selection process makes a mockery of the entire process and is a symptom of a dangerous level of bureaucratic rigidity within the administration.

Americans with Disabilities Act

An excellent analysis of the Americans with Disabilities Act of 1990 (ADA) was presented by Lydia Long in her paper, "The Americans with Disabilities Act of 1990 and law enforcement employment: notes and comments." The following discussion was excerpted from that paper.

The Americans with Disabilities Act became effective for most employers on July 26, 1992. The ADA prohibits discrimination against persons with disabilities who can perform, with or without accommodation, the "essential functions of the employment position." The act affects agencies who have 15 or more employees for each working day in each of 20 or more calendar weeks in the current or preceding calender year. Since many law enforcement agencies are included in the provisions of ADA, the potential for liability will be considerable unless the agencies take positive steps to meet the requirements of the act.

The act provides precise definitions for people who qualify for protection. Regarding this law, the term *disability* means, with respect to an individual:

(1) a physical or mental impairment that substantially *limits* one or more of the major life activities of such individual;

(2) a record of such an impairment; or

(3) being regarded as having such an impairment.

To be protected by Public Law 101-336, a person must fulfill the foregoing disability requirements. Someone with 20/100 vision, for example, is not protected; someone who is blind is protected. A person with a "bad leg" probably does not qualify under these standards, but a paraplegic does qualify. The enactment of the ADA has created much concern among police departments concerned that they will be required to hire large numbers of people who are disabled and who will not be able to perform adequately in a police job (Blackburn, 1991). The number of people protected by this act who actually apply for positions in police departments will probably be relatively few. The liability issue, however, will remain.

The primary concerns with ADA as applied to public safety officer positions lie in three areas. First of the major concerns involves placing the burden of proof on the law enforcement agency to show that a particular physical or mental criterion for a public safety officer position is job related and consistent with business necessity.

Unless an exception is provided in the ADA for public safety officer positions, law enforcement agencies will be required to make hiring decisions on the basis of a law that presumes that the functions of all job positions can be precisely defined.

The opposing view to this first primary concern points to the various provisions of ADA that provide for adequate safeguards against forced hiring of unqualified applicants. ADA provides for an employing agency to make pre-employment inquiries into the ability of an applicant to perform job-related tasks. ADA also provides for medical examinations after offering a job but before starting work and allows conditional job offers based on passing the medical examination.

Additionally, the act provides for defenses against charges of discrimination arising from employment actions. Such defenses are based on showing that the employer's actions were based on "job-related" and "business necessity" standards. An additional safeguard is built into ADA that permits a requirement that a person not pose a direct threat to the health and safety of other employees. The counterargument to the law enforcement concern is that these provisions adequately protect the police from forced hiring of unqualified applicants.

A second major concern of law enforcement officials centers on the prohibition against considering past illegal drug use in hiring public safety officers. Police authorities are especially concerned with this provision since most departments screen out applicants with a history of illegal drug use. Further, ADA provides applicants who test positive during a test for illegal drugs with a cause of action against the public safety agency if the laboratory conducting the test is determined to have erred.

By implication, the ADA would prohibit public safety agencies from considering an applicant's criminal conviction for possession or use of illegal drugs in rejecting the applicant. From the perspective of law enforcement, the courts will eventually rule that the consideration of prior criminal convictions, even if they are for illegal drug use, does not violate the act, at least to the extent that it is applied to law enforcement agencies (Blackburn, 1991). Under the law as written, however, litigation on the topic is a virtual certainty.

This second concern of law enforcement officials is also challenged by those who argue against any type of public safety exemptions from the provisions of ADA. The act provides for drug testing to determine if a person is still using illegal drugs. The act also contains provisions for applying the same standard to all employees, including those who use illegal drugs. That provision would permit the discharge of an employee who had previously used illegal drugs and was found to be continuing that use after employment.

The third major law enforcement concern about the provisions of ADA centers on the requirements if public safety departments to provide the full range of possible accommodations to job applicants with disabilities at the time of hire, which would result in reducing the availability of "light-duty" positions for officers who sustain their disabilities in the course of their duties.

Police agencies argue that policing comprises persons holding positions of varying routine responsibilities in addition to their primary responsibilities of maintaining public safety. All must be prepared to respond quickly to any number of incidents that could be physically demanding or would require particularly acute agility or perceptive abilities.

Read literally in the context of public safety officer positions, this section of the act would require public safety agencies to hire people who are able to drive a patrol vehicle, answer a telephone, interview witnesses, present cases to the prosecutor, or wash fire vehicles, even if the same people could not be required to respond to the physically demanding emergencies and contingencies that persons holding such positions occasionally, although not routinely, encounter. Moreover, the public safety officer positions that carry the least likelihood of physical stress or exertion (e.g., investigators, court officers, desk officers) may have to be filled with persons who are unable to perform the more dangerous, physically demanding responsibilities of the public safety officer position.

The arguments against this position by the police are based on the fact that ADA contains provisions for "undue hardship." Those provisions include the cost and nature of any accommodations that would be required, as well as the size of the employing agency, the numbers of persons employed, the financial resources, and the overall impact on the operation of the facility or activity involved. It is likely that police departments could, in most cases, argue successfully against many accommodation issues. The courts have ruled that job relationship and business necessity can be proven through qualitative as well as quantitative measures. The use of expert testimony, for example, could be used to validate the lack of accommodation due to the physical requirements of the police job and related tasks.

A thorough analysis of this act reveals that when police can document and validate job requirements that preclude the employment of the disabled, they will be in compliance with ADA. If there are jobs and positions that cannot be so validated, the law enforcement field will be forced to join many other occupations in opening some of its doors to employment for some disabled persons.

Intellectual Capacity

Law enforcement is primarily an intellectual exercise. Certainly there are physical aspects of the occupation, but the most valuable skills an officer can possess are the ability to excel in communication, both oral and written, and the use of sound judgment. Officers must be able to read and understand laws and organizational policies so that these may be translated into effective actions on the street. All police activities result in reports by the police of action taken. The translation of written directives into effective actions is dependent on the ability to use good judgment. The officers who possess good communication skills and possess good judgment, therefore, will be far more successful than others who lack these skills.

The topic of good writing deserves special attention. Successful prosecution in a court of law requires competent investigative reports. In many jurisdictions each year, cases are either lost in court or must be dismissed by the prosecutor due to the inadequacy of the report. Even when the case is solid and based on valid evidence, failure of the officer to communicate the information gathered in a clear and concise manner may doom the case for presentation in court. In the large jurisdictions this is of major concern; the prosecutor is often required to make prosecutorial decisions in a matter of minutes based on nothing more than the police report. Police literacy is vital to effective investigative reporting and prosecution. Sound judgment is crucial to all aspects of the police role. The following case dramatically illustrates the effect of poor judgment.

Wagstaff v. *City of Maplewood* (1981)
615 S.W.2d 608 (Mo.App.)

Action was brought to recover against city for wrongful death of the decedent, who was shot by a city police officer while being interrogated by him. The Circuit Court, County of St. Louis, Arthur Litz, J., rendered a $25,000 judgment against the city, and it appealed.

On the day of his death, Thomas E. Brown and a friend, Bobby Duncan, went to the E. J. Drug Store. Brown asked Duncan to go into the store and "find out about" a money order that Brown had taken from E.J. Drug the day before. A store clerk recognized the stolen money order and summoned the police. Brown had entered the store shortly after Duncan and both men were apprehended and taken to the Maplewood police station.

Officer Zweifel, who drove Brown to the police station, testified that it was apparent to him that Brown was mentally retarded, due to Brown's mannerisms and his inability to remember his birth date. After Brown was identified in a lineup, he was placed, along with Duncan, in a room for questioning. Officers Pool and Polidori conducted the interrogation. Duncan testified that during the questioning Officer Polidori pointed his gun at him, then withdrew the gun, loaded it, and placed it in his holster. Officer Pool then accused Brown of stealing the money order, during which time Pool was handling his gun. Pool emptied his gun's cartridges onto a table, then asked Duncan and Brown each to pick a number. Brown said "one," Duncan said "ten" or "seven," then Pool "pointed the gun right at Tom, straight and shot him." Duncan did not see Pool put a bullet in the gun nor pull the trigger but only saw "Tom get shot and fall, fall back, and he was dead."

Opinion of the Court

The doctrine of respondeat superior renders an employer liable for negligent acts committed by the employee within the course of his employment. Where the employer sanctions the use of force under certain circumstances, he cannot escape liability when the employee, while intending to act for his employer, makes a negligent mistake of fact or in an excess of zeal uses more than necessary force, or commits an error of law as to his privilege, or does an act combining all of these errors. Officer Pool made a tragic, negligent mistake of fact, the precise nature of which is not revealed by the evidence. His mistake may have been in assuming that the gun was unloaded, that his finger was not on the trigger, or perhaps that the safety catch was engaged. Regardless of the nature of the mistake, it is one for which the city is liable.

Judgment affirmed.

Intelligence

The debate concerning how much intelligence should be possessed by police officers centers around two conflicting points of view. The first position argues in favor of requiring officers only to possess common sense. Those on this side of the dispute believe that anyone with common sense can perform police work and see no need for evidence of intellectual capacity. Using this argument simplifies the administrator's task in the selection process; it eliminates all attempts to measure intellectual capacity of candidates and allows the selection team to focus on physical characteristics.

There is a weakness in this argument; it is impossible to define or measure common sense. Common sense can refer to judgment, but if this is the intent, it should be labeled judgment. The fact, however, is that the term does not refer to judgment, but rather to the mental capacity to see things the way "I" see them. It means that I know the truth even though I may be uneducated and that those who disagree with me, lack the common sense to see this truth.

The other position argues the high emphasis that police work places on judgment and urges an attempt to identify and measure intelligence in potential officers. There is a problem with this viewpoint also; intelligence is difficult to measure adequately. Too often, intelligence is confused with education. Education is a different topic, which will be discussed later (see Chapter 12). Intelligence is an inherent trait that refers to the mental capacity of the person rather than the person's level of knowledge. The question concerning intelligence is not what the person already knows, but the capacity of this person to learn. The first item to be eliminated in the measure of intelligence, therefore, is amount of education; this is only an indication of intelligence in its evidence of past capacity to learn.

Intelligence examinations such as IQ tests are also questionable, since many have been shown to be culturally biased. Also, no one has yet identified the cut off level of an IQ test for the police. Thus, how does one measure intelligence? The most common solution to this problem is the police entrance examination, sometimes a civil service exam or some variation thereof. In principle, this exam tests memory, basic literacy, and to a lesser extent, judgment. Although there are some questions as to the soundness of this approach, if done correctly it is the best alternative currently in use. The problem with this form of testing, unfortunately, is its tendency to test knowledge rather than intelligence, but the solution to this problem has still not been found.

Education

The movement toward the education of police officers began in 1917 when August Vollmer recruited college graduates from the University of California at Berkeley to work for the Berkeley Police Department. Few other agencies adopted this concept until the 1960s, when social turmoil forced a reexamination of the police. The result was strong support for educated law enforcement personnel. According to Herman Goldstein, "Few efforts to improve police operations in recent years have received such enthusiastic and widespread support as the general notion that police officers should be college educated" (1977, p. 283). The reasons behind the pressure to require college education for police officers can be categorized as follows:

1. A high percentage of the American public have some college education. The police should be staffed at least with people representative of the average education level of the nation.

2. Since the most intelligent of the nation's youth go on to college in large numbers, by failing to recruit from college graduates, law enforcement not only limits the total number of potential candidates, but fails to recruit from the most intelligent members of the population. This is especially crucial considering the heavy emphasis that law enforcement places on obtaining administrative personnel by promotion through the ranks. The chief executive can never be brighter than the brightest recruit since police agencies rarely bring in outsiders.

3. College education hopefully exposes the student to other cultures and lifestyles and thus creates a more understanding and tolerant person. The less education a person has, the more likely the person is to have a narrow focus on life. This person is more apt to judge others from the basis of a rigid view of family and social class morality and folklore. In other words, less educated people tend to be less tolerant of those who are different. College education, it is hoped, will lessen the impact of "good ole boy" networks and "redneck policing." The belief is inherent in this part of the argument in the capacity of education to improve the person. Thus better people make better police officers. Another aspect of this argument is the ability of more education to increase the person's knowledge, thus improving the person's ability to make decisions. Again we see the argument that education makes better police officers.

4. Because of its failure to attract educated personnel in the past, police work has fostered an image of dullards in uniform, capable of little humanity and with an all-too-rapid willingness to resort to the nightstick and gun to maintain order. Although this image is untrue and unfair, it has caught on in the entertainment media. The continual flow of new fiction, written and filmed, literally overwhelms the public with gunslinging, pistol whipping, and bloodletting. The average officer, who is generally sympathetic to the needs of the public and rarely fires a gun in anger or strikes a suspect, is buried under this massive onslaught of hyped misinformation. Many hope that attracting personnel with college educations will enhance the badly worn police image.

5) Older Police Officers don't like young educated police.

There are those who oppose college education as a requirement for police employment. They base their position on two ideas. First, the attempt to bring more minorities into law enforcement would suffer from requiring a college education. Fewer minorities seek a college degree and those who do often receive more lucrative offers from employers in the private sector than law enforcement is capable of providing. College requirements may therefore result in the continuing exclusion of minority candidates from law enforcement. Many who argue this believe the quality of policing will be better improved through affirmative action and increased minority participation rather than through increased college educational requirements.

The second argument focuses on past police performance. Those who hold this view believe that many police officers perform very well without college education. Some openly state, "College will not make me a better police officer." They also argue that placing a rigid requirement for a college degree will eliminate many potentially excellent officers who possess sufficient intelligence for the job but lack the piece of paper granted by a university. Another aspect of this argument is the varying esteem with which colleges and universities are held. Some have observed the great variance in the quality of education provided by different colleges and universities. Undoubtedly, the proliferation of diploma mills designed to obtain federal funds through the now defunct Law Enforcement Education Program (LEEP) and the Veterans Education Program has hurt the reputation of higher education in general and law enforcement programs specifically. It is hard to argue for giving preference to someone who was practically given a college degree, with little or no academic effort, over a person without a degree. Thus the inability to evaluate the true effect of the college education leads some to question its utility as a requirement for police service. Of course, the ultimate form taken by this line of reasoning is the real or imagined fear of the educated officer by the uneducated officer. The hostility encountered by college-educated recruits in many agencies, often emanating from middle management, is very real even if it is irrational. Many of the foregoing arguments, especially the latter, are an attempt to justify the perceived threat to job security by those without higher education.

College education and law enforcement are discussed in greater depth in Chapter 12. For the time being it is enough to say that the arguments in favor of college-educated police officers far outweigh those against. College education should be a minimum requirement for all entry-level law enforcement positions.

RECRUITING

Full-scale professional recruiting is new to law enforcement. In the past, recruiting was conducted by placing a notice on the bulletin board at city hall or by a one- or two-week ad in the local paper. Tests were given at regularly scheduled intervals to anyone who happened to show up. From these applicants, those who were most successful on the exam were hired, even though these might be questionable. William Bopp identified this practice as choosing from "the best of the worst" and noted the consistency with which this happens when an agency engages in passive recruiting (1974, p. 143).

This has changed in most agencies, but not all. Recruiting is a science requiring active professional personnel. Successful recruiting lies in the willingness to go anywhere at practically any time to seek out those with high potential. Through the process of universal recruiting, certain areas will be more productive than others. The agency must identify these areas and cultivate them for future personnel requirements. Areas such as college campuses, military bases, and even shopping centers have been fruitful for many agencies. Also, there are currently a number of nationwide publications catering to potential candidates on a nationwide basis. Through the use of brochures, fliers, and electronic and print advertisements, the police recruiter can canvass the entire nation and increase both the quantity and quality of potential recruits, which is the goal of police recruiters.

The function of recruiting should never be confused with the selection function. Recruiting requires the gathering of as many applicants as possible. The selection function focus on the elimination of potential candidates through the screening process. The duties of these persons, or units, are in direct opposition to each other, and assigning recruiting and screening duties to the same person or team can place these people under intense pressure, created by the conflicting objectives. Recruiting is a separate and unique function and should be treated as such.

Affirmative Action

Affirmative action programs are designed to correct past hiring and promotion practices in both public and private organizations. In essence, these programs allow preference to be given to minorities and women, to offset past problems of discrimination. This subject is controversial with many sound arguments both for and against. Affirmative action is a fact of life, however, and must be treated as such.

The extent to which hiring practices have been seriously discriminatory can be observed adequately in one of the many contemporary works of nonfiction dealing with this situation. Joseph Wambaugh pointed out the lack of Mexican-American police officers employed by the San Diego Police Department in the past 10 years despite the heavy concentration of Mexican-Americans in the southern portion of California. As Wambaugh said "the San Diego Police Department just didn't seem to know where it *lived*"(1984, p. 207).

Racial and sexual discrimination led to affirmative action. Until a sense of equality is achieved in hiring practices, affirmative action will be necessary.

Recruiting Women and Minorities

The ability to attract women and minorities to a police organization is directly related to the perceptions that all personnel will have equal chances at promotion and choice assignments. Merely offering a position to women and minorities is not in and of itself enough. Most people entering the field of law enforcement want a full career, with the potential to take advantage of all opportunities .

The ability to recruit women and minorities is hampered by a number of obstacles. First, each group, be it female, African-American, Hispanic, or Oriental, has its own needs, desires, and fears. A plan designed to attract women will not succeed in hiring African-American men.

Second, police work has an unsavory reputation in many quarters. Among many inner-city African-Americans, the thought of becoming a police officer is offensive. There is deep-seated mistrust and hostility directed toward people in this career. It is very difficult to recruit minorities for employment with an agency that has a history of discrimination.

Among women, there is still the problem of sexual harassment. A January 10, 1993 segment of *60 Minutes* chronicled the allegations of sexual harassment within the Bureau of Alcohol, Tobacco, and Firearms. The allegations included female agents having sexual paraphernalia left on their desks, being physically accosted by other agents and supervisors, having used condoms placed in sandwiches, and being pressed for sexual favors by supervisors. It should be noted that the allegations were denied by high officials of ATF and investigations are still in progress.

Unfortunately, the complaints expressed by the ATF female officers are not unique. Many police agencies have poor reputations with regard to the treatment of female officers. As long as those practices persist, it will be difficult to convince women that they can have a fulfilling career with those agencies.

Women face still another problem. Research has shown that the public still regards police work as a male occupation. Citizens, including many women, view policewomen as less competent than their male counterparts (Sterling and Owen, 1982, p. 340). Having to overcome those perceptions may discourage many qualified women from viewing law enforcement as a possible career.

To date there is little research on the effectiveness of recruiting strategies for minorities and women. Logic dictates that a successful recruiting strategy would include sending recruiting officers of similar gender and race into locations where qualified candidates could be found. For women, college and university campuses seem to offer the most fruitful locations for recruitment. The same is frequently true of minorities. There are a number of institutions of higher education where the majority of students are racial minorities. African-American universities can be found throughout the nation, especially in the south, and there are a number of predominantly Hispanic universities in Texas and other southwestern and western states.

The reality of minority and female recruitment is that agencies must go where such recruits can be found. Passive recruitment, waiting for women and minorities to seek out the agency, has not worked very well. A two-pronged strategy would appear to offer the most opportunity. First, the agency must establish a solid reputation for equal treatment of all employees. Second, the agency must actively seek out qualified female and minority candidates in sufficient numbers to justify the expense of mobile recruiting.

SELECTION

The selection, or screening, process is designed to eliminate those potential candidates who fail to meet specified minimum standards for employment. The number of steps in the process varies from agency to agency depending on size, resources, and sophistication of the administration. There are anywhere from one to nine steps in the selection process (see Table 9-3). Each phase differs from the others in cost and purpose. Since cost is always a source of difficulty for public agencies, the steps in the selection procedure should be structured to eliminate the maximum number of candidates in the early (less costly) steps while placing the more costly procedures later in the process. The following procedures are recommended in the order in which they are provided. The relative costs, however, will vary from jurisdiction to jurisdiction and the administrator should vary the steps in accordance with those differences.

Application Forms

One of the most often overlooked screening devices is the application form. Often used to obtain background information from which to begin the screening process, when properly designed the application form can offer the most cost-effective type of screening. By carefully specifying job entrance requirements and requesting information directly related to these requirements, unqualified candidates will often eliminate themselves. In instances where unqualified candidates do not withdraw, a cursory examination of the application form will identify those failing to meet agency standards. Also, the form itself can serve a useful instrument when the background investigation is initiated; it serves the function of a road map to the candidate's past, thus providing the most useful information for obtaining information about the applicant's history.

It should be pointed out, however, that some information cannot be obtained through application forms. Laws concerning equal opportunity employment restrict an organization from requesting information that may be used to discriminate on the basis of race and sex.

Written Examinations

Another cost-effective method of screening recruits is the written examination. This is a relatively safe screening device due to the element of consistency in the written test procedures. The same level of knowledge and intellectual skills are required of all candidates. It appears to be fair to all applicants.

Unfortunately, there are problems with requiring a written examination. First, exams written by white middle-class personnel may contain unintended cultural bias. There is a natural tendency to address issues and problems from one's own perspectives. Individuals use language and examples with which they are most familiar, often resulting in the warping of statements toward a white middle-class perspective. This is such a subtle effect that administrators often believe that minority members fail the exam due to a lack of intelligence. The real reason may be minority applicants' unfamiliarity with the cultural differences of other groups..

Table 9-3
Screening Components

Procedure	Selectivity	Problems	Cost
Application form	High: self-selection and self-rejection of candidates coupled with early rejection of obviously unqualified candidates	None if well designed	Low
Written exam	High: eliminates large number of applicants who have problems analyzing written material	Weak relationship between test material and job perfomance	Low
Oral interviews	Medium: eliminates those who are weak in oral situations or who do not present themselves well	Subjective: vulnerable to challenge on basis of discrimination	Medium
Physical agility	High: eliminates those who lack sufficient physical conditioning or agility to pass test	Vulnerable to charge that entry standards are different from job requirements	Low
Background investigation	High: eliminates those with criminal record, poor work history, and weak character	None if done correctly	High
Medical exam	Medium: eliminates applicants for physical anomalies	Problems exist if physical condition is unrelated to job requirements	High
Polygraph	Medium: eliminates applicants for background problems not found in background investigation	Problems with reliability of the instrument; in some regions, polygraph is illegal	Medium: high if agency has polygraph examiner
Psychological	Low: eliminates applicants with undetected personality disorders	None so far. potential problem with the inability to determine appropriate personality type for police work	High
Probationary Period	Low: eliminates those who have passed all other steps, but who fail in real-world environment.	Dependent on random occurrence of events to develop informed opinion of performance	High: officer already screened

Another problem relates to the validity of the test itself. All entrance requirements must be job related to be valid. Applicants cannot be tested on their knowledge of the law or police procedure because they have not yet been trained in these areas. They must be evaluated on the basis of their potential to complete training and apply the often difficult abstractions presented by law and regulations. The difficulty lies in designing an examination to test potential rather than present knowledge, and to do so in a manner that does not involve cultural biases.

There are a number of civil service examinations currently in use that appear to be satisfactory. By focusing on memory, reading comprehension, and capability to resolve abstract problems, these exams appear to test potential. So far, these examinations have been upheld in court cases. Whether or not they are truly job related, however, is still open to question. As Larry Gaines and Victor Kappeler observed:

> It has been virtually impossible to develop written tests which predict which candidates will be "good" police officers. There are two reasons for this. First, there is little agreement in police circles as to what constitutes a good police officer, and even if there was agreement, a sufficiently sensitive written test to measure these traits probably would not be available. Second, since police departments screen out the unqualified or poor applicants, predictive validity studies are rarely feasible since the remaining officers are not representative of the potential selection population (1992, p. 118).

The bottom line is that research has not established any relationship between entrance test score and performance on the job. It may be asking too much of an entrance exam to predict future job performance. The issue of test validity remains crucial to continued use of the written exam, however, and test validity is best measured by how well it predicts job performance. The administrator would be well advised to pay close attention to future court cases dealing with preemployment examinations; this is a sensitive and controversial subject.

Interviews

The screening procedure most susceptible to abuse is the interview. It is ripe for abuse due to its less structured approach and the secrecy of the interviewer's deliberations. The interview itself may take a number of forms and appear at a variety of places in the screening process. There may be several different interviews by different personnel for different purposes. The cost of the interview is measured only in terms of time used by the interviewers. Thus cost-effectiveness is measured only on the basis of whether or not the time of the people involved could be better expended elsewhere.

The first type of interview is the personnel interview. This interview is conducted by a person assigned to the screening team. The purpose of this interview is to obtain further information about the candidate not already on the application. It is also used to clarify information on the application. Often, unqualified candidates apply because they do not know if they possess the required qualities. A quick, informal interview can usually determine if the candidate is really qualified or if perhaps this person neglected to report negative items or perhaps overemphasized good qualities. In any case, the personnel interview is usually a quick and inexpensive method of screening out the unqualified prior to the intensive screening processes.

The next type of interview is the oral board. The board is a panel interview designed to allow a group of people to interview a candidate simultaneously. This offers an excellent opportunity to observe the candidate under stress and to observe the person's ability to think and communicate with an array of different types of people. Generally, there are two kinds of oral boards, nonstress and stress. The *nonstress interview* is simply an interview. No direct attempt is made to place the candidate under stress, although even the nonstress interview is stressful to some extent. In nonstress interviews the focus of the process is on the gathering of information about the candidate and the attempt to assess the person's capability to fit into the agency.

The other style of oral board is the *stress interview.* In this form the interviewers take a position of hostility toward the candidate. The interviewers assume the role of adversaries attempting to force the candidate into a disqualifying mistake. The focus in this kind of process is emotional; the interviewers attempt to push the candidate verbally into an emotional outburst of some kind. Confusion, anger, despair, fear, and frustration are the goals of the stress interview, and success for the candidate means maintaining poise in the face of a verbal assault.

There are problems associated with interviews of all types, but it is difficult to find even a trace of justification for the stress interview. Anyone subjected to a sufficiently hostile, irrational attack can be goaded into an emotional response; this proves nothing. Also, stress interviews become so thoroughly preoccupied with generating emotional outbursts that they cease to gather useful information from the candidate. In short, the stress interview generates no useful information and generally manages to establish the candidate as having human qualities; a fact already known.

Other problems with interviews center around their unstructured nature. As with other employment requirements, interviews must be conducted consistently with all candidates to remain fair. The unstructured interview fails to accomplish this. Instead, it meanders around a variety of topics so that no two candidates are exposed to a similar experience. This is of questionable legality, especially if the final result is elimination of a disproportional number of minorities and women. The fear of legal attack has led many law enforcement agencies to retain the interview, but without using it to eliminate candidates. This is not practical; no agency can afford to maintain a screening procedure that does not screen. A better approach is to structure the interview to ensure its fairness to all candidates.

The structured interview is one in which the interviewers must ask the same questions of each candidate. This does not prohibit the interviewers from further enquiry into an area of concern discovered in the interview process, but it requires that each interview seek the same basic information.

The structuring of the interview also introduces another problem inherent in preemployment interviewing. The purpose of the interview is to establish the degree to which the candidate will fit into the agency's philosophy. The question arises as to whose philosophy is being used as the standard in this phase. Ideally, the administrator should outline the agency's philosophy. Unfortunately, this is rarely the case. Instead, the philosophy is determined by the interviewer. Often, the personnel conducting the interview do so without guidelines as to how it should proceed. As a result, they conform it to their own concepts of what is valuable in a police officer and may disregard the organizational ideals. This is one more reason for structuring the interview. By establishing structure, the chief executive determines organizational philosophy and all applicants can be measured against this standard. Interviewers can be trained to ask a specific list of questions and be able to identify those answers conforming to organizational standards.

Despite the extensive use of oral interviews, studies conducted on the oral interview process are not very encouraging. One such study found that validity problems in the oral interview process would pose a serious threat to the police agency in a discrimination suit (Gaines and Lewis, 1982).

In another study, researchers attempted to establish concurrent validity within the oral board process. They were unable to do so; none of the job-related factors had sufficiently high correlations with board scores (Falkenberg, Gaines, and Cox, 1990). A second problem appeared as a result of this study. The researchers found that female raters tended to discriminate against minority candidates. While the findings of these research projects are based on a single agency, administrators should be forewarned. The oral interview process is fraught with legal dangers that cannot be ignored.

There are ways to minimize the dangers of the oral interview. Gaines and Kappeler have identified four procedures that can be implemented that will enhance the legality of the interview process (1992, pp. 120–121):

1. The number of rating dimensions should be minimal; no more than five. This reduces the amount of rater information processing and decision making.

2. The raters should be trained so that they clearly understand the process and how responses should be graded.

3. The rating scales should use behavioral anchors (as opposed to numerical or adjectival scales) so that raters will have standards to compare with candidate responses.

4. Great care should be taken when selecting the rating dimensions. They should be clearly understood by the raters and amenable to measurement.

These steps will not eliminate legal problems totally but they will tend to make the oral interview a more objective process.

Physical Agility Tests

The physical agility test is a relative newcomer to most law enforcement agencies. Although most fire departments and some police agencies have used this form of testing for some time, only within the past 20 years have most agencies adopted the procedure. Oddly enough, it seems to have become very popular immediately following court decisions requiring the hiring of females for police work. Some might leap to the conclusion that physical agility courses were designed to eliminate potential female police officers.

Although the foregoing conclusion may or may not be true, a minimum requirement for physical fitness and coordination for police officers is legitimate. It is legitimate as long as the requirements are applied consistently to all officers performing the same duties and as long as applicants are given sufficient training and practice time to give the best possible personal performance. If the physical agility course results in the elimination of a candidate, it should be the course itself causing the failure rather than the method in which the test is administered. The course should also be related to the types of physical duties required as a routine part of the job. The course should be a fair measure of potential police performance.

Background Investigation

One of the more critical steps in the selection process is the background investigation. It is also the one step consistently done in a slipshod fashion. Of all the law enforcement agencies in this country, perhaps the federal government does the best job of investigating the history of job applicants. For the most part, background investigations are conducted by contacting references supplied by the candidate and running a computerized check of arrest and conviction records. Applicants from a different jurisdiction often do not even receive this type of an investigation.

The purpose of the background investigation is to assess the person's character based on past behavior. We can assume that anyone with any sense at all will provide positive character references. References are most useful when they provide names of the candidate's acquaintances not listed as references. These, and other names they can provide, offer a better and less biased source of information concerning the applicant. No background investigation should ever stop with an interview of listed character references; this is a waste of time and effort and serves no purpose. The background investigation should continue to expand until the investigator has sufficient information regarding the moral character and history of the applicant.

Medical Examination

The medical examination is necessary to ensure that the applicant is medically fit to perform the duties of the occupation. It also prevents the agency from hiring people with chronic medical problems that will prevent them from fulfilling a complete law enforcement career.

The medical exam, or physical as it is sometimes called, is also the subject of some controversy. Many agencies have physical requirements dating back over 50 years. Some of these are obsolete. For example, many police departments will still not take applicants with flat feet even though medical science has alleviated the problems associated with this condition. The problem with medical requirements is that many police organizations created their own standards based on the subjective assessment of police administrators or by attempting to adapt the physical requirements of the armed forces.

The proper method of determining adequate physiological standards is by submitting the job description to a panel of medical personnel to allow the experts to establish the requirements. Once again, as always, it appears that the major difficulty in setting standards is decision making by personnel lacking sufficient knowledge of the subject to make good decisions.

The medical exam is a necessary step, but the requirements must be realistic. Also, the exam must be conducted by physicians who can be trusted to be thorough. Too many physicals are done rapidly in a haphazard manner. This defeats the purpose of the exam while maintaining the high cost involved.

Polygraph Examination

The polygraph, or lie detector as it is incorrectly titled, is useful as a means of verifying information on the candidate's application. Although useful, this instrument is often relied upon instead of a good background investigation. The polygraph was not meant for this purpose; it is better used to verify information supported by other means.

A problem with the polygraph lies in its dependence on human judgment to assess the results of the test. This means that the outcome is based on subjective rather than objective criteria. The machine itself may never make a mistake, but operator abilities vary among people. The results of a polygraph exam alone should never be used to justify the elimination of an applicant; negative information should be supported by other sources before the value of the data is accepted. This, by the way, is a good rule to apply to polygraph tests in any situation, including criminal cases.

The polygraph can be very useful, but it has its limitations. The danger lies in believing that it is the ultimate in screening devices. The most appropriate way of thinking about the polygraph is its use as a truth verifier rather than a lie detector.

One other limitation on the use of the polygraph is imposed by regulation. Some states have prohibited the use of the polygraph in employment situations. Still others allow its use, but under severe restrictions. The polygraph may therefore not be an option in some organizations.

Psychological Examinations

The psychological examination has its uses. Like the polygraph, it also has its limitations. When first instituted, there were some who believed in the ability of the psychological exam to solve the problems of screening out mentally unfit officers. This overestimates the capacity of this type of test. The psychological test is based on the assumptions of a normal population distribution. Exams are created by testing thousands of "normal people" and computing the scores to determine the average. The same exam is then given to patients in a mental hospital or those who have been diagnosed as "abnormal." These scores are then computed to obtain an average. The two averages are compared to determine the range of scores. From this basis the exam is given and scores compared against previously established norms. The test is therefore able to identify those clearly in the normal range and those clearly in the abnormal range, but anything else is asking more than many tests can give. The value of the exam is its ability to pick out people with borderline psychological problems, and this alone makes the tests worthwhile.

The real problem, though, lies in the inability of the tests to predict those who while pyschologically healthy now may suffer pychological difficulties later under the pressure of the job. No psychological test has yet been devised to solve this problem. Psychological testing is useful, but it is no panacea.

Probationary Period

The probationary period is not normally considered a screening procedure, but it does fulfill a screening function. The probation period is the time period in which the organization can assess the new officer and determine if the person has the potential to make a good officer. This period should be at least one year in length after the completion of training. Ideally, this period should be 18 months or more. Sufficient time is needed to allow a careful evaluation of the new officer under the actual stress of the job. Since the ability to evaluate the officer is dependent on activities beyond the control of the administration, the organization must have enough time to allow for a sufficient number of incidents to determine the person's capabilities and to determine the officer's rate of growth in the job. Thus the longer the probationary period the better, within limitations, A 5 to 10 year probationary period seems a bit extreme.

Postentry Staffing

A few organizations have sought applicants for supervisory or managerial positions from outside the organization. This is a feasible concept that is not used often enough. In these cases the screening process should be similar, but with added emphasis on the background investigation. A review of the applicant's performance in his or her current position should provide a good understanding of this person's potential within the hiring organization.

STAFFING THE KNOWLEDGE-BASED DEPARTMENT

The police selection system just outlined is based on the traditional model of policing. The emphasis in the past has been on physical requirements rather than intellect or communication skills. This is changing, for very good reasons. Those reasons and the changing nature of police selection are discussed in this section.

Fallacies of the Selection Process

There is a significant difference in staffing a public service organization and recruiting soldiers. With the adoption of the military model by the police, the resulting hiring criteria were predictable. The military needs personnel who are capable of operating under inclement conditions miles away from either supplies or support. They must therefore be in top physical condition. As a general rule, soldiers are young.

Youth has several advantages. First, young people are usually in the physical prime of their lives. They are easily conditioned and find it easy to stay in good condition. Second, young people are more easily led. They are quicker to show respect and to follow orders.

The result of using the military philosophy as a hiring criterion for law enforcement was focus on youth and physical ability as the most important features of a new recruit. Only recently has the military placed any premium on evaluating intelligence. Unfortunately, the same is true of many police agencies.

An additional problem with the military is the fundamental belief that combat is a male occupation. Although this may or may not be true, the adoption of the military model for the police meant that women had a difficult time entering the ranks of law enforcement. For many, police work is seen as akin to combat—ergo, policing is a man's job.

Despite a growing body of research to the contrary, police agencies still put too much emphasis on age and physical ability as criteria for employment. There is still a deep-seated belief that police work is primarily a physical occupation. The sad fact is that too many police agencies pass over applicants with higher intellect and better communication skills for applicants with better physical qualifications. This has always been a questionable practice; in the future the result could be disastrous.

As mentioned above, a by-product of the military model is the emphasis on youth. Police agencies have demanded young officers; most have upper age limits at around 35 years. There are a number of problems with this. First, only recently have police agencies truly placed any emphasis on physical fitness. In many agencies the lack of emphasis on physical fitness is still all too apparent.

Scholars are beginning to ask the question, "If physical fitness is so important to police applicants, why is it not equally important to working officers?"

The answer is simple. Physical fitness is important to anyone wishing to maintain good personal health. Police work, however, requires only occasional exertions of physical energy; the police occupation is generally sedentary. Officers do not have to be in particularly good physical shape to perform effectively. The agency looks more professional if the officers are in good physical shape, and more administrators are beginning to believe strongly in physical fitness. The duties of a police officer, however, rarely require a high level of physical ability or fitness.

The second problem related to age is in the area of maturity. Major police agencies are placing young adults into situations they are not prepared to handle. Research has shown that police brutality is more a product of immaturity than of sadism or authoritarianism. Immature people strike out when they are threatened.

Most young police officers, including those with college educations, have had little experience with responsibility or authority prior to becoming police officers. According to police psychologist Larry Blum, today's police recruits have less prior work experience than their predecessors, and they lack a sense of mission or purpose (Krauss, 1986, p. 7). Moreover, because of the lack of work experience, many young officers frustrate easily and react badly to discipline. They tend to view work as a means to an end; it is seen as a job, not a commitment. Many times their reading and writing skills are sub-par and they tend to give highest priority to interests away from the job (Osborn, 1992, pp. 24–25). This is the reality of the current applicant pool.

Young people are recruited, sent to training classes (not much different from their college or high-school classrooms) and then sent into the inner city to interact with people whose values, life-styles, and communication styles may be very-different. These young officers become fearful; they overreact in tense situations.

Young officers are placed in these situations because of tradition and/or labor agreements. They may be the wrong people in the wrong place at the wrong time. The majority of major police departments in the United States make this mistake. The cost of this error is massive. There is a high turnover rate, especially among female officers, many of whom are even more stressed in this environment than their male counterparts. There is an increased level of police shootings, a high level of complaints of brutality, and abuse of authority. Neither the department nor the community is served by these policies, but they persist. At the heart of the problem is the fact that officers are too immature for these assignments.

The problem with age is exacerbated by the need for agencies to change. The military model brings people into the organization who are ripe for integration into the police subculture. They buy into police mythology "lock, stock, and barrel." The result is that the kinds of people being hired by law enforcement agencies are those who are most vulnerable to the seduction of the subculture and the least able to change. Police administrators are hiring the very people who will prevent agencies from evolving into more effective institutions.

Realities of the Future Labor Pool

There are a number of demographic trends that should serve as a warning to police administrators concerned with maintaining a full complement of sworn personnel. First, we are an aging society. Competition for young recruits will increase in all sectors of the economy. Second, the demand for college-educated personnel is increasing across all sectors of the economy. This is especially true of minorities. Third, one of the reasons for the increased demand for more educated personnel is rapidly evolving technology, which requires more sophisticated personnel.

Problem-oriented and community-oriented policing are knowledge-based models of policing. They require intelligence, maturity, and the ability to communicate both in writing and with the spoken word. Moreover, the adaptation of modern technology to such tasks as criminalistics, crime analysis, and patrol administration place uneducated officers at a severe disadvantage.

The future labor pool will be older and more heterogeneous; during the next 10 years, only 25 percent of those entering the work force will be white males; two-thirds will be female (Osborn, 1992, p. 22). By the year 2010, more than one-third of all American children will be African-American, Hispanic, or Asian (Trojanowicz and Carter, 1990, p. 6). By the year 2000, the percentage of the population between 16 and 24 will shrink from 30 percent to 16 percent (Creton, Rocha, and Luckins, 1988, p. 64). How police organizations match the people in this pool to their own needs will determine the effectiveness of those organizations.

In some respects, the changing face of the nation will benefit law enforcement. As the labor pool changes, so must police recruiting practices. Already the upper age limitation for law enforcement has come under attack.

In previous years, law enforcement agencies have been exempt from age discrimination laws. A recent study, however, has recommended that this exemption be lifted. According to the study:

> "The project team found from their review of duties that the responsibilities of public safety officers only occasionally involve direct threat to the well-being of citizens and/or fellow officers. It further found that the base rate for the occurrence of catastrophic medical events leading to sudden incapacitation in the workplace is generally low and not well predicted by age" (Epps, 1992, p. 14).

As a result of the study cited above and the growing recognition that age and physical fitness are meaningless predictors of police performance, upper age limitations will probably disappear in the near future. This is good news. Given the problems associated with immaturity, a better argument can be made for hiring officers 35 or older rather than those who are 35 or younger.

Another advantage of older officers is that they are less susceptible to the effects of occupational psychosis (see Chapter 8); they are less likely to be impressed with the subculture. More mature and perhaps better educated, these are the officers who are the most likely to support change—indeed, to demand change.

But where does a police administrator find older, educated applicants? Everywhere. The U.S. military is currently downsizing. Officers in their late 20s and early to mid-30s, all college educated and all with experience in positions of authority, are now available for police service. Moreover, this has always been the case. Reserve officers have always been subject to mandatory retirement at around age 30 to 40. The Air Force alone reduces its force by hundreds of officers each year.

Of course, this brings with it the possibility of hiring recruits who are oriented to a military philosophy. Since that is a philosophy that needs to change in law enforcement, a large influx of ex-military personnel could have some drawbacks. It is important, therefore, that such personnel who are selected for police work be able to adapt to a different philosophy. Given that these are educated, mature individuals, most of their impact on the organization should be positive.

The private sector is also a prime area for recruiting police candidates. Each year thousands of men and women discover that life in the business world can be ruthless, unfulfilling, and boring. Many would gladly seek employment in the field of law enforcement. Many police administrators would be amazed at the number of accountants, managers, and lawyers who would forsake the world of private industry for a career in law enforcement. Police administrators have never considered this a source for employees; they have never recruited from this group.

The fact is that police agencies have never really recruited anyone—not in the way that other industries recruit. That may change. If police agencies are to compete for the best and brightest, they will be forced to become much more aggressive in their recruiting strategies.

Identifying Realistic Qualifications

What precisely do the police do? We have dealt with that subject from Chapter 1 onward. The answer to the question is both simple and complex. In its simplest form, police officers communicate; they talk to people and write reports. In its more complex form, they do anything and everything asked of them by the public.

The first criterion for an effective law enforcement officer, therefore, is the ability to communicate effectively. Beyond that, the needs expand exponentially. The more knowledge the officer possesses about more topics, the greater the ability of this person to respond to a variety of complex situations. Moreover, the ever-increasing reliance on sophisticated technology requires officers with an understanding of both the uses and limitations of this technology.

The second criterion for an effective law enforcement officer, therefore, is education and training. Since training is provided by the agency, the new recruit must have the education prior to seeking employment with a police agency.

The effective police officer must be able to communicate with diverse groups and individuals, and must be able to empathize with those who have different values and different goals. This person must be able to function in crisis situations—must maintain control of internal emotions so that the situation can be controlled. In short, this person must have a good understanding of self and others and must bring calm and reason to situations where none exist.

The third criterion is maturity. Whether this is a product of age, experience, or family background, maturity is absolutely critical for dealing with the vast array of volatile emotions that occur in the course of handling disputes and criminal episodes.

From a physical perspective, police officers must be able to perform the following tasks:

1. *Walk and run.* Every officer at one time or another will probably walk a beat. All will be forced at some time to get out of the police car and walk up a flight of stairs or into a rural area for which there is no road. Sometimes an officer has to run a short distance.

2. *Drive a motor vehicle.* Every police officer will be expected to operate a motor vehicle. Any physical disability that prevents the applicant from doing this should disqualify the applicant from police work.

3. *Complete a 20- to 25-year career.* It is not reasonable to ask any organization, public or private, to employ someone whose physical condition may bring about forced medical retirement or recurring medical leaves. Chronic medical conditions, depending on their nature and severity, could be considered grounds for rejection.

4. *Use police equipment.* Every officer will be expected to use agency equipment including, but not limited to computer terminals or typewriters, radios, firearms, and any other items of equipment designed to enhance police effectiveness. Anyone who cannot use the equipment is at a disadvantage and should be denied employment with a police agency.

Within these limitations, police agencies should set their physical standards. They need be no more stringent. The nature of the modern police force does not require extensive physical qualifications. Intellect and communication skills are what is needed.

DISCUSSION QUESTIONS

1. Describe the job analysis process. Why is this important?

2. What impact has the military model had on police recruitment and hiring practices?

3. Discuss the utility of various screening devices that a police agency might employ in its selection process.

4. Should recruiting personnel and screening personnel be different? Why?

5. Should there be differences between hiring standards using the traditional police model versus those of the knowledge-based models? Why?

REFERENCES

Blackburn, D. (1991). "Provisions of ADA brings new challenges to police hiring practices," *Subject to Debate.,* Vol.3, No. 5.

Bopp, William J. (1974). *Police Personnel Management.* Boston: Holbrook Press.

Creton, Marvin J., Wanda Rocha, and Rebecca Luckins (1988). "Into the 21st century, longterm trends affecting the United States," *The Futurist,* July/August, pp. 62–67.

Epps, Cheryl Anthony (1992). "Penn State study recommends elimination of ADEA public safety exemption," *The Police Chief,* May, p. 14.

Falkenberg, S., L. K. Gaines, and T. C. Cox (1990). "The oral interview board: what does it measure?" *Journal of Police Science and Administration,* Vol. 17, No. 1, pp. 32–39.

Forkiotis, C. J. (1981). "Vision requirements and the police officer selection process," *The Police Chief,* November, p. 56.

Gaines, Larry K. and Victor E. Kappeler (1992). "Selection and testing," in Gary W. Cordner and Donnas Hale, eds., *What Works in Policing? Operations and Administration Examined.* Cincinnati, Ohio: Anderson Publishing Company and Academy of Criminal Justice Sciences, pp. 107–123.

_____ and B. R. Lewis (1982). "Reliability and validity of the oral interview board in police promotions: a research note," *Journal of Criminal Justice,* Vol. 10, pp. 63–79.

Goldstein, Herman (1977). *Policing a Free Society.* Cambridge, Mass.: Ballinger.

Holden, Richard N. (1984)."Vision standards for law enforcement: a descriptive study," *Journal of Police Science and Administration.* Vol. 12, No. 2, (June) pp. 125–129.

Holden, Richard N. (June, 1993) "Eyesight standards: Correcting the myths" *FBI Law Enforcement Bulletin*, Vol. 62, No .6., pp. 1–6.

Kraus, Robert A. (1986). *How Will the Changing Work Force Impact Law Enforcement Human Resources Practices in the Year 1995?:* Sacramento, California Commission on Peace Officer Standards and Training.

Long, Lydia (March 1992). "The Americans with Disabilities Act of 1990 and law enforcement employment: notes and comments," paper presented at the Academy of Criminal Justice Sciences Annual Conference, Pittsburgh, Pa.

Osborn, Ralph S. (1992). "Police recruitment: today's standard—tomorrow's challenge," *FBI Law Enforcement Bulletin,* June, pp. 21–25.

Robbins, Stephen P. (1980). *The Administrative Process,* 2nd ed. Englewood Cliffs, N. J.: Prentice Hall.

Sterling, B. and J. Owen, (June 1982). "Perceptions of demanding versus reasoning: male and female officers," *Personality and Social Psychology Bulletin,Vol.* 8, No.2, pp. 336–340.

Trojanowicz, Robert C. and David L.Carter (1990). "The changing face of America," *FBI Law Enforcement Bulletin,* January, p. 6.

Wambaugh, Joseph (1984). *Lines and Shadows.* New York: William Morrow.

Chapter 10

Labor Relations

L aw enforcement is a people business. Nowhere is this more evident than in the complex relationship between the operational personnel and management. An unfortunate legacy of American management during the early years of the nation's history is a basic distrust of management by labor. In far too many organizations the workers believe that the administration is out to get them, while the managers view the workers as undependable and untrustworthy. Rather than work together toward a common goal, many organizations are locked in mortal combat with themselves. When that happens in a police agency, the result is ineffectiveness, anger, and bitterness.

In this chapter we will look at the relationship between management and labor within police agencies. We will gain a better understanding of why and how problems develop between labor and management. Additionally, ways are identfed in which problems are resolved.

THE EVOLUTION OF POLICE UNIONS

Unionization in the public sector was quite a few years behind the development of the private-sector labor movement. There are several reasons for this slower development. First, the government had legal mechanisms available to squelch a fledgling labor movement where the private sector did not. Second, the general public held the opinion that public servants, especially police and fire personnel, were essential to the safety and welfare of the people. Labor actions, such as a strike, by these groups were seen as an attack on the people and were therefore unlawful.

As with private industry, the public was unaware of the working conditions that spawned labor organizations. It would take decades before private-sector unions were accepted. Police unions have not been fully accepted in some parts of the country today. The first real attempt at establishing a strong police labor organization occurred in Boston. The result was the Boston police strike of 1919.

The Boston Police Strike

The Boston police strike was one of those rare events that was projected beyond its own time and place. It propelled Calvin Coolidge, the previously unknown and unheralded governor of Massachusetts, into the White House. At the same time it all but crushed the fledgling police labor movement and made it virtually impossible for a large police organization to institute a labor strike, a situation that is still true today (Russell, 1975, p. 1).

The causes of the Boston police strike are all too easily identified. The mystery is why it took so long for dissatisfaction to bloom into action. The problems seem to stem from four factors crucial to effective management. First, the pay was atrocious. The average police officer made less than an unskilled worker. This problem was exacerbated by the rapid growth in the industrial sector. Unskilled factory workers not only made more money, but there was also the availability of as much overtime as a factory worker wanted or could handle.

The second factor was working conditions, most notably hours. Had the officers received the same pay as the unskilled laborers, they would have been hard pressed to engage in the same kinds of celebration. Police officers worked a 7-day week, with one day off in 15. Day men put in 73 hours a week, night men worked 83 hours, and wagon men 98. In addition, day men had to spend one additional night a week in the station on reserve. Even in their free time, police officers could not leave the city without permission (Russell, 1975, p. 50).

The third factor was the capriciousness of the extra duties. Officers were assigned to delivering unpaid tax bills, surveying rooming houses, taking the census, and watching the polls at elections. Additionally, they were assigned to every kind of function, from band concerts to parades, and Boston had numerous parades. More irksome was the way that patrolmen were treated by supervisors and administrators. Promotion was in the hands of the captains, who tended to promote those they liked without regard to competence or experience. Patrolmen were often sent on errands by captains and higher-ups. They were required to bring in lunches and Sunday dinners for the administrators. They would pick up "free" daily newspapers for the commanders. One superintendent even complained about his free newspaper arriving late (Russell, 1975, p. 51)!

Finally, the physical conditions of the 19 station houses were deplorable. The majority of these were old, overcrowded, decaying, rodent infested, and vermin ridden. Beds were used by at least two, sometimes four, men in succession in a 24-hour period. The man coming off-duty would merely push the sleeping man out of bed and take his place. Bedbugs and roaches swarmed in the sleeping quarters; at one station the bugs were so voracious that they ate the leather of the police helmets and belts (Russell, 1975, p. 52).

Complicating these factors was the ever-increasing demand for police service. In 1906 the police force had 1,358 officers; by 1917 the number was 1,877. During the same time span, however, arrests jumped from 49,906 to 108,556. Additional responsibilities were also added. For example, the Boston police was responsible for checking the background and character of some 20,000 potential jurors (Russell, 1975, p. 52). It was clear that the Boston police force had been stretched to its capacity and beyond. Something had to give.

In June 1919, the American Federation of Labor reversed its policy of not allowing police departments entities to join. The fire department had already affiliated with the AFL; the Boston police saw this as their opportunity to gain bargaining power. The city government, backed by the governor's office, issued an order directly outlawing police membership in any social or fraternal organization. The battle lines were being drawn. Against the orders of their commanders and governmental officials, a police union was formed. This led to disciplinary action, including suspensions and dismissals.

By September 1919 escalation was inevitable. The Boston police went on strike. By the time the strike ended, a mere 24 officers remained at their posts. What resulted was general rioting, looting, and sporadic violence as the less reputable members of Boston society seized the opportunity to run wild in an unpoliced city.

Those running within mobs had some degree of safety as order broke down. To the individual, however, being caught on the street was dangerous. Women were especially in peril. Lone women caught on the street were often beaten, robbed, and gang-raped, sometimes in front of hundreds of onlookers.

The strike started on a Tuesday. By Wednesday it became necessary to call in the Massachusetts State Guard to restore order. Bolstered by a force of volunteer police officers, including Harvard's football team, order was finally restored.

As for the striking police officers, they were dismissed from the force. Not one was ever rehired. Many had difficulty finding jobs elsewhere in the city; it seems that no one wanted to hire an ex Boston police officer. In the aftermath, antiunion feelings were so rampant that even the Boston firefighters quietly returned their union charter to the AFL. Police unionization had been set back 20 years (Gaines, Southerland, and Angell, 1991, p. 303).

Police Unions Today

The movement to unionize police agencies lay dormant for many years. It was not until the early 1960s that unions began to make major inroads in the public sector in general and the police in particular. This era had an especially profound impact on law enforcement, in terms of both size and public exposure.

The increase in police labor organizations was the result of a number of factors. Civil disobedience and rioting forced the police into the spotlight. This was not always good, but it did highlight the need for increased standards. With the movement toward police professionalism came the recognition that officers should receive salary and benefits comparable to those of private-sector workers.

Reliance on antiquated wage scales and inadequate procedures for obtaining increases in the wages added to the problem. The fact that the political structure of most police agencies provided no means for employee input into either wages or benefits made things worse (Stanley, 1972). In an era when citizens were voicing their complaints on any topic, especially the performance of the police, law enforcement officers found that they had no voice at all. They needed a voice; an organization that would speak for police officers as a collective body. The solution for many was a police organization. The union made a dramatic reappearance.

There were other factors that contributed to the growth of public-sector unions. Three additional developments have been attributed to this phenomenon (Thibault, Lynch, and McBride, 1990, p. 396):

> **1.** An expansion of governmental services coupled by an increase in government employees.
>
> **2.** A continued policy by the federal government that supported the right of public and private workers to unionize and bargain collectively. For the public sector, this culminated in 1962 with President Kennedy's signing of Executive Order 10988, which allowed most federal employees to organize unions and bargain collectively. Further refinements of Executive Order 10988 were signed by Presidents Johnson, Nixon, and Ford.
>
> **3.** A significant decline in union membership in the private sector. This trend forced many private union organizations to look for new membership, readily available in the public sector.

The 1980s, however, witnessed a slowdown in police unionism. Partly this was a product of the recession of 1981-1983. Unions began to realize that economic realities precluded any further dramatic gains in wages and benefits (Sapp, 1985: p. 418). That being the case, unions seemed less necessary to many officers; for many this is still true.

The Unionization Process

People do not join unions for positive reasons. The creation of a body whose sole purpose is to confront management is not done either lightly or in good cheer. In the past police officers, more than most, have rejected the very idea of joining a union. They have seen police unions as being antiethical to the public welfare. Believing that strikes or serious job actions were not in the public interest, police officers in many areas have consistently rejected the idea of a police union. That police officers have chosen to join a union, especially to the degree that they have done so over the past 20 years, is indicative of a troubled labor–management relationship.

The reasons for joining a union vary from agency to agency. In most cases, however, it can be traced to one or more of the following reasons (Crane, 1979; Sirene, 1981):

1. Unsatisfactory working conditions
2. Opportunity for advancement
3. Lack of grievance procedure
4. Low salary
5. Need to be recognized
6. Poor communications

Unionization is usually a by-product of perceived managerial arrogance and worker exploitation. Even where this is not the case, the officers may feel the need for an organization to represent their interests. Usually, this is because they do not feel the formal organization is providing that service in an adequate manner.

The creation of a police union does not, however, mean endless confrontations and job actions by police personnel. On the contrary, the confrontational phase of a police union is usually of short duration. As with formal organizations that go through phases, so, too, do unions evolve.

As the union evolves, it will change, as will its relationship with management. Allen Sapp has identified three phases of police union development: the initial phase, consolidation phase, and institutionalized phase (1985, p. 414).

Initial phase: encompasses the period of organization of the union through the period where it is recognized as a collective bargaining unit by the employer.

Consolidation phase: begins when the union gains a degree of acceptance by management and police officers and seeks to consolidate its position and power.

Institutionalized phase: the final phase in the development of a police union where the union becomes almost an integral part of the organizational structure of the employing agency.

The evolution of the police union is a fascinating process. At the beginning, the union is almost universally hostile to management. The union will attempt to gain power and prestige through confrontation. Initially, membership will be limited as only the most alienated of the officers will join. The organization's goals will be to attain acceptance by both management and other officers.

As the union develops, goals and activities change. The organization becomes larger and more accepted. It still opts for controversial activities but is more flexible in dealing with management. Rather than calling for strikes as in the initial phase, the more mature union uses less dramatic job actions.

Finally, the mature union evolves. This organization is very much in tune with police management. It has become coopted; it is, in a sense, part of the management team. The mature union seeks arbitration to resolve differences with management. Membership in the union is accepted and universal, but the members are less committed to the union or its goals. In effect, the union has become an institution in and of itself. It will have its own administrative staff, a fairly substantial budget, and its primary goal will be maintaining the organization in as noncontroversial an atmosphere as possible (Sapp, 1985, pp. 414–418).

Pros and Cons of Police Unions

The police labor movement has produced both positive and negative results. Most of the benefits have been to the advantage of the officers; the negative aspects appear to have affected management and the public. The first and most obvious product of the police labor movement has been in the area of wages and fringe benefits. Over the past 20 years, police salary scales have increased dramatically. This has been parallel to the growth and increased power of police labor organizations. Fringe benefits have also increased; many departments have benefit packages on a par with those in private industry.

The second result of the labor movement has been the creation of highly structured hiring, promotion, and grievance systems within police organizations. Those agencies with well-organized labor organizations quickly disposed of the "good ole boy" network for promotions and choice assignments. The necessity to negotiate promotion and job assignment processes effectively negated systems based on personal friendships and loyalties.

Finally, the necessity to negotiate salary and working conditions has forced management to adopt personnel practices that are acceptable to everyone. The arbitrariness of old management policies was an early victim of collective bargaining. Overall, the impact on police organizations internally has been positive.

Sadly, not all aspects of the labor movement have been good for law enforcement. From the perspective of management, some of the losses have been substantial. Highest on police administrators' list of complaints about collective bargaining agreements were the loss of management prerogatives; those organizational decisions traditionally reserved for management. In a national survey almost 50 percent of the administrators surveyed stated that management prerogatives had been lost as a result of collective bargaining (Sapp, Carter, and Stephens, 1990, p. 6).

The public has also suffered, but less directly. Some of the lost management prerogatives deal with discipline. In many unionized departments the chief executives argue that it is difficult to dismiss a bad officer; the procedural protections negotiated by unions for their members are often significant. Although this has undoubtedly provided protection against unjust accusations and punishment for police officers, it has also increased the difficulty level of a supervisor attempting to administer discipline. A chief of police in an east coast city, for example, remarked that under the terms of the labor contract, he was able to test his officers for drugs any time he wished as long as he gave the officers 30 days' notice that they were to be tested. Clearly, the notification process demanded by the union defeated the purpose of the drug testing program.

Moreover, in its attempt to gain wide acceptance, the union will often attempt to negotiate promotion and assignment processes that favor seniority over competence. The end result of effective bargaining on the part of the union may well be to reduce managerial effectiveness to the point where there is some question as to who runs the agency. The by-product of the management–labor impasse is sometimes institutionalized mediocrity; an organization dedicated more toward keeping the officers happy than to organizational effectiveness.

It need not be this way. Collective bargaining means just that—bargaining. By the admission of many police administrators, the majority of managerial pre-rogatives lost through the bargaining process have been lost due to bargaining ineptitude on the part of management. Too often, unprepared police administrators have found themselves negotiating against professional union negotiators. The result in those cases was that the managers "gave away the farm."

As the bargaining process has become more professional on both sides, the results of the bargaining have become more rational. The end result has been generally beneficial for both parties.

COLLECTIVE BARGAINING

Collective bargaining refers to right of employees to negotiate the conditions of their employment. Practically any aspect of the employment can be negotiated. In reality, however, there are aspects that are usually considered the sole domain of management. These areas are sometimes negotiated but only when the labor organization is overwhelmingly strong or management weak or indecisive.

The term *collective bargaining* refers to both process and outcome. It implies the existence of an organized employee group, contract negotiations, and a grievance procedure. The goal of this process is a contractual agreement suitable to both the employees and to management.

Standards concerning collective bargaining have been published by the Commission on Accreditation for Law Enforcement Agencies. These standards were developed because of the disparity found among agencies that engage in collective bargaining. The standards include the following (Commission on Accreditation for Law Enforcement Agencies, 1984):

1. Development of a written directive describing the role of the agency in the collective bargaining process

2. Establishment of a collective bargaining team with one member as the principal negotiator

3. Specification of the bargaining unit

4. Development of impasse-resolving procedures

5. Creation of ground rules prior to negotiation

6. Adoption of the principle of good faith bargaining based on the Taft-Hartley Act

7. A written record in the form of a contract or an agreement signed by both parties

8. Distribution of the agreement to all supervisory and management personnel

Obtaining the Right to Bargain

The first step in the negotiating process is the creation of an employee organization. This is not as easy as it sounds. Factions within the employee group may have different ideas about what is best for the employees. There are agencies with multiple labor organizations. Usually, these are very large agencies with multiple needs. A governmental body might be willing to negotiate with a police officer's union, sergeant's union and lieutenant's union, but few management teams will accede to negotiations with three different police officer's unions. There must be a single voice for the employee group. This is a basic organizational problem that must be overcome prior to gaining recognition. Also, there must be sufficient employee support to organize initially, or the entire effort is wasted.

Federal laws prohibit management from interfering with the creation of a labor union. Employees may form their own or they may vote to join one that already exists. There are advantages and disadvantages to each approach. Locally controlled organizations provide more autonomy for the members and are usually less expensive in terms of dues. They also lack the political clout of the fully developed nationally recognized union. There is a broad array of opinion on which is most useful to police officers. The diversity of thought can be seen through the data collected on 312 major police agencies, shown in Table 10-1 (Sapp and Carter, 1991a).

Merely because a group of employees wants to negotiate a contract does not mean that they will be allowed to do so. In some states there are legal restrictions that prohibit collective bargaining by public employees, especially those involved in public safety. Similarly, in right-to-work states, employees cannot be forced to join a union even after it establishes itself as the bargaining agent for the employee group. Since the strength of the union depends on the support of the members, less than total membership weakens the union's bargaining position.

Overcoming state regulations can only be overcome through a change in law. This has been accomplished in a variety of ways. First is to convince the legislature to enact a change in the laws. The most effective way of doing this is by a strong lobbying effort. Police officer organizations in some states have found it very useful to ally themselves with firefighter organizations for lobbying purposes. Firefighter organizations have become among the more sophisticated public employee labor groups. The combined lobbying efforts of police and firefighters have been reasonably effective in changing state laws that limited collective bargaining.

Table 10-1
Police Union Membership

Employee Organization	Frequency	Percent
Local only (police officer associations)	74	23.6
Fraternal Order of Police	70	22.4
State-wide police labor organizations	58	18.6
Police Benevolent Association	37	11.9
Regional and county associations	14	4.5
International Union of Police Associations	14	4.5
National Association of Police Organizations	10	3.2
International Brotherhood of Police Officers	8	2.6
American Federation of State, County, and Municipal Employees	8	2.6
International Union of Operating Engineers	6	1.9
AFL/CIO	6	1.9
Service Employees International Union	4	1.3
Teamsters Union	3	1.0
Total	**312**	**100%**

A second process, which has had a mixed success rate, is by way of voter referendum. By collecting sufficient signatures on a petition, police organizations have been able to place the issue before the voters. There are several disadvantages to this approach. First is that it is usually done on a local level; other organizations within the same state are not affected by the outcome. Each police labor organization must therefore fight the same battle within its own jurisdiction if it wishes collective bargaining rights. Second, the issue is left to the whim of the voters. To obtain the support of the voters often requires more than just getting the issue on the ballot. It also requires a concerted public relations and voter information effort. To be sure, there are always those who oppose collective bargaining for the police. They will mount an effort to defeat the proposal. Such battles sometimes leave political wounds that take a long time to heal.

It is not absolutely necessary to limit the referendum to one locale; the same approach can be used on a statewide basis. Usually, however, labor groups from only one or two jurisdictions are seeking the change. A statewide referendum faces the possibility of attracting opposition from other police officers. For that reason, and the costs associated with a statewide campaign, such referendums are almost always local option–type elections.

Contract Negotiation

The first problem confronting both management and labor in the negotiation process revolves around just who is management and who is labor. Some organizations have bargaining units for operatives, one for supervisors and still another for upper management. The negotiation process may therefore include more than two bargaining units. It gets even more complicated when civilian staff have their own union. Ideally, the bargaining unit represents all nonsupervisory personnel. The addition of managerial or supervisory bargaining units can complicate not only the bargaining process, but can also vastly increase the chief administrator's level of management difficulty.

From a practical standpoint it is better that management personnel be associated with management. This is also true of supervisors, who are more likely to support the position of management if they are part of the management team (NEI Committee of Management's Rights, 1987).

Another issue relates to the chief administrator's role in the negotiation process. Some chiefs expect to be an active participant on the management team; others prefer to act as merely an advisor. Still other chiefs prefer to be responsible for the implementation of the conditions of the contract only after it is approved. A danger exists in those cases where the chief is not involved. Many of the agencies that lost management prerogatives did so because the chief was not aware of what was being negotiated. The management negotiating team was not sufficiently aware of how police departments operate. As a result, they negotiated away functions that were traditionally management areas of control.

The process itself is usually a face-to-face negotiation between members of the bargaining unit(s) and management. The goal of this process is to obtain an agreement or understanding that will be enforced for an agreed-upon period of time. Often, when the process has been in place for a number of years, the process will focus only on new issues, such as salary increases or benefits. As long as they are still working to everyone's satisfaction, the other working arrangements will be left in place.

If there are issues that arise during the time frame of the contract but are not covered by the contract, a separate negotiation will usually be conducted. This is known as the *sidebar agreement* (More and Wegener, 1992, p. 512). It may also be necessary to negotiate interpretations of the agreement or definitions of terms. Simply because an agreement is approved does not mean that negotiation ends until the contract time frame has been exhausted.

The determination of who will represent the bargaining units is up to the participants. When a national labor organization represents the officers, the negotiation team is usually made up of professional negotiators. A mistake that is sometimes made by police administrators when first confronted by the need to negotiate is to attempt the process without the aid and advice of professionals in the field of negotiating for management.

Many believe that both the officers and managers of police departments have benefited from the collective bargaining process. It has replaced the arbitrary decision-making and rule setting with a mechanism that provides for the joint resolution of issues (More and Wegener, 1992, p. 511). The popularity of collective bargaining can be inferred from the fact that in 1982, the U.S. Bureau of Census estimated that about 50 percent of the police officers in the United States were engaged in some type of negotiation process (McAndrew, 1989). According to a recent survey of the nations largest police agencies, fully 55 percent had a formal collective bargaining agreement (Sapp and Carter, 1991b). This is indicative of a steady increase in the number of agencies opting for collective bargaining. This appears to be the wave of the future; it is certainly a reality of the present for a significant number of police organizations.

Impasse Resolution

Impasse, or conflict, resolution usually occurs when one of two conditions is present. There is either disagreement between management and labor over the terms of the contract or contract negotiations break down. An impasse implies that further negotiations are futile; there is no room left for compromise.

The recognition that negotiations have reached an impasse does not always come easily. Sometimes, one side gives the impression that it is willing to negotiate when its position is really locked in place. This may happen to either side and either may move to implement the resolution process.

If the impasse is not broken, labor must either concede the issue or take actions designed to force the issue. It is at this point that job actions are taken by labor to push management into either conceding the point or initiating a resolution technique. The actions taken by police labor organizations are varied. They include work slowdowns, speedups, picketing, media campaigns, and the extensive use of sick leave (Blue Flu) to press for the resolution of the conflict (Sapp and Carter, 1991b). Fortunately, the use of job actions is limited. Most of the time, resolution techniques are initiated before job actions are taken.

The three most common techniques for impasse resolution are (Thibault, Lynch, and McBride, 1990, p. 399):

1. *Mediation:* a noncoercive process in which a third party studies the issue in dispute between the two parties. This neutral works behind the scenes with the parties and attempts to act as a go-between in settling the dispute.

2. *Fact-finding:* another noncoercive procedure by which a third party gathers evidence between the two parties and then offers a solution. The recommendations may be publicly released in an effort to have community pressure enter into the settling of the dispute.

3. *Arbitration:* as opposed to fact-finding and mediation, a third-party process in which an official body or representative of a state arbitration board studies the issues in disputes and then makes a ruling. This decision may then be binding on both parties, depending on statute.

The most popular method of resolving such conflicts currently appears to be the use of binding arbitration (Sapp and Carter, 1991b). In this process a neutral arbitrator hears both arguments and renders a decision. There is no appeal from the arbitrator's decision; it is final. The power that makes the arbitration binding may be found in one of several documents. It may be found in the negotiated contract, state law, city or county ordinance, jurisdictional policy, or court decisions (Sapp and Carter, 1991b).

Those agencies that do not use binding arbitration have different mechanisms for resolving impasses. Sapp and Carter (1991b) identified a variety of techniques by which the conflicts are resolved: (1) mutual cooperation that involved further good-faith negotiations; (2) the use of special masters, outside mediators, and advisory arbitration: (3) local authority such as the civil service board, city manager, and so on; and (4) other conflict resolution techniques, such as fact finding.

Contract Management

The end product of the bargaining event is usually written into a document referred to as the *memorandum of agreement* or *memorandum of understanding*. This document may be defined as "a written agreement prepared by management and an employee organization reached through meet and confer procedures that concerns wages, hours, or working conditions. The agreement may be submitted to the appropriate determining body or a government official for ratification and implementation"(More and Wegener, 1992, p. 509).

Typically, the memorandum of understanding is a written agreement that remains in effect from 1 to 3 years. Once in effect, this document becomes the basis for the relationship between management and labor. The majority of the agreements found in such documents are clearly defined and become part of the routine process in which the agency conducts its affairs. There are occasions, however, when disputes arise over one of the terms of the agreement. Those cases are usually determined by arbitration.

It is management's responsibility to administer the organization in accordance with the terms of the agreement. A union's primary responsibility regarding management of a union contract is to represent the union membership when there is evidence that management is not fulfilling its obligations. This may include filing a grievance, initiating a civil suit, or beginning internal discussions with members about the desirability of a job action.

Like all contracts, the memorandum of understanding takes on a life of its own. Unforeseeable issues arise that sometimes alter the definitions of terms and conditions that were agreed on. That is one of the reasons for a one- to three-year time limit on such documents. With each contract new information is uncovered that adds more topics of negotiation for the next contract period. The process of evolution never stops. There is never a time when the last contract is good enough for the next contract period.

AREAS OF NEGOTIATION

There are a variety of areas that are frequently negotiated by police labor organizations and management. Some are legitimate and logical. Others, while of concern to labor, are open to question. Where collective bargaining exists it will routinely focus on salary and benefits, promotion and assignment, and the disciplinary process. We will look at each of the areas in more detail.

Salary and Benefits

The issues of salary and benefits is both the most accepted and the most long-standing of the areas open to negotiation. It is quite likely that salary and benefits were among the primary issues that first sparked the decision of police officers to organize into labor unions. The impact of collective bargaining on salary and benefits has been substantial. Even those agencies that do not have collective bargaining have had to adjust their wage and benefits packages to remain competitive with those organizations that do negotiate in this manner.

There are limitations on how much additional salary can be negotiated by labor. All governmental entities are required to function within the limitations of their budgets. Budgets are legislative enactments and are based on income produced from taxes and fees. Management cannot agree to a contract there are insufficient tax dollars to support. In all police organizations, between 85 and 90 percent of the budget is committed to personnel. That means that even a 1 percent raise in salary represents a significant increase in the agency's operating budget. If the tax base is stagnant or shrinking, the only means by which management can supply wage increase is if the legislative body raises taxes. This is not usually popular with the citizens and therefore is not popular with the legislators.

One of the reasons mentioned earlier for the drop in popularity of police labor organizations is the realization among police officers that there is indeed a bottom in the well. Even unions cannot force higher wages when there is no money to pay the bill.

Benefits became popular areas of negotiation when the limitations on salary negotiation first became apparent. With the rapidly increasing cost of health care, health insurance has become a central issue in labor negotiations. It is not just a matter of basic health care. The decision to include maternity care, dental plans, and eyesight are of major concern to employees. Does the agency pay only for the employee's coverage or include the employee's family? What will be the deductible portion of the medical plan, and what percentage of the total cost will the coverage provide? All of these issues plus a myriad of others complicate the negotiation process and have a profound impact on employee morale and the agency's budget.

Besides health care, retirement, vacation time, and sick leave have become more important in the negotiation process. In each of these, it is not just the amount of money or time that is negotiated, but the process in which it is used or made available to the personnel as well. Vacation time, for example, is typically a product of seniority. But will the senior officers be allowed to schedule all of their vacation before the junior officers have this opportunity, or will vacation time be scheduled in increments of a few days or weeks at a time? What about maternity leave; or, for that matter, paternity leave? These are all issues subject to negotiation.

Promotion and Assignment

Promotion and assignment are somewhat more problematic. Promotions are not subject to negotiation, but the procedures used to decide who will be promoted are. This is a major concern of police officers. The availability to grow, to gain stature both professionally and economically, is a central issue. The past has seen a promotion system that was little more than the old spoils system. It was based on preferential treatment or personal loyalty. Not just minorities and women suffered from the old system. Supervisors and administrators were selected on the basis of anything but ability; many were promoted due to seniority or through political connections.

It should come as little surprise that labor organizations targeted the promotion process as fair game in collective bargaining. Generally speaking, the result has been positive. The promotion processes that have resulted from negotiation have been fair and impartial. Both police organizations and management have benefited from this process.

The same cannot be said for work assignment. This is a subject that was better left out of the negotiation process. One of the results of a negotiated assignment process is inappropriate assignments. According to Robert C. Wadman and Robert K. Olson :

> A basic premise of all personnel administration holds that it is productive to have the best skilled, highest trained, and most experienced people in positions that have the greatest potential for accomplishing the organization's goals. This premise is not sustained in America's police organizations, however. With few exceptions, new officers are assigned to uniformed patrol in high-crime, lower income areas and during the nighttime when criminal activity is at its peak. Their days off come during the week (Walker, 1983, p. 120). Crime consistently occurs most often in the lower income neighborhoods of American cities on weekends, and during the hours of darkness (*Crime in the United States*, 1984, p. 5). Yet, the most experienced officers, especially those with collective bargaining agreements, tend to work daytime hours, in the lowest crime areas or in specialty positions and work weekdays.
>
> If an officer is fortunate enough to be promoted, he or she will usually be assigned to a supervisory position in the uniformed patrol division, during the nighttime, in a high-crime area, and with days off during the week. Therefore, the least experienced police officers are being supervised by the least experienced supervisors, in the high-crime areas and during the hours of peak crime occurrence (1990, pp. 15–16).

It is not only beat assignment and days off that are affected by collective bargaining. Assignment to specialized areas may be determined by a process created at the bargaining table as well as assignment to training programs. Some departments have found it difficult to civilianize some areas of the department, such as dispatcher, because there was a contract clause specifying how officers would be assigned to that and similar areas. The ability to streamline an organization or to redesign it in accordance with evolving community needs may therefore be drastically impeded by a collective bargaining agreement.

Discipline Procedures

Officers are always concerned about the discipline process. This is an area of great importance in an officer's professional life. It is equally important to management. The case below demonstrates the bad effects of an ineffective disciplinary process. Although it has not yet come to trial, it is typical of the kind of case currently being filed against the police.

McLin v. *City of Chicago* (1990)
742 F.Supp. 996 (N.D.Ill.)

Plaintiffs Calvin McLin and Joseph Weaver, both of whom are young black men, allege that they were waiting for a bus when two white members of the Chicago Police Department ordered them into a squad car, drove them around, verbally abused them, and ultimately dropped them off in a neighborhood that the officers knew to be hostile and dangerous for blacks. As a result, McLin and Weaver were allegedly assaulted by a group of white and Hispanic civilians. Plaintiffs have now filed this civil rights lawsuit against the white and Hispanic civilians; the individual police officers allegedly involved in the incident; Leroy Martin, the superintendent of police; David Fogel, the administrator of the office of Professional Standards (OPS) of the Chicago Police Department and the city of Chicago. Pending is a motion to dismiss filed by Martin, Fogel, and the city. For the reasons stated below, the motion is granted as to Martin and Fogel but denied as to the city.

Failure to Discipline

In count VI, the plaintiffs allege that the city, through its police department and policy-making officials, maintains a policy and custom of "failure to properly supervise, discipline, transfer, counsel, or otherwise control police officers engaged in the excessive use of force, including deadly force, particularly those who are repeatedly accused of such acts." The complaint further alleges that this policy or custom was maintained or implemented with deliberate indifference, and that it was the direct and proximate cause of plaintiffs' injuries because it encouraged defendants to commit the actions complained of against plaintiffs.

In support of this allegation, the complaint alleges the following facts:

1. For the past 15 years, the OPS has received approximately 2000 to 2500 excessive force complaints and has sustained and recommended discipline in only 5 percent of those complaints. Of the remaining complaints, 75 to 82 percent are classified "not sustained" even though, as the department has admitted, the majority of the complaints have merit.

2. The percentage of excessive force complaints that are sustained is further reduced on review by the superintendent of police and the police board.

3. In the few cases where complaints are sustained, the amount of discipline recommended and imposed is, by the superintendent's admission, grossly inadequate.

4. In most, if not all, of the lawsuits that allege excessive force, deadly force, or other police abuse and which result in verdicts or settlements for the victims, the police department and OPS impose no discipline and almost never reopen the investigation, and sometimes promote the officer involved. In most of these cases, the officers involved are "repeaters" who are subject to numerous complaints of excessive force.

5. After a jury found that the city had a policy and practice of abusing persons suspected of shooting police officers in *Wilson* v. *City of Chicago*, No. 86 C 2360, no officers were disciplined and no investigation was initiated to discipline those responsible for the policy.

6. Investigations conducted by the OPS are inadequate, with no cognizable standard of proof, and the investigators are inadequately trained and often have connections with law enforcement, including being applicants for employment by the police department.

7. The OPS and the police department destroy disciplinary files and records of all excessive force complaints after five years, with the exception of complaints that are sustained. This makes it difficult to identify patterns of brutality, to identify and discipline "repeaters," and to investigate thoroughly complaints of excessive force.

8. About 5 years ago, the department rescinded a general order that had required an officer who had three "sustained" or "not sustained" excessive force complaints within a 2-year period to receive psychological counseling. Since then, the department has rejected for counseling the vast majority of officers that OPS recommends for counseling after an allegation of excessive force.

9. In 1983, television station WMAQ-TV broadcast a series that identified numerous police officers as "repeaters" who had up to 30 complaints of excessive force lodged against them. None of those officers were disciplined, nor was any investigation initiated, as a result of that series.

10. Although the "repeaters" have been identified by the department and OPS, nothing has been done to address the problem of repeaters, the repeaters remain on the force, and the practices and procedures of the department and OPS protect the repeaters.

11. For many years, officers of the department have maintained a custom and practice of taking youths—particularly black youths—from one neighborhood and dropping them off in a different, hostile neighborhood, thereby placing the youths at risk of physical attack.

12. Martin, Fogel, and other high supervisory officials of the department have knowledge of the "drop-off" custom described in paragraph 11 but have failed to discipline officers who engage in this activity, thereby encouraging the practice.

13. Defendant Serio has had previous complaints of racially motivated police misconduct lodged against him, but he has never been properly disciplined, counseled, controlled, or supervised.

The court finds that plaintiffs' allegations in this case suffice to state a claim against the city for failure to discipline its police officers.

Code of Silence

In count VII, the plaintiffs allege that the city and high supervisory police officials, including Martin and Fogel, have been aware of a de facto policy or custom of a police code of silence. Pursuant to this code of silence, police officers refuse to report instances of police brutality and misconduct of which they are aware, and they remain silent or give false and misleading information during investigations in order to protect fellow officers.

The plaintiffs allege that the code of silence is evidenced by the following:

1. Martin and Fogel have admitted that such a code of silence exists within the department.

2. In the case of *Jones* v. *City of Chicago*, No. 83 C 2360 (N.D.Ill.), numerous police officers and detectives testified that they had testified hundreds of times in cases where excessive force was alleged and that in none of those cases had they ever admitted to seeing or participating in excessive use of force or other police misconduct. They further testified that the only officer who they had heard of having done so was Frank Laverty.

3. Police officials routinely make public statements in high-profile excessive and deadly force cases, in which they falsely exonerate the police officer before the completion of the investigation. Plaintiffs cite two specific examples of such alleged statements.

4. The record in the case of *Falk* v. *McNamara*, No. 88 C 7293 indicates that unidentified officers who participated in the infliction of excessive force are protected by the identified officers and other members of the department, who conceal the identities of the unidentified officers and destroy documents that would place them at the scene. The record further indicates that thedepartment and OPS fail to perform a basic and timely investigation when identification could be accomplished through documents and pictures.

5. When plaintiffs and their families first reported the facts that gave rise to this case to supervisory officials at the department's ninth district, those officials told plaintiffs that they should keep the incident quiet. Other ninth district officers, through their silence and other actions, have attempted to protect the responsible officers from detection and punishment.

6. While Martin and Fogel have publicly acknowledged the existence of a police code of silence, Fogel almost never recommends, and Martin almost never approves, discipline of officers charged with excessive force in instances where a civilian victim's version of an act of police misconduct is denied by an accused officer and that officer's partner, or where other police personnel do not contradict the accused officer's denial of the misconduct.

The court finds that plaintiffs' allegations concerning a code of silence properly state a claim under 42 U.S.C. §1983.

For the reasons stated above, defendants' motion to dismiss is granted as to defendants Martin and Fogel and denied with respect to the city of Chicago.

The primary concern of police labor organizations regarding discipline is that the process is fair and impartial. They want the rule and policies clearly stated and they want the adjudication procedures to reflect fundamental fairness. Unions do not object to discipline where it is warranted; they object to arbitrary discipline.

The first step in the creation of a disciplinary procedure is to define the *grounds for discipline*. These are written as organizational rules or regulations that either prohibit or require certain forms of behavior. The rules should be supported by organizational policy which states the department's philosophy on various responsibilities and tasks (Carter, 1991, p. 355).

Problems arise when the department attempts to control behavior with vague, ill-defined terms such as "conduct unbecoming an officer." There are far fewer problems when the offense is clearly defined and articulated. It must also be published internally. Every member of the agency must know what is required and what is prohibited or the process is invalid.

The next step to be negotiated is the adjudication process. This is necessary to determine if the complaint can be sustained. The hearing may be conducted by a command-level officer, supervisor, panel of officers, civilian review board, or a hybrid combination of these (Carter, 1991, p. 359). The process selected is, in many cases, a product of the collective bargaining agreement.

Finally, there must be an appellate process. The discipline process may produce a reprimand, suspension without pay, reduction in rank, or dismissal from the force. The officer must have some mechanism for appealing the decision. This procedure is also a product of direct negotiation between management and labor.

Management Prerogatives

There are areas not open to negotiation. The majority of union contracts will have a clause specifying the rights of management. These rights may not serve as the basis of a grievance by officers or the union as a whole, even though management does not exercise these rights on a frequent basis. According to the International Association of Chiefs of Police (IACP), such rights include the right to (IACP, 1977, pp. 80–81):

1. Establish departmental rules and procedures.

2. Schedule overtime work as required in the manner most advantageous to the employer.

3. Discipline and discharge for cause.

4. Lay off employees if the need arises.

5. Transfer employees and to transfer governmental operations.

6. Consolidate the operations of two or more departments and to reorganize the operations within a department.

The necessity of maintaining management rights is all too clear. The chief executive officer for the agency is charged with the responsibility for directing and controlling that agency. If the authority to direct is bargained away, the union will become the unit that manages the agency, but the chief will retain public accountability and responsibility. This is an impossible situation, one that will invariably result in abuse of police authority and police isolation from the public.

GRIEVANCE PROCEDURES

The grievance procedure describes the method by which grievances will be filed and how they will be adjudicated. Grievances may arise from disputes over a myriad of issues. They may dispute the administration of the contract over the handling of wages, benefits, or over any variety of issues concerning working conditions. Where there is broad-based acceptance of the right to file a grievance, almost anything that relates to working conditions can be grieved. An example of the types of grievances filed in a large police agency over 6-month period offers a good example (Thibault, Lynch, and McBride, 1990, p. 408):

1. Lack of interior or writing-light replacement bulbs in patrol vehicles.

2. Administration of first aid to a person suspected of having AIDS.

3. Transporting prisoners by only one officer in an uncaged vehicle.

4. An officer responding to fires and going inside to locate the cause of the alarm before the arrival of fire service personnel.

5. Not being allowed to wear leatherlike athletic wear in place of prescribed leather shoes.

6. The presence of rats in a locker room.

Initiating the Grievance

The procedures set in place for initiating a grievance will usually specify the person or office to which the grievance must be submitted and the time frame of submission. Some organizations provide multiple avenues of initiation. An officer wishing to file a grievance, for example, might have the choice of filing it with a union representative, member of the grievance panel, or directly with the chief of police. Usually, the grieving party can only use one of the avenues. Once the grievance is submitted, it will follow the organizational path set out by the contract specifications. The grieving party cannot normally file with more than one office, nor can this officer file one place, then have a change of mind and file the same grievance in another office.

The time allocated for the filing of a grievance will vary from agency to agency. The purpose of the time limit is to assure that the complaint is handled in a timely manner while the memories of all involved parties are still fresh. Allowing someone to file a grievance based on an incident that occurred years in the past would be an exercise in both futility and absurdity. The operating theory is that if a party feels aggrieved, that person should be offended now and should file the complaint now. The actual time frame allowed varies from around 5 days to 30 days, although extenuating circumstances may allow for more leeway.

Initially, the officer should attempt to resolve the problem by taking it directly to the supervisor. If the problem cannot be resolved there, the next step is to take the problem to the supervisor's supervisor. If these actions fail to result in a solution, a formal grievance should be submitted.

The formal grievance must usually be in writing. Moreover, many procedures require that the complaint state the facts, specify the portion of the contract believed to have been violated, and identify the offending party. Once the appropriate complaint has been filed in the appropriate manner, the resolution process can begin.

Grievance Arbitration

Grievance arbitration in large organizations can be a multilayered process. It may require an investigation and written response from each level in the chain of command. Or the grievance may go directly to a grievance committee. Some committees are comprised of members of a personnel committee. Other agencies form a grievance panel that meets only when a grievance is submitted.

The decision of the grievance panel should be made in a timely manner. A common practice is to require a written decision within 15 days of the receipt of the grievance. The response will usually state not only the findings but the reasons for the decision as well.

Finally, the decision will be submitted to the chief executive officer or civilian official, such as the city manager, for review. This person may approve, reject, or alter the decision. There is also a time limit on this decision; 15 to 20 days is about normal.

Grievance Outcomes

If the grievance relates to a disciplinary action, the results will be either to approve the discipline to be taken, modify it, or overturn the decision. Other issues may have a broader impact on the organization. Disciplinary actions usually involve only one or a handful of officers. A grievance filed on an issue related to working conditions in general, however, may have a much broader impact.

Grievances serve other purposes than just mediating differences of opinion between management and officers. They also provide a measure of contentment among officers. Numerous grievances are indicative of hostility toward management. They often serve as an indicator of the need for a greater action on the part of the administration. Police managers must adopt a problem-solving approach to the grievance process. They must look beyond the grievance itself toward broader issues of the management–labor relationship. Grievances can provide an indicator that one or more of the following is needed (More and Wegener, 1992, p. 513):

1. Is there a need for changes in policies, procedures, rules, regulations, or contract provisions?

2. Is there a need to provide managers with additional training?

3. Is there a need for providing officers with additional training?

4. Is there either a localized or a widespread supervisory problem?

5. Is there a problem attributable to employee misunderstanding of an operational need?

In the final analysis, the grievance is the mechanism by which terms and conditions of the labor contract are tested. It is here that obligations and definitions are clarified.

Where possible, grievances should be handled at the lowest possible organizational level. This saves time, resources, and egos. When that is not possible, the grievance process must work in a fair and effective manner. If it does, the management–labor relationship can be strengthened. When it does not work as it should, this relationship can deterorate into civil litigation and eventually, job actions on the part of labor. This is not a process that management should take lightly.

DISCUSSION QUESTIONS

1. Discuss the evolution of police labor unions. Why did it take so long for the police to unionize?

2. Why do police officers join a labor union? What does this say about police management?

3. Discuss the pros and cons of police unions.

4. Discuss the collective bargaining process. What areas are open to negotiation? What dangers are posed for management by this process?

5. Compare the advantages and disadvantages of the various impasse resolution techniques.

REFERENCES

Carter, David L. (1991). "Police disciplinary procedures: a review of selected police departments," in Thomas Barker and David L. Carter, eds. *Police Deviance,* 2nd ed. Cincinnati, Ohio: Anderson.

Commission on Accreditation for Law Enforcement Agencies (1984). *Standards for Law Enforcement Agencies.* Fairfax, Va.: The Commission.

Crane, Donald P. (1979). *Personnel: The Management of Human Resources,* 2nd ed. Belmont, Calif.: Wadsworth.

Federal Bureau of Investigation (1984). *Crime in the United States.* Washington, D.C.: U.S. Government Printing Office.

Gaines, Larry K., Mittie D. Southerland, and John E. Angell,(1991). *Police Administration.* New York: McGraw-Hill.

International Association of Chiefs of Police (1977). *Crucial Issues in Police Labor Relations,* Gaithersburg, Md.: IACP.

McAndrew, Ian (1989). "The negotiation process," in Peter C. Unsinger and Harry W. More, eds., _Police Management/Labor Relations._ Springfield, Ill.: Charles C Thomas.

More, Harry W., and W. Fred Wegener (1992). _Behavioral Police Management._ New York: Macmillan.

NEI Committee on Management Rights (1987). _Management Rights._ Washington, D.C.: National Executive Institute Associates.

Russell, Francis (1975). _A City in Terror: 1919, The Boston Police Strike._ New York: Viking Press.

Sapp, Allen D. (1985). "Police unionism as a developmental process," in Abraham Blumberg and Elaine Niederhoffer, eds., _The Ambivalent Force: Perspectives on the Police,_ 3rd ed. New York: Holt, Rinehart and Winston, pp. 412–419.

_____ and David L. Carter (1991a). "Police collective bargaining units and organizational affiliations," _Police Labor Monthly,_ Vol. 10, No. 3.

_____ and David L. Carter (1991b). "Conflict and conflict resolution in police collective bargaining," _The Police Forum,_ Vol. 1, No. 1 (November).

_____ and David L. Carter, and Darrell W. Stephens, (1990). _Police Labor Relations: Critical Findings._ Washington, D.C.: Police Executive Research Forum.

Sirene, Walt H. (1981). "Management: labor's effective organizer," _FBI Law Enforcement Bulletin,_ Vol. 52, No. 1.

Stanley, David T.(1972). _Managing Local Government under Union Pressure._ Washington, D.C.: The Brookings Institute.

Thibault, Edward A., Lawrence M. Lynch, and R. Bruce McBride, (1990). _Proactive Police Management,_ 2nd ed. Englewood Cliffs, N. J.: Prentice Hall.

Wadman, Robert C., and Robert K. Olson (1990). _Community Wellness: A New Theory of Policing._ A PERF Discussion Paper, Washington, D.C.: Police Executive Research Forum.

Walker, Samuel (1983). _The Police in America._ New York: McGraw-Hill.

Chapter 11

Policymaking and Ethics

R esearch in the area of job satisfaction has uncovered an alarming phenomenon concerning organizational policy and policymaking; policies consistently undermine agency morale and job satisfaction (Holden, 1980). Law enforcement officers frequently wonder on whose side their administration sits; theirs or the criminals. General order and policy manuals are often the size and complexity of major novels, yet major violations of policy and procedure plague the best of departments. Policies, which should be the finest of administrative tools, seem to be the administrator's poorest utilized instrument. Why this should happen is probably attributable to the manner in which policy is formulated.

This chapter focuses on the policymaking process, and we identify where this process goes astray and how it can be corrected. We also discuss the ethics of law enforcement and of management, for the ethics of the administrator is closely tied to the policies of the agency.

POLICIES

Policies are the agency's guidelines. Unlike procedures, which lay out a prescribed set of steps to be followed in certain well-defined circumstances, policies provide general direction in areas of officer discretion. They are aids to decision making, rather than premade decisions.

Policies are necessary for a number of reasons. First, the administrator, through the policymaking process, is able to communicate to the operative personnel administrative preference on a broad range of issues. Many police decisions are open ended; there are an unlimited number of options or enough different options to limit consistency among various personnel encountering similar incidents. Policy allows the administrator to establish priorities among the various objectives. You might say that it allows the officer an insight into the administration's thoughts on the subject at hand. Second, the administrator is legally accountable for actions of agency personnel. Where there is no policy there is greater likelihood of administrative liability for inappropriate actions by officers. We find policies necessary, therefore, to facilitate consistency of officer response to calls for service and to establish accountability for the actions of individual personnel.

Policymaking

Although policies are necessary for the effective management of a law enforcement agency, policymaking is far from an exact science. There are some in private industry who argue against organizational policies in any form. Robert Townsend, for example, said:

> Policy Manuals—Don't bother. If they're general, they're useless. If they're specific, they're how-to manuals—expensive to prepare and revise. The only people who read policy manuals are goldbricks and martinets. The goldbricks memorize them so they can say (a) "That's not in this department" or (b) "It's against company policy." The martinets use policy manuals to confine, frustrate, punish, and eventually drive out of the organization every imaginative, creative, adventuresome woman and man.
>
> If you have to have a policy manual, publish the Ten Commandments (1984, p. 176).

This approach may be considered a bit extreme for law enforcement. The lack of policy may suffice in a private organization, but public agencies are controlled by law and governmental regulation. Also, a member of the Avis Rent A Car organization, Townsend's firm at one time, is not in a position to take the life or freedom of a person as the police are. We must conclude, therefore, that policies and policy manuals are a fact of life for law enforcement agencies.

A point to be made in the quote above is the incredible hostility displayed toward policy manuals by a successful executive. This attitude corresponds closely with the attitude of law enforcement officers toward organization policy. Townsend is also not alone in his assessment of the harm done to the organization by policy manuals. The best-selling book on management by Thomas J. Peters and Robert H. Waterman, Jr., *In Search of Excellence,* although not going as far as Townsend, urges a less formal approach to management, with policy playing a decidedly minor role in administration (1982). Clearly, there has been a considerable reevaluation of the necessity for policies by private industry. Yet courts have consistently criticized police departments for a lack of policy. The police administrator is in a bind. The courts want written policies on every conceivable issue, but such policies are detrimental to the morale and effectiveness of the organization.

One might assume that a well-thought-out series of policies, precisely written and possessing clear objectives would be invaluable to a law enforcement administrator. Unfortunately, as in private industry, the idea of policy is better than the reality of policy.

The problem is usually a product of one or more of the following reasons:

1. Policy is formulated strictly at the top of the organization, with little or no input from those who must implement the policy. This is a common problem in quasi-military organizations such as law enforcement. This problem has been discussed before; it centers around managerial arrogance—the lack of belief in the ability of lower echelon personnel to make a meaningful contribution to the organization other than through the fulfillment of work objectives. The lower-echelon personnel are actually in a much better position to know good policy from bad than are the administrators, but nobody asks them.

2. Policy statements are vague or poorly written. This is a problem facing a large segment of our society. Good writing skills appear to be a vanishing art. Good policy requires clearly stated ideas. A concurrent problem is a severe lack of parsimony in the writing of policy. The manuals are too lengthy because the individual policies are too wordy. As mentioned previously, there exists a firearms policy of 14 pages, typed single-spaced. Is there really any policy requiring this many words? A policy this long is meaningless and you can bet it was not produced by a patrol-level officer.

3. There is no clear, concise reason for having the policy—no objective to be served. This is having a policy for the sake of having a policy. Usually, these come about because someone in a staff position was looking for a way to either justify a position or to pass some staff duty off on line personnel. These policies only complicate administration and confuse operatives.

4. Policy statements were written for the wrong reason, resulting in a detraction from effectiveness rather than the facilitating of achieving agency objectives. There are two distinct kinds of error under this category. First, administrators write policies to protect themselves rather than to provide guidance to operational officers. The goal here is not to facilitate effectiveness but to provide an administrative excuse when an officer makes a mistake. The second error concerns writing a policy to correct an individual problem. Individual problems should be handled on a case-by-case basis. Under no circumstance should a policy be designed to resolve a single rare issue involving one officer. Policies are to provide guidance in the achievement of organizational objectives by the entire organization. Sometimes, however, a single officer will make a mistake, causing the administrator to overreact and write a policy designed to prevent this occurrence from happening again. This is almost always a mistake. Policy written to control bad officers will invariably overrestrict good officers, thus increasing frustration and decreasing job satisfaction.

5. Policy statements are a product of evolution; each administrator adds to the policy manual without subtracting anything. The end result is a conglomeration of conflicting statements with vague definitions written in different styles for different eras. The majority of large law enforcement agencies in this country are probably guilty of this problem. There is a limit to the amount of information that one person can retain. Large, complex policy manuals are mentally indigestible. It should come as no surprise when officers in these agencies consistently violate the policies. They honestly cannot remember the vast amount of information or cannot incorporate all this material into day-to-day procedures.

The creation of a sound system of policies should be the immediate goal of every law enforcement administrator. The following guidelines for policy construction should be helpful in this regard.

1. Policy should be the product of thoughtful analysis. Training is also a form of policy. Where policy does not exist but the organization provides training, the training may become the policy. Consequently, when training and policy conflict, the officer may have the choice of accepting either; a point of view sometimes taken by the courts. Any position statement thus provided through training, memorandum, or formal policy may be interpreted as a policy statement. The objectives of the agency and resultant policies and procedures should be thought out carefully and evaluated by all segments of the organization. Those responsible for implementing the policies must be allowed to study and recommend alterations in policy. An unenforceable policy is worthless and a policy unacceptable to the officers will cause more problems than it solves.

2. The goals of the policy statements should always be to provide guidance for officers. All policies must be examined carefully to ensure no inconsistencies and to ensure that they clarify the agency's position on various topics.

3. Policies should be designed by using the same guidelines for setting priorities as those used in the design of training programs. The greater the potential harm to an individual, either inside or outside the organization, the greater the need for a policy.

4. Policies should be short general guidelines. Great care should be taken to make these statements as clear as possible. The guiding principle for a policy should be to clarify and simplify issues for the personnel. A policy should never complicate or confuse an issue.

5. Policies should be accurate statements of the organization's values and philosophies. This set of statements establishes the tone of the organization. The agency's commitment to ethics and the principles embodied in the Constitution should be clearly and forcefully stated in this document.

6. The design of a policy manual requires the understanding that there is a limitation on human memory. Policies should reflect this reality. Officers will remember those policies that are used frequently. Policies involving incidents that occur once every other year or so will not be remembered. Policies must therefore be written as guidance for routine incidents. Extraordinary incidents must be handled in a nonroutine manner. There are exceptions, of course. The use of deadly force is not routine for most officers, but they must be well acquainted with policies that guide the use of deadly force.

Problems that arise from too many policies may be alleviated somewhat by computerization. Providing patrol officers, or at the very least dispatchers, with computer terminals allows rapid access to a computerized version of the policy manual. The same is true for procedures. The dispatcher can access the computer and call up the appropriate policy or procedure while the officer is at the scene. That would relieve the officer of having to memorize large amounts of information and would greatly reduce the number of policy and procedural violations that occur at present.

Whether or not the agency is computerized, the policy manual must not become a morale crusher. It must be as short as humanly possible, and it must be written in clear and concise terms. To accept department policy, the officers must first understand department policy.

ETHICS

The concept of ethics dates back to the earliest of philosophers. Socrates, Plato, and Aristotle all devoted much of their writing and teaching to ethical thinking and ethical behavior. But what is ethics? Ethics is a philosophical issue concerned with right and wrong (Souryal, 1992, p. 49). The easiest and most straightforward answer for our purposes, however, is, "doing what is right." The more difficult problem is *determining* what is right. Which is the correct path when one is confronted with options?

The difficulty of making the correct choice is acknowledged by the fact that each profession has a code of conduct; a document that identifies what is acceptable behavior. However, people have to govern their lives by their own sense of right and wrong. Laws help, but laws cannot cover every aspect of the relationship between people. The following case demonstrates what happens when police officers lose sight of ethics as a basis for professional decision making.

Moore v. *City of Philadelphia* (1990)
571 A.2d 518 (Pa.Cmwlth.)

This action emanated from a series of incidents that occurred in January 1977 in the aftermath of a restaurant robbery. Officers Kuhlmeier and Romano conducted portions of the investigation, which included a search for Moore, a suspect in the robbery. Before encountering Moore, Kuhlmeier and Romano had several confrontations with the other appellees, which included, inter alia, late-night searches of their apartments under the guise of searching for Moore. When Moore was made aware of the fact that the police were searching for him, he turned himself into custody. In an effort to elicit a confession, Moore was physically abused by the police. The abuse included being slapped, punched, and kicked by the John Doe officers, who also attempted intimidation by using racially derogatory language. Additionally, Kuhlmeier and Romano forced Moore to strip to the waist and then placed him in a room (freezing room) with broken-out windows for almost an hour. All charges against Moore were dropped at the preliminary hearing.

Appellees brought action against the city and officers, seeking compensatory and punitive damages because of the tortuous conduct and constitutional violations committed by the officers. Appellees' complaint alleges that the officers committed assault and battery, false imprisonment, intentional infliction of emotional distress, trespass, and defamation. Appellees further allege violations of Pa. Const. Art. I, §§ 1, 8, 9, and 26, in that the officers committed unlawful searches of their person and possessions; violations of their civil rights to be free of arbitrary and unlawful state action; and other actions which deprived them of life, liberty, and property.

On appeal to this court, appellants make the argument that the trial court erred in denying judgment n.o.v. because the record as a whole does not reflect credible evidence to support a verdict especially so as to permit a punitive damage award against Kuhlmeier and Romano.

As to the specific claim that there was only "minimal" contact between Moore and the named officers so that punitive damages should not have been awarded, we find that Moore's testimony alone that Kuhlmeier and Romano placed him in a freezing room, if believed as the jury so did, demonstrated more than "minimal contact" and is truly abuse. Punitive damages are permitted to punish outrageous conduct. Such damages are proper punishment and deterrence for extreme behavior and are subject to strict judicial controls. We believe that the trial court properly upheld the jury's award of punitive damages because the officers' conduct was more than "minimal" and certainly was outrageous.

In this section we look at a variety of concepts that affect both individual and professional ethics. This is very important, for the police administrator for the organization will exhibit ethical conduct to the extent that it is demonstrated by management. Unethical managers, regardless of what other skills they may possess, produce unethical organizations.

Values

The value system of a society differs from group to group. In the United States there are various groupings of people according to economic class, such as upper, lower, and middle. The value systems differ from class to class. Each subculture will have specific values despite the existence of overriding religion or other factors. The ethics of an individual or group are also shaped by the values of the individual or group.

The political values of law enforcement personnel tend to lean toward the conservative. This is because, historically, police officers have come from working-class backgrounds and possess working-class values, which include maintaining self-respect, proving one's masculinity, "not taking any crap," and not being taken in (Wilson, 1968, pp. 33–34).

Twenty years earlier, Gunnar Myrdal described the American police officer as economically and socially insecure and always on the defensive, creating the impression that he is crude and hardboiled (1944, p. 540). Almost 20 years prior to that, A. L. Cornelius wrote (1929):

> Policemen as a class are usually not well educated, skilled mechanically, or industrially. They are men above average in physical strength and appearance who lack sufficient persistence to acquire an education or learn a trade.

Fortunately, this appears to be changing. More recent research shows that a larger proportion of police officers are the children of professional people, technical workers, and managers (Radelet, 1986, p.102). This may lead to a modification in the class value system of police officers. Overall, however, they are still overwhelmingly conservative.

The problem with the police value system and their attempt to force it on the public is the inevitability of the conflict this produces. The police do not have the luxury of dealing only with the middle class, who agree with their point of view. They must also tend to the needs of the lower and upper classes, whose value systems differ. As long as the officers realize that this represents a difference of opinion, of no great concern, the problem is minimal. When the police set themselves up as judges of values and beliefs, however, they usually manage to generate hostility and resentment.

The police cannot change the values of others. To attempt to do so, or to base decisions on an inappropriate value system, is futile and dysfunctional. Enforcement of laws is one thing and is a correct police function. Enforcement of social values is something quite different and not a duty of the police. The law enforcement officer must recognize the difference between law and values and react accordingly. The law enforcement administrator must know the difference to generate valid policies and to augment proper training programs.

Unfortunately, it is difficult for people to escape their values. These ideals and beliefs are established over a long period of time. They are a product of the family environment, social contacts, and education process in both school and church. Values are what people believe to be true about the nature of human beings and human society. Few people are willing to accept another person's truth blindly unless that truth corresponds to their own version of the truth.

As mentioned earlier, the police are conservative by nature, and this has some utility. There are also drawbacks. A rigid adherence to a conservative philosophy makes a person unsympathetic to entire classes, such as the poor and the homeless. Conservatives tend to be somewhat xenophobic; they distrust those who are different. This makes them potentially hostile to racial and ethnic minorities. As far back as the 1960s, research identified a close affinity between police work and support for radical-right politics, particularly when linked to racial unrest (Lipset, 1969, p. 76).

Conservative ideology teaches that everybody should work and support themselves and their families. It opposes welfare and any other program that uses taxes to help the less fortunate. Conservatives believe in rugged individualism and a strong adherence to rules. Those violating rules should be severely punished.

Police officers are not happy with the sentence handed down by a court unless it is severe. This may not be the best value system for a police officer, but it is one we have been stuck with for a long time. The late Los Angeles police chief William H. Parker once commented that the nation's police officers were "conservative, ultraconservative, and very right wing "(Lipset, 1969, p. 76).

To override individual value systems, with their inherent lack of flexibility, police administrators have begun to introduce organizational values. These values are an important component of police management. Earlier in the book we discussed value statements and their utility for police administration. By establishing an organizational value system, the administrator can overcome the negative effects of the personal value system. The new organizational value system can be designed to better reflect the needs of society.

Integrity

Integrity means firmness of character. It might be said that ethical people are those with integrity, but the concept is a little more complex. Integrity also embraces morality, honesty, trust, and honor.

Law enforcement personnel must have integrity. From the top of the organization to the bottom, there is no room for those who lack integrity. Unfortunately, there are a number of forces combining to erode the integrity of every law enforcement officer in the country, if not the world. These forces center on self-image and its relationship with a public simultaneously wanting both a high-integrity police agency free of political input and individual police officers occasionally open to bribes or personal favoritism.

Self-Image

Law enforcement agencies seek to impose their values on society at large. To do this, however, new officers must first be socialized into the values of the law enforcement agency. The first assault on the new officer's self-image, therefore, is the high-powered attempt at indoctrination into the police subculture. In short, the new recruit must be inculcated with the folklore, myths, and values of the organization. The new officers become in tune with the police value system; they develop the self-image of a police officer.

To a great extent, self-image will contribute to the individual's integrity. The stronger the self-image, the greater the integrity. Cynicism eats away self-image and ultimately, integrity. Because the self-image of the police is tied to society's image of the police organization, integrity among the officers will often rise and fall with the image of the agency. When the organization's image falls far enough, the officers may wish to disassociate themselves from the agency's image. Self-image may then be sacrificed for self-gratification as one by one each officer makes organizational goals subservient to personal desires. Lying, stealing, brutality, bribery, extortion, and sexual misadventures are all products of cynicism and low self-esteem.

The major concern of the police administrator should be the behavior–attitude relationship. Frequently, someone will complain, "He has a bad attitude." The implied cure for this problem is an attitude adjustment. Very often, attempts to correct an attitude problem fail because the problem is not one of attitude, but one of behavior. Earlier we discussed a person's need to rationalize or justify his or her role. They are compelled to justify behavior. Most of the time behavior comes first and attitude is simply a justification for the actions of the person. When this is the case, attacking the attitude is meaningless; the behavior must be altered. After a behavior change, the attitude will meekly follow along since it is now required to justify the new behavior. The successful manager focuses on behavior rather than attitude and realizes that the key to effective performance lies in maintaining standards of good behavior.

The law enforcement administrator has the power, and duty, to maintain a solid positive public image. It is the least that can be done for the morale and job satisfaction of the agency. The first step in this direction is the maintenance, by the chief executive, of a high level of personal integrity. The next step is ensuring the same standards in all personnel by decisive policies and actions geared to proper behavior by all members of the organization. No one can be exempted from high standards of personal integrity.

Corruption

The ultimate depth to which an employee can sink is epitomized by the corruption problem. The tragedy is that it need not happen. Very few people enter public service with an intent to steal. For the most part, people enter police service with the highest of motives, or at the very least with a desire to obtain job security (Radelet, 1986, pp. 87–89). All available evidence indicates that corruption occurs because the community encourages it and the department allows it, participates in it, or ignores the possibility of it happening (Goldstein, 1977, p. 187).

Nothing can destroy public confidence in a law enforcement agency faster than allegations of bribery and cover-up. It is in the best interest of the administrator and the agency to combat actively any type of corrupt activity. Simply letting everyone know that illegal practices will be dealt with harshly will facilitate the laying of a proper foundation for high-quality performance.

One of the better methods of minimizing corruption is by maintaining an open department. Corruption grows only when protected with a cloak of secrecy. The news media are marvelous institutions for keeping government agencies, including law enforcement organizations, honest. A major administrative blunder is to reject the media as friends and perceive them as enemies. The media may be the administrator's best friend. Although they do make mistakes, they also seek the truth. When others are attempting to protect the chief executive from bad news, the media can be counted on to provide this information. Often this is embarrassing to the administrator, but it is always necessary.

Justice

Justice can be defined as fairness: a concept that is easy to understand, but difficult to define operationally. Justice is a relative concept: What is just for one is often unjust for another. All administrators should strive to be just, even though the goal of attaining justice for everyone is an impossible one.

One of the principal objectives of the police is the ensuring of justice. The method employed is the application of the legal system, and occasionally, a less formal, discretionary innovative approach outside the system.We should not be overly concerned when the police fail to ensure justice; few really want it anyway. Victims want revenge, criminals want to go free, and police want recognition and to some extent revenge for the victim. Few really want justice, which is just as well since it is difficult to define or measure. Regardless of our inability to define justice, however, we can discuss the philosophies inherent in the idea as well as forces joining to blur our vision of this desirable, yet unattainable concept.

Might versus Right

Plato, the great philosopher of ancient Greece, clarified the opposing philosophies of justice approximately 300 years before the birth of Christ (Plato, 1952). He placed the idea on a continuum. On one end he placed the idea, *might makes right;* the strong are meant to rule over the weak. At the other end he placed the idea of *natural law;* all persons must live under and obey the law. No person or government may be above the law, and the function of government is to ensure the certainty and quality of the law. All other philosophical concepts fall between these ideals.

The first point of view stresses the inability of the weak to suffer injustice. Since the strong rules by right, anything done by the strong is just. The weak cannot suffer injustice but may cause injustice by failing to respond to the commands of the strong. By contrast, the strong cannot do injustice, only fail to assert sufficient force to maintain their control.

The second argument focuses on means being as important as ends. All must answer to a higher law. The concepts espoused in the U.S. Constitution, such as that all men are created equal and no man is above the law, are characteristic of this philosophical viewpoint.

Managerial philosophies fall on this same continuum. There are many managers who are contemptuous of lower-level employees. They take the authoritarian approach to leadership and believe that they rule by right. They cannot be wrong and cannot do injustice. They are the captains of the ships and can fail to exercise sufficient control only when things go wrong. Unfortunately, there are many such police executives, although they are usually ineffective.

More enlightened managers, on the other hand, fall at the opposite end of the justice continuum. These managers believe in the worth of people as individuals, and their philosophies are in harmony with the principles embodied in the Constitution.

Few people fall totally at either end; most fit somewhere in the middle. It is fair to say, however, that most police administrators probably fall closer to the might-makes-right end of the spectrum. This belief is based on the observation that police administration, both as described in popular texts on police management and through personal contact with officers and administrators, tends to use the classical approach to organization and management espoused by Max Weber early in the twentieth century

There is an interesting phenomenon attached to individual concepts of justice or management. Personnel at the lower end of the organization often prefer a democratic approach to management, or the idea of a higher natural law. Managers seem to prefer the more autocratic, or might-makes-right concept. Yet managers are merely people who worked their way up from the lower end to the top. The same people appear to have different philosophies at different periods of their career. Although this seems strange, there is an explanation for this behavior.

People seek power for themselves while attempting to deny it for others (see Chapter 4). Administrators want power but do not want to share it with underlings. Employees know that they cannot have power alone, thus are willing to share it with management, but do not want the administration to have uncontrolled power over them. What we are seeing is nothing more than self-serving behavior. As people move higher in the organization it becomes more to their advantage to adopt a more autocratic approach. Prior to their advancement it was to their advantage for management to maintain a democratic approach. There is no real mystery, just self-serving power struggles. All levels seek to gain sufficient might so that they may define what is right.

Perception versus Reality

As noted earlier, true justice is a noble, albeit impossible goal. Administrators must be aware, however, of the necessity of maintaining an image of justice, which is attainable. Real justice depends on one's point of view; it shifts forms and changes as a chameleon alters color, depending on individual perceptions. Apparent justice, on the other hand, is a more stable commodity.

All aspects of the organization's procedures must be perceived as fair. If the process appears fair, the result will be accepted. Conversely, if the process appears unfair, the result will not be accepted, no matter how worthwhile.

Fairness

If there is to be any stability in the organization at all, the administrator must be fair. Had they been fair in the past, many problems besetting police agencies today would not exist. Both the public and agency personnel have a right to expect a fair shake when it comes to hiring, firing, and promotions. This means impartiality and not creating situations favoring certain individuals.

Fairness must also be practiced constantly in dealings with the public. The necessity of treating citizens with respect and dignity cannot be overemphasized. By their very nature the police come into conflict with the public. This is to be expected; it is unavoidable. How the administration handles the conflict will determine, to a great extent, how the public perceives the agency. Citizen allegations against police officers provide some of the most sensitive problems confronted by the administrator. The chief executive has a responsibility to be fair and impartial to both the accuser and accused. In many ways the administrator's ability, or inability, to be fair will become obvious in these circumstances. This is a major administrative test; in no other situation will the administrator's vulnerability be so apparent. Both the public and agency employees will observe the administrator's handling of these situations. Failure in either direction will injure the administrator's credibility. If the chief executive cannot do anything else right, this person had better be fair.

Psychological Contract

A psychological contract can be defined as a set of unspecified mutual expectations between two or more people. It exists in every human relationship and is the basis for loyalty. The quickest way to destroy a good relationship is for one of the participants to violate the provisions of this pact.

An example is the relationship between a man and a woman. Once they begin dating seriously there is a mutual expectation of fidelity. Despite the modern ideas of open relationships, few will continue a relationship that lacks loyalty and trust. Friendships can withstand almost any crisis except a violation of trust.

The same is true of relationships between organizations and their employees. A major reason for the rise in numbers and strength of labor organizations is the constant, blatant disregard of the psychological contract by management. Organizations have historically demanded more loyalty from the worker than the organization was willing to give in return; thus we have labor unions.

If you closely observe union contracts, you will find benefits specified in writing which should have been provided willingly by management years ago. The purpose of the written contract is to force the organization to be just. The overriding flaw in labor–management relations is the unwillingness of either side to give more than the contract calls for. Each person or group does just enough to fulfill the minimum requirements of the contract and no more. In other words, no one is willing to acknowledge the existence of the psychological contract.

Managers must realize that there are obligations to the worker which must be met, regardless of their existence in a contract. The employee has a right to expect a safe work environment, decent hours, reasonable compensation, and equally important, the understanding that the employee is a person with individual problems, often superseding the job and requiring occasional empathy.

The employee must also accept certain obligations regardless of written agreements. The employer has a right to expect an honest effort, support for the agency's policies, and respect for the organization's property. The organization also has a right to expect employee support in times of crises and a willingness to promote the agency's image.

The administrator who disregards the expectations inherent in the psychological contract does so at great peril. Unwritten expectations are as important as written ones, maybe more so. Violations of written contracts can be rectified in court or with mediation. Violations of the psychological contract destroy trust and loyalty, and often cannot be corrected.

ETHICAL STANDARDS FOR LAW ENFORCEMENT

The implementation of sound agency policy requires the administrator to have a solid grasp on the ethical standards to be imposed on the organization. A good place to start is with the Code of Police Ethics, formulated at the International Association of Chiefs of Police (IACP) conference in Honolulu, Hawaii in 1957, and updated in 1989. With the permission and assistance of Sir John C. Hermon, the new Law Enforcement Code of Ethics and Police Code of Conduct borrow heavily from Royal Ulster Constabulary's "Professional Policing Ethics" *(The Police Chief,* 1992, p. 14):

Law Enforcement Code of Ethics

As a law enforcement officer, my fundamental duty is to serve the community; to safeguard lives and property; to protect the innocent against deception, the weak against oppression or intimidation and the peaceful against violence or disorder; and to respect the constitutional rights of all to liberty, equality and justice.

I will keep my private life unsullied as an example to all and will behave in a manner that does not bring discredit to me or my agency. I will maintain courageous calm in the face of danger, scorn or ridicule; develop self-restraint; and be constantly mindful of the welfare of others. Honest in thought and deed both in my personal and official life, I will be exemplary in obeying the law and the regulations of my department. Whatever I see or hear of a confidential nature or that is confided to me in my official capacity will be kept ever secret unless revelation is necessary in the performance of my duty.

I will never act officiously or permit personal feelings, prejudices, political beliefs, aspirations, animosities or friendships to influence my decisions. With no compromise for crime and with relentless prosecution of criminals, I will enforce the law courteously and appropriately without fear or favor, malice or ill will, never employing unnecessary force or violence and never accepting gratuities.

I recognize the badge of my office as a symbol of public faith, and I accept it as a public trust to be held so long as I am true to the ethics of police service. I will never engage in acts of corruption or bribery, nor will I condone such acts by other police officers. I will cooperate with all legally authorized agencies and their representatives in the pursuit of justice.

I know that I alone am responsible for my own standard of professional performance and will take every reasonable opportunity to enhance and improve my level of knowledge and competence.

I will constantly strive to achieve these objectives and ideals, dedicating myself before God to my chosen profession...law enforcement.

Police Code of Conduct

All law enforcement officers must be fully aware of the ethical responsibilities of their position and must strive constantly to live up to the highest possible standards of professional policing. The International Association of Chiefs of Police believes it important that police officers have clear advice and counsel available to assist them in performing their duties consistent with these standards, and has adopted the following ethical mandates as guidelines to meet these ends.

Primary Responsibilities of a Police Officer. A police officer acts as an official representative of government who is required and trusted to work within the law. The officer's powers and duties are conferred by statute. The fundamental duties of a police officer include serving the community, safeguarding lives and property, protecting the innocent, keeping the peace and ensuring the rights of all to liberty, equality and justice.

Performance of the Duties of a Police Officer. A police officer shall perform all duties impartially, without favor or affection or ill will and without regard to status, sex, race, religion, political belief, or aspiration. All citizens will be treated equally with courtesy, consideration, and dignity.

Officers will never allow personal feelings, animosities or friendships to influence official conduct. Laws will be enforced appropriately and courteously and, in carrying out their responsibilities, officers will strive to obtain maximum cooperation from the public. They will conduct themselves in appearance and deportment in such a manner as to inspire confidence and respect for the position of public trust they hold.

Discretion. A police officer will use responsibly the discretion vested in his position and exercise it within the law. The principle of reasonableness will guide the officer's determinations, and the officer will consider all surrounding circumstances in determining whether any legal action will be taken.

Consistent and wise use of discretion, based on professional policing competence, will do much to preserve good relationships and retain the confidence of the public. There can be difficulty in choosing between conflicting courses of action. It is important to remember that a timely word of advice rather than arrest —which may be correct in appropriate circumstances—can be a more effective means of achieving a desired end.

Use of Force. A police officer will never employ unnecessary force or violence and will use only such force in the discharge of duty as is reasonable is all circumstances.The use of force should be used only with the greatest restraint and only after discussion, negotiation, and persuasion have been found to be inappropriate or ineffective. While the use of force is occasionally unavoidable, every police officer will refrain from unnecessary infliction of pain or suffering and will never engage in cruel, degrading, or inhuman treatment of any person.

Confidentiality. Whatever a police officer sees, hears, or learns of that is of a confidential nature will be kept secret unless the performance of duty or legal provision requires otherwise. Members of the public have a right to security and privacy, and information obtained about them must not be improperly divulged.

Integrity. A police officer will not engage in acts of corruption or bribery, nor will an officer condone such acts by other police officers. The public demands that the integrity of police officers be above reproach. Police officers must therefore avoid any conduct that might compromise integrity and thus undercut the public confidence in a law enforcement agency. Officers will refuse to accept any gifts, presents, subscriptions, favors, gratuities, or promises that could be interpreted as seeking to cause the officer to refrain from performing official responsibilities honestly and within the law. Police officers must not receive private or special advantage from their official status. Respect from the public cannot be bought; it can only be earned and cultivated.

Cooperation with Other Police Officers and Agencies. Police officers will cooperate with all legally authorized agencies and their representatives in the pursuit of justice. An officer or agency may be one among many organizations that may provide law enforcement services to a jurisdiction. It is imperative that a police officer assist colleagues fully and completely with respect and consideration at all times.

Personal–Professional Capabilities. Police officers will be responsible for their own standard of professional performance and will take every reasonable opportunity to enhance and improve their level of knowledge and competence. Through study and experience, a police officer can acquire the high level of knowledge and competence that is essential for the efficient and effective performance of duty. The acquisition of knowledge is a never-ending process of personal and professional development that should be pursued constantly.

Private Life. Police officers will behave in a manner that does not bring discredit to their agencies or themselves. A police officer's character and conduct while off duty must always be exemplary, thus maintaining a position of respect in the community in which he or she lives and serves. The officer's personal behavior must be beyond reproach.

The Use of Force

Two issues probably cause more problems for police administrators in the creation of policies than any other topics. These are the use of force and gratuities. The case *Garner* v. *Tennessee* [105 S.Ct. 1694, 85 L.Ed. 2d 1 (1985)] has simplified the policies regarding the use of deadly force. It is no longer legal to use deadly force except in the following circumstances:

1. In cases of danger to the life of the officer.

2. In cases of danger to the life of a third party.

3. To prevent the escape of an perpetrator who has just committed or attempted to commit a life threatening offense.

4. To prevent the escape of a prisoner from a jail or corrections facility.

There really is no other legitimate justification for the use of deadly force by the police. The limitations listed above represent the basis for a sound policy on the use of deadly force.

Another issue, related to the use of force, is the topic of off-duty weapons. Many law enforcement agencies require their officers to carry weapons and identification at all times, in case of the necessity for taking emergency police action (Fyfe, 1985, pp. 334–335). The arguments for this kind of policy are:

1. Police officers are on duty 24 hours a day and should be prepared to act when needed.

2. Requiring off-duty officers to carry weapons increases the number of effective police officers on the street at any given time.

3. Police officers are subject to vendettas by criminals seeking revenge or attempting to prevent the officer from testifying in court; therefore, they need the means to protect themselves.

4. During the course of a criminal act, some criminals will automatically kill a person discovered to be a police officer.

The reasons for not allowing off-duty weapons are equally compelling:

1. The number of criminals seeking revenge on the police is more a product of fiction than of real life; the number of cases in which revenge against the police was a factor is so small that it is insignificant.

2. If the officer is carrying neither gun nor police identification, there is small chance that a person engaged in a criminal act will identify a person as an officer, and even if this should occur there is low likelihood that it will make any real difference in the outcome of the act.

3. Worker's compensation does not always cover injury to officers working in an off-duty capacity; therefore, an officer taking action off-duty is risking injury for which there may be no insurance protection.

4. In large departments officers do not know all other officers; on-duty personnel may not recognize off-duty personnel as officers and may treat them as armed suspects, increasing the chance of injury to both.

5. Many incidents involving shootings by off-duty officers occur in and around establishments serving alcoholic beverages; many of the officers involved were drinking alcoholic beverages prior to the shootings, thus increasing the probability of liability suits against the officer and department.

6. A primary source of stress for police officers is the inability to leave the job at work; officers need to be average citizens off-duty, and requiring them to carry weapons and identification prevents this from happening.

7. The weapon becomes addictive; officers become so accustomed to having it with them that they show symptoms of paranoia when they do not have the weapon, fearing even to leave their own homes.

8. Firearms training for on-duty weapons is inadequate. Few agencies provide training for off-duty firearms, thus decreasing the officer's level of competence (which is already none too good) with this weapon; a weapon that is usually of different make and caliber than the one the officer uses on-duty.

For the good of the officers themselves, not to mention the administration, all officers should be required to leave their guns and badges at the office and go home to their families as people in other occupations do. The benefits in terms of decreased job burnout, stress, and increased self-confidence of personnel will make this a sound long-range policy. The following case illustrates the fallacy of a policy requiring off-duty officers to carry firearms.

Marusa v. *District of Columbia* (1973)
484 F.2d 828

A shooting victim brought actions against the District of Columbia and its police chief and against a bar owner seeking to recover for injuries sustained when he was shot by a police officer with the officer's service revolver after the officer had allegedly consumed an excessive amount of liquor at the defendant owner's bar. The District of Columbia, Aubrey E. Robinson, Jr., J., granted the defendant's motion to dismiss; the plaintiff appealed.

On May 29, 1969, Officer Clark consumed an excessive amount of liquor in a bar on K Street, N.W., and that immediately after leaving the bar, the "grossly intoxicated" Clark shot Marusa with his service revolver.

Marusa sought to hold Officer Clark liable for the injuries he had inflicted. He sought to hold Chief Jerry V. Wilson liable for negligence in hiring Officer Clark and in failing to train and supervise him adequately. He sought to hold the District of Columbia liable for negligence of Chief Wilson. Finally, he sought damages for negligence from DeMiers Investments, Inc., the owner of the bar in which Officer Clark was drinking prior to the shooting.

Opinion of the Court

The fact that Officer Clark was out of uniform at the time of the alleged assault on Marusa does not affect our conclusion. Officer Clark's tort was made possible only through the use of his service revolver, which he carried by authority of the city government. Policemen are, in fact, not only authorized but required to carry their service revolvers, as well as their badges and identification cards, "at all times" (except in their homes), whether in or out of uniform. Clearly, the government has a duty to minimize the risk of injury to members of the public that is presented by this policy. Thus, if the officer misuses his weapon, a judge or jury might reasonably find that misuse to have been proximately caused by the government's negligence in hiring, training, or supervising the policeman.

Marusa also sought damages from DeMiers Investments, Inc., which operates a (now defunct) "singles" establishment known as "Wayne's Luv." Marusa alleges that on the night of the shooting Officer Clark was served so many drinks at Wayne's Luv that he became grossly intoxicated; that employees of Wayne's Luv knew or should have known at the time they served Officer Clark that he was intoxicated and might pose a danger to others; and that Clark's intoxication was proximately related to his assault on Marusa.

Under the District of Columbia Code, it is a criminal offense to serve alcoholic beverages to a person who is "intoxicated" or who "appears intoxicated." Marusa's complaint sets forth a prima facie case, subject, of course, to rebuttal, that DeMiers violated this statute in serving Officer Clark. It is settled law in this court that "violation of an ordinance intended to promote safety" can give rise to a negligence action.

From the facts alleged in Marusa's complaint, it appears that DeMiers violated a statutory duty owed to Marusa. That allegation is adequate at law to warrant a trial on the merits of Marusa's action against DeMiers.

The dismissals as to the District of Columbia, Chief Jerry V. Wilson, and DeMiers Investments, Inc. are reversed and the cases remanded for further proceedings consistent with this opinion.

Gratuities

The problem of gratuities is delicate for most agencies. The policy itself is not the cause of concern; most departments prohibit the acceptance of gratuities in any form. The problem is the reluctance by supervisors to enforce the policy. No one wants to fire an officer for accepting a free cup of coffee. Even free coffee poses a dilemma for the administrator, however, for the ability of human beings to rationalize inappropriate behavior can be seen with exceptional clarity on this issue. The reasons for accepting free coffee are as follows:

1. I cannot be bribed for a lousy cup of coffee.

2. The businessman provides coffee in return for my being here to prevent criminal activity. In other words, he is buying extra police protection for free coffee.

3. It is too embarrassing to argue with a person intent on giving the coffee away.

4. Since I do not get paid very much, the restaurant owner is providing a service willingly to compensate for my lack of benefits.

5. The owner likes police officers and it would be an insult to one of our few friends to refuse the kind offer.

The administrator should see these arguments for what they are: attempts to rationalize improper behavior. They are also nonsense. Police officers are bought every day for free coffee. Admittedly, the bribe is not very large, but the payback is not large either; occasionally ignoring a parking violation by the owner or taking the owner's side in disputes with customers. The police get paid enough to buy their own coffee, and police protection should be provided equally to all citizens.

How is the administrator to face this problem? Through a two-pronged approach. The issue is not solely a police problem; the public is also involved. Since the policy involves the local business people, they should be informed of the policy. Most people will not tempt officers with gifts if they know that it is against agency policy and the policy is enforced. The administrator should first make the policy clear to the officers—NO GRATUITIES. This message should then be placed in the local newspaper and submitted to the local chamber of commerce. Once the public understands that the administrator is serious about this, most offers of gifts to officers should stop. For those still offered, the policy should be enforced when an officer either ignores the policy or does not take it seriously. Through consistency and determination, this policy can be enforced and should be for the betterment of the organization.

One final statement about policy and ethics and we will move on to another subject. The Law Enforcement Code of Ethics leaves nothing out of this relatively short statement of philosophy. A law enforcement administrator could easily take this statement, attach a procedure for filing complaints and grievances, and in less than five pages have a perfectly useful organizational policy. There may be a few additions, depending on the needs of individual agencies, but overall this code covers everything that an officer needs to know about policy and ethics. More important, it makes the point simply and clearly.

DISCUSSION QUESTIONS

1. Discuss the uses and necessities of departmental policies.

2. Why do policies create such a wide variety of problems for police agencies?

3. Discuss the errors committed by administrators in the creation of department policy.

4. Discuss the impact of the police value system on police management.

5. What is the psychological contract? Why is it important to the police administrator?

REFERENCES

Anon. (1992) "The Evolution of the Law Enforcement Code of Ethics," *The Police Chief,* January, pp. 14–17.

Cornelius, A.L. (1929). *Cross Examination.* Indianapolis, Ind.: Bobbs.

Fyfe, James J. (1985). "Always prepared: police off-duty guns," in Abraham S. Blumberg and Elaine Neiderhoffer eds., *The Ambivalent Force: Perspectives on the Police,* 3rd ed. New York: Holt, Rinehart and Winston, pp. 334–340.

Goldstein, Herman (1977). *Policing a Free Society.* Cambridge, Mass.: Ballinger.

Graham, Gerald (1984). "Consistency, fairness are keys to effective discipline," *The Kansas City Star,* May 27, p. 10D.

Holden, Richard N. (1980). *A Study of Job Satisfaction and Motivation in the Houston Police Department.* Dissertation. Huntsville, Tex.: Sam Houston State University.

Lipset, Seymour Martin (1969). "Why cops hate liberals—and vice versa," *Atlantic Monthly,* Vol. 223, No. 3.

Myrdal, Gunnar (1944). *An American Dilemma.* New York: Harper & Row.

Peters, Thomas J., and Robert H. Waterman, Jr. (1982). *In Search of Excellence.* New York: Warner Books.

Plato (1952). *The Republic,* translated by Benjamin Jowett, in *Plato,* The Great Books of the Western World Series Chicago: Encyclopaedia Britannica.

Radelet, Louis A. (1986). *The Police and the Community,* 4th ed. Encino, Calif.: Glencoe.

Souryal, Sam S. (1992). *Ethics in Criminal Justice: In Search of the Truth.* Cincinnati, Ohio: Anderson.

Townsend, Robert (1984). *Further Up the Organization.* New York: Alfred A. Knopf.

Wilson, James Q. (1968). *Varieties of Police Behavior: The Management of Law and Order in Eight Communities.* Cambridge, Mass.: Harvard University Press.

Chapter 12

Training
and Education

The most important process for ensuring organizational effectiveness is training. Despite this, most law enforcement agencies allocate less than 1 percent of their budget to training programs. This borders on criminal negligence; one cannot expect adequate policing from untrained officers regardless of their dedication.

The secret to successful management is good personnel. Proper training assures that the agency's personnel know how to do their jobs. The training must be adequate for the task. There is an old saying, "practice makes perfect," which is in error. A more accurate statement is, "perfect practice makes perfect." The training program must be focused on the realities of police work rather than the myths. It is all too easy to train officers for the wrong job, or to train officers to do the right job in the wrong manner. Training must therefore be based on the same job description that we discussed in staffing. To train personnel to perform a job effectively, you must first define the job accurately.

There is a price to be paid for having improperly trained officers. The following case provides a good example of those consequences.

Bordanaro v. *McLeod* (1989)
871 F.2d 1151 (1st Cir.)

Off-duty Everett policeman John McLeod became involved in an altercation with plaintiff Alfred "Da" Mattuchio while at a local bar/motel. McLeod was beaten and thrown out of the bar. The officer then called the police department for backup and the entire department, five officers, responded to the scene. The Chelsea Police Department also responded to the call.

Upon arrival, the officers shouted threats to the plaintiffs and demanded entry. Before the manager could open the doors, the police shattered the glass with their nightsticks. Fearing for the safety of the plaintiffs, the manager sent them upstairs to Room 209 while he went to unlock the doors. Once the doors had been opened, the police rushed into the motel and mounted the stairs in pursuit of the plaintiffs.

The manager and owner of the motel offered to open the door with a pass key. Instead of accepting their offer, Officers McLeod, Macauda, and Aiello assaulted and beat Guttardaro and the manager. The police officers were armed with nightsticks, clubs, bats, tire irons, and a fire axe in addition to their service revolvers. They banged repeatedly on the door, demanding entry and continuing to threaten the plaintiffs. A hole was hastily drilled in the door, through which mace was injected into the room. Soon thereafter, Officer McClusky fired two shots from his pistol through the door.

After forced entry to the room, officers savagely beat the heads and bodies of the unarmed plaintiffs until most were reduced to an unconscious or semiconscious state. McLeod repeatedly slammed Vincent Bordanaro's head against the wall and clubbed the other plaintiffs with a bat, all the while stating again and again, "Remember my name, John McLeod, don't forget it." Vincent Bordanaro died as a result of the repeated blows to his head.

A jury returned a verdict against Everett, its mayor, and its chief of police. Following the trial the district judge awarded attorneys' fees to the plaintiffs as prevailing parties under 42 U.S.C. §1988. The defendants appealed.

On appeal the defendants claimed that the evidence was insufficient as a matter of law to find either the municipality or its supervisory officials liable under Section 1983. Reviewing the testimonial evidence the court stated that the jury could have reasonably found that:

1. The sergeant had been present at either about "20 or 30" or "50 or 60" situations involving door breakdowns over his 24-year tenure as a police officer.

2. A 12-pound sledgehammer was provided by the city of Everett for use in breaking down doors.

3. Numerous occasions in which doors were broken down by Everett officers involved the unconstitutional practice of breaking down doors without a warrant when attempting to arrest a felon.

4. The scenario at the King Arthur Motel appeared no different than any of the previous breakdowns made over the years.

5. In breaking down the door at the King Arthur Motel, the officers were following what had been accepted departmental practice in the past.

The court further stated that although there was no direct evidence that the chief of police had actual knowledge of this policy of breaking down doors without a warrant, the evidence does support a finding of his constructive knowledge of that practice. The evidence is sufficient to prove that the chief should have known of the unconstitutional arrest practice. Therefore, the jury's imposition of Section 1983 liability on Everett based on this unconstitutional custom is affirmed.

The court also addressed the issue of whether Everett officials were deliberately indifferent to the need for better recruitment, training, supervision, and discipline of the city's police force. The court made the following observations:

1. The city of Everett was operating under a set of rules and regulations promulgated in 1951 and last distributed to the officers in the mid–1960s.

2. Aside from emergency medical instruction, Everett officers received little or no formal training after completing their initial police academy courses.

3. The city of Everett discouraged officers from seeking out supplementary training courses.

4. Massachusetts state law provided that police officers who enrolled in college law enforcement courses were to receive increased monetary benefits from their employers. The police officers of Everett were forced to sue the city to compel it to provide these benefits.

5. There was no supervisory or command training required on promotion to a higher rank.

6. Since few rules or guideposts for conduct were in force, the organization of the police department placed too much discretion at all operating levels.

7. Background checks of prospective officers were superficial at best, and failed to reach minimal levels of acceptability.

8. The chief of police failed to make written, monthly reports to the mayor concerning the department, as was required by city ordinance.

9. In the past, discipline had been meted out haphazardly, inconsistently, and infrequently to Everett officers.

10. No disciplinary actions were instituted against the officers involved in this incident until over one month after the episode.

11. A full, *internal* investigation by the Everett Police Department did not occur until over one year after the King Arthur incident.

12. The chief's review of civil grievances filed against Everett officers for their misconduct fell well below accepted levels.

13. Everett officials had given little attention to instances of police misconduct in the past.

14. The chief and the mayor had received oral and written requests for better training and organizational improvements prior to the incident at King Arthur.

The court stated that "based on all the foregoing, the jury was well within its discretion in finding that the recruitment, training, supervision or discipline of Everett police officers was grossly and flagrantly deficient."

In this chapter we concentrate on the necessity for training, learning theories, topics for training, training techniques, training design, and specialized training. We conclude with a discussion of training versus education.

NECESSITY FOR TRAINING

Training is necessary for the fulfillment of employee potential. Without training, the best of officers is inadequate at best, incompetent at worst. The foundation of effective law enforcement is established with a good training program.

There are a number of factors involved in the police milieu; which is the subject of this section. These factors are social evolution, legal mandates, maximizing performance, and prolonging employee service.

Social Evolution

Law enforcement is the art of maintaining order in an ever-changing society. Many police practices considered effective 20 years ago have no place in today's police agency. Times change and agency procedures must change accordingly. This means that not only must training programs for new officers be designed for today's world, but the organization must acknowledge the obsolescence of old training programs and be prepared to retrain senior officers on a continuous basis.

On-the-job training alone is not suited to an ever-changing environment. While nothing can substitute for experience, not all officers learn from their mistakes and many are unwilling to admit old practices are failures. New techniques and ideas must be taught in formal training programs and then applied to the street. Senior officers must be shown why the old procedures are in error and why new methods are superior.

Social trends also dictate the necessity for adequate training. Prior to the 1960s, police training focused on law enforcement and firearms. The social upheaval of the 1960s exposed the narrowness of police training where it existed and uncovered the insanity of the failure to train the police properly. Since this period, law enforcement training has been improving throughout the nation, although at an erratic pace. The focus of modern training, however, is not isolated to laws, procedures, and physical aspects of the job. Social skills are also required and these are beginning to receive their share of attention. In the 1970s the trend was toward social awareness and sensitivity training. In the 1980s, social awareness was out and more refined techniques of law enforcement and physical skills returned, but with more intensity and expertise than before. In the 1990s we are back to social skills with emphasis on multicultural sensitivity.

It is no longer acceptable merely to give police officers a badge and gun and send them out to maintain law and order. The requirements of the police function need a higher-caliber officer than was needed in the past. Today's officer must know more about more things than did the police officer of yesterday. The law enforcement administrator must hire people with better qualifications than were possessed by the chief's peers when they began their careers. Police training programs must be designed to turn out officers with more knowledge of the job than is possessed by the chief. As knowledge increases exponentially with time, so must each recruit class know more about the job than the preceding class. Also, as techniques become more refined and new procedures developed, these must be incorporated into the training program. Since the administrative officers are rarely involved in the updating of patrol and investigative techniques, new recruits should begin to know more than the administrators know about the job.

The goal of the training program should be to turn out employees who know as much as their instructors in the teacher's areas of specialization, and more than any single instructor through the accumulation of knowledge in a variety of topics. In short, the recruit should know more than any single instructor. Since the instructor should know more than anyone else in the organization, on graduation from the academy, the recruit should possess the most current knowledge in the agency.

Of course, until the knowledge is applied to actual situations it is simply an unused tool. The ability to apply classroom instruction competently to real-world situations is the mark of the effective officer. The classroom instruction must, however, be designed to meet the changing needs of society and to present the employee with the most appropriate information to do the job adequately.

Legal Mandates

By its very name, law enforcement indicates knowledge of the law in its most current form. The police officer must know as much about the law and legal procedures as do attorneys specializing in criminal matters. To accomplish this means that the police must be kept constantly aware of changes in the laws or procedures. They must be aware of issues determined in appellate court decisions as well as controversy surrounding certain laws and their enforcement. This requires constant training in law and procedure, sometimes on a daily basis, since the frequency of court-ordered change is unpredictable.

Criminal law is not the only factor to be considered by police administrators. The steady growth in civil suits aimed at public agencies, especially the police, has mandated the training of officers in the law of civil liability. Not only must the officers know how to perform the job, they must also be aware of the possible cost of improper performance.

Finally, the administrator must be aware of the ominous trend in civil suits against law enforcement agencies and administrators concerning poor training. The failure to train personnel adequately makes the administrator legally responsible for the improper actions of these poorly trained persons. The law in its many guises therefore requires an adequate police training program.

Maximizing Performance

The best reason for training is the ability to guide employee discretion and judgment. Without training, the employees are on their own. It is inconceivable that police managers would complain about poor performance when the poor performer was untrained. Training is the most certain method of instilling organizational values and pride in the individual officer. It is vastly superior to policies, which tend to be impersonal and sometimes vague. Training allows for questions and clarification.

Ultimately, a good training program does far more than prepare employees for the job; it socializes them into the ideology and values of the organization. The better a person is trained, the less supervision is required to assure proper behavior. The less supervision required, the more resources and personnel can be focused on doing the job instead of supervising those who do the job.

Training increases effectiveness by increasing the quality of the individual officer's performance while releasing personnel from costly and time-consuming supervisory activities. As in industry, the higher the quality of the work done on the line, the less there is need for quality control personnel. Resources spent on training should create the ability to lessen the resources devoted to supervision.

Training is one of the keys to organizational success. No amount of dedication or written guidelines can act as a substitute. With professional sports franchises, the games are won and lost on the practice field. This is equally true of other organizations, especially law enforcement. Unfortunately, this has been only recognized recently.

Prolonging Employee Service

Turnover is the curse of law enforcement. It takes thousands of dollars in training and several years' experience to prepare a new officer properly for the job. When a competent employee resigns, a vacuum is created that cannot be filled before the training and experience combine to provide an employee capable of competent performance.

One reason for the high turnover rate is frustration on the part of police officers regarding the police organization. There are a number of sources from which the frustration is generated. One of the most predominant is the bureaucratic nature of police organizations. Through a myriad of policies and procedures, officers find themselves tied up in procedural manuals they are unable to decipher. Also, as has been observed previously, police agencies tend to be top heavy—or at least middle management heavy. This usually generates autocracy in its worst form; dozens of little Hitlers permeate the organization, successfully stifling any creative thought or suggestion that might come out of the lower ranks.

A second source of the frustration is the confusion that many police officers have over the role of the police and how it meshes with the role of the courts. Law enforcement operates on an immediate timetable; decisions must be made now to resolve an immediate situation. The court time frame is future and past oriented, with little consideration given to the present. The court makes decisions based on their future effects by considering past court decisions of a similar nature. The deliberative process in the court setting is relatively slow compared to the high-speed police process. These different time frames ensure an inability of the court and police personnel to fully understand each other. This results in frustration on the part of both. However, court personnel are better educated and often have a better view of the entire criminal justice process than do the police. Also, the court decisions affect the police more noticeably than vice versa. In other words, the court is in a better position to frustrate the police than the police are to frustrate the court.

The third source of frustration comes from the nature of the job itself. Police work tends to be reactive; police take action after a crime has occurred. Officers receive many requests for help prior to a criminal event. Most of the time they must refuse to provide the aid requested even though they are convinced that a crime will occur if they do not act.

A similar problem lies in the inability to solve most crimes. People sometimes join police agencies with the expectation of solving crimes. Only after they get on the street do they realize that most crimes are solved when there is an eyewitness. Most thefts, including burglary, are not solved at all. The patrol officer may spend a good portion of the day writing police reports of theft cases for which there will be no solution. The frustration in these instances is compounded by the anger and frustration of the victim, which is often released at the expense of the investigating officer. The officer cannot help the victim in these cases, a fact known to the victim. The officer not only feels helpless, but is often made to feel incompetent.

Sufficient frustration and the officer will seek employment elsewhere. Contrary to the popular notion of employee turnover as a result of poor pay, inadequate benefits, or pressure from a spouse, which are sometimes excuses for changing jobs, police officers seek other jobs when they no longer enjoy police work. Frustration takes the fun out of law enforcement. Anything the administrator can do to relieve frustration will lessen employee turnover.

Adequate training can lessen the frustration in all of the areas noted above. First, adequate training can lessen the need for restrictive policies and repressive supervision. Even if the administrator feels insecure without a substantial array of middle management, some of these people can be transformed into more enlightened managers with adequate managerial training. Training can be used to generate and sell necessary policies and procedures. Most of all, training serves as a basis for self-esteem and confidence, both of which reduce frustration.

Second, training can provide a better understanding of the nature of the court and corrections system, thus alleviating the frustration associated with a lack of knowledge of how these institutions function. Not knowing why an event occurred is more frustrating than possessing this knowledge. Providing officers with an understanding of the pitfalls associated with police actions and their consequent results within the remainder of the system can do much to insulate the officer from the frustration of dealing with the other agencies of justice. Dealing with known quantities is always less frustrating than dealing with the unknown.

The third problem is a more difficult problem, for providing a sure solution would mean changing the nature and function of the police occupation. Regardless of the amount of training provided, many aspects of police work will still be reactive by design. Training, however, can provide the officer with an understanding of the limitations of the job before these are faced as frustrations. By altering the officer's expectations, the frustrations of the job can also be reduced.

Frustration is caused by goal blocking. Finding the solution to crimes is a goal of every police officer, but the lack of meaningful evidence frustrates this goal. Understanding when a goal can be achieved and when one should be discarded can do much to limit frustration. It is also helpful for the officer to understand the inability of the police to solve all of the problems of the people they encounter. If the officers can be taught to act as competently as they can, when they can, and not to worry about those situations they cannot alter, the training unit will have accomplished a major feat in the reduction of frustration. The net result will be reduced employee turnover.

CONTEMPORARY TRAINING MODELS

There are two basic forms of police academy, the military model and the collegiate style. Of these two, the military style is older. The *collegiate style* was primarily the result of the need to bring officers from diverse agencies together in a regional training format. Both models have benefits and both have disadvantages. The *military style* is strong in the inculcation of discipline and the establishing of a strong esprit d'corps. The collegiate style is geared more toward the informal classroom approach with an emphasis on discussion. Of the two styles, the collegiate is the better approach for preparing new police officers.

Because the police organization is built along military lines, however, there has been the tendency to structure police training academies similarly. The police boot camp style of academy is still a salient feature of the traditional police organization. The curriculum suffers from this philosophy. Rather than focus on the skills, the officers really need to accomplish their jobs, they are trained in accordance with the myth that they are soldiers in a war against crime.

Discipline and acquiescence to command are stressed where creativity and imagination are needed. Officers are schooled in firearms and self-defense. What they need are oral and writing skills. Police academies that are designed along military lines are archaic and dysfunctional. They teach the wrong lessons for the wrong reasons. Yet they continue. Why do they still exist despite the knowledge that they are outmoded? Paramilitary philosophy; there are those who believe that if an organization looks like a military unit, it must be a military unit. In reality, police organizations look military only because an arbitrary decision was made to make them look that way.

The better approach to police training is designed along lines similar to the college experience. Training is provided through a variety of techniques, but the salient feature is the positive environment provided for learning.

The academy experience is not a military boot camp; even the military has altered its approach to training over the past 20 years. The purpose of the academy is to provide knowledge and skills necessary for the recruit to perform competently in an independent manner. It cannot be stressed strongly enough that academies stressing high discipline crush the initiative and creativity out of recruits. Police work is an occupation requiring motivation, imagination, and initiative. These traits are not found in organizations obsessed with militarylike discipline. Boot camp training does a good job of teaching chain of command, saluting, and personal appearance. They also teach recruits not to question orders, even if they know that the orders are wrong; not to challenge authority, even when the senior officer is incompetent; and to not rock the boat, even when the boat needs to be sunk.

The boot camp approach to police training literally pushes the recruit into the arms of the police subculture. It does this by stressing group loyalty over duty, form over substance, and adherence to command over respect for constitutional values. Much of what is wrong in law enforcement starts with academy systems that are dysfunctional.

With that in mind, we proceed into a discussion of the factors that are involved with police training, including training topics and training techniques.

TRAINING TOPICS

The selection of topics for training is not to be taken lightly. For years police training has focused on the law enforcement aspect of the occupation. This is despite the fact that the vast majority of police work has little to do with law enforcement. Law enforcement is important, as are techniques of self-defense and firearm utilization. However, other subjects are equally important and deserve attention. In this section we discuss the proper selection of subjects to be included in a police training program. Actual topics will not be covered because each agency has unique problems and the training program should be tailored to specific situations whenever possible. Instead, we discuss how topics should be selected, and some examples are offered.

Since police work is concerned primarily with decision making, it is natural to identify topics based on the amount of harm that can be caused by faulty decision making in given areas. Training priorities should therefore be directed in accordance with potential for harm either to officers or to members of society. The following guidelines are offered in order of highest priority: physical harm, minor legal actions, routine decisions, role understanding, social understanding, and skill enhancement.

Physical Harm

The police are given the power of life and death in certain circumstances. As with the fictional character, James Bond, they are literally licensed to kill. Because of this awesome power and responsibility, the law enforcement administrator must place life and death decision making at the top of the list of priorities for training. This includes knowledge of the law regarding the use of force, knowledge of agency policy regarding the use of force, proper decision making under extreme stress, and proper use of tools of force (weapons, restraint devices, etc.).

Even though the vast majority of officers never fire their weapons in armed confrontations with suspects, the potential for accidentally injuring or killing an innocent citizen is serious enough to make weapons handling a major subject of any police training program.

Although firearms is not the only topic within a training module dealing with the use of force, it offers a good example of what can go wrong in a training program. The following problems are not limited to weapons, but are most obvious in this context. First, the state of weapons training among law enforcement agencies in this country is not comforting. A 1984 study of police firearms training programs found the following (Shenkman, 1984, p. 12):

1. The vast majority of law enforcement agencies do not require night firing as a part of their training programs, despite the prevalence of armed confrontation between officers and suspects during hours of darkness.

2. Only a few agencies use multiple selection targets which force the officer to make a rapid decision concerning proper or improper targeting. Also, only a few agencies use moving targets or make any attempt to simulate real combat conditions.

3. Only 20 percent of the nation's police agencies use regular service-type ammunition in training. Eighty percent of the nation's officers are trained with "wad cutters," practice rounds of low power; this makes these officers woefully unprepared for the noise, kick, and trajectory of real service ammunition when it is used in a combat situation. A full 75 percent allow the qualification course to be completed using wad cutters.

4. The majority of the nation's law enforcement agencies require their officers to qualify only twice a year.

5. Police officers in the study missed their intended target between 75 and 90 percent of the time in real combat situations.

While the study cited above focused on the physical act of firing a weapon, another study looked at the decision-making process of patrol officers in the shooting events. The study found the following factors considered in the decision to shoot (Brown, 1984, p. 140):

1. The real danger, in terms of risk to the officer or another of serious injury or death, presented by the actual situation.

2. The officer's perceptions of danger inherent in a situation.

3. The state law governing the use of a firearm to apprehend criminal suspects.

4. The police department's policies regulating the use of a firearm by a police officer.

5. The individual values of the officer.

6. The seriousness of the offense.

A disturbing aspect of the study cited above, is the additional finding regarding officers who have tendencies toward using a firearm. Mike Brown discovered that younger officers—those caught up in the John Wayne syndrome— are more likely than older officers to make the decision to use firearms more rapidly, and to do so under questionable circumstances. As Brown observes, the disturbing factor is the tendency of police agencies to assign officers to geographic areas and by shift according to seniority. This results in the agency placing those most prone to the rapid use of deadly force in areas and at times where deadly force can be most frequently justified in the mind of the officer.

What we observe by taking this quick glance at firearms training tells us a great deal about the state of police training in this country in general and about weapons training specifically. First, the need to train officers in the proper handling of weapons was recognized much earlier in the history of police training than most other topics. Despite this, firearms training is still sporadic and generally ineffective. Where it is done at all, it is often done wrong (see the discussion of trained incapacity in Chapter 8).

From the above we can see the need for improved firearms training, but what about the state of other police training. If the remaining topics are as poorly designed as weapons training, the police in this country are in big trouble. Fortunately, such is not the case. Weapons utilization brings almost every aspect of the officer's mental and physical capacity into play at the same time. A vast amount of information must be processed rapidly and a decision reached while nearly every muscle in the body must act simultaneously in a concerted manner to remove the weapon from the holster, aim it, and fire. The situation, the law, department policy, the officer's values, and firearms training must all come together at the same time. No other decision or act by an officer requires that all these elements be processed at the same time and with such speed. Also, no other action by an officer generates such emotional upheaval within the individual. Police shootings are rarely done through a process of cold calculation; they are most often high-speed actions accompanied by intense anger or fear. It stands to reason, therefore, that firearms training should be far more intricate and complicated than it appears through casual observance.

Other training topics do not present this vast array of factors for immediate consideration. Some are covered exceptionally well in training programs, given the limited time within which many programs are forced to operate. Firearms is not the only subject dealing with the potential for harm. Restraint techniques may also be improperly applied, as well as self-defense methods. Each must be considered in any training program.

Another aspect of the police responsibility for physical safety is knowledge of first aid. The police are in the unique position of being the first respondents to the scene of the majority of emergencies. Thus, whereas the police are sometimes empowered to kill, they are also responsible for saving lives whenever possible. Failure to provide proper first-aid training for officers is to deny people seriously injured or ill and in need of immediate competent help the emergency care necessary for their survival.

The police function and how it relates to the physical safety of officers and citizens should be the highest-priority item in any police training package. Both officer and citizen safety as well as the protection of officers from claims of civil liability demand such a training priority. There has been a shift in focus in the courts in police shooting cases, for example. Policy and training is now a proper subject for litigation in cases involving police shootings (Hall, 1984, p. 31). This is also true of any situation involving police force of any other kind, as the following case demonstrates.

City of Amarillo v. *Langley* (1983)
651 S.W.2d 906 (Tex.App. 7 Dist.)

Action was brought for injuries sustained in a collision that occurred when a patrol car drove in front of two motorcycles being pursued by police. The 108th District Court, Potter County, Edward B. Nobles, J., entered judgment for injured motorcyclists, and the defendant city appealed.

The litigation is based on a violent encounter between two motorcycles and a police car. Thomas E. Langley and John Langley were driving their respective motorcycles through downtown Amarillo with Jada Malone as a passenger on the back of Tom Langley's motorcycle, at approximately 3:00 A.M. on June 29, 1975. When the Langleys rolled through a red light on 6th Street, Amarillo police officer Jerry Ashford gave chase in his patrol car and broadcast his pursuit of the motorcycles. Policemen Ronald Hudson and Richard Webb, in a second patrol car, turned onto 6th Street toward the oncoming motorcycles and placed the car diagonally across the street in a maneuver described as a deterrent block. Tom Langley and Jada Malone collided with the blocking car and were seriously injured. John Langley turned his motorcycle sharply to the left and missed the patrol car but collided with a parked car and was also seriously injured.

Opinion of the Court
The chief of police and several police officers testified that the police department uses a deterrent block as an accepted method of stopping a person fleeing arrest, regardless of the nature of the crime or offense. They also testified that the deterrent block used in this case was proper. Thus there is evidence that by either policy or custom the city sanctioned the use of a deterrent block.

Within the framework of what a reasonable police officer would do, the jury was entitled to believe that policeman Hudson attempted to arrest two traffic offenders by driving his vehicle across a substantial segment of the lane in which they were traveling, and that he did so at night without turning on warning beacons, and that he did so a few seconds before they arrived at his location when he knew they were traveling at a high rate of speed. Being entitled to believe that testimony, the jury was entitled to find, and did find, that Officer Hudson used greater force than was reasonably necessary (i.e., excessive force).

We conclude, therefore, that Jada Malone and the Langley brothers established a section 1983 cause of action against the city of Amarillo.

Legal Actions

Arrests and traffic citations are routine occurrences for police officers. To the public, however, these are major events in their lives and cause great discomfort. At the least an arrest or citation presents a significant inconvenience to the person receiving the unwanted police attention. Often, the event is more than just an inconvenience, it represents a substantial financial burden in terms of court fees or legal costs. Add to this the embarrassment and public humiliation that sometimes follows such an event, and it takes little imagination to conceive of the potentially damaging consequences of a police mistake.

Since the potential for mistake, or abuse, is accompanied by serious consequences for the person victimized by the error, the law enforcement administrator must take every precaution to assure a minimum of errors of this type. Police officers are human and will make mistakes, but a sound training program focused on all aspects of criminal investigation and arrest can minimize the problem. This training should also consider the sensitivity of the situations. The law enforcement function can be fulfilled without harassment and vindictiveness.

The second-priority topics are those concerning decisions by police officers that have a profound impact on the lives of the people affected. When the police are in a position to inflict mental harm, they must be thoroughly trained to ensure that they perform properly, but with as little injury done to the innocent as possible. It is also not the function of the police to inflict harm on the guilty. They should take aggressive legal actions in as humane a method as possible.

Routine Decisions

The vast majority of police work is routine. The training program should strive to identify those functions within the agency that are common occurrences and teach the officers the most appropriate method of response. Often, policies are used for this purpose. This is an error; this is the way in which policy manuals grow to monumental sizes. Training is a much better and more certain approach for handling routine functions. It is more useful because it allows for discussion of the problem, and as new techniques are discovered or as the situation changes, requiring new responses, the training can be adapted rapidly.

Included in routine decisions are the vast array of human relations problems (family, business, and neighborhood disputes) confronting the police officer daily. The entire order maintenance spectrum can usually be identified under this heading, which would also include such duties as traffic control and accident investigation as well as monitoring businesses requiring legal supervision, such as bars and gambling facilities. As a result, more training time may be spent in this area than in all others, depending on the agency.

Role Understanding

A large amount of police frustration is the result of the police trying to be something they are not. A lack of understanding of their proper role can create unnecessary stress in the officers. The training program should strive to identify the proper role for officers within that agency. Officers should be taught what the agency is trying to accomplish and what their responsibilities are regarding the organization's mission.

For the officer's own mental health, emphasis should be placed on what can and cannot be accomplished by the police. The training program should be totally geared to accomplishing the possible.

Social Understanding

Understanding the police role is important only if the officer understands where the police organization fits into society as a whole. The social milieu of each jurisdiction is different. The training program should be designed to provide each officer with an understanding of the social composition of the jurisdiction and the competing values inherent within the various groups making up the population.

The police value system must mesh with the value system of the jurisdiction being policed. Where there is no synchronized value system, one usually finds hostility and resentment between the police and their public. This is most often found where there is no attempt by the police to understand their jurisdiction, which allows the police subculture to dictate the police values in an arbitrary and rigid manner.

The training program must make an attempt to foster understanding of the community among the officers. The training officer cannot teach the public to understand the police. If there is to be social harmony between police and policed, the agency must work to generate understanding among the law enforcement personnel of their society.

Skill Enhancement

There are a variety of skills that each officer should possess. Such things as reading, writing, thinking critically, and using tools of the trade must be practiced constantly for improvement and to prevent a degeneration of the skills. More than simply teaching the basics, the training program must therefore allow for a continual practice of necessary skills to foster ever-increasing capabilities.

Police officers spend the majority of their time communicating. They are either talking with people or writing reports. They must be able to speak and write well. Some years ago an assistant district attorney of a large city stated that approximately 10 percent of the felony cases he received were dropped because he could not read the report or the report was so poorly written as to be of no benefit in proceeding with the case. That level of incompetence in the use of the written word is unacceptable for a professional police department.

The ability to communicate well also reduces the danger to police officers and citizens. Officers with the ability to talk with people have less need of force.

Officers who articulate their instructions clearly and concisely obtain rapid control of situations. Those officers who are not so articulate frequently lose control, therefore allowing a tense situation to degenerate into one that is volatile. The ability to communicate is, in many ways, a much more vital skill than the ability to shoot a weapon.

TRAINING TECHNIQUES

The training technique adopted will depend on the subject matter as well as the time and resources available. Among the approaches available to the instructor are on-the-job training, programmed learning, job rotation, lecture, simulation, role playing, self-instruction, and seminars.

On-the-Job Training

On-the-job training is self-explanatory. The person is placed on the job, usually under the supervision of an experienced person, and allowed to learn by doing. This is one of the most common training formats among law enforcement agencies. It can be extremely useful, especially in situations with little capacity for injury or damage, such as in industrial or routine jobs. The drawbacks as they affect the police lie in the learning-by-making-mistakes aspect of on-the-job training. Police officers make occasional errors; rookies often make more than their fair share. Police mistakes often translate into mental or physical injury to an innocent person. There is an old saying that, "doctors bury their mistakes while lawyers send theirs to prison." Police officers do a little of both.

On-the-job training in police work has one further problem area; it is dependent on random situations. An officer can be in the field for several years on a small agency and never encounter a situation calling for competent training. On-the-job training is therefore sporadic when applied to law enforcement agencies; some officers receive exceptional training, other receive none at all.

Despite these limitations, all new law enforcement officers should receive on-the-job training after they graduate from the police academy and before they are allowed to do police work on their own. This is the point where the field training officer (FTO) is best utilized. Each new officer is assigned to a FTO for several months for training and evaluation. When used well, this provides excellent supplemental training to the academy and gives the agency an opportunity to observe the recruit in actual situations.

Programmed Learning

Programmed learning is a form of structured self-instruction. The training information is contained within a question/answer format. The student reads the information and is then asked to respond to questions about the information just read. Answers are provided to the questions, providing immediate feedback. This is highly useful for technical information such as legal issues or identification techniques. It is less useful for developing physical skills, which cannot be adequately developed without hands-on application. For intellectual development, however, programmed learning is a competent technique.

Job Rotation

One of the better methods of developing an understanding of the entire organization is through job rotation. Each officer is assigned a short tour of duty within each unit of the agency. This works very well with recruits who have not yet begun to identify with a single function of the organization.

Job rotation has the further advantage of introducing new officers to a variety of different personnel within the overall organization, thus facilitating their entry and acceptance into the organization.

Lecture

Lecture is a very cost-effective method for conveying information to a large group of people. It allows for a single instructor to reach a room full of people. As with programmed learning, it is useful for providing technical information. It is also useful for setting the stage for the training of physical skills, such as firearms. The lecture is given first, then practice is allowed.

The limitations on the lecture technique should be of concern to anyone involved in training. It is one of the least effective of all teaching methods. It is usually tailored to a speed of presentation far below the student's capacity to hear and comprehend. The students frequently allow their minds to wander and lose much of the information. Also, the attention span of the students is limited. After about 20 to 30 minutes, students begin to lose interest. The size of the class can also affect the individual student's willingness to participate, thus reducing the availability of feedback. In short, there are times when the lecture format must be used, but it should be used with caution and with its limitations kept in mind.

Simulation

Simulation is a very useful training technique. It has the advantage of allowing the trainee to respond to real-world situations without danger of causing harm. An additional advantage lies in the ability to alter situational variables to test possible responses. Simulation techniques include field exercises such as riot control or tactical responses and computerized problem-solving games. The limitations on simulation training are only those of the creativity of the person designing the exercises, and resources available to increase the reality of the situations.

Role Playing

A technique similar to simulations training is role playing. By requiring employees to act out various roles in problem situations, greater understanding is derived for all people involved. This is a useful method of teaching officers techniques for resolving interpersonal disputes. Role playing has sometimes been combined with simulation to enhance realism. For example, some agencies have hired professional actors and actresses to act out various situations involving interpersonal conflict. The new officers are then introduced into the arena to resolve the problem. This offers the officers a unique opportunity to experience the emotional stress involved in such a situation while testing their own interpersonal skills in a tense situation. Afterward, a debriefing session with all participants can serve to highlight the feelings of each person as the scenario progressed. This is an excellent method for training techniques in conflict resolution.

Self-Instruction

Self-instruction is the most cost-effective means of teaching any topic. The topic is assigned and the trainee seeks out the necessary information and learns it individually without personal contact with an instructor. Unfortunately, self-instruction is totally dependent on the motivation of the student. Lacking motivation, or some means of coercion by the instructor, most people simply will not learn the material.

Self-instruction is most often utilized with general orders and policy promulgation. New policies and procedures are issued and each officer must assimilate the new data. As might be expected, the degree to which this information is learned varies from person to person.

Seminars

Seminars differ from lectures in the format used. Within a seminar each student is expected to contribute something to the class. Unlike lectures, where the instructor presents the information to the students, the seminar stresses the presentation of information by students with the instructor acting as referee or moderator. Seminars are good educational formats when the structure is well thought out and the instructor maintains a sharp focus on the direction taken by the class. One of the dangers of the seminar is the tendency to drift off topic. For technical information, such as a discussion of legal issues, the seminar is a reasonably good approach.

TRAINING DESIGN

The training program should be designed carefully with a purpose always uppermost in the construction. There are three elements to a good training program: goal identification, skill development, and deficiency correction. These terms should be self-explanatory, but some discussion is appropriate. *Goal identification* means that the instructor has a specific objective or group of objectives in mind for the training module. It is not sufficient to have a general goal in mind; the goal must be specific. Otherwise, the course of instruction will drift about with no clear path to follow.

Skill development refers to the ability of the program to enhance specific skills relevant to the goals of the module. For example, a firearms program may have as a goal the training of each officer to use a weapon proficiently. Skill development will focus on actual practice in the use of the weapon.

Finally, *deficiency correction* focuses on a system of evaluation and feedback which allows the person to identify problem areas and work on these problems specifically to improve performance. Each training program must identify weaknesses and allow for improvement.

All training programs should follow the pattern outlined above. Time and research has demonstrated the validity in this approach. As long as these rules are kept in mind when training modules are designed, there should be few flaws in the structure of the training.

Specialized Training

Training serves a number of useful purposes, but it must be geared for the audience served. The types of training that should be provided by a law enforcement agency are varied. All personnel should undergo recruit training, with emphasis placed on topics as discussed above. After the initial training, however, all officers should undergo serious advanced training at various points in their careers. Every officer must be subjected to an ongoing training regimen to maintain skills learned previously and to receive new information as it becomes available. To this end, in-service training in specialized areas must be provided for all personnel. Also, a variety of specialized schools are available on a nationwide basis. Law enforcement administrators should take full advantage of these courses to provide as much high-quality training as is possible for agency personnel.

Finally, middle management and senior-level administrators should be required to attend management training programs. More organizational problems are generated by poor management than from any other source. Although this will probably always be the case, many problems can be alleviated by a sound managerial training program.

Training is not a one-time proposition. It is insufficient to provide a minimum of recruit training and hope that there will be no necessity for further instruction. Basic training merely lays the foundation for effective performance; continual training is the secret for maximum organizational performance.

EDUCATION

The debate over the value of education versus training has raged since the first police academy was founded and is not likely to be resolved here. Both have a place in law enforcement organizations. Training is concerned with the teaching of concepts to be applied directly on the job. Education focuses on a deeper understanding of the concepts under discussion and incorporates theory, philosophy, and history of the subject.

To differentiate the two concepts further, a person could be trained to operate a piece of machinery, such as a Breathalyzer without any knowledge of why it works. Alternatively, the person could be taught the history and theory of the instrument without being shown its operation. In other words, in the first case the person was trained about use of the Breathalyzer and in the second case was educated about the technology. The issue becomes confused because many programs integrate training and education by laying a solid theoretical foundation for the topic prior to training a person in the operation of the instrument. In this case the person is both trained and educated.

Education in the broad sense, however, implies much more than background in occupational concepts. The educated person is one who possesses knowledge of a variety of topics beyond the narrow confines of the occupation. The question for the police administrator is whether or not police officers should be educated, trained, or both. It is absolutely crucial for all law enforcement personnel to be trained in the fundamentals of the occupation, but how much education should the officer have?

There has been a consensus developing among scholars and police administrators on this topic. As far back as the early 1930s, the Wickersham Commission stated the need for a professional police force; one that was educated (National Commission on Law Observance and Enforcement, 1931). In 1973, the National Advisory Commission on Criminal Justice Goals and Standards made the same recommendation.

For the past 50 years, presidential task forces have been calling for college-educated police officers. How many departments took the call seriously? In 1989 the most comprehensive study yet done on the state of police education was commissioned by the Police Executive Research Forum, a national association made up of college-educated chief executives of the nation's largest police agencies. The PERF study provided the clearest picture of education level among the police and of the benefits of educated officers (Carter, Sapp, and Stephens, 1989).

From the PERF study a picture emerges of ever-increasing reliance on college education by major police agencies. Table 12-1 illustrates the breakdown, by race, of college education among the police (Sapp and Carter, 1992, p. 311).

Table 12-1
Education Level of Police Officers by Race (Percent)

	Blacks	*Hispanics*	*Whites*	*Other*
No college	28.2%	27.3%	34.1%	19.4%
One year	36.3%	49.6%	20.5%	36.1%
Two years	9.8%	6.5%	15.6%	13.6%
Three years	8.2%	4.7%	6.9%	13.3%
Four years	8.9%	6.7%	9.2%	9.6%
Graduate degree	8.6%	5.2%	3.7%	8.0%

Additionally, female officers in this study, who accounted for only 12.1 percent of the population sample, averaged a full year of education more than that of their male counterparts.

The following advantages of a college education for a police officer were identified (Sapp and Carter, 1992, pp. 300–301):

1. Greater knowledge of procedures, functions, and principles relevant to [the officers'] present and future assignments.

2. Better appreciation of their professional role and its importance in the criminal justice system as well as in society.

3. More desirable psychological makeup, which includes such qualities as alertness, empathy, flexibility, initiative, and intelligence.

4. Greater range of interpersonal skills centered in the ability to communicate, to be responsive to others, and to exercise benevolent leadership.

5. Greater ability to analyze situations, to exercise discretion independently, and to make judicious decisions.

6. Strong moral character which reflects a sense of conscience and the qualities of [honesty], reliability, and tolerance.

7. More desirable system of personal values consistent with the police function in a democratic society.

These factors suggest that college education helps to produce a more professional police officer (Sapp and Carter, 1992, p. 301).

There are counterarguments to college-educated police officers. The negative arguments can be summarized as follows (O'Rourke, 1971, p. 12):

1. Many good officers do not have degrees.

2. Many poor officers do have degrees.

3. Degree requirements will negatively affect minority recruitment.

4. Degreed officers will be bored with the job.

5. Degreed officers will expect special treatment.

6. College-educated officers cause animosity within the ranks.

7. Officers without college can develop necessary people skills through in-service and on-the-job training.

8. Police departments cannot competitively recruit college graduates.

Although the foregoing concerns are real, most are based on either myth or past experience when there were few college-educated police officers. As the percentage of degreed officers has increased, most of the concerns listed above have decreased.

Possibly the most frequent arguments are the first two. It is true that there are good officers without degrees and bad officers with degrees, but is that con-

Table 12-2

Advantages and Disadvantages of College Educated Police Officers

Traits of College-Educated officers	Strongly agree (+2)	Agree (+1)	Disagree (-1)	Strongly disagree (-2)	Mean score
Communicates better with the community	140	30	29	0	+1.17
More likely to leave job	29	121	297	23	-0.35
Writes better reports	130	302	37	2	+1.11
Less likely to question orders	1	69	344	53	-0.81
More effective performance	43	257	169	1	+1.00
Disruptive to promotion system	4	34	299	131	-1.11
More citizen complaints	2	6	343	113	-1.20
Requests reassignment	3	62	67	27	-0.77
More initiative in police tasks	36	292	138	3	+0.47
Less likely to make arrests	1	40	332	95	-1.03
More professional	62	303	101	2	+0.69
Writes more traffic tickets	2	53	395	14	-0.79
Uses discretion unwisely	3	53	337	75	-0.91
Less likely to be promoted	4	9	311	144	-1.24
Better decision maker	37	304	124	2	-0.54
More respect from community	34	225	200	7	+0.16
Less sensitive to racial/ ethnic groups	8	48	325	87	-0.93
Higher morale	10	176	270	12	-0.21
Fewer absences	11	154	291	7	-0.28
More disciplinary problems	2	15	376	70	-1.07

sistently true across the entire spectrum of officers? In an attempt to get at the real differences between college-educated and non-college-educated officers, the PERF study asked administrators their opinions regarding the performance of college-educated officers on a whole range of police activities. The results are demonstrated in Table 12-2 (page 299). The mean score represents the degree to which the survey respondents agree with the statement. (Carter, Sapp, and Stephens, 1989, p. 47):

On the basis of this survey, it would appear that there is a growing consensus among police administrators that the educated officer is more valuable to the police organization than one who is not educated. As a result of the study above, the Police Executive Research Forum passed, by a nearly unanimous vote, a resolution calling for the immediate implementation of a phased plan of college education for law enforcement officers, with the ultimate goal of requiring a four-year degree from an accredited college as a minimum entry requirement. This same resolution called for immediate implementation of requirements for college education for law enforcement officers promoted beyond the rank of patrol officer (Anon., 1989).

There are, however, still some unanswered questions. Is the college requirement legal? What is the impact of a college requirement on minority recruiting?

The answer to the first question is "yes"; the college requirement is legal. The landmark case regarding such a requirement is *Davis* v. *Dallas*.

Davis v. *City of Dallas* (1985)
777 F.2d 205 (5th Cir.)

The Dallas Police Department required that applicants for positions on its police force, at the time of application, (1) must have completed 45 semester hours of college credit with at least a "C" average at an accredited college or university, (2) must not have had a history of "recent or excessive marijuana usage" as determined by the department's marijuana usage chart, and (3) must not have been convicted of more than three hazardous traffic violations in the 12 months, nor convicted of more than six such violations in the 24 months preceding the date of application. Once the applicant had been hired, he or she was required to complete academy training, field training, and probation successfully before attaining permanent status.

Brenda Davis and Cynthia Jane Durbin brought action against the city of Dallas. Davis alleged that she was denied employment because of her race (she was black). Durbin alleged that she was dismissed from the department because of her gender. The police department claimed that Davis was dismissed because she falsified her application; Durbin allegedly performed inadequately during the field training process. In July 1978 both cases were certified as class actions. Davis also applied for injunctive relief to prevent the city from using discriminatory selection criteria in future police officer hiring. Injunctive relief was denied.

The Circuit Court ruled that:

1. The city's requirement that applicants for positions on its police force must have completed 45 semester hours of college credit at an accredited college or university with at least a "C" average, despite its statistically significant disparate impact on blacks, was justified by business necessity where police officers combined aspects of both professionalism and significant public risk and responsibility.

2. Because of the professional nature of the job of a major city police officer, coupled with the risks and public responsibility inherent in that position, empirical evidence is not required to validate the job relatedness of requirement that applicants for the position of police officer must have completed 45 semester hours of college credit at an accredited college or university with at least a "C" average.

3. The district court's findings that the city had shown sufficient job relatedness or business necessity for the requirement that applicants for the position of police officer must have completed 45 semester hours of college credit at an accredited college or university with at least a "C" average were not clearly erroneous.

4. The district court's findings that the requirement that applicants for the position of police officer in a major city not have a history of recent or excessive marijuana use was job related, despite the contention that it had a disparate impact on black applicants, was not clearly erroneous.

5. The district court's finding that the city's requirement that applicants for the position of police officer not have more than three convictions for hazardous traffic violations in the preceding 12 months or 6 convictions in the preceding 24 months, was job related, despite the contention that it had disparate impact on blacks.

The plaintiffs appealed to the U.S. Supreme Court. Relying on expert testimony from police administrators and academicians, the Court noted that national commissions had consistently recommended college credit as a minimum requirement for police officer. The Court upheld the lower court decisions and rejected the arguments of Davis and Durbin.

The problem associated with minority recruitment is more difficult to address. A smaller percentage of minorities go to college, and the competition between the public and private sectors to hire minority college graduates is intense. Despite this, the PERF study found that the proportion of black and Hispanic officers on a nationwide basis was roughly the equivalent of the proportion of black and Hispanic people in the general population (12.3 percent black officers compared with 12.1 percent blacks in the general population; 6.4 percent Hispanic compared with 8 percent Hispanic population) (Carter, Sapp, and Stephens, 1989, p. xxi).

The statistics above do not mean that all departments have a proportional representation of minority officers; that is far from true. It does mean that more minorities are seeking careers in law enforcement. Many of these people are college educated. The necessity of hiring minority officers is a pressing one. What is required is creativity in the recruiting process. It is no longer sufficient to advertise a position and see who applies for the job. Minority recruitment requires aggressive techniques, especially if the target is college-educated minorities.

Moreover, departments have successfully established that college education is a *bona fide occupational qualification* (BFOQ). In other words, departments are free to adopt educational standards as long as the standards are job related

(Gaines and Kappeler, 1992, p. 113). This means that other considerations are less important than college education. This does not lessen the responsibility, and necessity, for hiring minorities; it merely places the emphasis on hiring educated officers.

Clearly, the time has come for police agencies to require college education as a minimum entry-level criterion. Some agencies have even gone so far as to require graduate degrees for promotion to administrative positions. In an ever-changing and increasingly technical society, a high school diploma is no longer sufficient to meet the needs of the modern professional police department.

DISCUSSION QUESTIONS

1. Why is training so important to the creation of a modern police agency?

2. Discuss the various objectives of a police training program. Which is most important? Why?

3. Discuss the various techniques of training. Which is most appropriate for teaching procedures for handling domestic disputes? Why? Which is more effective for teaching the criminal code? Why?

4. Compare and contrast training and education. Which is more important for police officers? Why? Should a college degree be required of all police officers? Why?

REFERENCES

Anon. (1989). "Police and higher education," *Subject to Debate,* Vol. 3, No. 4

Brown, Michael F. (1984). "Use of deadly force by patrol officers: training implications," *Journal of Police Science and Administration.* Vol. 12, No. 2, pp. 133–40.

Carter, David L., Allen D. Sapp, and Darrell L. Stephens (1989). *The State of Police Education: Policy Directions for the 21st Century.* Washington, D.C.: Police Executive Research Forum.

Gaines, Larry K. and Victor E. Kappeler (1992). "Selection and testing," in Gary W. Cordner and Donna Hale, eds., *What Works in Policing: Operations and Administration Examined.* Cincinnati, Ohio: Anderson Publishing Company and the Academy of Criminal Justice Sciences, pp. 107–124.

Hall, John C. (1984). "Deadly force: the common law and the constitution," *FBI Law Enforcement Bulletin,* April, pp. 26–31.

National Advisory Commission on Criminal Justice Goals and Standards (1973). *Police.* Washington, D.C.: U.S. Government Printing Office.

National Commission on Law Observance and Enforcement (1931). *Report on the Police.* Washington, D.C.: U.S. Government Printing Office.

O'Rourke, W. J. (1971). "Should all policemen be college trained?" *The Police Chief,* Vol. 38, No. 12.

Sapp, Allen D. and David L.Carter (1992). "Police and higher education," in Richard N. Holden, ed., *Law Enforcement: An Introduction.* Englewood Cliffs, N.J.: Prentice Hall.

Shenkman, Frederick A. (1984). "Police handgun training and qualification: a question of validity," *FBI Law Enforcement Bulletin,* April, pp. 7–12.

Chapter 13

Organizational Control

A ll organizations must control their activities, and the management must be aware of how to design effective control systems. Control systems coordinate the activities of all organization members. These systems provide methods of integration and measurement. Control ensures that all members of the agency are coordinated through standards, rules, norms, budgets, and reporting systems. Control offers the mechanism for providing order to the diverse activities of the agency (Aldag and Stearns, 1991, pp. 569–570).

Although we tend to think of control as an objective process, the reactions of those subject to controls may sometimes be emotional and tinged with resentment. This occurs because control behaviors are designed to hold the members of the organization accountable for their actions and decisions. To determine if objectives are being met, it is people whose performance must be reviewed (DuBrin, Ireland, and Williams, 1989, p. 447). It is the placing of the person under a critical spotlight that triggers defensive behavior. This is unfortunate but necessary for effective management.

CONTROL NETWORK

A number of factors interact to form the control network. The first of these is the list of components that make up the control system. These are called the *elements of control*. The second factor is composed of the *functions of control*: how the elements are used. Third is the *control cycle*: the time frame in which the elements are engaged in the process. With this in mind we take a closer look at the control process.

Elements of Control

All organizations share elements of control. This is despite the fact that agencies develop their own unique control systems. This occurs because the elements can be defined in different ways. How they are defined determines the character of the individual control system. All control systems are made up of the following elements (Aldag and Stearns, 1991, pp. 571–572):

> *Monitoring systems*: measure and assess ongoing activities to determine the actual performance.
>
> *Evaluation systems*: compare the actual performance with the desired performance.
>
> *Feedback*: provides the necessary information from the evaluation systems to management, which determines if corrective actions are necessary.
>
> *Standards, rules, regulations*: serve to set guidelines for activities and decisions.
>
> *Goals*: communicate what performance is expected.
>
> *Corrective actions:* are exerted to bring actual behavior back into line with expected behavior.
>
> *Influence techniques:* are used to control behavior.
>
> *Rewards:* help the effectiveness of the control system by rewarding the desired behavior.

All of these elements will be found in a comprehensive control system. What will differ will be the way that each element is used and the individual design features of each.

Functions of Control

There are four interrelated functions served by control systems in organizations. Each function is necessary if the control system is to be effective. These functions are *overseeing, comparing, correcting deviations,* and *influencing future decisions* (see Table 13-1) (Aldag and Stearns, 1991, p. 572).

Overseeing

Overseeing is the means by which a control system monitor ongoing activities to ensure that they are being conducted in accordance with organizational guidelines. Normally, overseeing is a supervisory activity and is particularly useful when the activity being monitored is well understood by both worker and supervisor. Overseeing also occurs when the supervisor and officer are in close proximity to one another, although the availability of modern communications technology is changing this to some degree.

Table 13-1

Functions of Control

Function	Purpose	Methods
Overseeing	To ensure that appropriate action is taking place.	Observing Conferring
Comparing	To determine the degree of agreement between the actual performance and the desired performance and assess the significance of any deviation.	Measuring Collecting data Evaluating Disseminating Reporting information
Correcting Deviations	To correct unacceptable deviations from desired performance.	Immediate Basic
Influencing Future Decisions	To provide feedback to management to assess future goals.	Reporting Goal setting

Comparing

Comparing the actual performance with the expected performance does not necessarily occur when the supervisor and officer are in close proximity. This can be done in isolation. The person responsible for the comparison must, however, have access to information that demonstrates the performance of the person as well as information that states the expectations. Comparing involves measuring, collecting data, evaluating, disseminating information, and reporting to the decision makers.

"An important aspect of comparing is assessing the significance of any deviation from the plan" (Aldag and Stearns, 1991, p. 572). It is normal for there to be differences between what is and what should be. No plan is perfect. It is difficult, however, to know how much deviation should be allowed before engaging the mechanisms for correction. The amount of deviation allowed will often depend on the activity. Issues concerning the use of deadly force by police officers, for example, would be expected to have less tolerance for deviation than would issues concerning the handling of stray animals.

Correcting Deviations

There are two types of corrective action: immediate corrective action and basic corrective action. *Immediate corrective action* is taken to solve an immediate problem. An example might be to remove an officer from duty who is found to be intoxicated. *Basic corrective action* is designed to influence performance in the future. It involves an analysis of the causes for the deviation so that any corrective action taken results in a permanent solution to the problem.

Influencing Future Decisions

A good control system provides management with sufficient feedback to prepare for the future. It maintains organizational momentum by influencing and rewarding employees. By learning from past and present mistakes, the system allows for actions that help control future activities. Knowing that many officers are poor writers, for example, allows the administrator to alter the screening process to increase the importance of writing skills on future applicants.

Control Cycle

The control cycle is the composite of the elements of the control system linked together to form a system. Components of the system are structured into a specific time frame. The first three steps in the cycle are designed to energize the organization. These steps get the agency and its personnel moving in the right direction. The beginning of the cycle occurs with the development of goals and objectives. In this phase the organization determines what is to be accomplished. Next, standards and rules are promulgated. This sets the organizational guidelines that determine how the goals will be achieved. The third step occurs when the agency personnel actually engage in behavior that performs the required activities.

The second series of actions comprise the evaluative and reinforcement process. In step 4, the actions of the first three phases achieve measurable results. In step 5 those results are measured and compared with the goals and objectives. Step 5 may be one of two different actions, depending on the comparisons conducted in step 4. If there is sufficient deviance from the goals and objectives, corrective action is taken. The results are again measured after this action. If more correction is needed, it is applied. If not, the next step is evaluation of the overall process and reward for productive behavior. The cycle then begins again.

ASSESSING ORGANIZATIONAL EFFECTIVENESS

According to Robert Albanese, "Organizational effectiveness is the degree to which an organization's performance meets standards that are relevant to the persons or groups making the evaluation" (1988, p. 639). The critical question is: Which people will evaluate the effectiveness of a police agency? The public evaluation may be somewhat different from that of the police chief. The police officers will have their own evaluation, as will any labor union that is involved with the police. Moreover, the media will frequently develop their own evaluation, and that will have a dramatic impact on the evaluation of the public and government officials.

The criteria by which organizational effectiveness is judged is varied, as Table 13-2 demonstrates (Campbell, 1977, pp. 36–39). There is no single standard of measure for organizational effectiveness. As the table suggests, any evaluative system must take into account multiple criteria. We must be aware, however, that in some cases there will be an overlap of criteria. For example, the relationship between morale and turnover are typically very strong in an organization. The relationship in that case, however, is inverse. That is, as morale

Table 13-2

Criteria Used to Assess Organizational Effectiveness

Absenteeism	Motivation
Accidents	Overall effectiveness
Achievement emphasis	Participation and shared influence
Conflict–cohesion	Planning and goal setting
Control	Productivity
Efficiency	Profit
Evaluation by external groups	Quality
Flexibility–adaptation	Readiness
Goal consensus	Role and norm congruence
Growth	Satisfaction
Information management	Stability
Internalization of goals	Training and development emphasis
Managerial interpersonal skills	Turnover
Managerial task skills	Utilization of environment
Morale	Value of human resources

drops, turnover is likely to rise. Moreover, evaluations of effectiveness are bound by the evaluator's values, preferences and motivations. For this reason organizational effectiveness is a subjective comparison of performance versus goals (Albanese, 1988, p. 640). It might be said that effectiveness is in the eye of the beholder.

Guidelines for Assessing Organizational Effectiveness

The existence of such a multitude of criteria for assessing organizational effectiveness complicates the assessment process. What is needed are some guidelines for developing an assessment model. When we know what we are trying to accomplish, evaluation of effectiveness gets much simpler.

To help resolve this dilemma, Kim Cameron and David Whetten have suggested seven organizational-effectiveness guidelines (1983, pp. 269–274):

Frame of reference. You must know who is doing the evaluation and that person's or group's perspective. In other words, which of the agency's constituencies is doing the evaluation, and what criteria are being used?

Domain of activity. What domain of activity is being assessed? Most police departments operate in different domains and serve different constituencies. A police agency may have a superb tactical force but be weak in investigations. When assessing effectiveness, be clear about differences in the domain served by the organization.

Level of analysis. Judgments about the effectiveness of an organization can be made at several levels: the individual patrol officer, the traffic unit, or the entire organization. Assessing the performance of the records unit is one task; determining how well the agency treats its employee is a very different task.

Purpose. For what reason is effectiveness being judged? For example, is the reason behind the evaluation to reduce the number of sworn officers in the agency, or is it to determine the direction the agency should move as it grows? The purpose of the evaluation will have a dramatic impact on the ability to evaluate adequately the organization's effectiveness. The purpose can influence the kind of data that will be made available, the data sources that will be appropriate, and the amount of cooperation or resistance to be encountered.

Time frame. What time frame is being used? Police agencies operate in a world of the present. Rarely do they become involved in efforts for long-term effectiveness. Short-range objectives dominate these organizations. Other organizations may do the opposite: seek to maximize long-term survival at the expense of short-term profit. Whichever is used, the evaluation must be specific about the time frame used. Evaluating long-range effectiveness is different from measuring short-term effectiveness. The assessment model must take this into account.

Type of data used. Objective data gathered from the agency's organizational records can be quantified and may reflect the agency's "official" transactions. Subjective data gathered from interviews of questionnaires, however, may provide valuable and rich information if safeguards are used to prevent bias.

Referent used. What is the referent against which effectiveness is judged? Is the comparison used that of against a similar organization, against the organization's stated goals, against an idealized standard, or against its own past performance? The referent used can make a difference in the assessment outcome. An agency may look very effective when its performance is compared with past performance. The same performance may be evaluated as ineffective when compared against its stated goals. Since judgments about the effectiveness of an organization can differ widely depending on which referent is used, it is important to be clear about the referent used.

The foregoing criteria can help an administrator to understand and develop models for assessment. All managers should be aware of these criteria, especially when the agency is being evaluated by external constituencies. Similarly, these criteria provide for a series of models to be used in a comprehensive evaluation of the entire organization.

For a day-to-day assessment, however, a simpler approach is called for. What the police administrator needs is some "rules of thumb." These have been provided by R. M. Seers through a series of questions the administrator can ask about the organization (1976, pp. 50–63):

1. *To what extent are we applying our limited resources toward the attainment of our various goals?* Sometimes, especially in police agencies, resources are distributed throughout the organization without recognizing that the goals may be independent of the allocation. As a result some goals may be unfunded, or activities may be funded that fail to support a goal.

2. *Is there a clear relationship between the amount of resources we spend on the various goals and the importance of each goal?* If the agency is committed to community service and traffic enforcement, are the two goals considered to be equal? Is the commitment reflected in the allocation of resources?

3. *What kind of return on investment, per goal, are we getting on our resources?* Some organizational goals, considered more important, may have a lower return on investment than lesser goals. For example, property crime units will consistently produce a lower percentage of case closures than crimes against persons. Property crime investigation will, therefore, have a lower return on investment, but the number of property crimes committed as opposed to those crimes against individuals will make clearance of property crimes a high-priority goal. Other goals may be too expensive for the return they generate. Each goal must be evaluated in terms of commitment of resources.

4. *Is the entire organization working together for goal attainment?* Frequently, units within the organization engage in activities that are more helpful to them than to the overall organization. For example, purchasing units may be more interested in a purchasing system that simplifies their job than one that provides supplies for the organization in an efficient and timely manner. The administrator must always be mindful of the many ways by which units can undermine the ability of the organization to fulfill its goals.

5. *Is the "fit" between the organization and its environment changing?* Environments sometimes become unstable for organizations over time. Neighborhoods change, as does the racial–cultural makeup of the jurisdiction. As the environment shifts, so should the goals of the organization.

Errors in Assessment

We need to remember that measures of effectiveness are often subjective in nature. It is absolutely critical to define clearly what is being measured and how. There are two common errors associated with evaluating police effectiveness. These are confusing efficiency with effectiveness and the related tendency to fall into the activity trap.

Effectiveness Versus Efficiency

Effectiveness is defined as doing the right job, while *efficiency* is doing the job right. Measuring effectiveness is a complex process. Much of what police officers do they do individually and without supervision. It is often difficult to assess the effectiveness of either the unit or the individual officer.

Efficiency is much easier to measure. It is a simple ratio of input to output. For example, if 100 calls for service were received in one shift and those 100 calls were responded to by uniformed patrol in a timely manner, we would assume that the patrol unit was efficient. But was it effective?

A good criminal or traffic accident investigation can be a time-consuming process if done right. The demand to get the report finished so that the officer can get back in service, however, can undermine the officer's effectiveness for the sake of efficiency. The result is a poor investigation that someone else—an investigator—will be required to reconduct if the investigation is to be effective. A lack of effectiveness in patrol will therefore result in a lack of either efficiency or effectiveness in investigations. The outcome of the investigation will be sacrificed for the sake of a hurried input.

Police agencies consistently sacrifice effectiveness for efficiency. The perceived need to get officers to calls quickly, for the sake of public relations, sacrifices their effectiveness and results in poor public relations.

The primary focus of the police organization must be effectiveness. If something must be sacrificed, let it be efficiency.

The Activity Trap

In assessing both organization and individual performance, the most common error of police organizations is that of the activity trap. This is the tendency to measure the worth of a person or unit by its level of activity. Police departments count things. They have a long history of collecting data that are easy to collect rather than collect the data they need for measuring effectiveness. They have an equally long history of keeping score cards on people and units. Traffic officers are measured on number of citations issued and accidents worked; patrol officers on calls answered, citations issued, and arrests made; and investigators on cases closed.

Anyone who has been in a police agency for any length of time knows that these measures are indicative of absolutely nothing. Calls for service, traffic accidents, workable cases, and even traffic citations are as much the product of beat, shift, and random occurrence as they are of anything. The only variable under the control of the officer is the willingness to act on the event occurring in the officer's presence.

But tabulating scores is easy; therefore, it has become the primary measure of an officer or organizational element. How absurd can this get? Some 20 years ago it was widely believed by officers of the Washington State Patrol that promotion was based on the level of the officer's activity. Washington is a state with only two interstate highways. Only one of these, Interstate 5, has a heavy traffic flow. To get promoted therefore required an assignment on Interstate 5. To be assigned to the rural areas of eastern Washington was to be denied a chance for promotion permanently through no other reason than location of assignment. If the officer's beliefs were true (and there is no guarantee it was true; all police agencies are rife with myths and inaccurate rumors), that agency had let the activity trap badly warp its promotion process.

The activity trap is alive and well because police agencies have been unable, or unwilling, to develop meaningful measures of effectiveness. They have opted for counting things that are easy to count and have convinced themselves that making marks on an activity sheet is related to high-quality policing. It is not. The measure of a police officer is not in the number of citations issued, arrests made, or calls serviced. The true measure of an officer is in the relationship of the officer to the public, the sound use of discretion, and the ability to transform departmental policy, public law, training, and experience into professional responses to the police role. While these abilities are more difficult to measure, they are what policing is all about. Substituting numbers for these qualities does no justice to either the officer or the agency.

ASSESSING PERSONNEL PERFORMANCE

Ultimately, assessing organizational effectiveness is dependent on the effectiveness of individuals. This is especially true with police agencies; a large amount of the work involves face-to-face interactions with citizens and individual officers.

Performance appraisals are a controversial aspect of administration. The performance appraisal, or personnel evaluation, is a systematic evaluation of an employee by a supervisor or some other person familiar with this person's performance on the job. Performance appraisals are usually made by use of a standardized form adapted by the agency. Usually, the ratings are made at periodic intervals. A performance appraisal thus becomes a permanent part of an employee's record with the organization and is part of the record used by management in subsequent promotion, transfer, or termination decisions.

Are performance appraisals necessary? Most argue that they are; there are few management texts that do not state their need and provide information on how they should be done. That information will also be provided here. Before we begin that discussion, however, a word of warning will be provided. One of the world's leading management consultant's and the person considered to be the father of the Japanese management system, W. Edwards Deming, strongly opposes performance appraisal. He argues that:

> "...performance appraisals encourage short-term performance at the expense of long-term planning. They discourage risk-taking, build fear, undermine teamwork, and pit people against each other for the same rewards."
>
> Such evaluations, Dr. Deming says, leave "people bitter, despondent, dejected, some even depressed, all unfit for work for weeks after receipt of rating, unable to comprehend why they are inferior. It is unfair, as it ascribes to the people in a group differences that may be caused totally by the system that they work in."
>
> An insidious side effect is that they also increase reliance on numbers. Because they measure short-term results, there is a tendency to consider only evidence that can be counted (Walton, 1986, p. 91).

The Deming management method focuses on group efforts for evaluation. In a police department setting, the assessment process would focus on unit effectiveness rather than individual performance. Would this work for the police? It has for every other organization that has used this method. What has to be remembered is that the police disciplinary system is not geared to the performance appraisal. It is more attuned to the complaint investigation system. In reality, the performance appraisal accomplishes very little for a police agency. With that in mind we will look at the types and limitations of the performance appraisal.

There is no one right way to evaluate individual performance. The kinds of appraisal system used vary in both complexity and format. What works for one organization may not work elsewhere. The only thing that all appraisal systems have in common is that they are a system; that is they have several parts and must work together (Bernardin and Beatty, 1982). It is not the intent here to promote a single appraisal style. Instead, we look at a number of factors that go into the creation and operation of an appraisal system.

Purpose of Evaluation

Why evaluate personnel when the appraisal process is fraught with the potential for hurt feelings and disenchantment? There are a number of reasons why performance appraisals must be conducted. First, a number of personnel decisions depend on performance appraisals. To some extent, job assignment, promotion, and disciplinary decisions all depend on a sound appraisal process. Second, if employees are to improve their future performance, they need to know how they have performed in the past. Finally, individual performance is evaluated so that an evaluation can be made on policies and procedures that influence officer behavior (Aldag and Stearns, 1991, p. 318). The failure of a police agency to conduct an effective appraisal system can have tragic consequences, as the following case demonstrates.

Bonsignore v. *City of New York* (1981)
521 F.Supp. 394

The wife of a police officer who was shot and severely injured by a police officer who then committed suicide brought action against the city alleging that her injuries and her husband's death were caused by the city's negligence in requiring police officers to carry a gun. A jury awarded $300,000 in compensatory damages for negligence and $125,000 in punitive damages, but rejected wrongful death claim. The city moved for judgment notwithstanding verdict and, alternatively, for new trial, and the plaintiff moved for a new trial on the issue of compensatory damages.

On the morning of December 20, 1976, Blaise Bonsignore, a 23-year veteran of the New York City Police Department, shot and severely injured his wife, Virginia Bonsignore the plaintiff, and then committed suicide by shooting himself in the head. The plaintiff was struck by five bullets, which inflicted brain damage and caused minor motor dysfunction; several fragments remain in her body and brain. The weapon used in the shootings was Bonsignore's .32-caliber "off-duty" revolver, which as a police officer he was obliged to have in his possession 24 hours a day. The plaintiff brought this diversity law suit on her own behalf and on behalf of her daughters, alleging that her injuries and her husband's death were caused by the negligence of New York City in requiring Bonsignore to carry a gun.

Opinion of the Court

The plaintiff amply demonstrated at the trial the hazards of allowing unstable police officers to carry firearms. Between 1973 and 1976, when 14 officers were killed by criminals, 17 committed suicide and 2 were killed by other officers; these suicides were all accomplished with guns. When Bonsignore joined the department in 1953, it did not require incoming officers to undergo any type of psychological examination as to their fitness to carry guns and otherwise perform their duties. In the 23 years that Bonsignore was on the force, he was never given a psychological examination.

The police department had psychological procedures that might have identified Bonsignore as a problem, but testimony indicated that these programs had not been validated for reliability and that the police officer's code of silence would have prevented another officer from identifying Bonsignore as potential trouble for fear of jeopardizing Bonsignore's career. Thus the EWS (early warning system) failed to identify Bonsignore even though he had compiled a record of excessive sick leaves, even though his superiors had not filled in performance-rating data on his evaluation forms, and even though he had been assigned to the position of precinct attendant for an unusually lengthy period of time (all of these were supposedly indicators of emotional instability designed to activate the EWS). The position of precinct attendant, or "broom" as it is called in the force, is classified as a limited-duty assignment: It usually indicates mental or physical disability. Department regulations required the committee on personnel to investigate police officers who are assigned to limited-duty assignments for more than one year and to report its findings to the commissioner. Yet though Bonsignore was the Nineteenth Precinct's "broom" for 13 years, his situation was never investigated. Further, it was conceded by deputy inspector Bernard McCrann that there was a general attitude in the department that going to the psychological services unit would harm an officer's career. Other testimony revealed that because of concern over job security, promotion, and self-esteem, police officers will not voluntarily seek psychological help.

The jury could have found the defendant liable either because the department "failed to address itself with due diligence to the problem of reasonably ensuring that police officers are fit to carry guns without endangering themselves or the public" or because "the measures that it adopted for that purpose were so deficient that no reasonable person could accept the city's judgment." The jury predicated liability on the latter rationale, and the record contains ample evidence to support the jury's finding.

Motion for judgment and retrial is denied. Opinion affirmed.

Types of Performance Appraisal

When we speak of performance appraisals we are usually referring to supervisory evaluation of subordinates. It should be noted, however, that others may conduct appraisals as well. In private industry there is a growing use of both subordinate appraisal of supervisors and peer evaluations (Aldag and Stearns, 1991, p. 320).

Researchers have noted that subordinates are in a much better position than administrators to evaluate supervisors. Moreover, co-workers know a great deal more about the performance of their peers than do the supervisors. Consistently, subordinates are tougher evaluators than are supervisors. A problem that arises with this approach is the difficulty with which supervisors and peers deal with criticisms from peers and subordinates. Supervisors especially tend to ignore the ratings (Reibstein, 1988, p. 15).

There are three major ways by which performance may be analyzed. Appraisal can focus on traits, behaviors, or accomplishments (Aldag and Stearns, 1991, p. 318).

Traits and Personal Characteristics

Despite all the criticisms leveled at performance appraisal for being too subjective, the trait approach is still widely used today (Bernadarin and Klatt, 1985, pp. 79–86). Using this system, the supervisor is asked to rate a subordinate on such traits as friendliness, efficiency, and reliability. Frequently, the mechanism of evaluation is a form in which there are check-off boxes marked excellent, above average, average, below average, and poor (or some similar array of choices).

These systems are popular because they can be done rapidly and are easy to complete. They also have some problems. For example, "superior" and "average" may mean different things to different people. Moreover, supervisors may be unwilling to give low ratings on personality traits, especially when the rating will be shown to the person being evaluated.

Behavioral Approach

This system involves the recording of specific employee actions. One such system, the *critical incidents approach*, is based on the recording of only those good and bad incidents that were extraordinary. Sometimes the list is generated by the accumulation of such incidents by a group of officers over a long period of time. This allows the supervisor access to a detailed list of such actions. With this list, the supervisor is equipped to make adequate evaluations by comparing incidents on the master list with those of the subordinates.

A newer and somewhat related approach, the *behaviorally anchored rating scale* (BARS), presents a list of possible employee actions, ranging from very desirable to very undesirable (Aldag and Stearns, 1991, p. 319). An example of good police performance would be: "This officer routinely checks automobiles parked in suspicious locations late at night." An example of poor performance could be: "Officer takes coffee break at same time every shift regardless of number of calls for service on hold."

Results Approach

This system focuses on what the employee is supposed to accomplish on the job (Aldag and Stearns, 1991, p. 320). The negative aspect of this system is that it is time consuming and more complicated than trait scales. The advantage is that this evaluation relates directly to the goals of the organization. This means that organizational effectiveness can be evaluated from this process while agency goals and objectives are reinforced.

Sources of Error

Performance appraisals require human beings to judge other human beings; hence raters are prone to commit judgment errors. The problem lies not so much with the rating instrument as with the raters (Rice, 1985, pp. 30–36). Some raters, for example, deliberately distort their ratings and in the process defeat the purpose of the system. One author argued that "manager motivation for doing appraisal is what needs attention, not building a better mousetrap" (Albanese, 1988, p. 384).

There are five common rater errors: halo error, leniency, strictness, central tendency, and recency bias (Latham and Wexley, 1981). *Halo error* occurs when a rater's assessment of an employee on one dimension influences the ratings on other dimensions. An example of this would be to evaluate an officer's performance based on a pleasant personality. The officer may be an easy person with which to get along but may also be weak in a number of other areas of performance. Halo error is also somewhat of a misnomer. It is halo error if the officer is evaluated too high due to a single characteristic. The officers may have horns, however, rather than a halo if the single aspect is viewed negatively by the rater (Albanese, 1988, p. 385).

Leniency occurs when all officers in one unit are rated high by the supervisor. This poses a problem when officers in this unit are compared with those of another unit. Both the promotion process and assignment rotation can be effected by the inflated ratings of one unit.

Strictness is the opposite of leniency. This happens when a rater is overly tough. All officers within a unit are rated artificially low, thus putting them at a disadvantage in the promotion process and other personnel decisions.

One of the more common errors is that of *central tendency.* This occurs when the supervisors rates every subordinate as average. This happens when the rater is unable or unwilling to commit the time required to evaluate each employee accurately. This is most popular with supervisors because, with the exception of leniency, it is the least confrontational of the approaches to performance appraisal. Unlike leniency, which is likely to draw the attention of upper management, the error central tendency is less likely to attract administrative criticism.

Recency bias refers to the tendency to recall events from only the most recent past when evaluating performance. This is a real problem in appraisal systems that occur only once per year (Albanese, 1988, p. 386). Table 13-3 offers a summary of rater errors.

Evaluation Cycle

To fully understand performance appraisals, we need to understand the evaluation process. There are seven steps in the appraisal of employee performance (see Illustration 13-1).

Table 13-3
Rating Errors

Error	*Description*
Halo error	Rate employee on basis of a single performance dimension.
Leniency	Use high end of rating scale.
Strictness	Use low end of rating scale.
Central tendency	Rate all employees as average.
Recency bias	Remember only recent performance behavior.

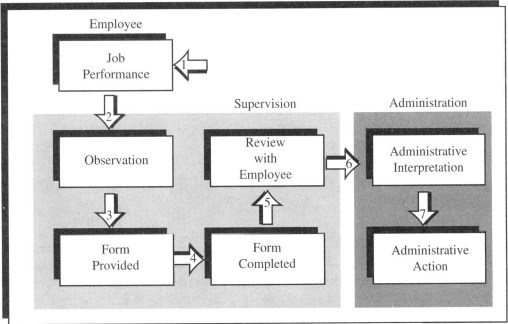

Illustration 13-1 The Evaluation Cycle.

The seven steps are described as follows:

1. The employee performs the job. How well this is done is influenced by personal ability, the job environment, time, and an error component due to chance.

2. The evaluator observes the employee. This is influenced by the position of the observer, frequency of the observations, predisposition of the observer, and random error. There are also sources of variation in the observation of people. Evaluators tend to look for behavior in conformance with the evaluator's prejudices. Supervisors tend to interpret what they observe according to their own predisposition. They also remember those observations and interpretations in conformance with their beliefs longer.

3. The evaluator is given the evaluation form to complete.

4. The evaluator recalls the previous observations and records them.

5. The contents of the report are communicated to the employee.

6. The report is forwarded to the central unit, where it is interpreted.

7. The various administrative actions follow the final interpretation.

Legally and Scientifically Defensible Appraisal Systems

An appraisal system cannot be arbitrary or capricious. It must be fair; it must conform to both legal guidelines and scientific principles of assessment. Legal and scientific requirements are mutually supportive because both strive for objectivity and accuracy. The following guidelines are offered as considerations for the design and implementation of an appraisal system (DuBrin, Ireland, and Williams, 1989, pp. 316–317):

1. Appraisal of job performance must be based on an analysis of job requirements as reflected in the performance standards.

2. Appraisal of job performance becomes reasonable only when performance standards have been communicated and understood by employees.

3. Appraisal systems that emphasize work behaviors rather than personal traits are more likely to be sustained by the courts. Measuring job performance in terms of personal appearance or subjective traits such as "dependable" are difficult to defend. They are more defensible, however, if they are supported with objective behavior-oriented measures such as "gets assignments accomplished promptly."

4. Clearly defined individual dimensions of job performance (such as creativity) should be rated rather than undefined global measures of job performance.

5. Courts tend to look more favorably on appraisal systems that include communication and feedback components of the system.

6. Appraisal systems must be validated (correlated with job performance).

7. An appeal mechanism must be provided if an employee disagrees with a manager's appraisal.

8. Appraisal systems should be kept current by updating job descriptions to ensure that performance is being measured against current expectations.

9. Appraisal systems should be written, documented, and filed, and personnel decisions should be consistent with the appraisals given to employees.

10. From the perspective of equal employment opportunity, an employer has little cause for legal concern unless the performance appraisal system has a disproportionately negative impact on a protected class.

Other authors suggest additional safeguards. Albanese argues that in addition to the above, the system should meet three more criteria (1988, pp. 384–385). He argues that the organization assess *rater validity*. This is not always easily done; it requires training and rater development concurrent with the development of the assessment system. Second is the need to use *more than one rater*. This not only helps to establish rater validity, but also helps to cancel out rater biases. Finally, Albanese argues that raters should *document extreme ratings*. It is one thing to rate a person as superior; it is quite another problem to document the reasons for that rating. No extreme rating, either high or low, should be given without a documentable reason for the rating.

If these guidelines are followed, the personnel appraisal system should be reasonably effective. It will never be perfect; that is not possible. If the system is objective and job related, however, it will accomplish its mission.

THE INEFFECTIVE EMPLOYEE

One of the principal goals of the performance appraisal is to identify poor performance so that it can be corrected. A system that merely identifies substandard performance but has no mechanism for correction is a meaningless system. In this section we look at the causes of poor performance and how it can be addressed.

Factors Contributing to Poor Performance

Most managers tend to attribute substandard performance to a single cause. The theory is that the officer has a problem (singular) and if that problem can be solved, everything will be all right. Moreover, managers almost always blame the employee for poor performance (Brown and Mitchell, 1986, p. 423). In fact, most cases of poor performance are the result of a combination of situational factors. These factors can be divided into individual and organizational factors (DuBrin, Ireland, and Williams, 1989, pp. 418–419; Miner, 1985; Green, 1979; Dubrin, 1987, p. 459).

Individual Factors

1. *Insufficient intellectual ability.* Employee lacks the mental capacity to handle the complexities of the job.

2. *Insufficient job knowledge.* Training and/or experience insufficient to handle job.

3. *Low work motivation, work ethic.* Employee has low personal work standards, not interested in job.

4. *Job stress.* Employee's internal equilibrium is disturbed by one or more factors in the work setting, including excessive work demands, heavy conflict, job insecurity, and conflicting demands (Motowildo, Packard, and Manning, 1986, pp. 618–629).

5. *Job burnout.* Conscientious employee becomes apathetic, bored, cynical, and feels depleted because of long-term job stress and the feeling that rewards in the job have gone stale (Jackson, Schwab, and Schuler, 1986, pp. 630–641).

6. *Obsolescence.* Manager or specialist who was effective in past becomes ineffective because of technical deficiencies in his or her own field or inadequate interpersonal skills (Bracker and Pearson, 1986, pp. 109–116).

7. *Physical limitations.* Employees may have insufficient physical strength or dexterity to handle the job adequately.

8. *Alcoholism or drug abuse.* Employee lacks good judgment and misses work because of drug or alcohol dependence.

9. *Cigarette addiction.* Employee is fatigued, wastes time searching for cigarettes and lighting them, burns and stains company property, and creates morale problems because of cigarette addiction (Solomon, 1983, p. 101).

10. *Emotional illness and personality disorder.* Employee experiences inner conflicts and counterproductive behavior such as delusional thinking, disruptive anxiety, depression, excessive euphoria, lying, cheating, stealing, abrasiveness, and compulsive gambling.

11. *Family and personal problems.* Employee is unable to attend to job because of preoccupation with family crisis, fights, breakup of key relationship, misfortune of loved one, or severe financial problems.

12. *Absenteeism or tardiness.* Employee loses time from work for a variety of reasons (other than alcoholism or drug abuse), including dissatisfaction, job stress, or family problems.

13. *Co-worker romance.* Two romantically involved workers (including supervisor and subordinate) may become so involved with each other that they divert time and energy from regular job responsibilities, and their behavior may disrupt the work of others (Warfield, 1987, pp. 22–35).

Organizational Factors

1. *Ergonomics problems.* Poor fit between the human requirements of the job and the machinery (Brooks, 1986, pp. 59–64).

2. *Inadequate communication.* Manager does not clearly communicate job expectations and/or does not provide candid feedback about performance deficiencies, resulting in the employee strengthening the unproductive behavior.

3. *Counterproductive work group influences.* Group pressure or ostracism make it difficult for the employee to engage in cooperative effort.

4. *Organizational culture.* Agency has a history of not imposing sanctions on employees who perform poorly. When the situation demands better performance, many employees may not respond to the new challenge.

5. *Counterproductive work environment and organizational support.* Employee does not have the proper tools, support, budget, or authority to accomplish the job.

6. *Manager's leadership style.* Manager's leadership style does not fit the employee's requirements, such as when an inexperienced employee does not receive close-enough supervision and thus learns key tasks incorrectly.

Stress Reduction

One of the causes of poor performance requires more in-depth analysis. Stress has been the subject of much discussion over the past decade. A large number of the physical and emotional problems that cause poor performance are attributed to stress. Many believe that the law enforcement occupation is one of the most stressful of careers (More and Wegener, 1992, p.184). Others question that appraisal. The research is sketchy; some studies show higher rates of heart problems, suicide, and divorce for police officers, whereas other studies refute those findings.

From a management perspective, whether or not police work is stressful is not really important. What is important is the recognition that stress is present in everyone's life. Even if there were no organizationally induced stress, police officers are still faced with the same stresses that affect everyone else. Family problems, money problems, and personal frustrations would exist without any contributions from the job. However, since there is ample evidence that police organizations, with their rigid bureaucratic structure, create frustration among the officers, it must be acknowledged that the work environment adds to the stress of police employees.

Of equal importance is understanding that in the past, the focus of stress reduction programs has been on sworn officers only. The belief that policing is a high-stress occupation has led police administrators to assume that only sworn personnel are subject to stress; therefore, only sworn personnel have need of a stress reduction program. The more appropriate view is that policing in and of itself is not stressful; life is stressful. Every member of the police organization, civilian and sworn, must be provided with a comprehensive stress reduction program. No one within the organization is immune from the effects of stress.

It is to the advantage of both the organization and the employees to provide a program of stress reduction. Again, it is less important to place the blame for the causes of stress than it is to address the physical and emotional by-products of stress.

Symptoms of Stress

There are a number of behavioral symptoms related to rising levels of stress. These include use of tobacco products, alcohol abuse, drug abuse, appetite disorders, and sometimes an increase in the number of accidents (More and Wegener, 1992, p. 203). According to one study, managers can detect stress-induced behavior by observing the work of individual officers. The following list was developed to aid managers in identifying stress-related problems (More and Unsinger, 1987):

1. Excessive absenteeism

2. Unreported absences

3. Arriving late and leaving early

4. Poor quality of work

5. Erratic work performance

6. Failure to meet work standards

7. Friction with co-workers

8. Increased accident rates

In addition to work-related symptoms of stress, there are personal problems that may appear as well. These include marital discord, family conflict, sleep disturbances, sexual dysfunction, and depression (Quick and Quick, 1984).

Stress Reduction Programs

Not all stress-related problems can be solved by management. Employees at all levels must be held responsible for taking charge of their own lives. However, management can observe and diagnose behavioral problems. This information can then be used help the employee see the problem more clearly and implement a solution to the problem.

Employee assistance programs (EAPs) can be very useful in treating many stress-related problems. The following areas have been identified as being amenable to a successful assistance program (Stratton, 1987):

1. Alcoholism

2. Substance abuse

3. Job stress

4. Job burnout

5. Anxiety.

6. Depression

7. Parent-child conflict

8. Single parenting

9. Grief

10. Smoking.

11. Nutrition.

12. Exercise

13. Weight control

14 Divorce

15. Separation

16. Police shootings.

Assistance programs may include professional counselors or may provide for peer counselors. The theory behind peer counseling is that an employee can learn more from a peer who has gone through a similar experience. In these programs, the peer counselors should be trained by professional psychologists.

One of the most direct, and in many cases effective approaches to stress reduction is through physical fitness. A growing number of departments are implementing fitness programs. This is partly to negate the buildup of stress. Also, police administrators have recognized that many police medical problems are more a by-product of life-style than of stress.

Modern policing is done mostly sitting down, especially in patrol. Long hours of riding in a motor vehicle while eating a high-calorie (junk food) diet at odd hours has produced many officers who are overweight and in poor physical condition. These factors may play a larger role in creating problems such as coronary distress among some officers than is produced by stress. Fitness programs address the problems created by the sedentary life-style of police officers. Maintaining physical fitness also does much toward maintaining a person's emotional fitness.

Given the rising cost of medical care and the costs associated with lost employee work hours, it is important that police administrators take the necessary steps to minimize employee health problems. Preventive measures such as fitness programs offer one of the most cost-effective means of accomplishing this goal. Employee assistance programs are useful after a problem has been diagnosed; this is also a feasible means of addressing the needs of both employee and organization. The role that stress plays in employee misbehavior should not be overlooked. Often, an employee undergoing stress can be saved with a good stress reduction program.

Where stress is not the cause of the problem, or when stress reduction techniques prove futile, the disciplinary process should be invoked. Despite the benefit to the organization in salvaging an employee, the public must not be sacrificed by the process. Police brutality that is the result of police stress is still brutality and must be treated as such. Stress is a physiological problem that can and should be treated, but the police administrator cannot allow stress to become a standardized defense for inappropriate behavior.

Citizen Complaints and Citizen Review

All organizations have the means to identify poor performance internally. The police, however, are more likely to come into conflict with members of the public than are other occupations. The police–community relationship is dependent on the ability of individual officers to relate well to the public they serve.

Unlike many private organizations, where internal measures of productivity are all that is important, the police officer may look good internally while performing poorly externally. Citizen input has therefore become a key issue in police control systems. Unfortunately, civilian review has not proven to be the hoped-for panacea. In this section we discuss the forms and limitations of citizen-based control systems.

Civilian Review

The concept of civilian review boards was first proposed during the 1950s. It originated with the belief, among some, that existing means for seeking redress against police misconduct were not effective (Goldstein, 1977). The types of boards proposed, and sometimes created, were varied. They included everything from civilian-dominated boards, external to the department, to internal police committees with citizen participation (West, 1991, p. 376).

In 1967, the President's Commission compared four civilian review boards. The results of this comparison were not encouraging. The assessment was that the boards were essentially only advisory bodies having little authority (*Task Force Reports*, 1967, pp. 200–202).

The two most notable attempts during this era were the Philadelphia Police Advisory Board (PAB) and the New York City Civilian Complaint Review Board (CCRB). Both were notable for a variety of reasons, not the least of which was the storm of police protest that surrounded them. The PAB was subjected to a number of law suits instigated by police organizations, including the Fraternal Order of Police (FOP). It finally died as the result of an election that brought to power a mayor opposed to any form of civilian review of the police. The PAB had lasted nine years (Halpern, 1974, pp. 561–582).

The New York experiment lasted only four months during 1966. Again the police organized to fight the CCRB. They were successful in putting a referendum before the people of the city. By a margin of 3:1, the CCRB was defeated (Walker, 1983, p. 239).

Because of the polarizing effect of civilian review boards, many police administrators in the late 1960s started looking for a less volatile approach. They wanted some way to get civilian oversight without the friction that appeared with the creation of civilian review boards. The result was the idea of the police ombudsman (West, 1991, p. 381). A number of proposals were put forth to create this office. The concept was structured on the Scandinavian model. The idea was that an individual—the ombudsman—would have the authority to investigate complaints against the police and enact reforms. Several problems with the concept appeared immediately. First was the question of how the ombudsman would be selected. The potential for the position to create political mischief was obvious. As can be imagined, there were a wide variety of opinions on the topic (Barton, 1970, p. 468).

What is more important, however, was the recognition that the problem was not so much what shape the review system took—either civilian review board or ombudsman—but how to persuade the police to accept any system of civilian review (West, 1991, p. 382).

The primary arguments against civilian review were based on the belief that police officers possess unique skills, training, and experience that make it impossible for civilians to make good decisions about police behavior. Additionally, civilian review boards were seen as a threat to morale. Many expressed the worry that civilian review would make officers feel restrained from taking appropriate action due to a fear that the civilian reviewers would not understand their actions (Hudson, 1971, p. 521).

Not every argument was negative. Even the staunchest opponents of civilian review had to admit that there was public distrust of the police investigating themselves. The strongest argument for a civilian review process, therefore, was its potential enhancement of the legitimacy of the review process and, indeed, the legitimacy of the police themselves in the eyes of the community (Kerstetter, 1985, p. 164). Attaining legitimacy in the eyes of the public was seen as crucial to enhancing the public's perception of the police. The dilemma facing law enforcement administrators during the turbulent era of the late 1960s and early 1970s, therefore, was how to enhance the public's perception of the police while maintaining the support of the police officers.

Throughout the majority of the United States, the 1970s was an era in which there was still distrust of civilian review. An exception to this prevailing negativism was the Kansas City, Missouri Police Department. In 1970 the Office of Citizen Complaints (OCC) was formed. This was not the only such office formed during the 1970s. San Jose, California instituted an ombudsman, and Berkeley, California created a police review commission (West, 1991, pp. 388–389).

Over the next 20 years civilian review boards proliferated. The past five years alone has seen a tremendous growth in both the number and types of such institutions. Obviously, the idea of citizens reviewing police actions has finally been accepted by both citizens and the police.

Contemporary Complaint Investigation Models

Previous research has found that there are currently three types of civilian review agency in use among U.S. law enforcement agencies (Walker and Bumphus, 1991, p. 3):

Class I: (a) Initial investigation and fact-finding by nonsworn personnel; (b) review of investigative report and recommendation for action by nonsworn person or board consisting of a majority of nonsworn persons.

Class II: (a) Initial investigation and fact-finding by sworn police officers; (b) review of investigative report and recommendation for action by a nonsworn person or board that consists of a majority of nonsworn persons.

Class III: (a) Initial investigation and fact-finding by sworn police officers; (b) review of investigative report and recommendation for action by sworn officers; (c)opportunity for the citizen who is dissatisfied with the final disposition of the complaint to appeal to a board that includes nonsworn persons.

Unfortunately, while there is a growing abundance of literature that describes the citizen review processes, little research has been conducted that measures the effectiveness of this process. The most current broad-based evaluation of civilian review systems points out that there is a lack of available research on (1) the effectiveness of civilian review, (2) the administration of civilian review procedures, and (3) the politics of civilian review (Walker and Bumphus, 1991, pp. 5–6).

What little research does exist is mostly public opinion research that, while having some utility, studies attitudes rather than effectiveness. One such study, conducted by Perez and published in 1978, included the Kansas City, Missouri Police Department; San Jose, California; Berkeley, California Police Review Commission; Berkeley, California Police Department; Oakland, California; and the Contra Costa County Sheriff's Office. The survey used in that project attempted to measure satisfaction with the complaint investigation process. Table 13–4 reproduces the results of that research (Kerstetter, 1985, p. 162).

A problem that surfaced with this study was that with the exception of the Berkeley PRC, there was a close correlation between the results of the investigation and the satisfaction expressed. People whose complaints were substantiated were satisfied; those whose complaints were unsubstantiated were not satisfied (Kerstetter, 1985, p. 161).

Compounding the problems inherent in studying the effectiveness of the citizen complaint process is the lack of realistic expectations on the part of the public. Nationwide, the number of citizen complaints substantiated against police officers is very low; it hovers somewhere around 15 percent. Available research indicates that police officers act legally and responsibly in the vast majority of their contacts with citizens. Moreover, there are invariably cases in which there is a legitimate grievance but one that fails to be substantiated due to

Table 13-4

Satisfaction with Investigative Procedures (Percent)

Agency *(very or fairly)*	*Impartial or mostly)*	*Thorough*	*Fair (completely*
San Jose	21.6%	28.1%	13.6%
Kansas City	17.9%	21.9%	15.7%
Berkeley PRC	64.9%	85.7%	73.3%
Berkeley PD	29.4%	47.0%	35.3%
Oakland	9.5%	23.1%	11.5%
Contra Costa SO	31.8%	21.7%	39.1%

a lack of sufficient information. Given the combination of these factors, the result is a low substantiation rate for citizen complaints; a situation that is bound to increase citizen dissatisfaction with the process because the outcomes are predictably in the police officers' favor (Kerstetter, 1985, p. 175).

There is very little research that provides a reason for the low percentage of substantiated complaints. Quite likely the explanation lies in several facets of human behavior. First, few, if any, police agencies communicate adequately to the public the powers, responsibilities, and objectives of the police. In a large number of cases, the citizen simply is not aware of whether the officer is right or wrong. If the action angers the citizen, it generates a complaint.

Second, many people are reluctant to accept responsibility for the bad events in their lives. If it is not their fault, the responsibility must reside elsewhere. In those events where a police officer intervenes to their detriment, it is likely that the officer is given the blame.

Third, the complainant does not always seek justice, but instead may seek revenge. The police have been the instrument of their pain and they wish to return the favor. Unfortunately for the police image, failing to get revenge, these people also assume that they received no justice. It must be remembered that justice is relative to the perceptions of the individual. Dealing with citizens' complaints may always be a no-win situation for any police agency, regardless of the system for handling citizen complaints.

Managing the Ineffective Employee

Managing the ineffective employee can be a difficult task. Typically, problem employees consume a disproportionate share of the manager's time. The management model presented below is based on the accumulated wisdom of administrators and researchers. The idea is to salvage the poor performers and return them to being fully productive (DuBrin, Ireland, and Williams, 1989, p. 420).

Definition of Effective Performance

The first step in the management of all employees is defining what is acceptable performance. Where goal setting is used, this is a fairly easy process. Where the goals and objectives are vague and ill defined, however, this can be a difficult process. One cannot accuse an employee of poor performance where there are no performance standards. To correct poor performance, therefore, requires defining good performance. This is the standard by which the employee's future performance must be measured.

Identifying Deviation from Acceptable Performance

Supervisors must be alert to deviations from normal performance. There are symptoms that astute managers can detect fairly quickly if they are attuned to their subordinates. Symptoms of poor performance problems include citizen complaints, negative comments by co-workers, late reports, an increase in errors in the handling of assignments, lethargy, and lack of concentration, to name a few. These and other changes in performance or personality signal the development of a problem. The sooner the problem is detected, the greater the likelihood of correcting the problem and saving the employee.

Formulation of Diagnosis with Employee

As soon as the problem is detected, it must be brought to the attention of the employee. This is a painful process and one of the reasons why supervisors tend to overlook problems until they are too serious to ignore. It is painful because most supervisors are uncomfortable in confrontational situations, especially with co-workers. This discomfort frequently translates into a tendency to put off the confrontation as long as possible. Unfortunately, the longer the discussion is delayed, the deeper the employee is likely to sink into the problem.

Nobody likes to be confronted with his or her own mistakes, including the manager. This person should therefore empathize with the employee's feelings. The meeting between the two should not be combative, but should be a straightforward attempt to get the employee to look at the problem and how that is influencing performance. The manager must focus on the behavior, not the person.

The goal of this meeting is to develop a definition of the problem that is agreed to by both manager and employee. The employee must develop the diagnosis or this person is likely to reject it as imposed by someone who does not understand the problem.

Selection of Remedial Action

The manager and employee must agree to an action that will correct the improper behavior. Sometimes outside specialists can be of some use here. Otherwise, this a process involving the manager and the employee. Once more, the employee must buy into the remedial action or the end result will be another form of game playing.

Implementation of Remedial Activity

The implementation process is usually one of two types: (1) those that managers can usually carry out by themselves, and (2) those carried out in the context of a formal organizational program.

The major strategies that managers can use by themselves are (Dubrin, Ireland, and Williams, 1989, pp. 422–424):

1. *Corrective discipline.* This is the most important, and in many ways powerful, tool of management. In essence it states, "shape up or ship out."

2. *Decision-making leave.* This is time off with pay. It allows the employee to think through his or her problems. The employee is given time off and asked to decide whether or not to stay with the job. If the decision is affirmative, an action plan is developed to improve performance.

3. *Counseling by manager.* This is not psychological counseling. It is job counseling designed to allow the employee to make discoveries about him/herself and the perceptions of others.

4. *Improve communication.* Increase the amount of two-way communication between manager and employee concerning the duties of the job and performance expectations.

5. *Increase motivation.* Motivation techniques are employed to improve performance. Rewards may be offered for improvement; punishments, for continued substandard performance.

6. *Job rotation.* If the problems stem from staleness or burnout, rotating the employee to a different job may have a positive effect on performance.

7. *Demotion.* If the employee is in a position beyond that person's capacity, demotion back to an activity where the employee was competent will be effective. The problem with this is the shock to the employee's ego, but it may be a necessary step if the person is to be salvaged. Despite its potential for effectiveness, this approach may be limited by civil service regulations or labor contracts.

8. *Lower performance standards.* Sometimes the problem is unrealistically high standards of performance. In these cases the easiest approach is to lower those standards.

Formal organizational programs are sometimes available for employees who are having problems. Such programs might consist of (DuBrin, Ireland, and Williams, 1989, pp. 424–426):

1. *Employee assistance programs.* In private industry this has become the most popular technique for a formal approach to performance problem (Hellan, 1986, pp. 51–54). The assumption is that professional counselors are better at solving employee problems than are managers. This has the added advantage of keeping the manager out of the employee's personal problems.

2. *Third-party counseling.* Usually applied only to upper-level managers, the third-party counselor helps both the superior and subordinate resolve a problem. The consultant diagnoses the problem, counsels the poor performer, and makes recommendations to other managers.

3. *Stress management programs.* These programs are designed to alleviate the impact of job-related stress. Such programs include physical exercise, relaxation techniques, monitoring of stress levels, and coping techniques (Weigel and Pinsky, 1982, pp. 56–60).

4. *Fitness and wellness programs.* A program that is related to stress management is the wellness program. Such programs encourage employees to remain physically and mentally healthy (Falkenberg, 1987, pp. 511–552). This program helps employees prevent health problems. One research project found that employees who stay in an exercise and nutrition program for two and one-half years or more have 40 percent lower hospitalization costs than other employees. Also, absenteeism dropped 18 percent for the physically fit workers (Frick, 1987, p. 1D).

5. *Behavior modeling.* The idea is to teach skills by having others imitate the actions of those who perform the task correctly. This technique has been useful in teaching skills such as interviewing, dealing with employee conflicts, terminating employees, and improving work habits. Behavior modeling typically includes six stages (Bittel and Ramsey, 1983, p. 43):

> **a.** Presentation of the concept.
>
> **b.** Step-by-step demonstration on cassette or film of actions the person can take to handle the situation.
>
> **c.** Rehearsal of skills in a supportive environment.
>
> **d.** Supportive feedback from peers and modeling specialists.
>
> **e.** Commitment to transfer the learning to the actual job situation.
>
> **f.** Followup to evaluate any problems encountered and to suggest ways to overcome them.

6. *Job redesign.* This is useful when the problem is caused by faulty job design. An example of this might be when the job specifications require the officer to report to multiple supervisors, who make conflicting demands. This is certain to result in performance failure. The solution in this case would be to redesign the job so that the officer reports to only one supervisor for all aspects of the job.

7. *Training and development.* A common antidote for poor performance is to send the employee to a training or development program. This is especially useful when the problem stems from the employee's lack of understanding of the job.

Reevaluation of Performance After Time Interval

The techniques discussed above will not automatically lead to improved performance. It is always necessary to reevaluate the poor performer at least once after the remedial activity. The discussion of this evaluation offers an excellent opportunity to praise the improvement, encourage the person's progress, or discuss problems that are being encountered as the person attempts to improve performance. The evaluation will also tell management if the remedial technique has been successful. If not, the decision must be made whether to try something different or begin the termination process.

Corrective Discipline

Corrective discipline is a positive method for improving poor performance. This approach allows the employee to correct the problem behavior before punishment is applied. Employees are told that their behavior is unacceptable and that corrections must be made if they want to stay with the organization (Asherman, 1982, p. 530; McConnell, 1986, pp. 64–71). A key element of corrective discipline is that the employee and the manager share the responsibility for solving the performance problem.

There are six stages in corrective discipline. These are described below (Dubrin, Ireland, and Williams, 1989, p. 427):

1. *Early intervention.* The manager should begin to work with the poor performer as soon as the problem appears and preferably no later than the second or third occurrence of the problem.

2. *Problem identification.* Poor performers must be identified in specific behavioral terms. Managers should avoid generalities about the person's attitude and should not use such terms as "lazy" or "bullheaded."

3. *Clarity of expectations.* The employee should know precisely what is expected in terms of improvement. The clearer the expectations, the less opportunity for ambiguity and confusion.

4. *Feedback.* Shortly after the disciplinary session, the employee needs to be informed orally or in writing as to how well this person is meeting expectations. Documentation of progress is important, particularly if the employee does not improve and eventually has to be terminated

5. *Positive reinforcement.* The manager should reward the employee for all improvements to help sustain the good performance. Everyday reinforcers such as praise, a handshake, or a favorable note to the file are usually adequate.

6. *Follow-up.* The employee's progress should continue to be observed and discussions should be held about how much progress is being made. When the employee begins to perform satisfactorily, the issue should be dropped. To be fully rehabilitated, the employee must feel that his or her behavior in no longer being singled out for scrutiny.

Corrective versus Summary and Progressive Discipline

Corrective discipline is the positive approach to discipline. The two negative forms of discipline are summary discipline and progressive discipline. *Summary discipline* is the immediate termination of an employee's employment. This is not done lightly and is subject to the terms of the labor contract and labor law. Grounds for immediate termination are provided by a gross violation of departmental policy. Frequently, this includes a violation of state or federal statute. Such violations include but are not limited to theft, sabotage, possession or sale of illicit drugs, rape, murder, or other felonies. In police agencies, unwarranted use of deadly force or being intoxicated on duty may also provide this justification.

Progressive discipline is a system of escalated penalties made known to employees in advance and imposed with increasing severity for repeated infractions (Madsen and Knudsen-Fields, 1987, pp. 17–24). The sequence of penalties usually proceeds in the order (1) oral warning, (2) written warning, (3) disciplinary layoff or suspension, and (4) discharge. Progressive discipline involves less counseling than does corrective discipline, but does recognize the importance of giving an employee a second chance.

Termination

The decision to fire an employee is one of the most difficult tasks faced by an administrator. At times, however, the termination of an employee's job can benefit both the employee and the organization. As with any controversial decision, there are arguments both for and against firing substandard performers (DuBrin, Ireland, and Williams, 1989, pp. 432–434).

Pros of Termination

1. *The shock may be therapeutic.* After being fired, the employee may realize that he or she must improve in order to earn a living.

2. *Department morale may show a spurt.* Effective co-workers may be happy to know that one must carry a fair share of the work load in order to remain employed.

3. *Fired employees often wind up finding a job for which they are better suited and often improve their occupational status.* Not everyone is meant to be a police officer. Many people find better jobs in private industry.

4. *Firing a poor performer usually creates a job opening for a more deserving and better qualified employee.* Getting rid of "deadwood" thus creates new opportunities in an era where opportunities do not abound.

5. *Firing a substandard performer may increase the productivity of employees who are not fired.* Such an act conveys the message that the organization sets high limits of acceptable performance and sees that they are enforced.

Cons of Termination

1. *Firing may be considered an admission of error in the selection, training, and management of human resources.* If a given substandard performer had been selected and trained properly, the dismissal would not have been necessary.

2. *If an employee is wrongfully discharged, the result can be costly litigation.* Currently one-half of all law suits against organizations for wrongful discharge are brought by nonmanagement personnel. Moreover, a number of former employees won subsequent libel suits against their former employers for comments that damaged their reputations (Corbett, 1986, p. 19–23; Gillot, 1986).

3. *Firing may lead to job stress for co-workers of the fired employee.* Co-workers may become fearful and anxious because they fear they will be the next to be fired.

4. *The organization that fires too many employees develops a poor reputation that may lead to problems in recruiting high calibre employees in the future.* Security-conscious people tend to avoid applying for work at agencies with a reputation for readily firing employees.

The most difficult management decision relates to poor performance. Obviously, those employees engaged in criminal activity or wantonly violating major department policy should be fired without hesitation. Poor performers reside in the management "gray area." Many are nice people who just do not seem to perform well. The decision to take remedial action or to terminate is one that has long-term consequences. The administrator should have sound organizational and legal reasoning for whichever course of action is taken.

DISCUSSION QUESTIONS

1. How does an effective control system work? Why is it necessary?

2. Discuss the problems related to the assessment of organizational effectiveness.

3. What is the activity trap? Why is it such a severe problem for law enforcement?

4. Discuss the problems inherent in the design and implementation of a performance appraisal system.

5. In designing a plan to deal with an ineffective performer, why is it necessary to know the cause of the problem? At what point should the decision to terminate an employee be made?

REFERENCES

Albanese, Robert (1988). *Management.* Cincinnati, Ohio: South-Western.

Aldag, Ramon J., and Timothy M. Stearns (1991). *Management,* 2nd ed. Cincinnati, Ohio: South-Western.

Asherman, Ira G. (1982). "The corrective discipline process," *Personnel Journal*, Vol. 65, No. 7, p. 530.

Barton, P. G. (1970). "Civilian review boards and the handling of complaints against the police," *University of Toronto Law Journal,* Vol. 20, p. 468.

Bernadin, H. J., and R.W. Beatty (1982). *Performance Appraisal: Assessing Human Behavior at Work.* Reading, Mass: Kent.

Bernshein, H. J., and L. A. Klatt (1985) "Management appraisal systems: has practice caught up to the state of the art?" *Personnel Administrator*, November, pp.78–86.

Bittel, Lester R., and Jackson E. Ramsey (1983). "What to do about misfit supervisors," *Management Review,* Vol. 72, No. 3, p. 43.

Bracker, Jeffrey S,. and John H.Pearson (1986). "Worker obsolescence: the human resource dilemma of the 80's," *Personnel Administrator,* Vol. 31, No. 12, pp. 109–116.

Brooks, Gail E. (1986). "VDT's and health risks: what unions are doing," *Personnel,* Vol. 63, No. 7, pp. 59–64.

Brown, Karen A., and Terence R. Mitchell (1986). "Influence of task interdependence and number of poor performers on diagnosis and causes of poor performance," *Academy of Management Journal,* Vol. 29, No. 2 (June), p. 423.

Cameron, Kim, and David A.Whetten (1983). "Some conclusions about organizational effectiveness," in Kim Cameron and David A.Whetten, eds. *Organizational Effectiveness: A Comparison of Multiple Models.* New York: Academic Press, pp. 269–274.

Campbell, J. P. (1977). "On the nature of organizational effectiveness," in P. S. Goodman and J. M. Pennings, eds., *New Perspectives on Organizational Effectiveness.* San Francisco: Jossey-Bass.

Corbett, Lawrence P. (1986). "Avoiding wrongful discharge suits," *Management Solutions,* Vol. 31, No. 6, pp. 19–23.

Dubrin, Andrew J. (1987). *The Practice of Supervision: Achieving Results through People,* 2nd ed. Plano, Tex.: Business Publications.

_____, R. Duane Ireland, and J. Clifton Williams (1989). *Management and Organization.* Cincinnati, Ohio: South-Western.

Falkenberg, Loren E. (1987). "Employee fitness programs: their impact on the employee and the organization," *Academy of Management Review,* Vol. 12, No. 3 (July), pp. 511–522.

Frick, Robert (1987). "Corporations finding healthy employees mean lower costs," *Rochester Democrat and Chronicle,* March 30, p. 1D.

Gillott, Roger (1986). "More fired workers suing their former bosses," *Associated Press,* September 23.

Goldstein, Herman (1977). *Policing a Free Society.* Cambridge, Mass.: Ballinger.

Green, S. G. (1979). "Causes of ineffective performance," *Proceedings of the Midwest Academy of Management,* April, pp. 38–48.

Halpern, S. C. (1974). "Police employee organizations and accountability procedures in three cities: some reflections on police policy-making," *Law and Society Review,* Vol. 8, No. 4 (Summer), pp. 561–582.

Hellan, Richard T. (1986). "An EAP update: a perspective for the 80's," *Personnel Journal,* Vol. 65, No. 6, pp. 51–54.

Hudson, J. R. (1971). "Police review boards and police accountability," *Law and Contemporary Problems,* Vol. 36, No. 4 (Autumn), p. 521.

Jackson, Susan E., Richard L. Schwab, and Randall S. Schuler (1986). "Toward an understanding of the burnout phenomenon," *Journal of Applied Psychology,* Vol. 71, No. 4, pp. 630–641.

Kerstetter, Wayne A. (1985). "Who disciplines the police? Who should?" in W .A. Geller, ed, *Police Leadership in America: Crisis and Opportunity.* Chicago: American Bar Foundation.

Latham, G. P. and K. N. Wexley (1981). *Increasing Productivity through Performance Appraisal.* Reading, Mass.: Addison-Wesley.

Madsen, Roger B., and Barbara Knudsen-Fields (May, 1987). "Productive progressive discipline procedures," *Management Solutions,* Vol. 32, No. 5, pp. 17–24.

McConnell, Patrick L. (1986). "Is your discipline process the victim of RED tape?" *Personnel Management,* Vol. 65, No. 3, pp. 64–71

Miner, John B. (1985). *People Problems: The Executive Answer Book.* New York: Random House.

More, Harry W., and Peter C.Unsinger (1987). *Police Managerial Use of Psychology and Psychologists.* Springfield, Ill.: Charles C Thomas.

_____, and W. Fred Wegener, (1992). *Behavioral Police Management.* New York: Macmillan.

Motowildo, Stephen J., John S. Packard, and Michael R. Manning (1986). "Occupational stress: its causes and consequences for job performance," _Journal of Applied Psychology_, Vol 71, No. 4, November, pp. 618–629.

Quick, James, and Jonathan D. Quick, (1984). _Organizational Stress and Preventive Management._ New York: McGraw-Hill.

Reibstein, L. (1988). "Firms ask workers to rate their bosses," _The Wall Street Journal,_ June 13, p. 15.

Rice, B. (1985). "Performance reviews: the job nobody likes," _Psychology Today,_ September, pp. 30–36.

Seers, R. M. (1976). "When is an organization effective?" _Organizational Dynamics,_ Autumn, pp. 50–63.

Solomon, Lewis C. (1983). "The other side of the smoking worker controversy," _Personnel Administrator,_ Vol. 28, No. 3, pp. 72–101.

Stratton, John G. (1987). "Employee assistance programs: a profitable approach for employees and organizations," in Harry W. More and Peter C. Unsinger, eds., _Police Managerial Use of Psychology and Psychologists._ Springfield, Ill.: Charles C Thomas.

Task Force Reports: The Police (1967): President's Commission on Law Enforcement and Administration of Jobs, Washington, D.C.: Government Printing Office.

Walker, Samuel (1983). _The Police in America._ New York: McGraw-Hill, p. 239.

Walker, Samuel, and Vic W. Bumphus (1991). _Civilian Review of the Police: A National Survey of the 50 Largest Cities, 1991._ Omaha, Neb.: Department of Criminal Justice, University of Nebraska at Omaha, p. 3.

Walton, Mary (1986). _The Deming Management Method._ New York: Perigee.

Warfield, Andrea (1987). "Co-worker romances: impact on the work group and and on career-oriented women," _Personnel,_ Vol. 64, No. 5, pp. 22–35.

Weigel, Randy and Sheldon Pinsky, (1982). "Managing stress: a model for the human resource staff," _Personnel Administration,_ Vol. 27, No. 2, pp. 56–60.

West, Paul (1991). "Investigation and review of complaints against police officers: an overview of issues and philosophies," in Thomas Barker and David Carter, eds., _Police Deviance,_ 2nd ed. Cincinnati, Ohio: Anderson, pp. 373–404.

Chapter 14

Administration: The Future

In this chapter we conclude our discussion with a number of issues. First we look at the future. An attempt is made to make some sense out of the ever-shifting social and technological trends. Finally, we identify some practical, straightforward rules of thumb for managing police organizations today and tomorrow.

WHERE ARE WE GOING?

The world is changing rapidly and the United States has not been exempted from this process. Eastern Europe is rapidly moving toward a form of democracy and the People's Republic of China is attempting to normalize relations with the Western nations. How this will affect us as a nation is not yet known. We do know that tomorrow will not be like today. In this chapter we focus on what tomorrow is likely to be from the perspective of the police administrator. Demographics will factor prominently in determining the face of the future. While this chapter does not evaluate all demographic trends, it seems worthwhile to look at one of the more powerful forces that will almost certainly be at work. This country is rapidly aging. Policing an older population is different from attempting to police the young.

Aging is not the only change that the nation will experience. The racial/ethnic mix will change immensely over the coming century. These changes may cause shifts in political and economic power. Moreover, the tendency of American companies to export jobs while importing products will more than likely generate a variety of economic crises over that same period. The most predictable change, however, is that the population is aging. To get a feeling for the future, therefore, we examine the social/economic impact of an aging society.

America Tomorrow

The post–World War II baby boomers are now entering middle age. When this huge population cohort hits retirement age the effect on American society will be profound. In just 20 years the 50–64 age group will increase by 25 percent and the 75 and older group will increase by 26 percent (Ostroff, 1989, p. 26). By 2030, a full 25 percent of the population will be elderly. By 2050 no less than 5 percent of the population will be 85 or older (Anon., 1988a, p. 8).

In the time between the reaching of elderly status and until the demise of a significant segment of the elderly, political decisions will be determined by this group. This will occur because of several factors. First, a larger portion of the elderly vote than do members of the younger generations. Second, the elderly will also be parents, grandparents, and great grandparents. They will have some influence on the voting behavior of their children and grand children. For some 20 to 30 years, the elderly vote will be the most powerful political block in the nation. Because people tend to vote for their own self-interests, we can anticipate a wave of legislation designed to provide services for the elderly.

The above-mentioned legislation will have some associated costs that the younger generation will be forced to bear. First, retirement systems will be under a terrible burden. Currently, a person paying into a retirement system derives far more from that system than is put into the system. In effect, when one pays into a retirement system, that person is paying the retirement benefits of a person currently on retirement. When there are more people in the work force than on retirement, the system works well. That will not be the case 30 years from now. There will be so many retired people that both private and government retirement systems will be hard pressed to fulfill their obligations. This includes the Social Security system. Retirement systems will be forced to increase the employee withholding amounts to meet the increased demand.

Second, the elderly have increased health needs. Medical costs and insurance are already rising at a frightening pace. Currently, we spend three times more money on the elderly than we do on children (Anon., 1988a, p. 8). Much of that cost is reflected in health care. That ratio should increase as the nation ages. In 30 years the costs of basic medical care may be well beyond the capacity of all but the very wealthy. At some point the elderly will address this issue at the ballot box. The results could be a form of national health insurance paid for by the taxes of the younger, employed generations.

At the very least, the government's priorities will reflect the needs of the elderly. There will not be enough tax dollars to provide everything that the elderly demand and also fully fund all other aspects of government. Health care will eat government budgets to the bone. Other services, such as the police, may find hard times ahead.

The elderly are fearful of crime. They worry more about crime than any other age group. It should not be a surprise that in those states where the average of the population is above the national median, crime and criminals are dealt with more harshly.

As the nation ages, the attitude toward crime will harden. Louder cries for the death penalty may be heard. There may be strong demands for longer prison sentences and less parole and probation. Should these things occur, the prison systems will be tasked beyond their capacity to function.

Demands for police protection and other services will also increase. Crime and the fear of crime will, quite likely, rank second only to health issues in the minds of the elderly. This time period will probably be remembered as the era of the highest taxes in the nation's history, which means that it may also produce the most violent anti-tax protests since the Boston Tea Party. This is mere speculation, however; in truth, we know that the elderly fear crime and want it dealt with harshly. That will continue and as the population ages, that philosophy will, more and more, become the philosophy of the nation.

Crime Trends

With each passing week it becomes more evident that tomorrow will not be like yesterday. The future will present society with problems of ever-increasing complexity. It should be painfully obvious that poverty is not going to be eradicated or even dealt with effectively. At the same time, evolving technology will increase the wealth and influence of those who understand and control the world of science. To quote an old cliche, "The rich will get richer, the poor will get poorer." The technology wave will not only ensure this process but will create an ever-widening gap between the educated and illiterate. As Iran has rejected Western modernizations, so too may our poor reject a world dominated by technocrats.

Drugs, a global economy beyond the ability of any nation to control, and terrorism are all part of this future. As William Tafoya stated when speaking of drug abuse, spouse/child abuse, urban unrest, and terrorism "These are the types of crimes that, like a cancer, literally spread throughout society, unmindful of geographic or political boundaries. They are the kind of crimes that reciprocate with other social ills and exacerbate already debilitated conditions; they evoke situational fear" (Tafoya, 1986, p. 304). The challenge to law enforcement will be immense; so too will be the gratitude of society to those who can and will meet these challenges.

The intensity of specific crimes will also change over time. It is chic to speak of crime in the singular. The reality is that there are many different types of criminal behavior. Changes in demographics, economics, and values will cause the frequency of some crimes to decrease while others increase. Georgette

Bennett has made an array of predictions for the future of crime, including the following (Bennett, 1987, p. 582):

1. The computer will be the single greatest crime generator in the future.

2. The concentration of crime in the United States will continue to be in the sun-belt.

3. Low birth rates and high work rates will leave a plethora of unguarded homes ripe for daylight burglary.

4. The growing service economy will create many part-time jobs, which combined with fewer student dropouts will mean less crime.

5. More abusive families will emerge as the number of single, poor, young, and undereducated mothers grows.

6. Industries with workers of older ages will experience less theft.

7. The growth in elderly population will increase medical quackery and insurance fraud.

8. Fear of AIDS will reduce the demand for streetwalkers.

Technology and Crime

Predicting social changes is a dangerous business. It is an arena where the person uttering the prophecies can easily appear foolish. Predicting technological change, however, is safer. Even though we cannot say exactly what changes will occur, we know there will be changes. Most of these will reflect improvements in existing technology. The focus in this section will be on those technical areas that have had the greatest past influence on the police.

The evolving weapons technology presents the most serious challenge to the police. It is difficult to be a terrorist with only a baseball bat. The greater the firepower, the greater the ability of an individual or small group to inflict death and destruction.

The world will not see safer and saner weapons. On the contrary, the future will see deadlier and more efficient weapons. Among the destructive instruments that police agencies may have to face are such items as hand-held rockets, computer viruses, electromagnetic pulse generators, and liquid metal embrittlement agents (Cretron, 1989, pp. 20–24).

The Stinger hand-held rocket is a small, lightweight, highly reliable rocket. It will become increasingly available to terrorist groups and is an effective means for shooting down airplanes of all types.

Computer viruses have already been introduced and have caused irreparable harm to many computer programs. Much of this has been done as a lark or as a challenge. Terrorists or criminals may use such techniques for more sinister purposes in the future.

Electronic pulse generators provide a means of attacking a computer. Such a device can be connected to a power line that feeds the computer under attack. The mechanism sends a powerful electronic pulse through the electrical circuit. This pulse can destroy the computer's memory bank.

Possibly the most frightening of the newly developed weapons are liquid metal embrittlement agents (LMEs). This agent, when applied to metal, makes it brittle. The metal loses its resiliency and begins to crack and crumble under stress. It takes little imagination to understand what effect such an agent would have on the wing of a commercial aircraft in flight or to any metallic structure.

In addition to these weapons, both biological and chemical weapons are becoming both more available and deadlier. Chlorine gas, for example, can be produced from seawater and is available to almost any group desiring such a product.

In summary, law enforcement will be required to deal with a wider variety of weapons that are more specialized and more effective. Police agencies will have to be better trained in far more areas of weapon expertise than they are now.

Bombs

The Provisional Irish Republican Army has aptly demonstrated what a little kerosene and fertilizer can do when properly mixed. Until they established a means to obtain more sophisticated bombs, they killed and maimed in Northern Ireland with just those two items. Explosive materials have become much more deadly and efficient. Today, a small amount of military plastic explosives can do incredible damage. Plastic explosives are easily hidden, fairly stable (making them safe to handle), and relatively easy to obtain.

It is not encouraging to note that weapons designers are working to improve explosives. These improvements include more explosive power, increased stability, and better triggering mechanisms. Bombing in the future will be more destructive, more accessible, and more of a problem for the police.

Firearms

There seems to be a belief among many people that everyone should own an automatic weapon. Assault rifles and machine guns are the current fad among gun enthusiasts. It takes little imagination to guess the difficulties this poses for the police in the future. Shootouts with criminals equipped with handguns were dangerous. Facing adversaries armed with military assault rifles substantially increases the risk to both police and innocent citizens.

Increasing police weaponry is really not a sound solution to the problem. In a gun battle, the police are usually not in a position to unleash the fury of an automatic weapon at an armed opponent. Most gun battles take place in an urban setting. Firing off a clip of ammunition in the direction of a criminal will, sooner or later, result in the killing of an innocent bystander. The police are therefore limited in their ability to respond to sophisticated weaponry.

Social Turmoil

Technology is neutral; it does not choose to kill or maim. It is only when a person chooses to use the technology for lethal purposes that it poses a danger. The real problems confronting law enforcement over the next 50 years will be social fragmentation. In a given society, violence is proportional to the level of sociopolitical instability within that society.

The United States is fragmenting socially. The division of wealth is badly skewed toward a shrinking proportion of the population. The number of poor is growing. The middle class is disappearing. Minority groups vie with each other and the white majority for jobs and political power. Racial unrest and bigotry is expanding and the result is the development of militant factions within each racial/ethnic group. The future portends great trauma for the nation. Two results of this fragmentation will be increased terrorism and urban unrest.

Terrorism

Terrorism will be with us because there are an increasing number of alienated people in the world. Also, we have a tendency to view the world of terrorism as an international conspiracy controlled and manipulated by a handful of regimes. This is simply not true. In every location experiencing terrorism, there is a history of perceived repression or disenfranchisement. Until the conditions causing terrorism are addressed, country by country, the problem will continue. As Frank Hagan has stated, terrorism is likely to increase as a "tool of cheap 'diplomatic leverage' and as authoritarian and democratic regimes resort to ideological justifications in their power maintenance" (Hagan, 1990, p. 581).

Terrorism is also dependent on both the media and technology. As weapons technology improves, it becomes possible for smaller groups of terrorists (or even individuals) to inflict greater damage, injury, and death. Since it can be reasonably expected that weapons and explosives technology will continue to evolve into more efficient designs, we can conclude that terrorism will experience a comparable increase in effectiveness.

The same is true of the media. We are no longer faced with a few major news networks controlling what we see and hear. Satellite communications make it possible for events to be televised within hours, or even minutes, of the actual event. The increasing number of news services combined with the competitive nature of broadcast journalism makes it almost a certainty that terrorist groups will be able to publicize whatever message they wish, in almost any format.

The degree to which the media complicates the problems associated with terrorism can be seen by a quick review of past media practices that have aggravated terrorist situations. According to the Vice President's Task Force on Combatting Terrorism, the media practices that can lead to problems during a terrorist incident are (*Public Report of the Vice President's Task Force,* 1986, p. 19):

1. Saturation television coverage, which can limit or preempt the government's options.

2. Political dialogue with the terrorists.

3. Coverage of obviously staged events.

4. Becoming part of the incident and participating in negotiations. The media in the role of arbiter usurp the legal responsibilities of the government.

5. Payments to terrorist groups or supporters for interviews or access.

6. Coverage of military plans or deployments in response to terrorist incidents.

Censorship is not an option open to us under our form of government. The relationship between the government and the media must be one of mutual understanding. Clearly, terrorism will test that relationship extensively in the future.

Given the growing alienation of the poor in this country, the urban ghettos seem a likely spawning ground for what could be our most serious confrontation with terrorism in the future. But this is not the only source of potential trouble. At least three other groups have been identified as possibly becoming increasingly terroristic: the antiabortionists, drug dealers, and right- wingers (Creton, 1989, pp. 20–24). While these disparate organizations have little in common with one another, they share one commonality, the willingness to use violence.

Some antiabortion forces have engaged in violence to make their point. Emotional issues such as abortion can provide the impetus for mobilization of large segments of society. The abortion controversy could well lead to terrorism. Of equal concern is the likelihood of counterterrorism from pro-choice groups. Militancy on the part of one faction could incite militancy on the part of the opposition. The police will be in the middle.

While the growing drug problem has been discussed, we have not looked at drug dealers as potential sources of terrorism. In Colombia, the drug lords have aggressively attacked police and court officials in an attempt to persuade them that investigation and prosecution of drug cases was not in their best interest. Such a scenario could be played out in this country as well. Drug gangs are well armed with the most sophisticated military weapons, have the resources to field an army, and are willing to take on the justice system in a head-to-head confrontation. The gangs are currently too busy fighting each other to go aggressively after police or judges. That could change in the future. If it does, drug gangs certainly pose a terroristic threat.

Historically, the United States has had to deal with issues raised by right-wing extremists. Some of these groups are seeking to return to a time when white males had the majority of the power and money. Such groups are not likely to sit back and quietly accept the growth in political and economic power of minority groups. There is a real possibility that membership among these groups will increase. Concurrent with membership increases we can expect growing militancy. Thus far the primary targets have been African Americans and Jews. Future extremists are likely to target Asians and Hispanics.

Urban Unrest

Dwellers of the urban ghetto have three major disadvantages. First, some areas lack a strong tradition in favor of education. Role models, unfortunately, often include drug pushers and pimps. Second, the majority of families are broken, with children raised by single parents or grandparents. Third, the lack of available work and the availability of welfare has stripped away some of the strengths of the work ethic. More and more, inner-city residents are faced with fewer opportunities and more hostility. This indicates a serious problem developing in the inner cities of the nation. These conditions have led several researchers to predict massive urban unrest and civil disorder by the year 1999 (Tafoya, 1986, pp. 372–373).

The scope of the problem can be seen in numbers. In 1986 it was estimated that there were over 32 million people living in poverty in the United States. Ten million of these people had jobs, but the wages earned were not sufficient to meet basic needs (Anon., 1988b, pp. 6–7). This number is growing. At the bottom layer of this mass of people are the homeless. One study found 229,000 homeless citizens in just 20 cities (Anon., 1989, pp. 3-4). This represents an army of the disenfranchised: people with no resources, no prospects, and no hope. The impact on law enforcement will be severe. The major focus of police activities is, and always has been, street crime. Street crime is closely associated with urban poverty (Sykes, 1980).

THE POLICE OF THE FUTURE

The emerging police organization is one that will retain some vestiges of traditional policing but will be completely different in other areas. The emphasis will be on identifying community problems and solving those problems in cooperation with various community organizations. The police must once more merge into the governmental structure as a team member rather than as an isolated strike force.

The new police officer must be better educated, better trained, and have a more thorough understanding of the police role within a multifaceted society.

The goals of the emerging police will focus on social ills and the causes of crime. Crime control will still be their concern, but crime prevention will be their reason for existing. The new police must see the Constitution not as an impediment to effective law enforcement, but as the primary foundation for the American way of life. The police must not see the Constitution as just another set of laws, but as the ultimate law, never to be knowingly ignored or violated.

The organizational structure of tomorrow's police must take these factors into account. To do that, however, requires an understanding of the mistakes of the past. Despite the increased training and professionalism of law enforcement personnel in this country, the effectiveness of the police in reducing crime has been decreasing steadily. Concurrently, the isolation of the police from the community they serve has been increasing steadily. What have we been doing wrong? What must be done to correct the problems associated with police management?

The answer lies in the very structure of the traditional police organization. The very premises on which the police are built are factors that contribute to the problems. Law enforcement agencies must change, but will they?

Varieties of Police Administration

When discussing law enforcement, there is a tendency to speak in the singular, as if there were but one police agency and one style of organization. That is not true. The police of the United States are represented by tens of thousands of different agencies at the federal, state, and local levels. They have different levels of resources, personnel, and responsibility.

Discussing the changing face of U.S. law enforcement is difficult because there is no single such creature. The police are a multifaced organism. Because there is no one single police organization, there is also no single future for police agencies in the United States. Among the future police in this country, there will be a variety of organizational types. Rather than becoming more alike, law enforcement will become further fragmented, with each agency altering its design and structure in response to the pressures of that jurisdiction.

The forces that will shape future departments are already at work. In this section we look at possible outcomes.

Why Police Management Must Change

Current police practices are a failure. Each year brings more crime and fewer clearances. It is not that crime rates are increasing, in many cases it is the opposite. But crime rates are expressed as a ratio. Real crime is increasing as the population base increases. The number of police officers is not increasing in proportion to the number of the population, therefore; police caseloads are increasing at a steady pace.

Despite the move toward professionalism, the police have become increasingly isolated from the public they serve. To some extent, technology has been responsible for this condition. When police officers were moved into cars, they began to lose touch with the public. When administrators provided air-conditioners, the officers raised their windows, adding another shield between them and the people. When it became more comfortable to stay in the car than to get out of the car, police officers ceased to be involved with the citizens of their community.

As a group, many police officers are unaware of the changes outside their jurisdiction and do not belong to professional organizations that promote learning through continued research. Indeed, few police officers and administrators read much material of a professional or scholarly nature.

At this time it is doubtful that more than 20 percent of the nation's police executives understand either problem-oriented or community-oriented policing. It would be surprising if more than 5 percent of the nation's officers have even heard those terms used. Why should they? The terms are not used in the press, and the overwhelming majority of police officers do not read textbooks or professional journals unless they are required for promotion.

To some extent police administrators have been successful in obtaining requirements for higher education for police officers. Where this has failed is in the inculcation of a professional mind-set. Police leaders have failed to convince the nation's police officers, including many managers, of the necessity for continued learning, especially for continued self-education. Many law enforcement officers and managers are not only isolated from the community, they are isolated from each other. Moreover, they are isolated professionally. They learn only from their own mistakes.

The failure of the police to adapt to changing social conditions, to take full advantage of advanced technology, and to grasp the failures of their past will cost them heavily in the future. The public is losing faith, not only with the police but with the entire justice system. Private security is expanding rapidlyand is gradually taking responsibility for areas once thought to be the primary domain of law enforcement. In 50 years law enforcement and security forces may change positions relative to status. It may be the security forces who are seen as professional and the police who are seen as minimum-wage "door shakers" and night watchmen.

The security companies have the resources and ability to adapt to the needs of the customer. Who do citizens call when there is trouble? Do they call someone who is working for the citizen and striving to please, or someone who may be less responsive? If the police as a group do not change, there is a real possibility that law enforcement, as an institution, may become obsolete within the next century.

Why Police Management Cannot Change

Police administration is a charismatic endeavor. It is charismatic because the chief executive officer of a police agency is primarily a politician. This person stays in office only as long as the respect of both the civil administration and the police officers can be maintained. Once lost, for either, the tenure of the police executive tends be short-lived. Changes must therefore meet the approval of both groups.

As we discussed in Chapter 9, police organizations often employ the type of person who is most resistant to change. This fact, enhanced by a budgeting system that does not reward effectiveness, represents a powerful force toward stagnation. Overcoming this force requires a truly effective administrator.

Unfortunately, succession is not influenced by the chief executive officer. A successful administrator can see everything accomplished go up in smoke with the appointment of a new chief, one who is from the traditional school of police management. The average tenure for police chiefs in this country is loosely estimated at around three years. That is not enough time to make permanent changes.

Moreover, political forces work against police change. Problem-oriented and community-oriented policing are frequently, and inappropriately, seen as "peacetime" police models. When crime is low and the streets calm, the public want "friendly" community-oriented officers who talk to kids in schools and coach kids'sports. When crime is high, especially violent crime, the public wants "kick-butt" policing. They want the officers in the streets collaring criminals.

Politicians elected on a tough anticrime platform demand traditional policing techniques. The police administrator who is unwilling to take this step will almost invariably be replaced by a chief who will take the department in that direction. When problem- or community-oriented policing is most needed, therefore, is when it is most likely to be eliminated and replaced by the "old ways."

Courts may also be a force against police change. Because each time a civil suit is filed it includes the chief executive officer, law enforcement agencies are trying to protect themselves with a vast array of policies and procedures and ever- increasing supervision. This is detrimental to both contemporary policing models and to effective policing (see Chapters 8 and 11). But court decisions will force police agencies to engage in further rulification. That will be one more impediment to administrative change.

Finally, as we discussed earlier, we are a long way from a professional police force or management system. There are still too many undereducated officers and administrators,too many who are locked into their own narrow view of the world. Sadly, in 50 years police departments may look identical to police organizations of today.

The Gift and Curse of Technology

Law enforcement is currently going through a technological transition period. In the past, paperwork meant forms and reports written on real paper. The future will see fewer and fewer paper reports and larger numbers of electronic reports. The current transition phase is one in which the computers are in place- but the personnel are not yet aware of the capabilities of the equipment. In most police agencies computers are little more than expensive typewriters and filing cabinets.

Real computerization will occur when police administrators learn that the true benefits of the computer lie with its ability to analyze and collate information. That time is rapidly approaching. Computers have not yet revolutionized policing, but they will in the future. That future is not very far away.

There is a downside to the computer revolution. There are serious shortcomings in computerized files that are not likely to be corrected in the near future. By the year 2000, it is expected that such systems will be the target of legal action. Because the inaccuracies and inadequacies are expected to be pervasive, a further projection is that the police will lose the majority of these lawsuits to well-prepared plaintiffs (Tafoya, 1986, p. 373). The following case provides a demonstration of this problem.

Powe v. City of Chicago (1981)
664 F.2d 639

Plaintiff-appellant Andrew Powe filed this lawsuit against the city of Chicago and the county of Cook under section 1983, 42 U.S.C. section 1983. The district court granted defendant's motion for summary judgment. Powe appealed.

In February 1972, Powe was the victim of an armed robbery committed by Ernest Brooks, who took, among other things, Powe's wallet containing his identification. Brooks was later arrested for another crime, and using Powe's stolen identification, he pleaded guilty and was sentenced to two years' probation under the name "Andrew Powe." He then violated probation and a probation violation arrest warrant was issued by the Cook County Adult Probation Department on December 20, 1974, for the arrest of "Andrew Powe, a/k/a/ Ernest Brooks." The warrant was lodged with the Cook County sheriff's fugitive warrants Section and was placed as a "stop order" with the Chicago Police Department "without adequate specificity to identify the intended arrestee."

On November 25, 1975, the real Andrew Powe was stopped by Chicago police for a traffic offense. The police made a routine computer check and Powe was arrested under the warrant noted above. Powe was unable to post bond until the following day; therefore, he spent the night in jail. On December 1, 1975 Powe went before a judge and explained the situation. The case was continued so that the prosecutor could investigate. On December 30, 1975, the prosecutor verified Powe's story and he was discharged.

Three months later, on March 8, 1976, Powe was once again stopped by Chicago police for a traffic violation and once again was arrested on the outstanding warrant. This time Powe spent the night in jail, but the mistake was discovered when an employee of the adult probation office stated that he was the wrong man. Despite this, Powe was not released promptly, but was held in custody for "many" additional hours prior to being released.

Following the second arrest, Powe filed this lawsuit. Thereafter, he was arrested twice more on the same warrant, once in January 1977 and again on November 5, 1977. In this lawsuit he seeks damages and injunctive relief, under section 1983 and under pendent state counts of negligence and respondeat superior, for all four of his arrests and for his retention in custody by the Chicago police, on the occasion of his second arrest, after they were notified that he was not the man sought under the warrant.

Opinion of the Court

The Fourth Amendment guarantees that no person shall be arrested unless there is good reason to believe that he or she has committed a particular crime. By the terms of the Fourth Amendment, an arrest warrant based on probable cause and particularly describing the person to be seized is sufficient cause to make an arrest. But an arrest warrant that, by way of description, simply gives one or two of several names which, for all the authorities know, the arrestee might or might not be using, does not provide sufficient information on which an arrest may be made.

We therefore hold that the complaint adequately alleges that the probation-violation warrant was invalid for failure to satisfy the Fourth Amendment's particularity requirement. The dismissal of that portion was erroneous and is reversed.

The second complaint, prolonged detention by the Chicago police, is unsubstantiated by evidence that the Chicago police regularly, as a matter of practice, detain arrestees for an unreasonable time after it is clear that there is no longer any cause to hold them. Nor can we draw such an inference from the allegation of a single incident of undue detention. We conclude that Powe has not made out a claim against the city of Chicago for his continued detention on the occasion of his second arrest. The decision of District Court concerning this portion of the complaint is affirmed.

Moreover, at least one researcher has predicted that by the year 2000, local law enforcement could be overwhelmed by sophisticated crime and may be reduced to taking preliminary reports (Tafoya, 1986, p. 373). Evolving communications provide both a boon and a bane to law enforcement. Microelectronics have allowed the development of police radios that can be worn as headsets. This allows officers in tactical situations to maintain constant contact while keeping their hands free to handle people, weapons, or other instruments. Range is increasing, as is the clarity of communications.

The installation of video cameras in police cars has already proved to be beneficial in a number of police–citizen encounters across the nation. Eventually, the cameras will be live action rather than videotape instruments. It is just a matter of time until the cameras are small enough to attach to helmets worn by street officers. When that occurs, the dispatchers and commanders will be able to monitor situations live. That will bring a whole new dimension to police management.

The downside is that communications does not evolve just for the police. It also serves the criminal and the media. Police monitoring has become a form of entertainment for many citizens. Similarly, police scanners serve a more sinister purpose for the criminal. It is relatively easy in most jurisdictions to track patrol officers and their vehicles.

Enhanced communications technology will also bring a new dimension to public access of police news. Many people now monitor police radio broadcasts. The ability to monitor live video broadcasts could have long-reaching effects on police operations.

Computer-to-computer communications allows officers to fully utilize the department's databank from a patrol vehicle. A vast array of information can be made available to patrol officers while in their cars, and it is no farther away than their fingertips. This is already available in some jurisdictions. Within 20 years it will be available to the majority of police agencies.

It might be concluded that better communications means better reporting by the media. That may or may not be true. What will happen is that there will be more reporters and they will be at scenes faster and with better equipment. Police officers may be forced to deal with the media at any given situation more rapidly than they are prepared to do. It is likely that the press will begin to arrive at major scenes, with a full array of broadcasting equipment, before the police. If this occurs, police administrators will be required to take an in-depth look at the police–media relationship, for it will become more important than it is already. The following case demonstrates what happens when the police fail to understand the rights of the press.

Connell v. Town of Hudson (1990)
733 F.Supp. 465 (D.N.H.)

In this civil action, David W. ("Nick") Connell claims that officials of the town of Hudson, New Hampshire, violated his constitutional rights by ordering him away from the scene of an accident and threatening to arrest him if he persisted in taking pictures.

David Connell, a Ferry Street resident and freelance reporter for the *Hudson News,* heard a collision, grabbed his camera, and rushed to the scene of an accident. From a distance of approximately 25 feet, Connell took a few preliminary pictures. A police officer asked him to move farther away. Connell left the scene to get a telephoto lens, then returned to another area farther from the accident, as the officer had instructed. After taking a few pictures from that spot, Connell moved to a closer position, approximately 30 yards away from the cars. Connell moved again and set up a tripod on a neighbor's lawn about 40 yards from the accident. Another officer approached, and the following exchange took place.

"The officer came over to me and his words were, as I recall: 'We've been patient with you long enough and you'll have to take your camera and go down—and he indicated a point about where they had the barrier was. You'll have to go down there. You can photograph there if you want.'"

And I said: "I believe I have a right to photograph from here" (indicating his location).

And he says: "You do not. If you don't move, I'll put you in handcuffs and take you to—put you in jail."

Connell moved "under protest." He then got permission to enter a nearby house where he had seen people watching from a second-story window. As he prepared to take pictures from that window, an officer told him to stop photographing and leave the building. When Connell refused to leave, the officer went to police chief Albert Brackett.

"I went to—back to my—to the window and recommenced trying to set my camera up. And then police chief Brackett, being briefed that I had been not exactly cooperative, came to the window and reiterated all of the preceding demands that I stop photographing, that I come down out of the building, that they did not need a warrant."

"And I asked him why—under what pretext—he would arrest me, what had I done wrong. And he says the charge would be for disturbing the peace."

"I said: 'That can't be. I'm not disturbing anybody's peace. I'm just photographing through a telephoto lens.'"

"And he insisted that he was right, that what he was doing was legal and that I had to do it."

"So I said, Well, I recognize who you are and your position. You're acting chief of police. In deference to that, I will come down and desist from photographing but I want you to understand that it's under protest and it is not the end of it.'"

The plaintiff asserts that the events described above violated rights guaranteed him by the First and Fourth Amendments to the U.S. Constitution. Plaintiff's Fourth Amendment argument is not persuasive.

Nothing in the record suggests that Connell was prevented from leaving the scene at any time. The court therefore rejects his Fourth Amendment claim. The court does, however, find merit in plaintiff's First Amendment claim.To resolve the issue raised in the instant case, the court must determine whether the restrictions placed on Nick Connell were reasonably justified. The court finds that they were not.

The undisputed facts demonstrate that Connell followed all instructions reasonably designed to prevent interference with police and emergency activities. Although he may have crossed a police perimeter, that perimeter was not clearly delineated, and, when asked to move, he moved. He left the scene to retrieve a telephoto lens that would enable him to take the pictures he needed from a distance. And he did not thereafter improperly approach the accident area. It is hard to imagine how Connell could have interfered with police or emergency activities by taking pictures from the second floor of the house that others were using to view the accident.

Defendants' most persuasive argument is that emergency personnel refused to remove Mrs. Cote's body until Connell stopped taking pictures. But even that fact does not provide the justification necessary to withstand judicial scrutiny.

Defendants make much of their argument that the limitation placed on Nick Connell's picture taking were reasonable because Connell's action invaded Donna Cote's right to privacy. The court does not accept defendants' paternalistic view of police authority.The court also rejects defendants' assertion that Chief Brackett is protected by qualified immunity.

Reasonable police officers understand that their authority has well-defined limits. At the time of this incident, Albert Brackett., the acting chief of Hudson's police department, can be fairly held to the understanding that he could not chase a photographer away from an accident unless that photographer was unreasonably interfering with police activity. The record in the instant case suggests no such interference.

The defendants also argue that this suit may not be maintained against the town of Hudson because the plaintiff has not demonstrated that the actions about which he complains result from town "policy" or "custom."

Identification of policymaking officials for this purpose is a question of state law. Under New Hampshire law, a police chief has "authority to direct and control all employees of his department in their normal course of duty." The court has little difficulty concluding that Chief Brackett's conduct during the July 9, 1987 confrontation represented town of Hudson policy.

Moreover, the letter from town administrator Alice Monchamp manifests the town's support for Chief Brackett's action, and, as the plaintiff points out, the defendants have admitted that "at all relevant times defendant Brackett and other police officers present at the accident scene described in the plaintiff's complaint were carrying out the lawful policy, practices and custom of the defendant town of Hudson."

Accordingly, for the reasons stated hereinabove, the court declares that David Connell's rights, protected from government intrusion by the First Amendment to the U.S. Constitution, were violated by town of Hudson police when they ordered him to stop taking pictures from positions that did not interfere with police activity.

Profit-Motivated Policing

There is one trend that is already having a dramatic influence on police operations and management. Due to civil seizure laws, law enforcement agencies have discovered a source of revenue outside their authorized budgets. They can now seize property that is the result of criminal activity or is used in the commission of a crime. The emphasis of this law is on drug enforcement. Because it is a civil process, the burden of proof and trial procedures shift to the substantial benefit of the state. The law enforcement agencies keep all or a substantial portion of the property seized. This is a legal, but often questionable process.

The theory behind this law is that it provides law enforcement with the resources to better enforce the drug laws. The theory is enhanced by the arguments of law enforcement administrators that without the additional resources they are less effective than with those resources. Statistical information would seem to bear this out. Police agencies do make more arrests and seizures when they are the recipients of the seized items.

But is this what is really happening? Partly, but the primary reason that drug enforcement increases when the police keep the items seized may be a shift in priorities. Drug enforcement becomes a profit-making enterprise where traffic enforcement and theft investigations do not. It is reputed that one police agency in the southeastern portion of the country adds 20 million dollars a year to their resource base as a result of drug-related seizures.

In truth, drug enforcement—as with all vice offenses—has always had a low priority among the police. These priorities, however, have shifted dramatically in the past 15 years due to civil seizure laws. Police priorities in some agencies now reflect the profit motive. Profit-based management is a different type of management from the public service orientation of law enforcement. Police administrators are ill suited to deal with nonbudgeted funds. The potential for misuse and mismanagement is high when there is an unpredictable and unaccounted for flow of large sums of money and property into an agency.

The reason these laws are questionable is the almost certain abuse that will take place with these laws. There is no philosophical problem with denying criminals the proceeds of their crime; it is a logical action for the government to take. The issue is who should receive the benefits of justice system activity.

Over 2000 years ago the Roman courts rewarded those who filed criminal charges against others by giving them a portion of the condemned person's property. Until the Romans discovered their mistake, the result was an overloaded and badly abused court system. Up until the mid-twentieth century, police officers in the United States were awarded a portion of the fines they collected, and in many cases, budgets were built around enforcement activity. The result was the infamous speed trap and law enforcement for personal gain.

Legislators, both state and federal, have now upped the ante. Farms, houses, airplanes, ships, boats, and automobiles have become police property for the taking. Some police departments take in more cash than the local banks. And the public is told it is okay; it is the only way the police can fight drug trafficking.

The reality is that those who stand to profit personally from a decision to take a person's property cannot be the ones to make the decision to take that property. To allow that to happen is to invite corruption and mismanagement on a monumental scale.

Civil forfeiture is with us for the time being. While it exists many police managers will have a different set of priorities and management problems than have existed in the past. Police chiefs will have to make decisions and answer questions never before posed. Some departments will lose substantial portions of their budget as city and county governments inevitably begin to reallocate budgets to take advantage of the seized resources (Government may rationalize that if a police department gets 20 million dollars in seizures, why not shift 10 million dollars of the police budget to the fire department? Both gain that way.)

Eventually, civil forfeiture will either be eliminated or redesigned so that the police do not benefit directly. That will happen because the public outcry over the misuse of these laws will rattle the halls of the legislatures from Alaska to Washington, D.C. Unfortunately, the image of U.S. law enforcement will take a hard battering in the process. Civil forfeiture has allowed police departments to stick their hands in the cookie jar. Sooner or later the public is going to slap that hand. Many police chiefs are going to be looking for new jobs when it happens. That is a shame, but greed makes a poor value statement for a police agency.

DISCUSSION QUESTIONS

1. Discuss the demographic factors that will change the nature of policing in the future.

2. Discuss the social factors that will affect policing in the future.

3. What impact will evolving technology have on policing?

4. From the perspective of a police manager, discuss the pros and cons of asset forfeiture laws.

5. Harland Cleveland once said, "Future executives will be decision brokers rather than decision makers"(1972, p. 13). What are the implications of this statement for police administrators?

REFERENCES

Anon.(1988a) "Coming soon: elderly America." *Population Today,* Vol. 16, No.10, p. 8.

_____ "The ten million working poor"(1988b). *Population Today,* Vol. 16, No. 2, pp. 6–7.

_____ (1989) "Another winter for the homeless," *Population Today,* Vol. 17, No. 2, pp. 3–4.

Bennett, Georgette (1987). *Crimewarps: The Future of Crime in America.* Garden City, N.Y.: Anchor Books, Doubleday, 1987. As cited in Frank E. Hagan, *Introduction to Criminology* , 2nd ed. Chicago: Nelson-Hall, 1990, pp. 581–582.

Cleveland, Harland (1972). *The Future Executive.* New York: Harper & Row.

Cretron, Marvin J. (1989). "The growing threat of terrorism,"*The Futurist,* July–August, pp. 20–24.

Hagan, Frank E. (1990). *Introduction to Criminology* , 2nd ed. Chicago: Nelson-Hall.

Ostroff, Jeff (1989). "An aging market," *American Demographics,* May, pp. 26–27.

Public Report of the Vice President's Task Force on Combatting Terrorism (1986). Washington, D.C.: U.S. Government Printing Office, February, p. 19.

Sykes, Gresham M. (1980). *The Future of Crime.* Rockville, Md.: National Institute of Mental Health.

Tafoya, William L. (1986). "The future of law enforcement," Chapter 5 of *A Delphi Forecast of the Future of Law Enforcement.* Dissertation for the University of Maryland. Ann Arbor, Mich.: University Microfilms, International.

Prologue

Whether or not police organizations change, police administrators must have a game plan. They must develop a set of administrative philosophies and proceed from that basis. The following section is predicated on that idea. This section might be titled, "ground rules for administrators." It is a summary of information presented earlier and is intended to provide easy-to-remember rules of thumb for good management. These ideas are valid for police managers in all police organizational models.

THE ADMINISTRATIVE FUNCTION

The issues in this section revolve around the administrator and duties performed by this person. The administrator may be the most important member of the agency; effective organizations consistently have good leadership (Peters and Waterman, 1982).

If It's Not Broke, Don't Fix It

There is a natural human tendency to overadjust or oversupervise. When something is working well, it should be left alone. Problems are generated by constant tinkering. The number of businesses to fail because they continued to change after they had found a successful formula is staggering. The almost certain shifting of a flexible organization toward a rigid bureaucracy is the product of constant tinkering and poor decision making.

There are two primary reasons for administrators initiating unnecessary change. First is the belief in change for the sake of change. This is especially prevalent among new managers. They feel that they were brought in to make changes, so they make changes. Sometimes it takes years to overcome the destruction brought on by these mad scientists of organizational change. Second, administrators brought in from other organizations, for some strange reason, believe that the form they learned there is the only right form. They immediately attempt to reorganize the new organization into their old one. Sadly, the old form probably did not work all that well in the other organization, but it almost never works in the new one.

Change is necessary for continued growth of the organization. Change, however, must be for the right reasons and in the right direction. Change for the sake of change or to recreate an old organization by transforming a new one is always wrong. The administrator will have enough problems fixing those things not functioning properly. There is no need to expend precious time and resources correcting something needing no correcting.

Administrators Exist to Solve Problems, Not Create Them

Administrators exist to serve those who do the work, not vice versa. The administrator's duty is to grease the wheels of organization, to make the worker's job easier, and to remove obstacles from the path of industry. Encouragement and advice are the manager's stock in trade.

The administrator's function is not to bark orders to underlings, browbeat workers, stand in the way of progress, shift more burdens to the worker, take credit for others' efforts, invent roadblocks to performance, or invent new methods of alienating, demoralizing, and offending every man and woman on whom the organization depends.

At the very beginning of this book, W. Edwards Deming was quoted as stating, "Eighty-five percent of an organization's problems are caused by management." If a person cannot manage effectively, that person should do nothing. That manager will come out better than most of his or her counterparts. In short, the administrator should, "lead, follow, or get the hell out of the way."

Face Problems Head On or Later On

Day-to-day management consists of making decisions. The vast majority of these are minor problems and can be handled quickly. The secret to maintaining harmony in the organization is to resolve these issues quickly. Few large problems pop up instantly; they need time to develop. This is due to the nature of large problems. They are usually created by the combining of various small concerns into a multifaceted issue and need time to fester and generate hostility and frustration. Prison riots do not occur because of a single event; the event only provides the spark in a volatile environment. The same is true of job actions by union employees. Strikes often take years to develop; it takes a great amount of frustration and anger for a police officer to violate an oath and walk off the job.

A side benefit to solving small problems promptly is the gaining of employee respect and support. Resentment builds toward the administration when small problems are allowed to fester. Often these problems are so small that no one will complain for fear of being petty, but the resentment will grow anyway. When those rare giant problems occur without warning, the difference between whether the administrator survives or not often depends on employee support. The major issue may have nothing to do with past small issues, but if there is sufficient employee resentment, the workers may seize the crisis as an excuse for eliminating the boss. The crisis may be the excuse in this situation, but the reason is a failure to solve small problems promptly.

The point of this is self-explanatory; Managers ignore small problems at their own risk. For those who want to slay dragons, that's their business, but dragons are much easier to kill when they are fresh out of the egg.

Secrecy Protects Incompetence and Little Else

There are two types of information subject to secrecy in a law enforcement agency:

1. Sensitive information about individuals discovered in the course of legitimate police activities which is, simply stated, no one's business. This includes intelligence information based on rumor and innuendo.

2. Tactical information concerning police response to specific types of crimes or targets of crimes. This includes information uncovered during an investigation necessarily kept secret to enhance investigation or prosecution.

Nothing else concerning the law enforcement function is private information. A natural attribute of bureaucracies is secrecy. The reason for this is brutally simple. Organizations protect themselves from embarrassment by controlling information concerning organizational activities. Law enforcement agencies are public service agencies and the public has a right to know what transpires within those agencies. The administrator has an obligation to allow the public access to the inner workings of the agency. Does this mean that the administrator and the department will be embarrassed by what is discovered? Absolutely; the major reason that public service agencies, especially police organizations, have been able to function in such a backward ineffective manner for so long is their ability to hide their ineffectiveness from the public.

Positive change comes when an organization is no longer able to maintain an image of effectiveness in the face of hard data to the contrary. How long can corrupt, brutal, and incompetent officers survive with the public and media having full access to their actions and decisions? How many times can an administrator make the same mistake when the error is publicized. Embarrassment is a valuable organizational tool. No one wants to be humiliated; the very possibility of it happening is sufficient to make most people consider their decisions a little longer.

Secrecy breeds cover-ups and political behavior. Remember, there are bad officers because good officers protect them. There is a saying with regard to decisions, "Make every decision as if it will appear on the six o'clock news." Competence needs and deserves public recognition; incompetence needs secrecy. Since the administrator does not need incompetence, secrecy is an unwise policy.

Take the Job Seriously, Never Yourself

The headline above is good advice for everyone, but especially for administrative personnel. The drift toward administrative arrogance is so subtle and steady it often occurs without the person noticing the development. Others notice, however, and once egomania sets in, effectiveness goes out. The administrator is not the organization. This person is merely another member of the team with a different set of duties and responsibilities. A challenge to administrative decisions is not a challenge to the administrator's character, intelligence, or dedication. It merely represents a difference of opinion.

The symbols of success—authority, power, responsibility, large office, private secretary, and personal car—are attached to the office, not the person. They were there before the current manager and they will be there after that person is gone. Managers are neither all-knowing nor terminally stupid. Their best chance for success lies in the accomplishments of others; this is the reality of administration. This has been acknowledged in a hundred ways in a thousand organizations. There is an old truism in U.S. Navy that "The chiefs run the Navy"—note, not the admirals, captains, ensigns, or even the president of the United States, but the chiefs, those senior enlisted members of the organization with operational responsibilities. Smart naval officers have always known this and they lead their units accordingly. In law enforcement, the patrol-level officers are the department, they are all the public sees. Effective administrators know this and manage their agencies accordingly. The following case demonstrates the willingness of the courts to support police work that is conducted within the limits of law and policy.

Alberts v. *City of New York* (1982)
549 F.Supp. 227

A $3.5 million action was brought by the plaintiff against the city, police department, and arresting officers to recover damages arising out of alleged assault and battery and false arrest. The complaint was dismissed by the District Court, Keven Thomas Duffy, J.

On August 8, 1980 at approximately 9:30 P.M. a van driven by Kosmas Bidales was stopped for running a red light by police officers James Ogletree and Hillery Simmons, who were in a marked patrol car on Amsterdam Avenue near 168th Street. Ogletree left Simmons behind in the patrol car, walked to the driver's side of the van, and asked to see Bidales' driver's license and registration. Ms. Gloria Alberts, the plaintiff, was seated in the passenger side of the van and was in the middle of a vociferous argument with Mr. Bidales when Officer Ogletree approached the van. The plaintiff, who was shouting obscenities when the van pulled over, now directed her foul language at the police officer. Ogletree warned Ms. Alberts that if she persisted in her verbal abuse he "was going to lock her up." Ms. Alberts did not heed the officer's warning. Ogletree then walked to the passenger's side of the van to confront the plaintiff and to again warn her: "You keep on and I'm going to lock you up." At that point Ms. Alberts struck the officer in the face with her hand, the officer countered by striking her back with his hand, and Ms. Alberts struck back. Officer Ogletree then told the plaintiff that she was under arrest, and he opened the van door. Ms. Alberts refused to be led out of the van by the officer, and to avoid him she moved into the space between the van seats, simultaneously kicking the officer in the stomach and groin area. At this point, to restrain the plaintiff, Ogletree punched Ms. Alberts with full force on her left cheek. This blow quieted the plaintiff. She was then placed under arrest for disorderly conduct, harassment of an officer, and resisting arrest. She was transported to the 34th precinct station, where she was subjected to a strip search in the presence of a matron as a standard booking procedure. As a result of the injury suffered to the plaintiff during her altercation with Ogletree, she missed two weeks of work and lost vacation and sick leave benefits. She suffered no permanent damage.

Opinion of the Court

To maintain her suit against the police department, the plaintiff was obliged to prove at trial that Ms. Alberts' injuries resulted from a policy or custom of the New York City Police Department, or that policymaking officials of the police department were directly involved in her arrest. This burden was not met. Furthermore, although plaintiff's amended complaint alleged otherwise, there was no evidence at the trial establishing either negligent supervision of policemen or a police department policy to encourage lawless conduct.

The remaining defendant is police officer James Ogletree. Plaintiff argues that this officer's alleged false arrest and assault of Ms. Alberts was a violation of section 1983. In recognition of the inherent discretion that must be afforded police officers to promote effective law enforcement, the law entitles a police officer "to qualified immunity from an assessment of damages against him if he acted with a reasonable and good faith belief that he had acted lawfully." The plaintiff argues that her arrest lacked the requisite probable cause and therefore could not be defended on the basis of "reasonable and good faith belief that he had acted lawfully." This burden has not been met. The arrest of Ms. Alberts was justified by her behavior and was based on probable cause. Ample evidence supports Ogletree's "good faith" and probable cause arrest on these charges.

The conduct of Ogletree is not to be condoned and it appeared at trial with the benefit of hindsight that other means might have been available to subdue the plaintiff. However, it is this court's duty not to scrutinize the officer's behavior but instead, to determine if the force utilized was excessive. The facts in this case lead to the undeniable conclusion that Ogletree's force was not excessive.

The plaintiff has failed to prove that any of the defendants violated her rights secured either by the constitution or by state law. The complaint is hereby dismissed.

DECISION MAKING

The most important decision that an administrator often makes is in the selection of who will make a decision. Sound administration requires sound decision making. The following guidelines focus on this process.

Those Who Must Live with Their Decisions Learn to Make Good Decisions

The rapidly evolving sophistication of police service is placing tremendous strain on the decision-making process in the larger agencies. Management is no longer capable of consistently making the best decisions regarding all aspects of the organization, if they ever were. Organizations are made up of people, and all people think. Nowhere is it carved in stone that management thinks better than labor.

We are speaking of delegation and its importance. The failure to trust the lower echelons with important decisions is a major factor in the failure of law enforcement policies. Those law enforcement administrators most out of touch with reality are those who often insist on making every decision personally. Those with a reputation for making a minimal number of decisional errors are those who delegate. When the person best suited to make the decision makes it, it is usually correct. The administrator who delegates can appear to be all-knowing. When one person, any person, attempts to make every decision—some in areas outside this person's immediate knowledge—many turn out badly. This person usually manages to create an impression of terminal stupidity.

Those Who Do the Job Know the Job

On the surface this headline appears to be a restatement of the preceding guideline. To some extent this is true, but this point is worth emphasizing on its own. As a person moves up in an organization, new skills are acquired and old skills and knowledge lost. Knowledge retained of the old responsibilities also becomes dated; changes are not incorporated because the person no longer needs to keep abreast of changes in operational matters. In short, those who know most about a problem are those who face the problem. This is true of administrators as well as operatives.

Administrators are necessary because those at the bottom of the organization rarely see things from an overall perspective. They concern themselves with the immediate problems they face in their own units. The administrator has to have a larger view and act on behalf of the whole, while operatives focus on the parts. In this sense the administrator acts as a mediator between the various factions of the organization. This person is constantly trying to coordinate the parts into a unified whole; this is a crucial administrative role.

When the problem is isolated in one organizational element, however, the people most attuned to the situation are the people in that element. This is the appropriate arena for the problem to be solved. There is probably nothing more ludicrous, and destructive, than a top-level administrator, 10 years removed from the street, attempting to force a desktop solution to a problem on an element operating in the field. This is the type of situation where an administrator gets a golden opportunity to provide a grand display of ignorance, embellished with a subsequent loss of employee respect.

People do not get smarter as they rise in an organization, they merely change duties and friends. Never forget; In any organization, the people doing the actual work know more about it than those who do not do it—whether they are inside or outside the organization. This is why some private firms require administrators to spend a week or two every year on the line—doing the job. It is also why a criticism of business schools is their philosophy that anyone can be taught to manage a factory without ever stepping foot on the floor of the production room (Walton, 1986, p. 92).

Facts are More Valuable than Opinion

The most ludicrous statement produced from managerial arrogance is: "I consider myself a good judge of character." Nonsense; people are all terrible judges of character because they do not judge character. They judge image and image is always controlled by the person being judged. People dress, speak, smile, and act in a manner calculated to establish an image. This image can be maintained as long as the actions are consistent with that image. If the image is maintained long enough, many will refuse to believe any information contradicting the image.

An old chief of police I once knew had a method for determining when employees were guilty of something with which they were accused. He said that when a person is innocent, this person will argue innocence and attempt to provide facts. The guilty will always feign hurt feelings and say, "You know I wouldn't do something like that."

That theory may or may not be true. One thing is certain: we rarely know anyone well enough to know what they are truly capable of. Anyone is capable of almost anything under the right circumstances. The administrator would be well advised to trust facts and disregard emotions and character judgments.

There is now a large body of evidence supporting the heavy influence of physical appearance on our judgment of character. As early as grade school, children begin to judge others by how they look. Attractive people are judged as good; the unattractive are seen as bad. Attractive women are difficult to convict in court, and then receive shorter sentences than less attractive females. Tough, hard-looking men are easier to convict than small, quiet, pleasant types. It is relatively easy for the most savage rogue to manage an image totally different from his true character. It is also possible for people with a poor image to be extremely competent. People who don't believe this should spend some time in court. That is where defense attorneys dress their clients in business suits and get them fresh haircuts. Some attorneys go so far as to have the defendant's mother seated right behind her son. This is image management; it is intended to play on the juror's belief in their ability to judge character. Anybody can play the image game; the administrator is well advised to ignore such manipulation.

When it comes to managing people, the manager should not trust anything but the facts they have before them. If they rely on facts rather than judgment, managers will be right 99 percent of the time. If they rely on their own good judgment, they will frequently play the fool and will find themselves saying with depressing regularity, "Damn, I just didn't think him capable of that."

The Squeaky Wheel Gets the Grease

Allocation of resources is a major administrative instrument for effective management. The allocation decision also determines, to some extent, the effectiveness of the various elements within the organization. Budgetary decisions should always be made in accordance with organizational objectives. Unfortunately, it does not always work that way.

There is a tendency in all organizations to reward complainers. Those who cry the loudest or whine to the point of distraction often get more than their share of an agency's resources. The more emotional the argument, the greater the perceived need for more resources.

Emotion has nothing to do with need. Resources should be allocated based on demonstrated need, not on the amount of tears shed by the unit manager making the request. Often, the truly effective personnel suffer in silence. They make their case and accept the final decision in a mature manner. Instead of being rewarded for professionalism, they are punished by having to watch badly needed resources being diverted to less important areas.

Emotion is not the only problem with allocation decisions. Proximity also plays a role in this process. The more time the chief executive spends with lower-level managers, the more likely it is that these managers will be favored with extra resources. This happens because close proximity allows more opportunity for those close to the chief to state their case for additional resources.

Administrators must allocate resources based on organizational objectives and real needs. Whining and unequal proximity of lower-level managers must not influence this process. The primary rule that each administrator must keep in mind is: *The squeaky wheel does not always get the grease; sometimes it gets replaced.*

ORGANIZATION

The guidelines on organization focus on structure and goals. The elements of the organizational structure are similar to Frederick Herzberg's hygiene factors (see Chapter 3); the right structure will not necessarily make the agency effective, but the wrong structures will ensure ineffectiveness. According to Deming, "It is possible and in fact fairly easy for an organization to go downhill and out of business making the wrong product or offering the wrong service, even though everyone in the organization performs with devotion." (Walton, 1986, p. 57).

Formality: The Curse of Bureaucracy

Let us look at the problems associated with formal communications. First, formal implies one-way; there is no such thing as one-way communication. By its definition, communication implies more than one person is involved. Formal communication is always written and always slow. Dynamic organizations rely on speed in both communication and actions. Formality requires a specific vocabulary, repleat with hidden meanings and standard phraseology.

The horror stories surrounding bureaucracy provide a strong reason to restrict formality in organizations to only those situations where required. During the height of the siege of Leningrad it is reputed that the military command wanted to transform a factory making one type of bottled product into one making Molotov cocktails (firebombs). According to the story, they were required to send an envoy through the German lines to Moscow to get written permission to make the change. That's bureaucracy.

During the Napoleonic Wars, Great Britain created an office to watch the coast of the English Channel in order to notify the military in case Napoleon attempted an invasion. The British are reputed to have abandoned this post sometime after World War II. That's a long time to worry about Napoleon.

Every organization and nation has similar stories and they highlight the same problem, bureaucracy. Formality is a curse—sometimes a necessary curse—but always a curse. Remember that; when there is an option between formality and informality, the manager should choose to be informal.

Less is Best

Top-heavy organizations are bad news; they just do not work. By the same standard, too many layers of hierarchy also destroy effectiveness. The people who make the key decisions—top administrators—must be close to the point at which the job is accomplished. Middle management gets in the way, often becoming a roadblock between the administrator and operative in the field.

In top-heavy organizations the chief executive will invariably be surrounded by a thick layer of management personnel, insulating the chief from those in the trenches. At its worse a sort of organizational malaise sets in where the administration begins to feel it is an "us versus them" situation regarding labor.

The patrol-level officers are not the chief administrator's enemies; they are the people who get the job done. The administrator will only recognize this through intense personal contact with operatives in the field. Too many people in the administration will prevent this interaction from happening. The chief executive will be too busy watching all those managers maneuvering for power and resources to establish the necessary contacts with those on the job.

In our society, with highly developed computers, fewer managers are needed to handle decisions and the flow of information. Given the current status of municipal, state, and federal budgets, law enforcement agencies can ill afford whole office loads of paper pushers. Too often, this is all that middle managers are. The agency should take a hard look at which managerial services are essential and which are superfluous. Some years ago the Kansas City, Missouri Police Department eliminated the rank of lieutenant totally. This had no negative consequences and some positive effects. This is a first easy step with which most agencies can begin.

When a heavily layered bureaucracy is created, a feudal kingdom is established with numerous fiefdoms occupying the building. If feudalism was all that practical, it would not have died out in the Middle Ages. Why feed a dinosaur? They are supposed to be extinct. If tax dollars were tied to performance, many law enforcement agencies would also be extinct, for many police organizations have much in common with the dinosaur.

Do What You Do Best

One of W. Edwards Deming's seven deadly sins of management is *a lack of constancy of purpose* (Walton, 1986, p. 36). An organization that has no long-range plans for staying in business produces managerial insecurity. This leads to organizational insecurity. Police organizations are frequently guilty of this error. Many do not know why they are in business; they do not know what they need to accomplish. Police leadership must have focus. They must know what they are attempting to accomplish and have a long-range plan for its accomplishment.

The past 20 years has witnessed a meteoric rise in the number of private security organizations. Of course, there is nothing new about private security; during the mid nineteenth century such agencies as Pinkerton's were actually more effective, and respected, than most local police of the time. Today, the advent of modern methods of policing and the growth in scientific techniques have supposedly made private security unable to compete with publicly funded police organizations. Considering the constitutional powers granted public peace officers as opposed to the mere rights and duties of citizenship granted the private operations, one has to wonder how private security can survive at all, much less grow. The reason is that private security organizations cater to the people who pay the bill. They do not concern themselves with fairness, justice, or equality under the law. They are not worried about conviction rates or public image.

Law enforcement is a public service. The police administrator cannot ignore the wants and needs of the public. Unfortunately, too many law enforcement agencies are so caught up in the production of numbers and the enlarging of the budget that they have little time left for dealing with the public.

Hardly a day goes by where the media do not report a meeting or call for a meeting between police administrators and citizens' groups across this nation. Minority groups have concerns; business groups have concerns; average citizens have concerns: All want to get support from the police. These concerns are real; the people involved are not just troublemakers or radicals. These are real people; they have problems and want help. If the chief executive cannot do anything else, he or she should at least listen to their concerns. All such groups are well qualified to recognize the problems of the community.

Informality and Flexibility

In autocratic organizations only management is allowed to think, which is why these organizations lag behind in innovations and new developments. Eliminating the titles and insignias of rank and requiring that all address each other by first names constitutes the first step. The chain of command should be used only for the submission of formal reports and requests. This will create an atmosphere of innovation and creativity and administrators will be amazed at how many good ideas patrol-level officers have. An added benefit of this is the blow that will be struck at administrative arrogance while increasing job satisfaction and morale at all levels.

Productivity through People

Chief executives of law enforcement agencies usually do not make arrests, issue citations, investigate criminal acts, search for missing persons, take lost property reports, or patrol the streets. The only contribution made to these efforts by administrators is through resource and personnel allocation, policymaking, and encouragement. The officers at the lower end of the spectrum get the job done, those at the upper end act as cheerleaders and spectators.

Anything the administrator can do to make the job easier for the officers should be done. Anything that makes the officers on the street feel better about themselves and their agency should be done. Anything that detracts from their effectiveness should be eliminated. Anything that causes them to lose self-esteem or respect for the agency should be changed. They are the department—not the chief. Their effectiveness is both the agency's and the chief's. Good people do good work-if left alone. Help them and the administrator helps the community and the administrator. Hinder them and the administrator becomes a leader without followers—a third world general shining with medals and brass, laughed at by both the personnel and the community.

While those who succeed should be rewarded, it is even more important not to reward underachievers. When quality of work is not a consideration in the allocation of rewards, quality will not be important to the people who do the work.

One of the most difficult and distasteful aspects of management is the use of negative sanctions. The decision to dismiss someone from the organization can be stressful for both parties, but it is often necessary. One of the true tests of executive courage is the willingness to fire nonproductive employees.

Many police administrators have found it useful to use labor unions, police associations, or civil service as a crutch. They argue that these organizations prevent the administrator from removing incompetent personnel. This is nonsense; these groups require that the administrator have the facts of the case in order and that he or she proceed in an impartial manner. They do not prevent the removal of poor employees.

Robert Townsend may have said it best when he observed that "performances are distributed along a bell-shaped curve; a few outstanding ones at one end, the vast majority of satisfactory ones in the middle, and a few undeniably lousies at the other end" (1984, p. 73). It should be a goal of the chief executive to reward the achievers and get rid of the lousies. In an organization dependent on its public image, as are the police, the poor employee can literally destroy the effectiveness of the organization. The agency cannot afford to keep this person and there is no good reason to do so. Every authorized position must be filled by those capable and willing to do the right job in the right manner.

Build Bridges Rather than Barriers

Hostility is bred in isolation. In the majority of police agencies in this country a note of discord exists. Patrol officers and detectives do not like each other. Service personnel consider traffic officers too lowly to engage in conversation. Tactical officers speak only to other tactical officers. Anger and resentment grow best when an organization is subdivided into fiefdoms and housed to prevent people from different units from speaking to each other directly.

These walls should be torn down. Work periods should be structured to facilitate face-to-face communication. All personnel should be forced to attend briefings with each other. Problems should be solved by bringing those involved together. Interunit work groups should be utilized to create an organization of friends and colleagues rather than of cliques.

Emotional barriers can sometimes be removed by destroying physical barriers. Sometimes merely placing two feuding units in the same office will solve the problem. Some organizations have replaced elevators with escalators to enhance face-to-face communication. Just seeing each other and saying good morning can reduce friction.

COMMUNICATION

Communication is the lubricant for the wheels of progress. People must talk to each other if there is to be coordination and a minimum of duplication of effort. The following guidelines summarize the most useful communication formats.

Keep it Informal

There is a purpose for formal messages. Information important to the entire organization, requests needing clearance by a number of different units, statistical data, and formal complaints should be handled through the chain of command and must be in writing. Everything else should be resolved informally. We focused on this in the last section and will not dwell on it here, but when two units are having a problem, they do not need a mediator from above, nor do they need a staff meeting to formulate a new policy to resolve the dispute. The disputants need to sit down with each other and work it out. They should be locked in a room and told not to come out until they resolve the issue. They will get hungry and sleepy sooner or later; this does wonders for resolving problems. Let the people with the problems solve the problems. Administrators should not tie up the entire organization over an interelement conflict.If chiefs do nothing in their tenure but keep the personnel talking to each other, they will be far more successful than most of their peers.

If You Can't Say It to Their Face, Don't Say It

In the last section we discussed the importance of face-to-face communication. There is a reason. When people talk to each other personally, they use more than just words. They also communicate with a large variety of nonverbal signals, known as body language. Body language highlights the conversation. Clarity requires the accents provided by body language. Another reason for personal communication is the ability to ask questions and receive immediate clarification of vague or ambiguous information. It is not often even necessary to ask for clarification; the puzzled look on the face of the receiver of the information is sufficient to generate clarification from the sender. For no other reason than clarity, the majority of communication should be face to face.

Face-to-face communication serves another purpose. When people talk to others directly, they are speaking to a person. This is also true of telephone conversations, but without the nonverbal cues we are accustomed to monitoring. Written communications are the worst possible form of message. They are without emotions and conscience. A memo is written to a nonperson, for there is no immediate feedback. People will say things in writing that they would never dare tell someone to their face. Warfare by memorandum is a waste of time and resources, yet most large organizations go through one civil war after another with memos being the principal weapons.

When used properly (or improperly, depending on your frame of reference), tons of documents can be labeled FYI (for your information) with neat little routing slips, then dumped into the communication channels, burying necessary messages in a sea of junk. The two major reasons that important letters get lost or do not get acted on promptly is because: (1) they are thrown out with the junk mail, including all the FYIs, or (2) they are at the bottom of the pile of junk and the bureaucrat involved is too insecure to cull out the junk but insists on reading every piece—for reasons unknown.

Administration can be simplified with a simple rule—talk to people. Managers should not think in terms of communication. People do not communicate with others, they talk to them. Those who keep this simple concept in mind won't go wrong. An administrator should never write a letter when the person can be called; should never call a person who can be talked to face to face. Everyone in the organization should follow the same advice with people both inside and outside the organization.

THE SECRET OF SUCCESS

The secret of success is that there is no secret of success. What works well for one organization does not always translate well in another setting. There are some constants, however, which lead to effective organizations. These are the subject of our final discussion.

Good Training

Professional athletics also offer a good example of this rule. The average professional football team will spend some 20 to 25 hours practicing for every hour of playing time, not counting training camp and players practicing on their own. To excel at anything requires hours of training. This includes police work.

Like the administrator, the employees must know what business they are in. Judgment, although necessary, cannot be the sole source of knowledge for law enforcement officers. Judgment will tell a person that it is necessary to restart a person's heart and breathing when it stops, but only training will tell the person how it is done. Training, education, and practice are the tools used to transform good people into good employees. The better the training, the less the need for management or supervision.

Good Policies

Policies are the conscience of the organization. These represent the agency value structure; they are to the organization what the Ten Commandments are to Western religions. They should be kept short and clear. Ambiguity and excessive verbiage will kill their usefulness.

The rule regarding policies is simple. Does the chief know and understand every policy in the department, without looking through the manual? If not, neither does anyone else. All those midlevel bureaucrats who keep complaining about how patrol officers cannot read and understand policy have the luxury of sitting in their air-conditioned offices while they review the fine print in every dissertation on ambiguity and confusion that they helped to produce. Patrol officers do not have this luxury. They probably don't even have ready access to the manual, but they have to know it by heart. If the chief executive doesn't know it, why should anyone else?

There is a maximum amount of information that one person can absorb. The officers also have to remember state laws, federal laws, and city ordinances, as well as criminal procedure and a myriad of information concerning persons property and other events. The human brain can hold only so much. Administration should not be complicated with poor policy. One of the oldest rules of supervision applies to policymaking: *KISS—keep it short and simple.*

Stay Out Of The Way

If the department has good people, provides good training, and sets out clear policies, the major administrative concern will be how to spend time. One of the most difficult tasks of management is knowing when not to interfere with production. When things are going well, it should be left alone. Administrators should now have time to do what administrators were meant to do: get out of the office and talk to people. They should talk to anyone who will talk to them. Problems should be stopped before they start through the process of asking questions of those doing the work. Administrators should talk to community leaders, members of the media, politicians, and even schoolchildren. The manager should never interfere with those who are making the organization look good.

This does not mean that there will be no problems, for there will be sufficient complications to keep managers from getting bored. But always remember, the organization hired and trained these people as experts in their business; a business they now know more about than the administrative staff. The secret to effective management with highly motivated professionals is to give them encouragement and support and intervene only when it is clearly called for. If a situation comes up requiring administrative action, this should be done decisively; other than that, the manager should sit back and enjoy success.

Good People

Organizations are made up of people. Technology is nice, good equipment is helpful, but people are essential. Public administrators can learn a lot from professional athletics. The Dallas Cowboys and San Francisco Forty-niners did not achieve long-term success by wearing pretty uniforms or building fancy stadiums. They have continued success because they hire the best people they can get.

When Alfred Sloan turned General Motors into the most successful auto manufacturing firm in the world, he claimed that his major strength was in getting good people to work for him. This is the first key to effective management. The less a person is required to manage, the better the organization. Good people need less management than do poor or mediocre ones.

The path to effective management lies in identifying what the organization is in business for, identifying what kind of people are needed to fulfill the mission, and aggressively seeking out every person who might have what it takes to fulfill those expectations. No organization should accept less than the best. Police agencies are better off understaffed than having a full staff of which only 50 percent are competent. A good organization is one with good personnel.

REFERENCES

Peters, Thomas J., and Robert H. Waterman, Jr. (1982). *In Search of Excellence*. New York: Warner Books.

Townsend, Robert (1984). *Further Up the Organization*. New York: Alfred A. Knopf.

Walton, Mary (1986). *The Deming Management Method*. New York: Perigree.

Index